Improvement Science at Your Fingertips

A compilation of resources for coaches of improvement science

Brandon Bennett, Alicia Grunow, and Sandra Park

Version 2

This edition first published in 2022
© Improvement Collective and ISC LLC
All rights reserved. No part of this publication may be reproduced, stored in a retrieval system, or transmitted, in any form or by any means, electronic, mechanical, photocopying, recording or otherwise, except as permitted by law. Advice on how to obtain permission to reuse material from this title is available by emailing improvesciatyourfingertips@gmail.com.

The right of Brandon Bennett, Alicia Grunow and Sandra Park to be identified as the authors of this work has been asserted in accordance with law.

Library of Congress Cataloguing-in-Publication Data
Names: Bennett, Brandon K. author. | Grunow, Alicia J. author. | Park, Sandra R., author.
Title: Improvement science at your fingertips: a compilation of resources for coaches of improvement science / Brandon Bennett, Alicia Grunow, and Sandra Park.
Description: First edition. | San Francisco, CA: ISC LLC, 2022
    Includes bibliographical references and index.
Identifiers:
Library of Congress Control Number: 2022913840 | ISBN 979-8-9866679-0-4 (paperback)

About the Authors

Brandon Bennett, MPH, is the Principal Advisor for ISC LLC serving as an Improvement Advisor in the fields of Healthcare and Education. He has led and advised on diverse initiatives from disease specific processes to country-wide improvement programs. Brandon has published results-based and methodological papers on the application of Improvement Science methods and been a featured speaker at conferences around the world. He is currently Faculty for the IHI Improvement Advisor Professional Development Program, Faculty for the Improvement Collective's Improvement Science Coaching Course and is an Honorary Lecturer within the School of Medicine at the University of Lancashire in the United Kingdom. Brandon is a former Senior Fellow at the Carnegie Foundation for the Advancement of Teaching.

Alicia Grunow, PhD, Alicia Grunow is an Improvement Advisor and co-founder of the Improvement Collective. She started her career as a bilingual teacher in Denver Public Schools and then in New York City. Alicia was a Senior Managing Partner at the Carnegie Foundation, where she co-authored Learning to Improve; How America's Schools can Get Better at Getting Better. She holds a BA in psychology from Reed College, an Improvement Advisor certificate from the Institute for Healthcare Improvement, and a MA degree in Economics and PhD in Education from Stanford University.

Sandra Park, PhD, is an Improvement Advisor and co-founder of the Improvement Collective. She was previously a managing director at the Carnegie Foundation for the Advancement of Teaching, where she led the foundation's Building a Teaching Effectiveness Network (BTEN). Sandra previously taught elementary school in Oregon, Maryland, and Washington, D.C., and was director of programs at First Graduate in San Francisco. She holds a BA in sociology from Georgetown University, a teaching credential and MAT from Louis & Clark College, an EdM in administration and policy from the Harvard Graduate School of Education, a PhD in education policy from UC-Berkeley, and an Improvement Advisor certificate from the Institute for Healthcare Improvement.

Introduction

Welcome to version 2 of Improvement Science at your Fingertips: A compilation of resources for coaches of improvement science. Through our years of coaching improvement science, we have gathered and written several go-to resources that are helpful in guiding our coaching work. This is our attempt to put them all in one place for other improvement coaches to use. New to this edition is our online resource. All the one-page reference sheets, protocols, agendas, etc. found in the appendices can now also be found online at www.improvementcollective.com.

In the true spirit of iteration, we think of this book as a prototype version that will be improved by watching how it is used in practice. Therefore, we are really interested in how you mark it up, what you pull out to use for what purpose, and what additional pieces of paper you stick inside of it to use when coaching your teams. Please keep these notes and share them with us and we will improve the guide as a collective!

If you have suggestions or comments for us, we would love to hear them. We have future chapters planned, but also want to know what deserves treatment from your perspective. Please email us at improvesciatyourfingertips@gmail.com.

This guide is also a reflection of the collaborative nature of improvement. It is about pulling resources together from many sources. We owe a special thanks to friends and colleagues at the Carnegie Foundation for the Advancement of Teaching who provided early iterations on some of these documents and who created space for us to innovate from them. We look forward to learning from all of you and seeing the other tools and frameworks you add to this compilation.

Brandon, Alicia & Sandra

Table of Contents

About the Authors ii

Introduction iii

1. Conceptual Foundations 1

A Timeline of Quality Improvement in Different Fields 2
A Timeline of Quality Improvement Tools and Methods 3
System of Profound Knowledge 4
Six Principles for Educational Improvement 8
Kinds of Knowledge Needed to Improve 10
The Model for Improvement 12
Improvement Habits 16
Improvement Habit Look-Fors 17
Systems Framework 19
Equity Framework 20

2. Facilitating and Coaching Improvement Teams 21

Building Effective Improvement Teams 22
Defining Improvement Team Membership and Roles 27
Table 2.4 Improvement Team Roles 30
Building an Inclusive Table 31
Supporting the Development of Effective Improvement Teams 33
Stage 1: Commission an Improvement Team 34
Stage 2: Launching an Improvement Team 38
Stage 3: Engaging in Collective Improvement Work 41
Stage 4: Adjourning the Team 52
Conversational Capacity 53
Coaching Stances 60

3. Organizing Improvement Journeys 63

Organizing the Improvement Journey 64
Understanding the Current System 67
Focus Collective Efforts 71
Generate Change Ideas 76
Test Ideas in Practice 78
Sustain and Spread 80

4. Assessing Team Progress 85

Project Progress Score Rubric 86
Team Rubric 88

5. Improvement Methods and Tools I 91

Empathy Interviews 92
Empathy Observations 97
Journey Map 100
Process Map 102
Process Failure Analysis 108
Force Field Analysis 110
Cause and Effect Diagrams 120
Aim Statements 126
Theory of Practice Improvement: Driver Diagram 132
Scanning 140
Plan-Do-Study-Act Cycles 141
PDSA Ramps 150
Change Packages 155

6. Improvement Methods and Tools II: Data 163

The Measurement Tree 164
Visualizing Quantitative Information 171
Data Visualization Using Small Multiples 181
Ordered Bar Chart 185
Pareto Analysis 190
The Run Chart 198
Histograms 215
Box-and-Whisker Plots 225

Appendix A: Improvement Tools—Reference Sheets, Templates, and Checklists 233

Empathy Activities 234
Process Failure Analysis Reference Sheet 236
Process Failure Analysis Template 237
Process Map Reference Sheet 238
Force Field Analysis 240
Cause and Effect Diagram Reference Sheet 241
Cause and Effect Template 242
Aim Statements Reference Sheet 243
Theory of Practice Improvement: Driver Diagram Reference Guide 244
Driver Diagram Template 245
Plan-Do-Study-Act (PDSA) Cycle Reference Sheet 246
PDSA Template 1 248
PDSA Template 2 249
PDSA Template 3 250
PDSA Template 4 (2 pages) 251
PDSA Checklist and Coaching Plan 253

Planning PDSA Ramps......254
Assessing Scale for Testing......255
Visualizing Quantitative Information Reference Sheet......257
Pareto Analysis Reference Guide......259
Run chart Reference Sheet......260

Appendix B: Protocols and Agendas......263
Initiating Conversation: Sample Agenda (with questions and listen-fors)......264
Sample Agenda of Initial Launch Meetings......266
Huddle Protocol and Note Taking Form......267
Team Meeting Protocol......268
Data Conversation Protocol......269
Learning Consolidation Protocol......270

Appendix C: Improvement Journey — Forms, Templates, and One-Pagers......271
Improvement Journey Plan Template......272
Learning Plan Template......273
Investigation Summary Template......274
Investigation Summary Look-Fors......274
Charter Board Template......276
Charter Form......277
Charter Slide Deck Template......278
Charter Assessment......279
Improvement Routines......280
K-W-L Template......281
Talking Points One-Pager......282

1. Conceptual Foundations

Section 1 of Improvement Science at your fingertips orients readers to the history of Improvement Science and the fundamental principles that undergird the approach. For those readers who are new to the field of quality improvement or the study of improvement science some definitions are helpful. The first use of the term "The Science of Improvement" can be found in *The Improvement Guide: A Practical Approach to Enhancing Organizational Performance* by published in 1996. Today Improvement Science can be defined this way:

Improvement Science is an applied science meaning it is primarily concerned with applying scientific knowledge to practical problems.

Improvement Science proposes, studies, and applies methods for changing the design of systems seeking different and/or better results from their current status quo.

Improvement Science contends that "all improvement comes from developing, testing and implementing changes" (Improvement Knowledge) and that the specific changes needed to improve performance must flow from subject matter expertise (Research Knowledge, Professional Knowledge, Experiential Knowledge, see page 12 for more on Kinds of Knowledge needed to improve systems).[1]

In this section you will find some of the organizing frameworks that have broadly defined improvement science and which shape how coaches employing improvement science work with improvement teams. Readers may find in the following pages key lenses or perspectives for thinking about improvement journeys and may choose to apply these to problem-solving issues that arise when working with improvement teams.

Suggestions for further reading

- *The Improvement Guide* by Langley, Moen, Nolan, Nolan, Norman, and Provost
- *The New Economics for Industry, Government and Education* by W. Edwards Deming
- *Thinking in Systems: A Primer* by Donella H. Meadows edited by Diana Wright
- *Learning to Improve* by Bryk, Gomez, Grunow, and LeMahieu
- *Working to Improve: Seven Approaches to Quality Improvement in Education* by LeMahieu, Bryk, Grunow, and Gomez

---

[1] See Section 1: Kinds of Knowledge Needed to Improve for more information.

A Timeline of Quality Improvement in Different Fields

- Manufacturing — 1920s
- Agriculture — 1920s
- US Military — 1940s
- Civil Aviation — 1950s
- Energy — 1950s
- Japanese Automotive — 1970s
- Other Automotive — 1970s
- Healthcare — 1980s
- Education — 1980s

A Timeline of Quality Improvement Tools and Methods

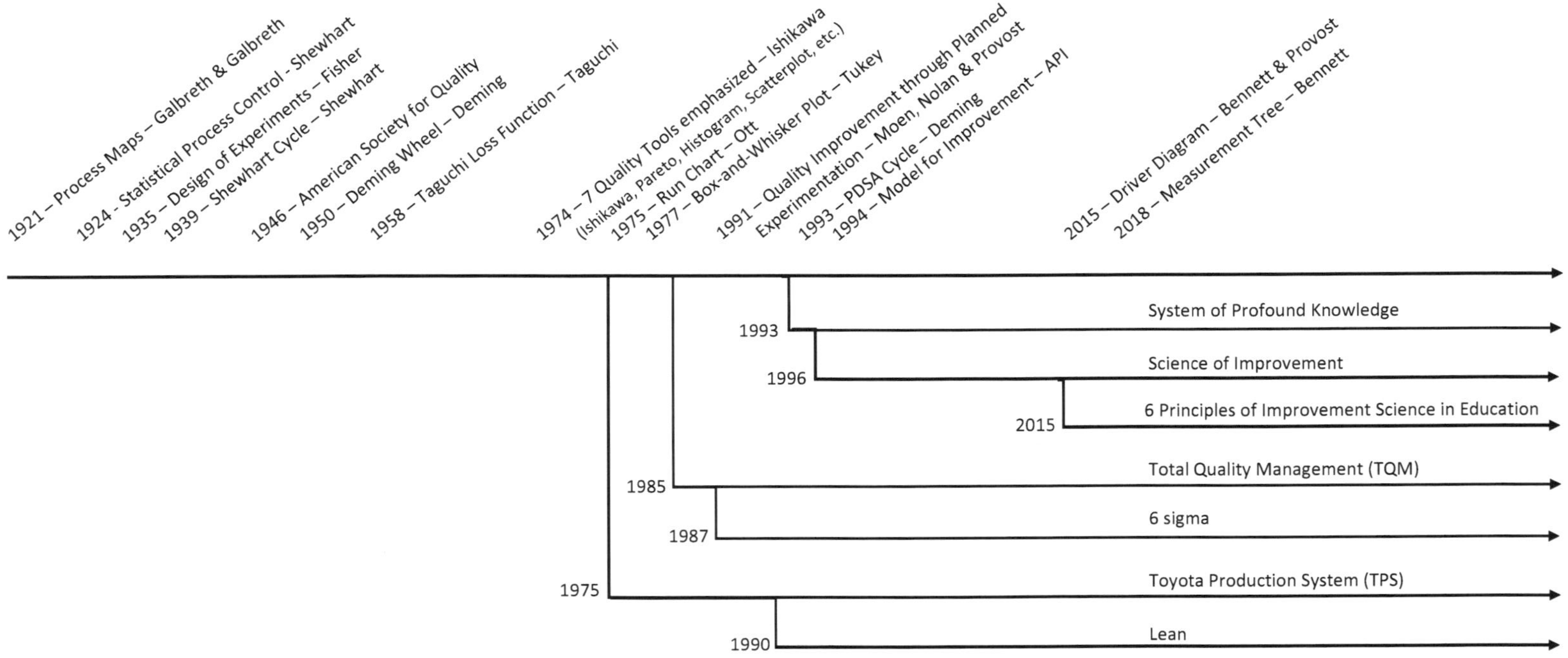

- 1921 – Process Maps – Galbreth & Galbreth
- 1924 – Statistical Process Control – Shewhart
- 1935 – Design of Experiments – Fisher
- 1939 – Shewhart Cycle – Shewhart
- 1946 – American Society for Quality
- 1950 – Deming Wheel – Deming
- 1958 – Taguchi Loss Function – Taguchi
- 1974 – 7 Quality Tools emphasized – Ishikawa (Ishikawa, pareto, Histogram, Scatterplot, etc.)
- 1975 – Run Chart – Ott
- 1977 – Box-and-Whisker Plot – Tukey
- 1991 – Quality Improvement through planned Experimentation – Moen, Nolan & Provost
- 1993 – PDSA Cycle – Deming
- 1994 – Model for Improvement – API
- 2015 – Driver Diagram – Bennett & Provost
- 2018 – Measurement Tree – Bennett

Branches (right side):
- System of Profound Knowledge
- Science of Improvement
- 6 Principles of Improvement Science in Education (2015)
- Total Quality Management (TQM)
- 6 sigma
- Toyota Production System (TPS)
- Lean

Nodes: 1975, 1985, 1987, 1990, 1993, 1996

System of Profound Knowledge

What do we really know about how our systems work? Conceptually we know they are complex. Experientially and from our own vantage points we know when they work and when they do not work. Often, we experience and can point to frustrating aspects in the design of systems, especially as we relate to them as workers, consumers, community members and leaders. But what of the whole? For most of us the depth and breadth are elusive, often seeming unimportant with some parts feeling far away, "not my problem and not in my locus of control." Real change though requires depth of knowledge, whether that is within ourselves as we personally try to improve, or as part of the systems in which we find ourselves as those leaders, workers, and community members.

After a lifetime of working to improve systems of all kinds W. Edwards Deming, a statistician and management consultant, proposed the System of Profound Knowledge (choosing "profound" to communicate the depth and breadth of knowledge this system could help create). This system proposed a way of thinking about and seeing our systems, a way of assisting us (people who are a part of a system) to develop the deep knowledge needed to effectively change our systems to produce the outcomes from them we desire.

Each category (Appreciation of a System, Understanding Variation, Theory of Knowledge, and Psychology) offers unique insights into our systems, both deepening and broadening our perspectives on what is, why and where in the system specific change can be brought to generate different, better outcomes for those the system serves.

Below are brief overviews of each category and in the pages that follow readers will find specific methods and tools linked to these categories. Pragmatic applications of which yield those valuable insights (depth of knowledge) needed to inform any improvement journey.

In 1992 Deming expressed the sentiment that these categories don't stand alone, they inform and "interact with each other." Knowledge of one category is incomplete without knowledge of the other categories. It is in using them all together that an advisor, coach, leader, or improvement team can obtain the clearest picture of the system they seek to improve.

Appreciation of a System (Systems Thinking)

"A system is an interdependent group of items, people, or processes working together toward a common purpose" (Langley et al, pg. 77). Systems Thinking comprises the theories, methods and tools used to understand systems. Donella Meadows wrote, "Once we see the relationship between structure and behavior, we can begin to understand how systems work, what makes them produce poor results, and how to shift them into better behavior patterns" (Meadows, pg. 1). For leaders and coaches of improvement, no insight could be more important than how a system is designed (its structure) and how it generates outcomes (its behavior). Investigators and improvers have a great many methods at their disposal for seeing the structure of a system, each creating a window into how our complex systems are designed and how the parts interact to create the outcomes we see from them. From empathy interviews to process maps to run charts, most tools exist for the purpose of helping us better see the design of our systems.[2]

Understanding Variation

"When a systems thinker encounters a problem, the first thing he or she does is look for data, time graphs, the history of the system. That's because long-term behavior provides clues to the underlying system structure. And structure is the key to understanding not just what is happening, but why" (Meadows, pg. 89). For systems thinkers, understanding variation is a key that unlocks the system. The use of tools like Shewhart Charts, Run Charts, and Pareto Analysis give deep insight into the outcomes of systems. When segmented in various ways (group, location, time, etc.) such tools reveal who the system is working for, who it is not, where the system is working, and where it is not. They also assist leaders and teams in asking and answering fundamental questions about the performance of the system, things like:

- Is the system stable, meaning predictable into the near future?
- If the system is unstable, where, for who and why?[3]
- If the system is stable, is its performance desirable or does it need improvement?

Answers to these questions are fundamental to the successful leadership, management, and improvement of systems.

Theory of Knowledge

"Remember, always, that everything you know, and everything everyone knows, is only a model" (Meadows, pg. 172). Our knowledge of systems, how they are designed, how they function, all of it, is always incomplete. Leaders, managers, and improvers are required to act on this incomplete knowledge, they are required to manage from a theory they have about why things are the way they are. "The theory of knowledge teaches us that a statement, if it conveys knowledge, predicts future outcome, with risk of being wrong, and that it fits without failure observations of the past" (Deming, pg. 102). Theory of Knowledge is about recognizing this fact of life and then managing from a place of humility; incorporating both a theory of our system (an explanation for why we see the outcomes we do), and a mechanism for learning whether our theory is true in practice. Tools like annotated process maps, driver diagrams, and PDSA cycles are all created and used to articulate a shared theory and to test that theory in practice. "Getting models out into the light of day, making them as rigorous as possible, testing them against the evidence, and being willing to scuttle them if they are no longer supported is nothing more than practicing the scientific method

---

[2] See Section 1: Systems Framework for more information on the Six Components of Systems Change

[3] Unstable systems are inherently in need of improvement. Without predictability, leaders cannot know who the system will work for, where, when, or for how long. Before even asking if the level of performance is good, stability is key to the successful management of systems. For a fuller treatment on assessing for stability the authors recommend multiple references explaining Shewhart's Theory of Common and Special Cause variation with the branch of statistics known as Statistical Process Control Methods. References include Economic Control of Quality of Manufactured Product by Walter Shewhart, The New Economics for Industry, Government and Education by W. Edwards Deming and The Health Care Data Guide: Learning from Data for Improvement by Lloyd Provost and Sandra Murray, among many others.

— something that is done too seldom even in science, and is done hardly at all in social science or management or government or everyday life" (Meadows, pg. 172).

Psychology (The Human Side of Change)

"People are born with a need for relationships with other people and need for love and esteem by others. One is born with a natural inclination to learn. Learning is a source of innovation. One inherits a right to enjoy his work. Good management helps us to nurture and preserve these positive innate attributes of people" (Deming, pg. 108). Returning to our definition of systems, "a system is an interdependent group of items, people..." (Langley et al. pg. 77), our social systems are not only made up of people, they are dependent on them. Understanding human motivation, understanding human interaction, appreciating psychological needs, are all key to successfully leading, managing, and improving systems. For coaches of improvement, every theory assumes something about the psychology of the people involved. Taking time to make explicit those assumptions, to incorporate them in clear fashion, and attend to them in the accomplishment of the work is critical to achieving the outcomes desired. Using critical skills, such as those described in chapters on conversational capacity or those on empathy interviews, observations and journey maps assist improvement teams in addressing the human side of change.

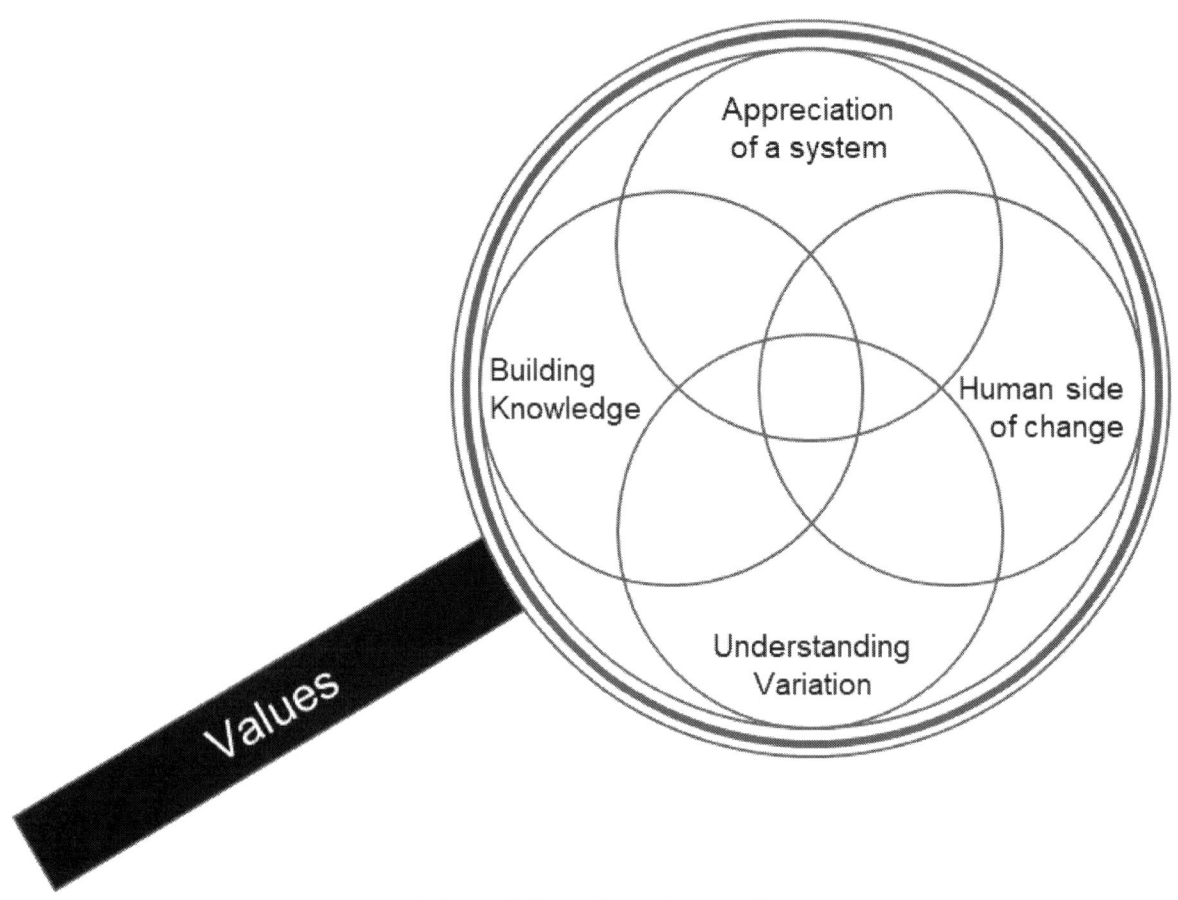

Adapted from Langley et al.

We can think of Deming's System of Profound Knowledge as a lens (pictured above) which leaders, improvement coaches and teams can apply to their systems. The goal is to magnify important sources of variation, to understand the system's structure and in doing so to develop a strong theory for how to improve its outcomes. But as with any lens, where we focus matters.

Values

We can think of our improvement lens as having a *focus* that guides *what* we look at, which outcomes are prioritized. In some ways the System of Profound Knowledge is agnostic about its own application. Leaders could use it to improve outcomes for community members, create efficiencies, and decrease inequalities. But the ideas can just as easily be used to increase oppression, focus solely on profitability, or increase disparities. Values matter. For leaders of improvement being explicit about values, what matters to the leadership of the system, is a critical choice. Improvement teams will follow the leader. If a leader commits to eliminating gaps in outcomes based on race or socio-economic class, improvement teams will use the lens to help uncover the structure of the system creating those disparate outcomes. If leaders hold back from naming such outcomes as important, improvement teams will too, even when those outcomes may represent especially important sources of variation in the system which require change.

Six Principles for Educational Improvement

From 2008-2020, the Carnegie Foundation for the Advancement of Teaching set out to develop and spread new ways of organizing improvement efforts in education. During the tenure of educational scholar Tony Bryk, the foundation generated a new model, Network Improvement Communities (or NICs), which combined an emphasis on the application of Improvement Science and the formation of networks as a means of accelerating progress.

Carnegie Foundation leaders laid out "six improvement principles" which form the foundation of the Network Improvement Community model in the 2015 book *Learning to Improve; How America's Schools Can Get Better at Getting Better.* The application of these six improvement principles is hypothesized to accelerate progress on important problems in education.

Be problem-focused and user-centered

Attend to variability

See the system

Embrace measurement

Learn through disciplined inquiry

Organize as networks

6 CORE PRINCIPLES OF IMPROVEMENT

Carnegie Foundation 2015

Be problem-focused and user-centered

Center improvement on the needs of the user. Clearly define the problem to solve and co-develop solutions with key participants.

Attend to variability

Expect and seek to understand variation. As solutions are tried, identify what works for whom under what set of conditions.

See the system

Ascribe to the underlying assumption that systems produce outcomes. Go and see how processes come together to produce the outcomes we see.

Embrace measurement

We cannot improve at scale what we cannot measure. Collect measures of key outcomes, processes and unintended consequences as feedback on improvement efforts.

Learn through disciplined inquiry

Treat ideas for change as hypotheses. Engage in iterative PDSA cycles to learn fast and improve quickly.

Organize as networks

Form as a network of diverse expertise committed to a common aim. Use the wisdom of crowds to accomplish more together.

The first five principles are inspired by the Science of Improvement as they apply to the field of education. They connect directly to the System of Profound Knowledge and the study of Improvement Science efforts in other fields. The sixth principle adds a focus on networks as a means of organizing the diverse expertise needed to make progress on complex educational problems.

Kinds of Knowledge Needed to Improve

Improving systems means changing their design. Effective design and redesign require teams to access and use a variety of different types of knowledge and expertise to succeed. Determining which types of knowledge needed during each phase of the improvement journey is an important job of any improvement coach.

Experiential Knowledge

People experience systems in different ways; how they experience and perceive their experiences matters. Experiential knowledge refers to the life experiences of those the improvement work seeks to help. Deeply understanding how students and families experience school, how patients experience care, how customers experience service, and the impact these experiences have on their lives is an essential part of the improvement process. This knowledge is most salient when trying to understand the system as well as when generating change ideas toward the design or redesign of the system.

Research Knowledge

What works to produce outcomes? What works to heal patients? What works when teaching children to read? Research knowledge is actively produced by those who investigate to understand, often connected to academia. Generally, research knowledge can be accessed through journal articles, books or direct interviews of scientists, researchers, and investigators connected to or interested in a particular problem of practice or field of study. This is generally knowledge about WHAT works and is a rich and important source of change ideas.

Professional Knowledge

People who work in systems have extensive knowledge about how those systems work and often, how they do not work. Professional knowledge is gained by being a part of the system. Professionals often have a mixture of both job and industry specific training as well as knowledge gained through years of practice in their field. Teachers and principals know how schools work, nurses and doctors understand how hospitals provide care, counselors and therapists are familiar with causes and treatments in the mental health space. This type of knowledge is important in understanding the system and generating change ideas.

Improvement Knowledge

With ideas for what might work to improve a system the question of how to change the system remains. Improvement knowledge is knowledge of the theory, and methods useful in designing and redesigning systems to produce different, hopefully better, outcomes for those the system serves. It is deeply rooted in the System of Profound Knowledge and the Science of Improvement, providing teams with a different way of seeing our organizations and in how to approach change. This is the knowledge this resource guide is all about!

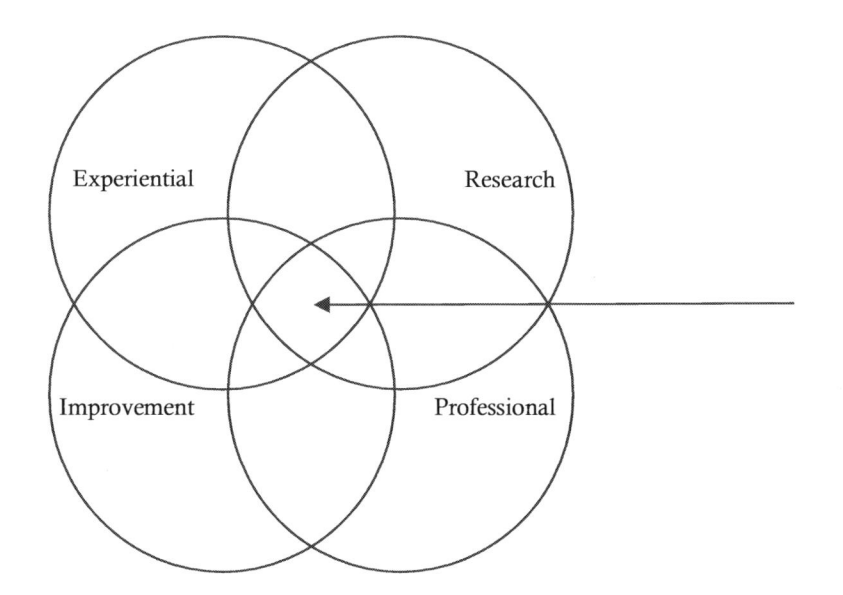

Opportunity for Success

Combine experiential, research, professional and improvement knowledge in creative ways to develop effective changes for improvement.

11

The Model for Improvement

Engine for systems learning and productive change

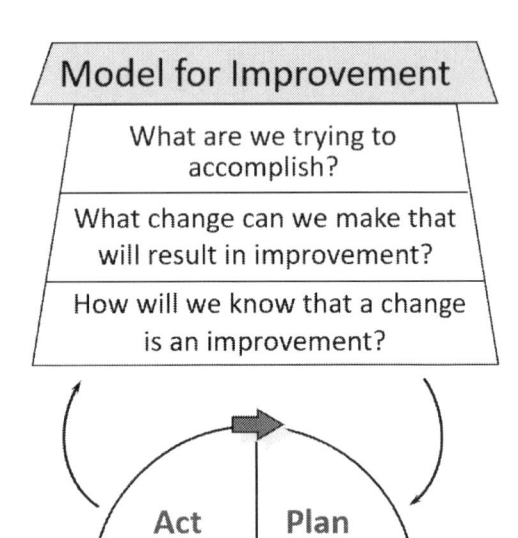

All improvement requires change, but not all change is an improvement. By what method can we realistically distinguish between the two? The Model for Improvement (MFI), presented here, is a pragmatic approach for systems learning, one that assists leaders and frontline workers in discovering which ideas actually lead to better performance and which, though seemingly good at face value, do not. The Model for Improvement is comprised of two main parts: the three questions and the Plan-Do-Study-Act (PDSA) Cycle. Each part is covered here with recommendations on how to apply the MFI in practice to assist team learning and improvement in practice.

The Three Questions[4]

The three questions associated with the Model for Improvement are:
1. What are we trying to accomplish?
2. What change can we make that will result in improvement?
3. How will we know that a change is an improvement?

Answering this trilogy of guiding questions is powerful for improvement teams and managers alike, bringing into focus an entire scope of improvement work for teams. The questions are frequently applied in two ways: to scope the journey and boundaries of an improvement initiative for a system and to guide the development of learning cycles. We will cover their latter use in the section below: Plan Do Study Act Cycle.

In scoping the journey and defining the boundaries the three questions are used by teams to develop a project or program charter which guides the work of improvement that individual teams do toward accomplishing improved outcomes for the system.

---

[4] The Carnegie Foundation for the Advancement of Teaching uses a slightly different wording (adding "specifically" to the first question and "and why" to the second) and swaps the order of the last two questions. The conceptual foundations remain the same however and which version is used is a matter of personal preference.

Question 1[5]

What are we trying to accomplish?

Many teams tasked with improvement will need guidance and facilitation in answering this question. While it may seem a simple task, this question can prove difficult in practice. To answer this question is to set a destination for the team. Often referred to as an Aim statement (see page 133), this first question challenges teams to consider their current level of performance, what level would constitute improved performance, for who in the system a change in performance is desired, and how long the team is giving themselves to learn their way into the destination described.

Question 2

What change can we make that will result in improvement?

At the start of this chapter it is noted that all improvement requires change. At the start of an improvement journey people on an improvement team are likely to have many ideas about how the system could look different. These might include the addition of new resources, the design or redesign of existing work pathways, or adjustments in the culture of the organization or workplace. Because people are different, perspectives will differ, both in terms of which ideas are likely to be important and in how much of one or another is needed to achieve a new level of performance. This question allows team members to dialogue, negotiating an initial theory of what might make the difference in improving performance in practice. Often teams find it helpful to articulate their theory of practice improvement in the form of a Driver Diagram (see page 139) which can visually represent their most current understanding of the leverage points producing the current outcome as well as their ideas about how to affect those leverage points to achieve a new or better outcome for the system.

Question 3

How will we know that a change is an improvement?

At the heart of all improvement journeys is the ability to understand if and when a system has changed its performance. This means the presence of empirical measurement, both of the outcome(s) and of the processes that are engaged to produce the outcome(s) of interest. The answer to this question then, is in the creation of a set, or family, of measures that will allow an improvement team to understand quickly, when the ideas they are trying in practice are having the intended result of improving the performance of the system. Measurement is a complex topic and so, again, the answer to this question is often complex. Teams starting on an improvement journey often find it helpful to conceptualize a family of measures in the form of a measurement tree (see page 172) in order to understand how measures relate to each other and how detecting a change in

---

[5] The three questions can be answered in any order and indeed facilitators and teams may find starting with different questions on different initiatives makes sense depending on contextual factors such as what is known about the problem being addressed, the level of evidence associated with change ideas or the directives of senior leaders or higher managers. The order presented here is one of convenience, with the hope that it will help readers discover meaning in practice and will apply them as makes the most sense within a given system.

performance in one or more of them can increase their degree of belief that their theory is on track to produce the improvements in performance they desire from their system.

Plan-Do-Study-Act-Cycle

At the heart of learning is discovery — discovery of new information about our environments, about the systems in which we work, about the interaction people have with their system and of the components of the system with each other. Discovery is often about curiosity, accident, and failure. Through history we have been moved forward scientifically by people who stumbled across a connection, noticed something in practice others had not, or who postulated what might work only to uncover in practice it did not. In the last 500 years our ability to discover has been greatly accelerated by scientific thinking, the forming of theories and hypotheses, observation or experimentation and subsequent revision of our theories when our hypotheses failed to be correct in practice. The Plan-Do-Study-Act (PDSA) cycle is a practical way of applying scientific thinking in complex social and operational environments. It is comprised of four elements that guide its user or team in a disciplined fashion toward uncovering evidence to support their theories of practice improvement.

The PDSA cycle begins with articulating the change and recording predictions about what we expect will happen (plan); attempting the change and documenting what in fact did happens (do); comparing the results to the predictions (study) and deciding on what to do next (act). In many instances, a PDSA cycle may not generate the results expected; but this failure to achieve predicted outcomes often provides clues as to what to try instead. This is turn becomes the basis for the next PDSA cycle—another mini-improvement experiment.

PDSA cycles can be applied along a continuum of scale to uncover whether individual ideas for change have utility in practice in one small corner of the system or whether an entire complex theory has value in producing a stated aim or outcome. Often it is used to rapidly try ideas in practice, finding conditions under which the idea fails to meet expectations but as evidence is built PDSA cycles can increase in duration, size, and scope to accommodate the desired learning (for more on PDSAs and the use of PDSAs to guide the scaling of changes see page 148 and 157).

In practice, the Model for Improvement is most useful when an aim of appropriate scale can be identified. In some cases, teams first engage in an investigation of the problem to identify where their change efforts might best be focused. At this point, the Model for Improvement becomes the main framework disciplining the change efforts of a team or community. Taken together these three disciplining questions structure the improvement effort and the PDSA cycles guides learning from practice to help improvement teams learn their way into actual improvements in system performance. The Model for Improvement also outlines a powerful way of thinking that becomes embedded in improvement communities over time.

References and Further Reading

- Langley G, Moen R, Nolan K, Nolan T, Norman C and Provost L. The Improvement Guide: A Practical Approach to Enhancing Organizational Performance, Jossey-Bass, 2009.
- Provost L, Murray S. The Health Care Data Guide: Learning Data for Improvement. San Francisco: Jossey-Bass, Publication, 2011.
- Moen R, Norman C. Circling Back: Clearing up myths about the Deming cycle and seeing how it keeps evolving, Quality Progress. 2010; 43(11):22
- Bryk, A.S., Gomez, L.M., Grunow, A. & LeMahieu, P. (2015). Learning to improve: How America's schools can get better at getting better. Cambridge, MA: Harvard Education Press.
- Ogrinc G, Shojania K. Building Knowledge, Asking Questions, BMJ Qual Saf 2014;23:265–267. doi:10.1136/bmjqs-2013-002703
- Taylor M, McNicholas C, Nicolay C, Darzi A, Bell D, Reed J. Systematic review of the application of the plan-do-study-act method to improve quality in healthcare. BMJ Qual Saf 2014; 23:290–8.

Improvement Habits

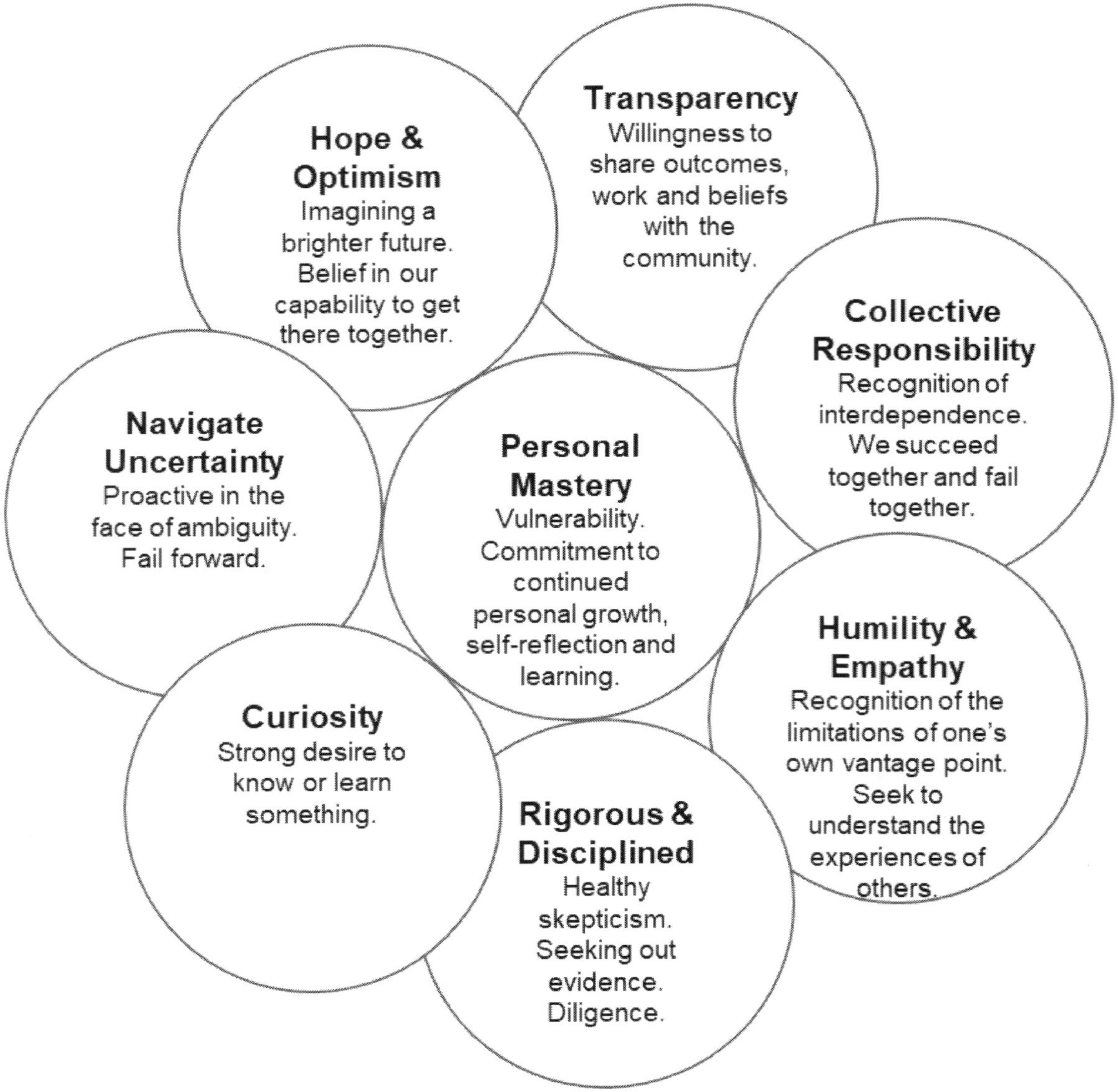

Collective Responsibility
Recognition of interdependence. We succeed together and fail together.

Humility & Empathy
Recognition of the limitations of one's own vantage point. Seek to understand the experiences of others.

Transparency
Willingness to share outcomes, work and beliefs with the community.

Personal Mastery
Vulnerability. Commitment to continued personal growth, self-reflection and learning.

Rigorous & Disciplined
Healthy skepticism. Seeking out evidence. Diligence.

Hope & Optimism
Imagining a brighter future. Belief in our capability to get there together.

Navigate Uncertainty
Proactive in the face of ambiguity. Fail forward.

Curiosity
Strong desire to know or learn something.

Improvement Habit Look-Fors

Habit	Look-Fors	Importance to Improvement
HOPE & OPTIMISM Imagining a brighter future. Belief in our capability to get there together.	**Maintains a strong sense of purpose** <ul><li>Refers to the "why"</li></ul> **Believes in the potential and good intentions of others** <ul><li>Frequently points out individuals and participants assets</li></ul> **Exhibits a sense of agency** <ul><li>Proposes possible paths forward</li><li>Finds own locus of control (avoids fatalistic thinking)</li><li>"We can do better"</li></ul>	Improvement in inherently optimistic; it assumes that we can create a different reality by working together in new ways. We also assume that the people working in the system have good intentions and are doing their best. Taken together this hopeful orientation to the work can restore the deep sense of purpose that brought people to the profession in the first place.
TRANSPARENCY Willingness to share outcomes, work, and beliefs openly with the community.	**Open to participation in shared environment** <ul><li>Share's data</li><li>Candid about thinking and assumptions even when it diverges from the rest of the group</li><li>Shares "work in progress"</li><li>Makes practice public</li></ul> **Openly acknowledges and talks about what is not working**	"If we cannot express our assumptions explicitly in ways that others can understand and build upon, there can be no larger process of testing those assumptions and building public knowledge." (Peter Senge)
COLLECTIVE RESPONSIBILITY Recognition of interdependence. We succeed together and fail together.	**Accepts responsibility for others** <ul><li>Uses "we" language</li><li>Comments on the work of others and offers support</li><li>Acknowledges individual impact on the success of the group</li></ul> **Pursues shared practice** <ul><li>Tests change ideas in common</li><li>Seeks out expertise of others who have solved similar problems</li><li>Documents learning so others can learn from it</li></ul> **Recognizes diverse forms of expertise**	The problems we set out to solve are typically complex, requiring action across typical organization boundaries. Solving these problems requires breaking down norms of individual practice, department silos, and "hero" models to solve our problems. Instead, we pursue a collective effort that engages diverse expertise and capitalizes on the learning of others working on similar problems.
HUMILITY & EMPATHY Recognition of the limitations of own vantage point. Seeks to understand the experiences of others.	**Open to feedback and learning from others** <ul><li>Accepts disconfirming evidence</li><li>Defers to expert knowledge when appropriate</li><li>Recognizes what you know and what you do not know</li></ul> **Values and actively seeks out different perspectives** <ul><li>Engages in "humble inquiry"; Asks and listens</li><li>Takes the time to "go and see"</li><li>Seeks out an understanding of user's experience</li></ul> **Recognizes the expertise of the front lines**	"Every system is perfectly designed to get the results it gets," Paul Batalden. Given this, there is no one person who is the cause of the problem or who can solve it alone. As a result, this means you must adopt a type of inquiry borne in a sincere sense of humility and empathy to see and understand the problem and possible solutions.

Habit	Look Fors	Importance to Improvement
RIGOROUS & DISCIPLINED Healthy skepticism. **Seeking out evidence.** Diligence.	**Maintains focus for sustained period of time on improving high-leverage area** • Says "no" to work or changes that detract from the focus **Exhibits scientific orientation to work** • Uses and respectfully probes for data or evidence to back claims and beliefs • Expresses a dose of doubt in the face of untested ideas • Actively tests change ideas under multiple conditions; seeks disconfirming evidence to "break" theory **Documents work consistently (PDSAs, data charts, progress reports)** **Adheres to improvement routines** **Attends to the details of practice**	One of the primary goals of improvement science is to generate new knowledge that can be spread. This requires more rigorous testing, adherence to a consistent rhythm of testing, and a more stringent evidence base than learning that happens through traditional professional learning communities and action-based research.
CURIOSITY **Strong desire to know or learn something**	**Openly wonders** • Poses authentic questions • Asks why • Generates multiple hypotheses to explain patterns in data **Proactively pursues learning** • Goes beyond "requirements"	Improvement pursues better outcomes as a learning journey. Curiosity propels the journey by continually posing questions about why things are the way they are and seeking out new knowledge that might lead to an improvement.
NAVIGATE UNCERTAINTY **Proactive in the face of ambiguity. Fail forward.**	**Toggles between the big picture and the next step** • Shifts between understanding complexity and moving forward **Leans into action** • Proposes concrete actions to avoid "analysis paralysis" • Willing to try a change or an improvement tool despite not being able to imagine exactly how it will work **Trusts the learning process** • Tries and iterates instead of looking for the perfect idea • Willingness to be wrong; approaches failures as an opportunity to learn	While we may be able articulate the end goal, the path to getting there is usually not linear or clear. Rather than letting the unknown paralyze us, we need to actively lean into the improvement process, trusting that it that will help us learn our way into how to solve the problem.
PERSONAL MASTERY **Vulnerability.** Commitment to continued personal growth, self-reflection, and learning.	**Able to balance personal vision for oneself with accurate assessment of current reality** • Articulates personal strengths and weaknesses **Able to engage in productive conflict** • Uses conversational capacity "candor" and "curiosity" skills • Recognizes triggers during conflict; takes responsibility • Actively pursues self-reflection **Recognizes own mental models and beliefs**	At its heart, improvement is about learning, and learning is inherently vulnerable. To learn with others and as an organization, you need to be a learner yourself. This involves knowing yourself and managing the personal emotions that this brings up for you.

Systems Framework

"Every system is perfectly designed to get exactly the results that it gets," is an axiom commonly used to describe a core belief at the foundation of Improvement Science. The core challenge for improvement teams and communities is to change their system to create outcomes different from the undesirable ones they currently experience.

The trick is systems are notoriously hard to see. Asking people to describe the system is akin to asking fish to describe the water they are swimming in. The following framework was developed to make the multi-dimensional components of systems which interact to create observable outcomes more visible to leaders and teams. In particular, the authors sought to explain the systems components that hold inequitable systems in place.[6]

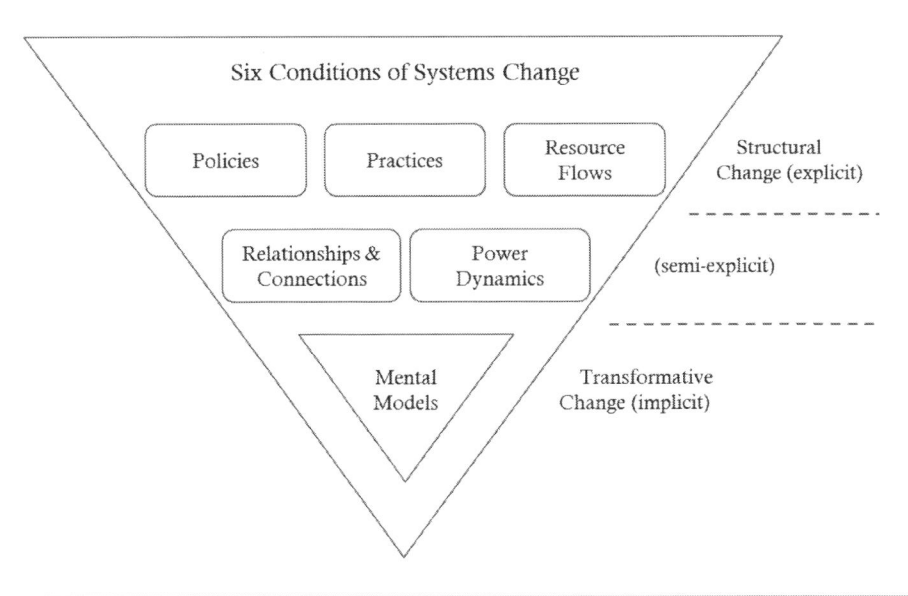

Six Conditions of Systems Change

- Policies
- Practices
- Resource Flows

Structural Change (explicit)

- Relationships & Connections
- Power Dynamics

(semi-explicit)

- Mental Models

Transformative Change (implicit)

Systems Change Conditions - Definitions

Policies: Government, institutional and organizational rules, regulations, and priorities that guide the entity's own and others' actions

Practices: Espoused activities of institutions, coalitions, networks, and other entities targeted to improving social and environmental progress. Also, within the entity, the procedures, guidelines, or informal shared habits that comprise their work.

Resource Flows: How money, people, knowledge, information, and other assets such as infrastructure are allocated and distributed.

Relationships & Connections: Quality of connections and communication occurring among actors in the system, especially among those with differing histories and viewpoints.

Power Dynamics: The distribution of decision-making power, authority, and both formal and informal influence among individuals and organizations.

Mental Models: Habits of thought - deeply held beliefs and assumptions and taken-for-granted ways of operating that influence how we think, what we do, and how we talk.

From Kania, J., Kramer, M., & Senge, P. (2018). *The Water of Systems Change.* FSG Report

---

[6] The Six Conditions of Systems Change is a complementary framework to use with the Lens of Systemic Oppression by the National Equity Project (see Section 1: Equity Framework). Both aim to support broad understandings of the individual, relational and structural components of systems that interact to produce inequitable outcomes.

Equity Framework

The pursuit of more equitable outcomes is the grounding purpose for many teams pursuing an improvement science approach. Pursuing equity requires shared equity values and clear, shared definitions of equity to ground improvement work. The National Equity Project provides a definition of equity that can serve as a starting place as teams and organizations define equity in their context.

Defining Equity

> Equity is the <u>state</u> that would be achieved if how one fares in society was no longer predictable by race, gender, class, language, and/or any other social/cultural factor.
>
> Equity in <u>practice</u> is each child/family receives what they need when they need it, to develop to their full intellectual, social, economic, and physical potential.

Pursuing equity also requires seeing the system that produces and sustains inequitable outcomes. The National Equity Project's Lens of Systemic Oppression provides a framework for identifying the multi-layered, reinforcing forces that come together to systematically advantage some while oppressing others. The framework offers a systems perspective that can guide improvement teams to better diagnose the causes of inequitable outcomes and build stronger theories of how to disrupt them.

THE LENS OF SYSTEMIC OPPRESSION

INDIVIDUAL   **SYSTEMIC**

INTERPERSONAL

INDIVIDUAL
A *person's* beliefs & actions that serve to perpetuate oppression
- conscious and unconscious
- externalized and internalized

The *interactions* between people - both within and across difference

INSTITUTIONAL
Policies and practices at the *organization* (or "sector") level that perpetuate oppression

STRUCTURAL
How these effects interact and accumulate *across institutions* - and across history

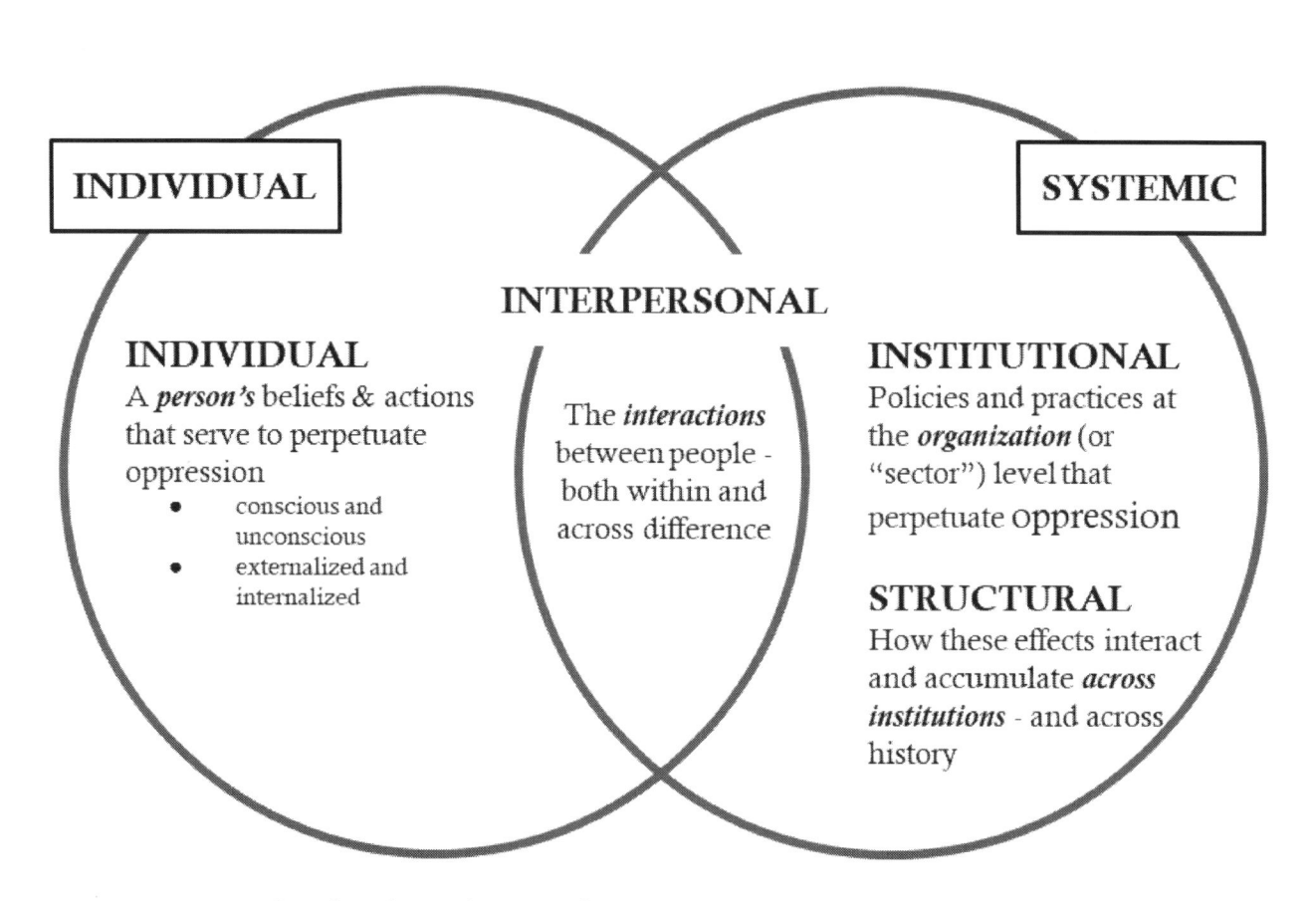

For more see: www.nationalequityproject.org/featured-resources/lens-of-systemic-oppression

2. Facilitating and Coaching Improvement Teams

For many, the attraction of an improvement science approach is the availability of practical tools and methods to guide improvement efforts. What is often less obvious is that in taking an improvement science approach, we are also signing on to a different way of working and relating to one together. This section provides guidance about the social infrastructure required by an improvement science approach.

Suggestions for further reading

- *Conversational Capacity* by Weber
- *The Wisdom of Teams* by Smith and Katzenbach
- *The Culture Code: The Secrets of Highly Successful Groups* by Coyle
- *The Team Handbook* by Scholtes
- *The Fifth Discipline: Team Learning* by Senge
- *The Art of Coaching Teams* by Aguilar
- *Difficult Conversations* by Patton, Stone, and Heen
- *Crucial Conversations* by Grenny, Patterson, McMillan, Switzler,, and Gregory

Building Effective Improvement Teams

If we want to build reliably effective teams, we need to manage the human side of the enterprise with the same level of rigor and discipline with which we manage the technical.

—Craig Weber

Improvement is by design a team sport. Gaps in performance are addressed by empowering teams of people to investigate critical systems problems, try out various solutions and spread what they learn to other parts of the organization. The secret sauce of an improvement team is their capacity to learn. This requires breaking down our typical silo-ed and individualistic ways of working in favor of a collective learning approach in which team members agree to come together to examine their individual perspectives and work toward shared solutions. By investing in improvement teams, organizations begin to break through bureaucratic structures and create a culture where everyone in the organization engages in collective learning to improve their work.

We are accustomed to touting the value of collaboration and putting people into teams, but we are less accustomed to the discipline of forming highly effective teams. For many, the tight form of collaboration that is entailed in working on an improvement team will entail a significant shift. In this chapter, we review what research has to say about teams and describe how the technical tools of improvement science are used to support the development of a high-functioning team.

Differentiating a group from a team

Not every group of people that comes together can or needs to be considered team. In the *Wisdom of Teams*, Katzenbach and Smith provide the following definition of a team:

> **Team**: A small number of people with complementary skills who are committed to a common purpose, set of performance goals, and shared approach for which they hold themselves mutually accountable" (Katzenbach and Smith 1993, pg. 41).

The defining feature of a team is a high level of mutual accountability and interdependency to achieve a shared purpose. Teams commit to joint goals and work products. Many of the groups that we commonly refer to as teams don't meet the conditions of this definition. Katzenback and Smith provide a continuum to distinguish different ways that people commonly work together.

Table 2.1 Ways that Small Groups of People Work Together

Working group	Pseudo team	Potential team	Real team	High-performing teams
Regularly interact to share information or perspectives but work remains individual	Has an opportunity to work collectively but has not focused and committed to collective performance.	Engaged in trying to improve its collective performance but lacks clarity about the purpose, goals or common approach.	Equally committed to a common purpose, goals, and working approach for which they hold themselves mutually accountable.	Outperforms expectations. Meet the conditions of real teams and has team members that are also deeply committed to one another's personal growth and success.

Source: The Wisdom of Teams

The advantage of organizing as a team is the magnified impact that the group can have by pooling their individual talents and skills. This impact includes enhanced performance results, work products, and meaningful learning. Along with these advantages come risks. In committing to becoming a "real team," individuals are assuming joint responsibility for collective goals and work products. They are opting into group discussions and debate that inevitably will involve conflict. This is less comfortable, takes time, and goes against many of our deep-seated values of individualism.

What makes for a high-performing team?

Many research studies have pursued an understanding of what produces *high-performing teams*. High-performing teams get results and outperform the expectations of individual group members. Said another way, they have developed a collective capacity that is higher than the sum of their individual capacities. This collective capacity enables them to outperform other teams on a wide range of tasks (Katzenback and Smith). High-performing teams develop a collective identity. They no longer appear as a collection of individuals but as a unit that acts together. And they represent themselves externally as a group. In the words of Katzenbach and Smith, high-performing teams are "a small group of people so committed to something larger than themselves that they will not be denied" (p. 259).

Contrary to popular thought, high-performing teams are not necessarily made up of high-performing individuals, nor are they composed of people with similar working styles (Gratton & Erickson, Duhigg). Several studies have tried to pinpoint the ways of working that characterize the difference between high-performing teams and their lower performing counterparts. Table 2.2 summarizes the distinguishing features from three different authors.

Google Study on Highly Effective teams	Katzenback and Smith Vital Signs of Highly Effective Teams	The Culture Code
Equality in the distribution of conversational turn taking (across tasks)

Social sensitivity: skilled at intuiting how other people feel based on tone of voice etc.

Psychological safety: safe to share things that scare us | Exceptional performance "outperform all reasonable expectations of the group, including those of the team members themselves"

High levels of enthusiasm and energy

Personal commitment that is willing to go the extra mile

Great stories of galvanizing events — turning points in their history where they overcame the odds

More fun and humor than ordinary teams | Establish purpose: Narratives create shared goals and values

Build safety: sending signals of connection that generate bonds of belonging and identity

Share vulnerability: Habits of mutual risk drive trusting cooperation |

Table 2.2 Distinguishing Features of High-Performing Teams

What these distinguishing features have in common is the development of relational practices that create a safe space for team members to engage openly and transparently with one another. The team experience is a positive one, characterized by laughter and connecting team members to a purpose that is larger than their individual work.

In supporting the development of high-functioning teams, attention to relational practices of a team goes hand-in-hand with attending to the structural aspects of a team. Common work routines and conversation protocols provide ways for each member to contribute. Conversations about shared performance goals and norms can provide a place for team members to share what is important to them. Structuring improvement work to enable quick learning and get early wins helps the team to have fun and create common stories that shape their collective identity. Most authors argue against investing in generic "relationship building activities" (i.e., a ropes course) that is disconnected from the core work of the team (Aguilar).

Defining *Improvement* Teams

Improvement teams are unique in that they are commissioned to solve specific *systems* problems. They are committed to *learning* their way into improvement and are disciplined by the application of improvement methodologies. The hallmarks of a successful improvement team are: (a) evidence of improved performance, (b) the discovery and documentation of key evidence-based practices and (c) an enhanced capability to improve.

In this sense, improvement teams are *real teams* and not a *working group* (see table 2.1 above). The theory and practice of improvement science provides improvement teams with specific technologies for achieving the elements in the definition of a team provided above. We describe each of these elements below noting how they are achieved on an improvement team.

> **(1) Committed to a common purpose and set of performance goals.** Improvement teams commit to a common aim statement that defines what will be improved, for whom and by when. During the *chartering* phase the improvement team articulates the motivation for the improvement work, crafts the aim statement and identifies measures to assess their progress. These are typically articulated in an *improvement charter.* Improvement teams have regular routines for updating the charter, reviewing data, and coming to joint decisions about where to focus next. These routines provide improvement teams with a mechanism for renewing and focusing attention on the collective goals of the group (see chapters on aim statements and charters in this guide).
>
> **(2) A small number of people with complementary *and the necessary* skills.** Improvement teams are made up of people with the *necessary* expertise to solve the problem they were commissioned to solve. The larger team literature emphasizes attention to the technical, interpersonal, and project management skills necessary for team functioning. These can either be selected for or can be developed through participation on the team. In defining the key technical skills, improvement science brings additional attention to the diverse *kinds of expertise* needed to achieve the systems problem at hand. This includes research, professional, and improvement expertise (see kinds of expertise on page 12). An important principle in improvement is those whose work practices are the object of change are actively involved in the improvement work. Initial work in understanding the system helps to identify key processes that impact the aim. Improvement teams focus their work on these processes and include people that engage in them daily.
>
> The research is clear that team functioning is inhibited when teams grow too large. Most researchers agree that effective teams *can* have up to 20 people but that teams with fewer than 10 people are much easier to manage (Katzenbach and Smith). Sutton and Rao use the "pizza rule": a team should not grow to a size where they can't share a pizza together. Smaller teams allow people to relate to one another individually and ease

collective decision making. For improvement teams, it can be hard to put together this small number requirement with the need to engage the diverse expertise necessary to address complex systems problems. More complex improvement initiatives require multiple improvement teams that come together to regularly share learning (see improvement team membership below).

(3) **Shared approach.** Improvement teams have a shared approach on four dimensions. (1) Like all real teams, they have agreements about roles, decision-making and how they will relate to one another. These need to be established up front and monitored throughout the work. (2) Improvement teams use a common improvement methodology to achieve their goals. Throughout this resource guide, we rely on the Model for Improvement as the core improvement methodology for teams, augmented with additional tools and methods that can be used to solve specific problems (see the overview of the Model for Improvement on page 14). However, *which* improvement methodology is used is less important than that the team ascribes to a *common* methodology. In most cases, team members build skills in an improvement methodology through work on the team. An outside improvement coach often supports this capacity building. (3) Part and parcel with an improvement methodology comes the distinctive rhythm of improvement work. Starting on page 43, we define the improvement team routines. They involve specific kinds of team meetings as well as work in between team meetings to learn in practice. The learning of the team is dependent on committing to this shared rhythm of learning. (4) Finally, improvement teams agree to work toward common practices and a shared theory of improvement. Improvement team members come together not just to share their individual perspectives, but to use evidence to design and determine standard practices that are used by all team members and often spread to others outside the team.

(4) **Mutual accountability.** In high-functioning teams, team members hold each other accountable for the development of work products and achieving the team's goals. Team-driven accountability requires high levels of commitment and trust. In an improvement approach, the learning of the team depends on the work that team members do in between team meetings. Team members bring back learning from learning cycles and data about their practice to debrief with the improvement team. Developing a sense of joint responsibility to the learning of the team is critical for effective improvement work.

In most organizations, working in an improvement team will feel different than other collaborative experiences. The common purpose and shared approach represent a much tighter form of collaboration than other typical workgroups like professional learning communities, communities of practice, committees, and working groups. In some cases, launching improvement teams will require taking a "pseudo team" or a "partial team" and supporting their development into a real team through applying improvement methods and routines. In other cases, launching improvement teams will require forming a team of people that don't often work together. Regardless, the development of a real team will take space and time. The methods and routines of improvement will help to create a distinctive team culture. Still, rigorous attention needs to be paid to ensure that these routines result in a social environment that supports the development of high-functioning teams.

References

Aguilar, E. (2016). *The Art of coaching teams: Building resilient communities that transform schools.* San Francisco, CA: Jossey Bass.

Coyle, D. (2018). *The culture code: The secrets of highly effective groups.* NY, NY: Bantam Books.

Duhigg, C. (2016). What Google learned from its quest to build the perfect team. *The New York Times Magazine.*

Gratton, L. & Erickson, T.J. Eight ways to build collaborative teams. *Harvard Business Review.* November 2007

Katzenbach, J.R. and Smith, D.K. (1993). *The wisdom of teams: Creating the high-performance organization.* Boston, MA: Harvard Business Review Press

Sutton, R. & Rao, H. (2014). *Scaling up excellence: Getting to more without settling for less.* NY, NY: Crown Business

Defining Improvement Team Membership and Roles

Defining the members of an improvement team usually happens simultaneously with selecting an aim for the improvement project. In an improvement approach, those whose work is the object of change are actively involved in making the change, contributing their perspectives, and testing out new ideas in practice. Aims are set by making key decisions about what part of the system will be worked on and what sites will be involved in the change. This has implications for who needs to be on the team.

Example. Leaders at La Casa en el Arbol High School set out to launch an improvement effort to increase the number of students who went directly to four-year colleges and universities. After investigating the problem, the leaders decided to start by focusing on FAFSA completion. They were surprised to find that only 45% of their graduating seniors successfully completed the FAFSA. Their initial aim was:

> Increase the number of seniors in La Casa en el Arbol High School with a completed FAFSA from 45% to 80% by June 1, 2020.

The leaders commissioned an improvement team made up of the school's two advisors, two teachers, and the school's vice principal. Together this team of five took responsibility for figuring out how to increase the FAFSA completion rate across the school.

Had the leaders selected a different starting point related to four-year college-going—such as decreasing the number of students who failed their math classes or increasing the number of 9th grade students who were on-track for success—they would have needed a different improvement team. An improvement team focused on 9th grade performance would necessarily be made up of a group of 9th grade teachers across subject areas and possibly the counselor. Attacking math success rates would require an improvement team mostly made up of math teachers across the school. Ultimately, addressing four-year college-going rates may require work on all these factors. If they had the organizational capacity, the school might opt to launch multiple improvement teams at the same time. If not, they would pick a starting place and evolve the focus and team over time.

Broadly speaking, the interdependency between the aim and team membership is managed in one of two ways. Sometimes the team is selected first, and the aim is built around this team. Other times, the aim is identified first, and a team is commissioned around achieving the aim. Table 2.3 summarizes these two approaches.

Table 2.3 Starting with the Aim vs. Starting with the Team

	When?	Advantages	Disadvantages
Start with the team, create an aim statement	Existing structure or group of people that are committed to working on something and want to use improvement methodologies to guide their work.	Ability to leverage existing commitments, relationships, and group structures for improvement work	The team may not be well situated to address the problem at hand. Teams' understanding of the problem may be constrained by what they can see or what is under their control.
Start with the aim statement, create a team	Improvement work is commissioned by leaders to make progress on an organizational problem or goal.	The improvement work is focused on an organizational priority. The team can be constructed to have the expertise necessary to make progress.	Requires time and energy to build a joint sense of purpose, collaborative structures and trusting relationships amongst team members.

In practice, leaders consider both the aims and the teams that are implied in selecting a starting point for an improvement initiative. Improvement initiatives benefit from early wins. Finding places where willing people and important yet fixable problems intersect is key for producing those early wins. Subsequent phases can build on these wins and tackle less fully formed teams and more difficult problems.

Evolving/Multiple Teams: Complex Team Structures

Regardless of how the initial team is selected, there is a need for flexibility in defining team membership. Particularly in larger improvement endeavors, the team structure will evolve as the improvement work evolves.

One time when team membership often shifts is between the understanding the problem phase of the improvement journey and introducing changes (see Chapter 3 for more on *improvement journeys*). Organizations will often begin with a broad problem of practice and spend the first phase of the improvement work trying to understand the causes of that problem. A key product of this phase of improvement is the identification of key leverage points in the system to drive improvement. As the improvement work shifts to making changes in those leverage points, new teams are often launched to test changes to each of these practices. The team involved in understanding the problem may therefore be different than the team responsible for making improvements.

Another natural evolution in team composition comes when the focus of improvement turns from developing/testing changes to spreading proven changes to a larger part of the organization. Many improvement efforts begin by engaging a single department or site in solving the problem at hand and then subsequently enlarging the effort to spreading what is learned to other departments or sites. This increase in scale of the improvement effort necessitates a rethinking of team structure and roles.

Larger improvement initiatives may also involve multiple teams working together simultaneously on a common improvement aim. These teams might be working toward similar aims in different locations (i.e., two different schools working on FAFSA completion rates). Or the improvement teams may be commissioned to work on different aspects of the problem (i.e., FAFSA completion rates and 9th grade on track). Typically, improvement teams working on different aspects of the problem would use a driver diagram to coordinate their improvement work (see Chapter 5 for more on *driver diagrams*).

Even for smaller improvement endeavors, team membership often changes. Along the improvement journey, the team may have new insights about the parts of the system that are producing the outcomes, and this may have implications for who needs to be part of the team. For example, an improvement team comprised of math teachers in La Casa en el Arbol High School set out to improve the passing rates of students in math. They began by working on mindsets and instructional practices to aid in the learning of math. Along the way they learned that many of the students were assigned to the wrong classes. Scheduling classes was the work of the counselors in the school. To solve these problems, they needed to engage counselors in their improvement effort.

Finally, improvement team membership may have to evolve because one of the members changes roles or leaves the organization. Whatever the reason that requires team membership to change, transition points are key pain points for improvement teams and should be carefully managed. New team members need space to connect to the purpose of the improvement effort and add their perspective. New relationships need to be built. They need to be brought up to speed on what they team has been learning and given opportunities to catch up on some of the skills that the team members have developed through engaging in the improvement work. The re-formation of teams or formation of new teams should prompt a refocus on the characteristics of what makes a successful team.

Defining Team Roles

In managing the diverse participation of improvement teams, it can be helpful to remember that not everyone who contributes to the team needs to be considered a *team member*. As a rule of thumb, *team members* attend all the team meetings and are actively involved in improvement work in between team meetings. The characteristics of an effective team described above apply to them. However, effective teams exist in a larger context that enable them to be effective. Team sponsors and Improvement Coaches are critical resources to improvement teams, but they may have a different rhythm for interacting with the improvement team. Finally, improvement teams need access to diverse forms of expertise and perspectives to inform their improvement work. It is not always practical for these people to be *on the* team and attend all team meetings. Rather, they can consult with the improvement team as their contribution is needed. Table 2.4 outlines different roles that people can play with regards to an improvement team.

Improvement Projects Focused on Equity

For improvement projects that are focused on equity, it is particularly important to pay attention to who is on the improvement team. For all improvement projects, integrating the voice and perspective of the people that the improvement work is intended to serve is critical. This is particularly true when the backgrounds of the people on the improvement team stand in stark contrast to the end-users. For equity-focused projects it is best practice to include a member of the community who the improvement work is intended to impact (i.e., student, parent, patient, etc.) directly on the improvement team. It is important to have rigorous routines for bringing the community's voice into the conversations and interpretations of the improvement team. Especially critical points include when the team is understanding the problem, selecting an aim, designing, or evaluating change ideas and interpreting data. Improvement teams may choose to enlarge their team meetings at critical times, maintain a key-users group and/or integrate practices of seeking out the user's voice into their improvement activities.

Table 2.4 Improvement Team Roles

ROLE	DESCRIPTION	RESPONSIBILITIES	SELECTION CRITERIA
Team Lead *(Team Members)*	The team lead is the point person for the team who takes initial responsibility for orchestrating the activities of the team, maintaining team records and communication with the rest of the organization. The role may become more shared as the team evolves.	-Maintains the charter -Schedule, plan, and facilitate team meetings -Makes sure work is on track -Coordinate and communicate with the sponsor and improvement coach	-Strong interpersonal skills (relationship oriented) -Strong organizational/project management skills (task oriented) -Knowledge of improvement and area of focus preferred -Job assignment allows for flexible time
Team Members (no more 5-7) *(Team Members)*	Team members carry out the work of the team. They are the people whose work processes are the object of change and are therefore well-situated to learn from trying changes in practice.	-Actively participate in improvement routines -Meets weekly with the improvement team -Collects, analyzes, and makes sense of data -Conducts inquiry cycles on their work -Shares and consolidates learning with team	-Represent the key areas affected by the project -Curious, open-minded, and proactive -Work well in a team setting -Informal leaders whose opinions are respected by peers
Team Sponsor *(Key Team Resources)*	The team sponsor commissions the improvement work. He or she provides the organizational conditions necessary for team success and connects the improvement work to organizational priorities.	-Meet monthly with the team or team lead -Provide time and space for improvement work -Celebrate accomplishments, remove barriers -Identify opportunities to spread learning	-Has some level of formal authority to the organization -Oversees the people and/or the focus area of the improvement work -Curious and able to create a safe-space for team learning
Improvement Coach *(Key Team Resources)*	The improvement coach helps the team improvement methodologies to make progress in the problem area. In some cases, they may double as the team lead or serve as the team lead in the beginning of the effort.	-Help launch the team and charter the project -Guide the team on what to engage in next -Facilitate and lead some team meetings -Build team members' skills with tools -Provide coaching and feedback	-Experience using improvement methodologies -Facilitation and teaching skills -Strong analytic skills -Relationship and task oriented -(preferred) Knowledge of the content area
Content Expert *(Optional Team Resources)*	Consults with the team to provide access to research and professional knowledge around the topic of interest.	-Provide access to resources -Identify key practices -Help the team make sense of what is being learned	-Well versed in the research literature related to the improvement effort -Pragmatic; capable of translating research knowledge to concrete practices
Key users *(Optional Team Resources)*	Having a user directly on the team can have a transformative effect. In lieu of adding a user as a team member, teams can identify key users that they return to regularly.	-React to change ideas -Share perspectives and experiences -Engage other users to capture their perspective	-Represents the user group of interest -Comfortable sharing with the team -Good relationship with team members and other peers
Tester *(Optional Team Resources)*	Teams may employ "testers" outside their team to test changes in contexts that are not under their sphere of influence	-Test changes, collect data, and report learning	-Curious and open-minded
Data Analyst *(Optional Team Resources)*	Consults with the team to provide data support	-Helps identify measures and data collection instruments -Guides or provides data visualizations	-Understands the use of data for improvement -Pragmatic

Building an Inclusive Table

(Adapted from The Chalkboard Project)

> *The best ideas emerge when the whole organizational ecosystem - not just its designers and engineers and certainly not just management — has room to experiment.*
> —Tim Brown

Far too often, only a few people are at the decision-making table. This might make decision-making faster and more efficient, but it means solutions come from an incomplete perspective and, as a result, are often ineffective. Broadening the table to involve people with different perspectives, especially those who are historically underserved, helps ensure that the decisions and solutions serve everyone in the system. Creating an inclusive design process is also one way to operationalize a commitment to equity. The Creative Action Lab summarizes the importance this way:

> People with different identities, perspectives, and backgrounds (e.g., race, religion, sexual orientation, etc.) will bring holistic insights into any setting, particularly through knowledge building, problem solving, and implementation. Also, each sector of society contributes different perspectives and knowledge bases that should be brought together to effectively approach problems. We especially need to include the individuals and communities affected, also known as living experts, who are often excluded from design and decision-making processes. (Equity Centered Community Design Field Guide)

How to Build an Inclusive Table

1. **Commit.** Be authentic and transparent in your call to include more voices at the table. Make sure those around you share this commitment.

2. **Get rid of excuses.** Bringing more people into the improvement process as true partners might require more time and more resources. Be wary of excuses that allow you to continue with the status quo.

3. **Assess the status quo.** Who is at the table? Who is not at the table? Are those most affected by the problem we seek to solve at our table? Why not? What conditions have we created that maintain everyone's ability to participate in meaningful ways? Be sure to ask these questions about historically excluded groups, such as students and families of color, LGBTQ educators, and families for whom English is a second language.

4. **Identify who to invite.** Think first about the types of people you want to invite, rather than individual names (for example, first-year teachers, high school freshmen of color, or parents of recently arrived immigrants). Consider reaching out to people you do not know before people you do know.

5. **Invite.** Start with the why; explain the purpose of what you are doing. Be specific about what their commitment would look like.

6. **Build trust and authenticity.** Acknowledge the various perspectives and backgrounds of everyone at the table. Establish and follow equitable team agreements so that you do not inadvertently do harm to people who have been historically excluded. An example of agreements could include:
    - Stay Engaged

- Speak Your Truth Responsibly
- Listen to Understand
- Be Willing to Do Things Differently and Experience Discomfort
- Expect and Accept Non-Closure
- Confidentiality

7. **Be inclusive.** Inviting people to the table does not count if they do not have a voice that is taken seriously once there. Facilitate activities that provide space for everyone to have a voice. Ensure collaborative decision-making. Understand and address the barriers of sharing power and/or access that prevents diverse co-creators from coming and working together. Acknowledge, understand, and utilize the strengths and the nature of the expertise each stakeholder brings, but do not confine their roles and input to these areas.

8. **Check in.** As you work together, continue to assess how you could increase the inclusiveness of your process and whether everyone there feels welcomed, valued, and has opportunities to fully participate. Be flexible and adjust.

Supporting the Development of Effective Improvement Teams

An improvement team goes through various stages of development during its lifecycle. One of the key roles of an improvement coach is to support the team through this journey, attending to key activities and practices specific to each stage.

- **Stage 1: Commission an improvement team**
  During this stage coaches primarily engage with organizational leaders to identify the focus of the improvement work and the members of the improvement team. Once the focal area and team have been determined, it is critical that the senior leaders clearly communicate the goals of the work to the team, identify it as a priority and provide the team the necessary time and space to do the work. This handoff at the end of commissioning is crucial to the successful launch of a team.
- **Stage 2: Launch an improvement team**
  During the launch, the improvement team begins to form as a team. Building relationships, aligning around a common purpose, and establishing a common working approach and norms are key goals of this phase. The improvement coach typically facilitates the launch, working closely with the team lead.
- **Stage 3: Engage in collective improvement work**
  This phase is the longest and where the team coalesces around the work. The coach's primary goal is to help the team establish and maintain the core improvement routines. In addition, the coach and/or team lead communicates regularly with the sponsor and other key stakeholders outside the team, providing updates, problem-solving issues that may arise, and securing additional resources, as necessary.
- **Stage 4: Adjourn the improvement team**
  This is an often a forgotten but important phase when organizational leaders recognize, celebrate, and share the efforts and learning of the improvement team.

Table 2.5. Stages of Development of an Improvement Team

Phase	Commission	Launch	Engage in collective improvement work	Adjourn
Key Goals	<ul><li>Identify focus for improvement work</li><li>Select and recruit the appropriate team members</li><li>Secure commitment from other key leaders and stakeholders</li><li>Come to a shared understanding of the improvement process</li><li>Secure time, space and supports for team</li><li>Once team solidified, communicate purpose and importance of work to entire team</li></ul>	<ul><li>Have team connect to purpose of improvement work</li><li>Have team members connect with each other</li><li>Establish a safe space for learning</li><li>Establish roles and rules for working together</li><li>Launch improvement routines</li></ul>	<ul><li>Design the improvement journey</li><li>Establish reliable and effective improvement routines<ul><li>Team meetings</li><li>Cycles of inquiry</li><li>Data collection and analysis</li><li>Data conversations</li></ul></li><li>Maintain charter</li><li>Build capability in improvement</li><li>Communicate regularly with sponsor and stakeholders</li></ul>	<ul><li>Document and share learning</li><li>Honor efforts</li><li>Celebrate accomplishments</li></ul>
Who	Organizational leaders	Improvement Coach Team Lead	Improvement Team	Organizational leaders

Stage 1: Commission an Improvement Team

The ultimate goal of the commissioning process is the activation of an improvement team that is empowered and supported to engage in improvement work focused on a goal important to the organization.

During the commissioning, the improvement coach works with organizational leaders to:
- Identify a focus for the improvement work
- Select and recruit the appropriate improvement team members
- Secure commitment from other key leaders and stakeholders
- Come to a shared understanding of the improvement process
- Secure time, space, and supports for improvement work
- Communicate purpose and importance of work to entire team, once team is solidified
- Establish a productive coaching relationship

The involvement of organizational leaders is critical during commissioning. They influence the focus of improvement work, aligning it with organizational priorities, and authorize teams to engage in improvement. It is critical that the organizational leaders who directly supervise improvement team members or oversee the departments involved in the chosen focus area are involved. These leaders can secure time and space for improvement work, remove barriers, and eventually spread what the improvement team learns to other parts of the organization. Successfully commissioning an improvement team can help set the stage for effective improvement work and create the conditions for the organization to capitalize on the investment.

How to commission a team

The improvement coach works with organizational leaders to clarify who will engage in the improvement work and its focus. The improvement coach plays a key role in translating the organization's need for improvement into a structure conducive to the improvement process. Commissioning often requires multiple back and forth conversations among organizational leaders and other key stakeholders to identify and agree upon a focus area for the work. The time and steps required for commissioning a team will depend on the existing working relationship between the improvement coach and the organization, the organization's knowledge of improvement and the internal dynamics of the organization. Figure 2.1 provides a general process to help the improvement coach guide the work of commissioning a team.

Figure 2.1. The Commissioning Process

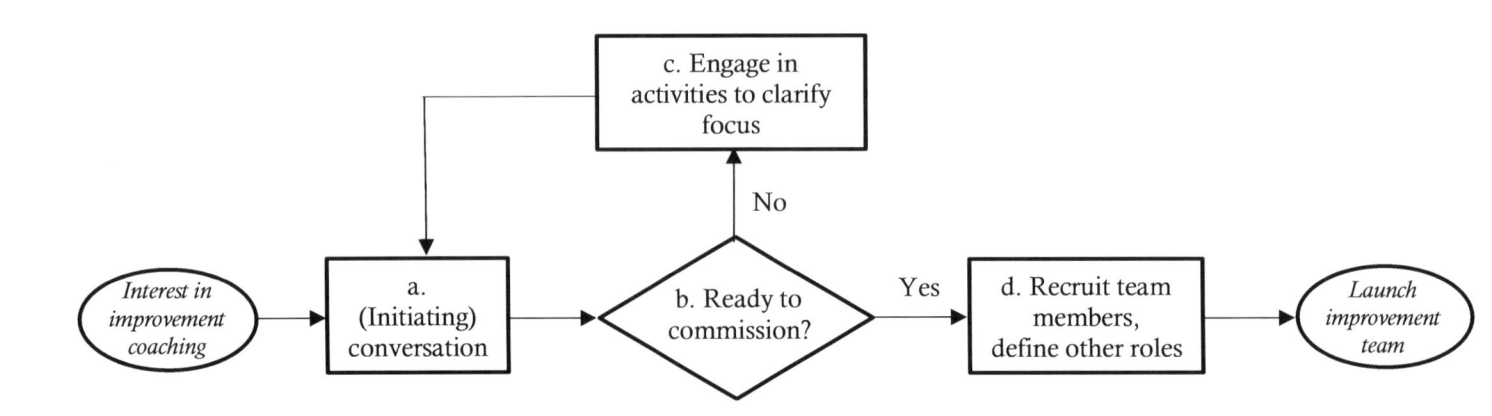

a. Initiating conversation

The initiating conversation is the first contact between those initiating the improvement work and the improvement coach. This is a facilitated conversation that can occur one-on-one or with a small team. The goal of this conversation is to build a relationship between the coach and the group or organization, probe potential areas of focus and improvement team members, and, most importantly, assess the group's readiness to commission a team.

During this conversation, the improvement coach will largely take an inquiry stance, asking questions to learn about the people and organization, understand the various motivations for improvement work, and soliciting information to inform the design of the improvement work. The coach will also need to provide information about what is entailed in taking an improvement science approach. Sharing this information and exploring how it applies to the goals of the organization will help the leaders make informed decisions about if and how to commission a team.

For key questions to probe information to provide during an initiating conversation, see the Initial Conversation: Sample Agenda on pg. 267. For a quick overview about the improvement science approach, see Talking Points about Improvement Science on pg. 284.

b. Assessing readiness to commission

Throughout the initiating conversation the improvement coach will get a sense of the group and if they are ready to begin recruiting individuals to the improvement effort. Table 2.6 provides some criteria for readiness to commission an improvement team.

> **Table 2.6. Criteria for Readiness to Commission an Improvement Team**
> ☐ Established a productive coaching relationship
> ☐ Have compelling focus, scope, and timeframe for improvement work
> ☐ Identified potential improvement team members for recruitment
> ☐ Secured commitment from key leaders on focus area, improvement approach and improvement team members. Identification of a sponsor
> ☐ Secured time, space and supports for the improvement team

c. Engaging in activities to clarify focus

In most cases, the initiating group will not have enough time, the right information, or the right people in the room to make all the necessary decisions in the first meeting. Additional work and follow-up conversations will be needed before recruiting the improvement team. These conversations may involve the same people or an expanded group of stakeholders whose commitment and perspective are necessary to make the key decisions. As an improvement coach, you may want the group to engage in activities either during these conversations or in between to help identify a shared focus and structure for the improvement work.

Typical activities to consider:

- **Organize a data conversation:** Have the relevant people pull data on the problem. Organize a data conversation at the next group meeting.

- **Gather more perspectives:** Have members of the group agree to go out and engage the necessary stakeholders 1:1 to seek their perspective. The original group can meet again and use this information to make decisions about improvement work.

- **Provide access to examples:** To help people see how improvement projects unfold, agree to bring back examples of improvement work and how it unfolded across multiple phases. Alternatively, mockup several different scenarios for how the proposed improvement work of the group could proceed.

d. Recruiting team and defining other roles

The final task in commissioning a team is to recruit members of the improvement team, identify a sponsor for the team, and identify and recruit other supporting roles (see Table 2.4 for more on improvement team roles). The sponsor is usually the one who recruits the improvement team members, often working in concert with the improvement coach. It is important to note that members should be recruited in the effort, not simply told to participate. Recruitment conversations should include highlighting why the improvement work is important to the organization and providing space for potential members to share their interests, perspectives, and concerns. It is also helpful for the sponsor to share how they will be supported and how their work portfolios will be adjusted to make room for the work.

Recruitment conversations can be held individually or as a team depending on who the potential members are and if the members currently work on a team together or not. If conversations are held individually, the sponsor should meet with the whole team after all the members have agreed to participate to reiterate the purpose of the work and how the team will be supported. This can be as part of the Launch Meeting (see next section) or a separate meeting before the launch. Either way, meeting with the improvement team at the beginning of a project is a keyway to acknowledge the importance of the improvement work and to formally establish the team.

You may also want to consider creating a formal document that outlines the improvement project. The sponsor could use this to talk through and get feedback on various aspects of the project when he/she meets with the team, and then have everyone sign off on when everyone is clear and in agreement about expectations, roles, and responsibilities.

Coaching Tips for Commissioning

- **Need for in-time decision making.** Much of the commissioning work requires in-time decisions from the coach about whether the group is ready to move forward or would benefit from additional activities to clarify the focus for the work. Spend time before the conversations anticipating where the team might struggle and map out different next steps for different scenarios.

- **Achieving appropriate level of clarity.** A specific aim statement for the improvement work does not need to be established in the commissioning phase. Rather, it is preferable that the improvement team has an active role in crafting the aim statement. In commissioning, the leaders just need to have enough clarity to feel comfortable with the direction of the improvement work, to justify the investment and to be able to identify the relevant team members. The improvement coach should circle back with the leaders as the aim statement develops to ensure that it fits with their vision of the improvement work.

- **Expect a mismatch between the team and the problem.** It is not uncommon for organizations new to improvement to initially select an improvement team that does not include the appropriate people to work on a common problem; for example, establishing an improvement team made up of district level personnel to solve problems that occur at school sites. This mismatch comes from traditional ways of thinking about how to solve problems. Leaders may need support identifying the appropriate improvement team and understanding how work at the local site could scale up to have impact on the district.

- **Get to commissioning the team as soon as possible.** The hope for actual improvement comes from improvement teams actively engaging in improving practice. Some leadership teams will have an easier time than others identifying a "good enough" starting point and feeling comfortable about having the focus evolve over time. Engaging a smaller group in the commissioning process can facilitate decision-making. However, this must be balanced with ensuring that you have the right people at the table to provide the improvement team with the necessary time and support.

- **Commissioning a multi-stakeholder team to do an organizational analysis of the problem.** In some cases, it will become clear in the commissioning phase that the senior leadership does not have a good understanding of what is happening in the area of focus or has conflicting opinions about whether or how to move forward. In this case, the improvement coach may advise the group to commit to a phase of improvement work dedicated to better understanding the problem, taken on by an improvement team made up of diverse stakeholders. Once a specific focus area is identified, the initial team adjourns (sometimes becoming an advisory group) and local teams are commissioned to identify and test changes within that focus area.

- **Up-commissioning.** Sometimes improvement work gets initiated by an existing group of individuals in the organization and not the organizational leadership. Either a team approaches an improvement coach, or an improvement coach seizes an opportunity to structure existing collaborative work using improvement methodologies. In this case, the improvement coach helps the team to "commission-up;" identify a sponsor, connect the work to the organization's goals, and secure the necessary supports. Many of the same guidelines described above can be followed. Initiating conversations still focus on what the group wants to accomplish and what it would mean to structure the work using improvement. The follow-up activities involve expanding team members, and/or identifying and engaging the leadership of the organization to support the work. Once the commissioning criteria are met, the team can move on to launching their improvement work.

Stage 2: Launching an Improvement Team

The launch of an improvement team is when the team initiates collective work and begins forming as an organized entity. Early interactions set the stage for how the improvement team will engage with one another and the improvement coach. During this stage, the improvement coach is trying to establish a distinct culture and collective working experience that is usually different than the larger organization in which it exists, and other teams or groups that members may have participated in. As a result, carefully crafting the launch experience is critical in establishing a new culture and ways of working together.

During the launch phase the improvement coach works with the team lead to facilitate the team to:
- Connect to the purpose of the improvement work
- Connect to each other
- Establish a safe space for learning
- Establish roles and rules for working together
- Establish coaching relationship
- Launch improvement routines

In addition to establishing a new culture, the launch phase is often used to introduce the improvement routines the team will engage in moving forward. The improvement coach should enter the launch with an outline of the improvement journey and how to structure the next phase of work. From the start, you want to build an expectation the team will learn by doing, not simply by talking. This is exemplified by establishing a team rhythm where members engage in improvement activities between meetings and bring back their learning. Therefore, the early meetings of the improvement team should balance team formation conversations with setting up the improvement work to be done during in between times.

Table 2.7 outlines potential activities that can be used in designing the launch of an improvement team. While paying attention to the feel and structure of the first team meeting is important, launching an improvement team usually does not occur in a single team meeting. Cultivating the culture, you seek to create and the routines necessary to engage in improvement work usually takes a few meetings to establish. As a result, as a coach you may want to include additional launching activities that reinforce specific norms and routines and continue to build team relationships into the opening series of meetings (Sample agendas in Appendix B). If possible, it is helpful to have a longer initial team meeting to allow more time for some of the discussions.

Table 2.7 Key Practices for Launching Improvement Teams

Key Practices	Why is this important?	Potential Activities
Connect to the purpose of the improvement work	Teams thrive when there is a high degree of commitment to the team's purpose and shared goals. Developing this commitment requires giving team members space to connect their personal goals and vision with that of the team. The sponsor will often set a general improvement focus with room for the team to add their perspective, language and shape the specific direction.	<ul><li>Each person tells a story of a student they taught (who made the breakthrough you are hoping for, that you hope to help through the improvement work, etc.)</li><li>The sponsor or leader of the organization personally shares why the work is important to the organization then asks (and listens) for team member perspectives (possible frame: "forces for…" "forces against…")</li><li>Go-round: Vision of the future Create a postcard or headline of the results of the improvement project.</li><li>Go-round: Reflections Here is where I am. Here is where I would like to be. This is what I think I would need.</li></ul>
Connect to each other	Effective teams have high levels of trust and personal connection. To develop trust, team members need to learn about each other's histories, passions, values, and skills and to in tern reveal these aspects of themselves.	<ul><li>Go-round: Something personal Examples include guilty pleasure, something I am passionate about, I am 95% sure I am the only one on this team who, etc.</li><li>Share personal stories about the topic area, struggle, journey as a professional</li><li>Check-ins: Integrate the practice of starting each time meeting with a check-in like "Share one word that describes how you are doing today."</li></ul>
Establish a safe space for learning	The improvement team's primary responsibility is to learn. Learning requires openness to see, admit and be curious about what is not working. The team environment needs to be a safe place to engage in this inherently "risky" activity of learning together.	<ul><li>Modeling by the sponsor, team lead, and coach: Err on the side of listening, share vulnerable stories, admit when you do not know, acknowledge when something does not go well, regularly ask for feedback</li><li>Create behavioral norms to support "lean into learning" (Start with go-round of myself as a learner or conversational capacity activity)</li><li>Facilitation structures for equal voice: Go-rounds, individual writes, chalk talks can help people feel more comfortable speaking up.</li></ul>
Establish roles and rules for working together	Team members need enough clarity on their roles and the structure of improvement work to understand how to meaningfully contribute. Attending to the operational aspects for joint work can also be beneficial.	<ul><li>Introduce an outline of the improvement journey, improvement routines and the roles of each team member</li><li>Create procedural norms for working together (how to deal with absences, preferences around communication).</li><li>Go-round: Gold mines and land mines for working on a team.</li></ul>
Launch improvement routines	The crux of improvement work occurs between team meetings. It is important to establish the rhythm of improvement work from the very beginning.	<ul><li>Establish a shared workspace</li><li>Schedule team meetings</li><li>Engage in an improvement activity (empathy interview, data collection etc.)</li></ul>
Establish a coaching relationship	For the team to "lean into learning" they need to see the improvement coach not as the singular "expert" on the team, but as a guide to the team's learning.	<ul><li>Erring on the side of listening</li><li>Sharing personal stories</li><li>Go-round: How do you like to be coached?</li><li>One on one conversations with each team member</li></ul>

Some of the activities are activities that the team engages in together to foster relationships and co-construct how they will work together. By facilitating these activities, the improvement coach enables all the team members (including the team lead) to fully engage in the conversation and can probe areas that need further discussion.

How the improvement coach and team lead "show-up" is equally important in shaping the emerging culture of the team. By modeling vulnerability, transparency and curiosity, the team lead and coach can foster connections and create a safe space for others to follow suit. In the beginning, both should err on the side of listening to prevent reinforcing the typical norm of coach and leader as the singular experts.

Finally, launching also involves helping the team understand what to expect in taking an improvement science approach. The improvement coach need not co-construct this with the team but can directly share information and ask for reactions. Improvement team members benefit from having timelines, an overview of the improvement journey, and the expectations of improvement work. For many people, the motivation to improve is more directly related to solving the problem at hand as opposed to engaging in a "new approach to improvement." Depending on a read of the team, the improvement coach may choose to downplay the details and new language of improvement science and opt instead for a general description of how the team will work together.

Coaching Tips for Launching Teams

- **Attend to the launch of the team, even for existing teams that already work together.** For teams that do already work together, it can be useful for members to learn each other's connection to this work and have new conversations about how they want to work together. The launch is a reflective and grounding phase that is useful for all teams.

- **Beware of "hollow activities" to build relationships.** Good relationship activities give people a chance to know each other in authentic ways. They are chosen purposefully for the work that needs to get done on the team. In *The Art of Coaching Teams*, Elena Aguilar outlines her considerations for choosing an activity: (a) the levels of trust on the team, (b) how the activity allows people to reveal who they are to each other, (c) a range of activities that use different modalities, (d) connection to what is done in the meeting and (e) the potential emotional impact (appropriately light or heavy).

- **Balancing the role of the improvement coach and the team lead.** In situations where there is an improvement coach and a team lead, the two should work together to launch the team. It can be helpful for the improvement coach to facilitate initiating activities so that the team lead can fully participate as a team member. However, if the coach is not going to be at all the team meetings, the team lead also should assume some of the role of leading team meetings. The two should think together about how to work out the appropriate balance.

- **Establishing rituals.** Consider establishing some rituals for your team meetings. Example rituals include starting with celebrations, ending with appreciations, ending with plus/deltas, trading off bringing food, etc. Rituals provide a chance to return to the purpose and common working agreements and can be anchors for creating a positive culture for the team.

References

Aguilar, E. (2016). *The Art of Coaching Teams; Building Resilient Communities that Transform Schools.* San Francisco, CA: Jossey-Bass

Stage 3: Engaging in Collective Improvement Work

Improvement science involves learning in practice to improve system performance. This learning is often organized broadly as a series of learning sessions and action periods. During a learning session—which can be as formal as a convening of multiple teams or as informal as a team meeting—the improvement team decides where to focus efforts, which improvement tools to use, and (if necessary) builds skills with specific improvement tools and methods. During the action periods, team members engage in improvement activities as part of their daily work.

The following diagram describes how one school district organized the efforts of its improvement teams over the course of a school year. Even for single teams, it can be useful to visualize the overall structure of the improvement effort to plan for the improvement journey.

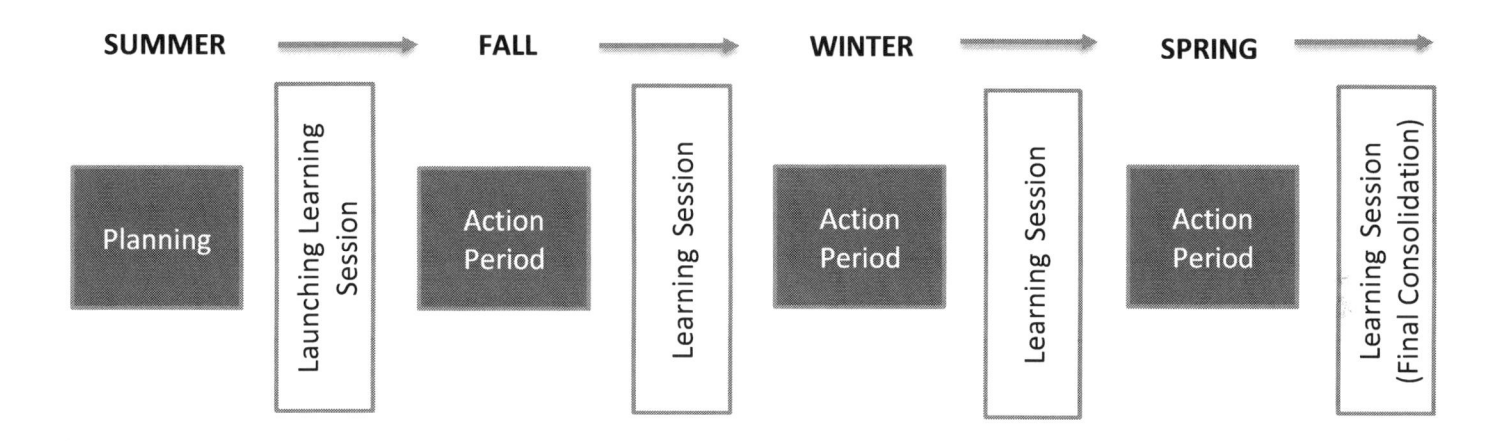

SUMMER → FALL → WINTER → SPRING →

Planning | Launching Learning Session | Action Period | Learning Session | Action Period | Learning Session | Action Period | Learning Session (Final Consolidation)

Five Key Improvement Routines

Integrating improvement activity into daily work is one of the trickiest parts of doing improvement; however, the only way a team will learn and make headway on its aim is if it establishes a consistent and reliable rhythm to the work, especially during the action periods. The following are five key improvement routines that will help discipline and drive the improvement team's learning. While each improvement routine has its own individual purpose, collectively they serve as the flywheel for propelling the team forward. If one of the routines is missing or happens only sporadically, the team's overall learning is diminished. As a result, it is critical that teams establish these routines as quickly as possible and for them to become part of the team's standard practice. To ensure their reliability and efficacy, the team may want to assess the quality of its individual improvement routines periodically.

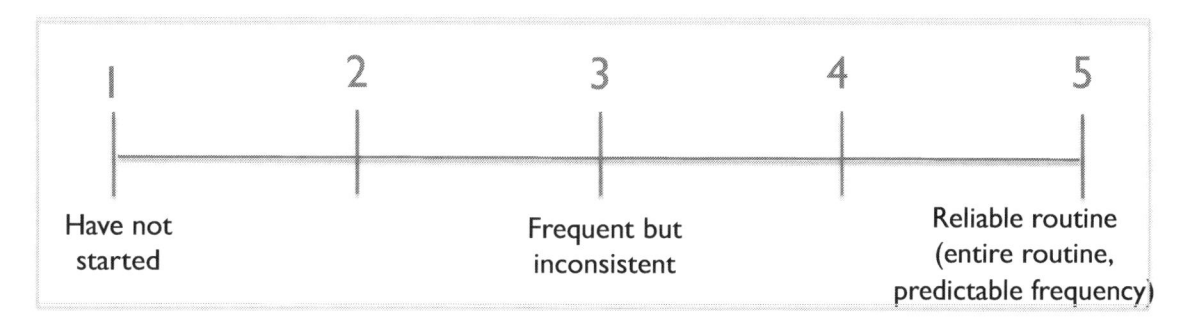

1 — Have not started
2
3 — Frequent but inconsistent
4
5 — Reliable routine (entire routine, predictable frequency)

Routine	Purpose	Timing and Frequency
Learning Cycles	Test changes in practice	Daily, weekly
Collecting, analyzing, and displaying data	See the system. Get valuable feedback to help guide change efforts.	Daily, weekly, monthly
Consolidation of learning	Build a collective understanding of what is learned. Create knowledge artifacts for others. Update theory.	Usually monthly (as part of team meeting)
Collective data conversations	Build shared understanding of performance. Generate hypotheses to test.	Usually monthly (as part of team meeting)
Huddles and Team Meetings	Huddles: Maintain testing momentum—share learning from PDSAs, articulate next steps, trouble-shoot issues that arise during testing, etc. Team meetings: To reflect on progress thus far—review data, consolidate learning from action period	Huddles: Usually, weekly Team meetings: Usually monthly

1) **Learning Cycles**

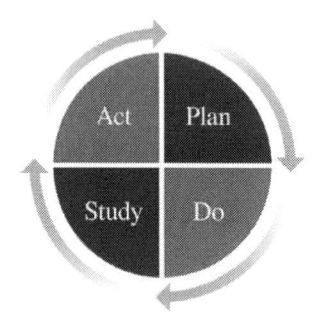

Of all the routines, running learning cycles is the most important. If you do not try ideas in practice, your team won't learn much. Most often, these learning cycles take the form of a PDSA. The basic steps of this routine are the Plan, Do, Study, Act components of the PDSA cycle. However, how the team enacts this routine may vary. Individual team members may plan and run their PDSAs independently from each other. Team members may plan their PDSAs together, either on the same or different change ideas, during a huddle or team meeting and then run them individually. Team members may plan a PDSA for another tester to run. Whatever the case may be, clearly identify who is responsible for running each step of the routine and by when.

Challenges in Running PDSAs
Below are a couple of common challenges that teams face in establishing a learning cycles routine. With either challenge, first take an inquiry stance to help you better understand why an improvement team is not running the test.

Challenges	Potential Causes and *How to Support*

Do not actually run the PDSAs they plan	- Unclear about how to do the change idea they are testing; change idea(s) is under specified
	  - *If they are unclear about the change idea, clarify what they need to do by talking them through the change idea and answering specific questions they might have, modeling the change idea, or having them observe another person doing it.*
	
	- They have not identified when, where, etc. they are going to run the test
	  - *Revisit the section of the form that asks them to articulate the logistics for running the test and plan it out with them.*
	
	- Unmotivated to do the test, do not see the value
	  - *There could be a few reasons why they are unmotivated—they are skeptical the change idea is going to work, they don't want to be a part of the team and were mandated to participate, or they find it too time consuming. There is no easy solution to this problem; the best thing you can do is listen carefully, make sure they feel heard and recognize their frustration, and then make a clear concrete suggestion that tries to address the underlying reason.*

Do not document their PDSAs	- Do not know how to fill out the form - Do not have time to fill out the form - Do not see the value in documenting their learning - *In all of these situations, you may want to do the documentation for them in the beginning, either by observing them run the test and/or debriefing the test quickly and writing down what they say, and then gradually have them take on more of the responsibility.*

One tricky challenge to be aware of occurs when your routine happens regularly but is not generating any learning. This is a sign that your routine is happening mechanistically—that people are just going through the motions and treating it more as a task rather than a learning opportunity. Sometimes this happens when the change ideas are weak or when certain tasks just need to be done (i.e., calendaring a meeting). It can also be a sign that team members are not fully committed to the work and have been mandated to participate. Revisiting change ideas and/or talking to the team about their reasons for or frustrations with being on the team may help address this challenge.

Applying Routine to Understanding the Problem
While learning cycles are most often associated with PDSAs, the routine can also be applied to understanding the problem. There may be moments when insights generated from running a PDSA cycle raises new questions or problems in need of deeper investigation. In these situations, a team may decide to run a learning cycle where they 1) clearly articulate a question they want to investigate, 2) decide what data and/or tool (empathy interview, survey, observation, etc.) they want to use, 3) make predictions about what they will discover, 4) run the investigation and 5) compare what they discovered with their predictions.

For example, when testing a formative reading assessment routine in a handful of schools in different districts, an improvement team discovered that teachers were being asked to administer multiple reading assessments required by various stakeholders—school, district, state. It prompted the team to ask, what are all the other assessments teachers are required to administer? They then ran a learning cycle to answer this question. They first made predictions about what reading assessments teachers were required to administer, how frequently, and for what purpose, and then surveyed the teachers to get data to compare against their predictions. What they discovered is the number of assessments that teachers were being required to administer were far more than they had predicted, and the assessments varied from school to school and district to district. This then prompted the team to have a conversation with the district leaders about how to address this problem.

2) **Collecting, Analyzing & Displaying Data**

Data collection ⇒ Data entry ⇒ Data analysis ⇒ Data display

Once you have defined your measures and created your data collection tools (tally sheet, exit form, etc.), it is important that you establish a regular routine for collecting, analyzing, and displaying your data. Above are the basic steps of the process; each step may need to be broken down into more detailed steps, depending on the complexity of your data collection process. In addition, you may have different data routines for different measures as exemplified below. Again, clearly articulating the steps, who is responsible for each step, and the timeframe in which they need to occur will help ensure greater reliability of the process.

Measure	Data collection	Data entry	Data Analysis	Data display
Class attendance	• Collected daily; teacher takes attendance at beginning of class period, notes number of students present in data collection form • Teacher gives form to team lead at end of week	• When team lead receives data from all five teachers, enters into spreadsheet	• Team lead determines average percent of students in attendance across all five classrooms for each day that week	• Team lead creates/updates run chart display for weekly huddle
Student sense of self-efficacy	• Collected every six weeks, students complete 1-minute paper survey at end of designated class period • Teacher gives surveys to team lead	• When team lead receives data from all five teachers, enters into spreadsheet	• Team lead determines average survey responses for each class	• Team lead creates run chart with aggregate (across all classrooms) and small multiples displays (each classroom) for learning session

Challenges in Collecting, Analyzing & Displaying Data
Below are a few common challenges that teams face in establishing a data collection routine which improvement coaches may want to look out for. Again, first take an inquiry stance and have them walk through their data collection routine, listening carefully for places where the routine breaks down and why.

Challenge	Potential Causes and *How to Support*

Integrating data collection and entry into individual's daily work routines	- Too burdensome and time-consuming
	  ○ *Process map work routine where data collection needs to happen. Identify step that data collection can be attached to.*
	  ○ *Create simple data collection form with clear directions.*
	  ○ *Have someone else (coach, another teacher, student) collect data.*

Not knowing what analyses to run or display to create	- Do not have clear operational definitions for their measures
	  ○ *Determine exactly what the data point is that is going to be plotted (e.g. average number of students who attend class per day across five classrooms) on their graph.*
	  ○ *Mockup potential data displays even before data collection begins to decide which display will be most helpful to the team.*

3) Collective Data Conversations

Reviewing and discussing your data displays serves as an important feedback loop for the improvement team in tracking its progress. It is critical that everyone on the team can participate equally in the conversation since each person will bring different perspectives to the data. Using a structured conversation protocol will help facilitate not only equity of participation but also in uncovering various assumptions, theories, and questions that team members have about the data that can serve as the basis for further investigation or testing.

Conversation Protocol
- *Note:* Questions answered through go-round, so everyone has opportunity to share
- Walk through the data—explain display (e.g., what is this a graph of what is represented on the different axes, etc.). Does everyone understand it?
- What do you see and notice? Stay descriptive.
- What hypotheses or explanations do you have about what you see? What alternative theories might exist?
- What questions does the data raise for you?

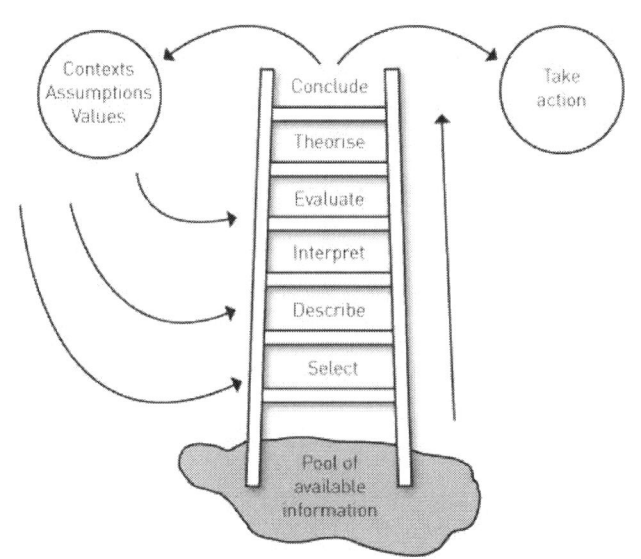

Challenges in Collective Data Conversations
The most common challenge that teams face is staying descriptive at the beginning of the conversation. They will quickly move up the ladder of inference and want to share their hypotheses and theories about what they see. Many of these theories will be based on previous experiences. It is important as a coach

that you push the team to generate as many different theories as possible to help team members see outside their mental models.

Often these conversations happen in tandem with the consolidation of learning since the data serves as critical evidence to draw on when revising your theory or informing next steps for your improvement team.

4) Consolidation of Learning

Every 4-6 weeks, the team should stop to reflect and consolidate what it is that they have <u>learned</u> from their testing and data collection.

Steps in consolidation

1) *Reflect individually on what was tested.* Before the team meets to consolidate its collective learning, individual team members should review their PDSAs since the last consolidation meeting and reflect on the following questions:
   - What did you test?
   - What did you predict?
   - What did you learn? What is your evidence? This can be drawn from the PDSAs or data displays.
   - What was surprising?

2) *Summarize what was tested across the team.* When the team meets, it should first summarize all the changes that have been tested during the previous action period: what change ideas were tested, how many PDSAs were run on each change idea.

3) *Synthesize key learnings, highlighting evidence.* The team should then synthesize key learnings from the PDSAs run on each change idea, and most importantly, the evidence to support these insights. Here, the team can draw on quantitative or qualitative data collected as part of the PDSAs and/or data displays of the associated family of measures.

   How the information is organized or documented when it is synthesized can be done using a variety of methods. Whatever method is used, the primary goal is to be able to see patterns, trends, or themes in what was learned that can help the team revise and update its theory and decide what to focus on in the next action period. Some common methods include affinity and matrix diagrams.

4) *Decide what to do with change ideas tested.* Based on what is learned, the team needs to decide how to proceed with the change ideas tested during the action period:
   - Abandon
   - Make adaptation(s) based on key learnings from the team and retest
   - Test in more contexts
   - Make a permanent part of the system

5) *Revise theory (driver diagram, process map, etc.).* The team should then revisit its theory of improvement and make any necessary revisions—add or drop a driver, change ideas, or process steps—given what is decided in Step 4. You do not necessarily need to revise your theory every time you consolidate. If there are multiple improvement teams testing around a common theory,

then the theory will more likely be revised every 4-6 months based on the learning over 2-3 action periods.

6) *Decide on what to focus on in the next action period.* Much of what happens in the next action period will also be driven by decisions in Step 4 as you continue to build evidence for your change ideas as they move up the testing ramp: Who is going to test what in the next action period, do we need identify other contexts for testing, what adaptions will we test, etc.

However, sometimes learning, especially that which is unexpected, may prompt the generation of new learning questions and a return to the "Understanding the current system" phase of the improvement journey. Or you may have built up enough evidence around a handful of change ideas that will require moving onto the "Spread and Scale" phase. As a result, you may decide to suspend PDSA cycles testing change ideas connected to your theory of improvement during the next action period to instead privilege a different set of learning cycles and activities focused on investigation or spread. Alternatively, a team might continue PDSA cycles and add these other activities as another strand of work that might further their learning during the action period.

5) Team Meetings/Huddles

Meeting regularly with your team helps maintain momentum around the work and holds members accountable to the team. There are typically two types of meetings that improvement teams engage in. Huddles serve as short team check-ins and are usually no longer than 30 minutes. During huddles, team members share key learnings from their most recent testing, articulate next steps, and help each other trouble-shoot issues that may arise. For the huddles to be executed in the given amount of time, it is good to have a clear protocol that helps members share out only the most important information in a disciplined way. See sample protocol later in this section. Team meetings usually happen monthly and are longer (60-90 minutes). Collective data conversations and consolidation of learning usually happen during these meetings.

What is important about these meetings is that they are focused on what the team is learning through their work. Project planning, scheduling, and handling other logistics, should either be done separately or should only take up a small portion of the agenda.

Putting the routines together

Taken together, these five improvement routines create a rhythm for team learning. It can be helpful to structure the routines around already existing events—like learning sessions. In some cases, teams use these events as the impetus for consolidation, in preparation to share with other teams. In other cases, teams go through multiple cycles of consolidation within each action period.

Improvement Routines 1   *Improvement Routines 2*

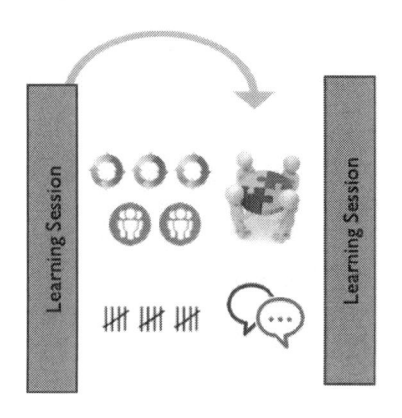

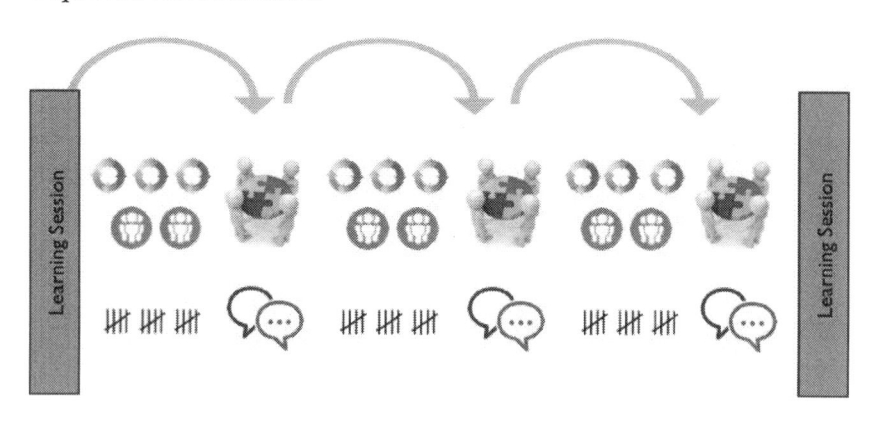

The role of the improvement coach in this stage

The improvement coach plays a key role in supporting collective improvement work. To support the team, the improvement coach:
- Designs the improvement journey
- Supports the development of reliable and effective improvement routines
- Builds capability in improvement
- Maintains the charter and shared workspace
- Maintains communication with stakeholders

Designing the improvement journey

The improvement coach will often sketch out a plan for the improvement journey up front, based on the nature of the improvement problem and time available. The plan includes delimited phases of the work to focus on understanding the problem, chartering the project, designing changes, and testing and building evidence. In addition, the timeframe for the improvement project can be divided up into action periods and moments for team consolidation, built around the natural rhythm of the improvement work and available team meetings. See Chapter 3: Improvement Journeys for more on how to design improvement journeys.

Supporting the development of reliable and effective improvement routines

The improvement coach helps the team first establish improvement routines and then effectively use those routines to support team learning. A sample planning document for improvement routines is below. In some cases, the coach may play a more active role in the improvement teams at the beginning of the improvement work and gradually transfer these responsibilities to the improvement team lead or team members.

Sample planning document for improvement routines

TEAM MTGS/ HUDDLES	Team Mtg Mon. 3/26 10 – 11 am	Huddle Mon. 4/2 10 – 10:30 am	Huddle Mon. 4/9 10 – 10:30 am	Huddle Mon. 4/16 10 – 10:30 am	Team Mtg Mon. 4/23 10 – 11 am	Huddle Mon. 5/7 10 – 10:30 am	Huddle Mon. 5/14 10 – 10:30 am	Team Mtg Mon. 5/21 10 – 11 am
TESTING	Put together plan for testing, generate change ideas 2 PDSAs	3 PDSAS	3 PDSAS	3 PDSAS		3 PDSAS	3 PDSAS	
CONSOLIDATE LEARNING					✓			✓
DATA COLLECTION	Collect student exit slips daily	Collect student exit slips daily	Collect student exit slips daily	Collect student exit slips daily	Collect student exit slips daily	Collect student exit slips daily	Collect student exit slips daily	Collect student exit slips daily
DATA CONVERSATION			✓		✓ (PROGRESS UPDATE)			✓ (PROGRESS UPDATE)
	LS4 MARCH 23-24	March 26-30	April 2-6	April 9-13	April 16-20	April 23-27	LS5 MAY 2-3	May 7-11	May 14-18	May 21-25	IMP REV MAY 31 - JUNE 1

Building capability in improvement

The improvement coach brings improvement expertise to the team. Through engaging in improvement routines, the team members each develop improvement capability that can be used for this and other improvement projects. In addition to helping the team make progress, the improvement coach also tracks the development of improvement skills and identifies areas of focus that will best support team members. This may include teaching specific skills, providing 1:1 coaching and providing feedback to the team. Developing the expertise of the improvement team lead is particularly important, as the team lead increasingly takes over the responsibilities of facilitating the team.

Maintaining the charter and shared workspace

In the early stages of the project, the improvement team develops a charter that contains the motivation, aim, measures, and initial theory of improvement. As the team learns, the charter becomes a place to document learning and update shared understandings. Consolidation meetings serve as a key mechanism for synthesizing the team's learning. The improvement coach (or the team lead) takes the responsibility of recording the new learning in the charter. It can be useful to use a slide format to record the charter and return to some of the key slides (like the purpose, or a student quote) at the beginning of team meetings. The slide deck can also become a presentation resource when the team is asked to share their work. In addition to the charter, improvement teams typically have a central repository to hold the key artifacts from their work. The improvement coach (or team lead) may also organize this repository as they update the charter.

Maintaining communication with key stakeholders

The improvement team lead or improvement coach is responsible for maintaining communication with the sponsor and other important stakeholders as the improvement work progresses. Monthly meetings with the sponsor are recommended.

Improvement Routine Planning (sample)

1) **TEAM MTGS/HUDDLES:** Identify how frequently you would like to meet as a team. If you can identify dates/times now, even better. Team meetings are usually for longer conversations (data conversations, consolidating learning from testing. Huddles are no more than 30 min and usually used to maintain testing momentum (share learning from tests, articulate next steps, trouble-shoot issues that arise during testing, etc.).
2) **TESTING:** Identify how frequently you will test—how many PDSAs can your team run each week given what you're testing? Write down the number for each week. Ideally, you will run a minimum of one PDSA per week.
3) **CONSOLIDATE LEARNING:** Identify when you would like to pause and consolidate what you have learned so far. Again, this will likely happen during a team meeting. Plan on consolidating once before LS5 and and once before the Improvement Reviews.
4) **DATA COLLECTION:** Identify how frequently you will collect data (daily? weekly? monthly?).
5) **DATA CONVERSATION:** Identify when you would like to review data with your team. Some teams like to review their data and consolidate learning at the same time; others like to review their data more frequently and allocate some time during huddles to do this.

	Team Mtg Mon. 3/26 10 – 11 am	Huddle Mon. 4/2 10 – 10:30 am	Huddle Mon. 4/9 10 – 10:30 am	Huddle Mon. 4/16 10 – 10:30 am	Team Mtg Mon. 4/23 10 – 11 am	Huddle Mon. 5/7 10 – 10:30 am	Huddle Mon. 5/14 10 – 10:30 am	Team Mtg Mon. 5/21 10 – 11 am	
TEAM MTGS/ HUDDLES									
TESTING	Put together plan for testing, generate change ideas 2 PDSAs	3 PDSAs	3 PDSAs	3 PDSAs		3 PDSAs	3 PDSAs		
CONSOLIDATE LEARNING					✓			✓	
DATA COLLECTION	Collect student exit slips daily	Collect student exit slips daily	Collect student exit slips daily	Collect student exit slips daily	Collect student exit slips daily	Collect student exit slips daily	Collect student exit slips daily	Collect student exit slips daily	
DATA CONVERSATION			✓		✓ (PROGRESS UPDATE)			✓	(PROGRESS UPDATE)
LS4 MARCH 23-24	March 26-30	April 2-6	April 9-13	April 16-20	April 23-27	LS5 MAY 2-3	May 7-11	May 14-18	May 21-25	**IMP REV MAY 31 - JUNE 1**

Stage 4: Adjourning the Team

The end of an improvement project should be recognized and celebrated. Closing out an improvement project involves:
- Celebrating accomplishments and honoring efforts
- Documenting the learning

The sponsor of the improvement project should take a lead role in closing out an improvement project. They may do this by holding a final "improvement review" to hear about what the team has learned and recommendations for the organization, providing a space for the improvement team to share their work with a larger audience, or attending a final team meeting to mark the end of the improvement work. The sharing can focus both on what the improvement team learned about doing improvement work and about the content area which was the improvement focus of the team. The sponsor can honor the learning by sharing how he or she might use the learning from the team.

A final consolidation and documentation of learning is particularly important as the improvement project adjourns. If the improvement work will continue to an additional phase, documentation of evidence-based changes and key elements of the improvement infrastructure will be critical for new teams taking on the work. Even if the improvement work will not continue, the learning that the team accumulated will often be useful to the organization later in time when they re-launch improvement work or return to this focus area. The team lead and improvement coach usually lead the team through a final consolidation and documentation of their improvement work.

Conversational Capacity

Teams can produce more than individuals precisely because they bring people together with different skills and experiences. Improvement teams that work across organizational silos bring multiple vantage points to a given problem. While it is easy to recognize the advantages of diverse expertise, leveraging this is hard to do in practice. People's differences often get in the way of a team's functioning instead of enhancing it.

Where these differences often manifest themselves are in team conversations. Team conversations serve as the foundation of collective learning. They are how teams develop shared understandings of the work, make decisions, and hold each other accountable. According to Craig Weber in his book *Conversational Capacity*, "a team's conversational capacity isn't just another aspect of teamwork—it defines it. A team that cannot talk about its most pressing issues is not really a team at all. It's just a group of people that can't work together effectively when it counts" (pg. 30). As a coach, one of the most important responsibilities is to facilitate effective team conversations. Doing so will dramatically accelerate the learning of the team.

To facilitate good team conversations requires you to first appreciate and understand the unique ways in which each team member sees and understands the world. The *ladder of inference* is a concept developed by Chris Argyris, the late professor of organizational behavior at Harvard Business School, that illustrates how our mind makes sense of our everyday experiences.

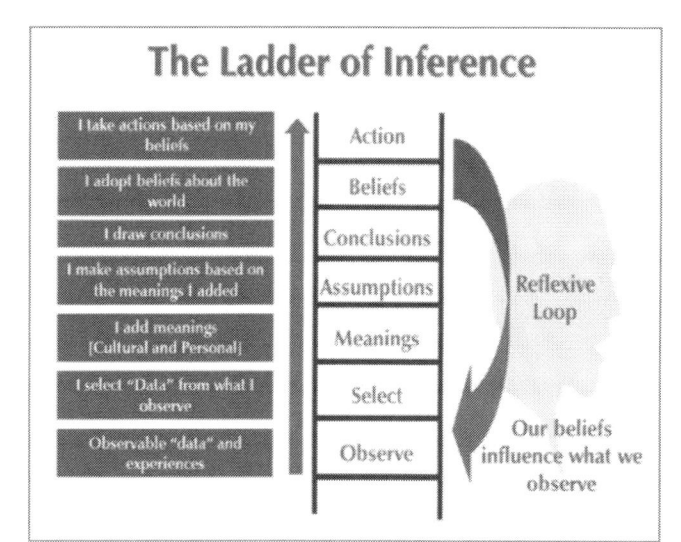

At the bottom of the ladder sits all the observable data our sensory inputs take in at any given moment. Because of the mind's cognitive limitations, it necessarily moves up the ladder and selects a slice of the observable data to focus its attention, ignoring the rest. From there it uses multiple filters—educational and cultural backgrounds, emotional states, vocation—to make inferences, develop assumptions, and draw conclusions about these observations. This shapes our beliefs and subsequent actions, which in turn, influences what observable data we take in.

Weber uses the example of two men visiting Chicago for the first time. After wandering around and exploring downtown for about hour, one man describes the city as a "dump," while the other describes it as "beautiful." Neither statement is right or wrong, but rather a reflection of the filters each uses to make sense of its observations of the city. The man who calls the city a "dump" is a cop; the slice of the city he sees is the "graffiti", "suspicious behavior", "double parked cars", "jaywalkers", and "expired registration tags". The other man who sees the city as "beautiful" is an architect whose attention is drawn to the "buildings, historical landmarks, and design." Neither is even aware of how their filters shape what observable data they attend to and the conclusions they subsequently draw. (Weber, pg. 128)

What is problematic is that instead of recognizing the inherent limits of what we see, "our default tendency to assume our ladder is correct, and that other people need to correct their erroneous perceptions. Failing to appreciate the degree to which we filter our 'reality,' we tend to hold our ladders as truth rather than as hypotheses" (Weber, pg. 129). Thus, when team members hold on to their ladders as truths, conflict usually ensues, which hampers the team's ability to function effectively.

A team's ability to surface and manage clashing ladders is largely dependent on its ability to have open, honest conversations. Weber refers to this as the team's **conversational capacity** — "the ability to have balanced, non-defensive dialogue about tough subjects and in challenging circumstances" (Weber, pg. 15). While individual skills regarding communication and reflection are critical for conversational capacity, Weber is clear in defining conversational capacity as a *collective capacity* that the team must build and take collective responsibility for. Engaging in conversations where multiple perspectives are surfaced and discussed allows the team to collectively see and understand well beyond what any one person can observe.

Defining a Team's Conversational Capacity

Too often conversations about complex or difficult topics do not spur honest and non-defensive conversations. This is particularly true when trying to solve systems problems. "Systems thinking is particularly prone to evoking defensiveness because of its central message, that our actions create our reality" (Senge, pg. 237). These conversations often challenge the tacit and explicit beliefs that form the top rungs of our ladders and shape how we see and understand the world, which can feel uncomfortable and unsettling. As a result, the conversation either breaks down or becomes polarized because individuals fear being vulnerable and open to the possibility of being wrong.

The conversational capacity of a team develops over time as team members learn to trust each other, and the team is established as a safe place to express and explore differing points of view. One measure of conversational capacity is the difficulty level of issues that a team can effectively manage. In the early stages, team members may be honest about relatively low stakes topics, but more sensitive topics may remain off limits or only be discussed in dyads of trusted parties outside the context of the team. The hallmark of high conversational capacity is the ability to stay in a productive conversation as the issues become more challenging.

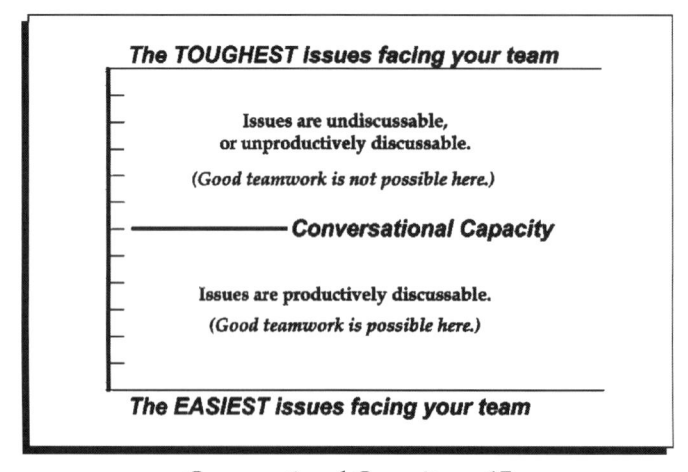

```
The TOUGHEST issues facing your team

        Issues are undiscussable,
        or unproductively discussable.
        (Good teamwork is not possible here.)

        ─────── Conversational Capacity

        Issues are productively discussable.
        (Good teamwork is possible here.)

The EASIEST issues facing your team
```

Conversational Capacity, p.17

As mentioned earlier, engaging in productive conversations requires the team to surface and examine conflicting ladders of inference among team members. However, conflict naturally produces a fight or flight response for most of us — either we double down and more fiercely defend our point of view or back off and keep our views to ourselves. The goal of conversational capacity is to combat these "winning" or "minimizing" behaviors and replace them with candor and curiosity. What is particularly challenging is that being candid and curious are two states of mind that do not easily co-exist under stress.

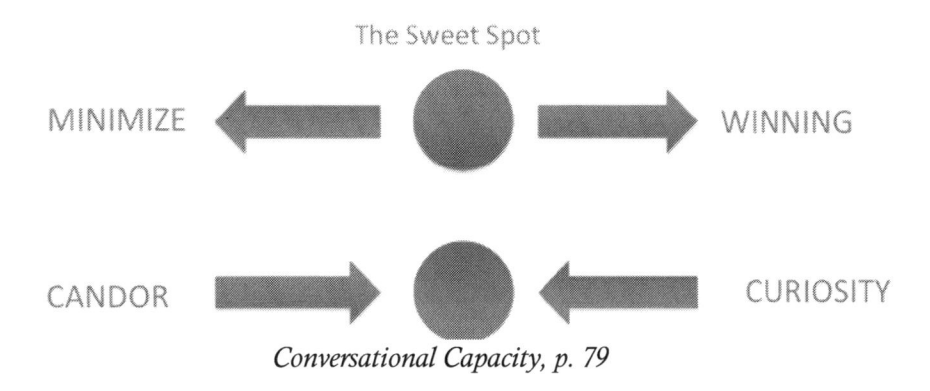

```
                        The Sweet Spot
    MINIMIZE  ⟵         ●        ⟶  WINNING


    CANDOR    ⟶         ●        ⟵  CURIOSITY
```
Conversational Capacity, p. 79

When we minimize, instead of being candid we subvert our true opinions and perspectives in the spirit of keeping the peace. When we win, we try to force our perspective onto others, ignoring their ideas or opinions. "This is the most insidious problem affecting our teams, work relationships, and organizations: our conflicting ladders of inference and the minimize and win tendencies we use to manage them" (Weber, pg. 132). It is important to note, that our tendency to minimize or win is an emotional response, not an intentional one. The desire for fight or flight in the face of conflict is strong. And while we might have some tendencies toward one or the other, we all engage in both depending on the circumstance.

Minimizing Behaviors	**Winning Behaviors**
Cover up our views, ideas, or concerns	We state our positions as facts
We feign agreement or support	We dismiss or discount alternative views
We engage in hallway conversations	We solicit support
Ease in	We do little genuine listening
Ask leading questions	Do not inquire into alternative points of view
Avoid the issue	
Use third party examples	We interrupt
Deliberately ambiguous	Display aggressive or dismissive body language
Submissive body language	
Unilaterally control the issue to keep it safe	Use hyperbole
Use email to raise an issue	Demonize people with different views
We make excuses for people	Pull rank
	Ask dismissive or belittling questions to put down views we do not like
	Unilaterally control the situation to win

Conversational Capacity: Summary of Typical Minimizing and Winning Behaviors (pp. 41-44, 51-53)

Conversational Capacity Skills

The real gift of Weber's book is that he breaks down the discipline of good, honest conversations into a practical capacity with four specific skills and mindsets that can be observed and practiced within a team. The first two skills involve clearly articulating our thinking. They are at the heart of being candid. The second two skills involve inquiring into the perspectives of others. They are at the heart of being curious. Combined, the skills push us to surface the different ladders of inference that team members bring to the conversation. They encourage members to share their positions as theories based on the data and experiences, they are drawing from, to test them with the team and then to ask others to do the same. They keep conversations in the sweet spot, especially when the topics become more challenging.

> **Conversational capacity skills**
> 1. Stating our clear *position*
> 2. Explaining the underlying *thinking* that informs our position
> 3. *Testing* our perspective
> 4. *Inquiring* into the perspectives of others

1. **Stating our clear position.** Stating our clear position means being transparent about what we believe and being able to articulate it succinctly. It takes time and effort to articulate our theories and even when we know our point of view it can be common to hedge our opinions with phrases like "I wonder if.." or "Don't you think…"
   Examples of clearly stating our opinion include:
   - Option B is the best decision.
   - I think there is a better way to do this.
   - We need to include a student voice in the discussion.
   - We do not have any evidence that the change is an improvement.

2. **Explaining the underlying thinking that informs our position.** When we state our position, we also need to make transparent the data we used to come to the position. The "data" is sometimes traditional forms of data, but more often is based on our past experiences. Making our thinking visible opens it up to influence by others.

3. **Testing our perspective.** We maintain curiosity by remembering that our perspectives are hypotheses that can be tested. We can present our positions in ways that invite others to share and challenge our hypotheses. Examples of what this sounds like:
   - Is there a better way to make sense of this?
   - That is how I see the problem. What does this look like from your perspective?
   - I would really like to hear from someone that has an opinion that challenges me.

4. **Inquiring into the perspectives of others.** The more diverse views on the table, the better the team's learning will be. Part of being a good conversational participant is helping to pull out the ideas of others. This is particularly helpful for people that have views that are divergent from your own. Examples:
   - Help me expand my thinking on this. Tell me how you see *x*.

- o What have you seen or heard that leads you to think *y*?

Developing Your Team's Conversational Capacity

Personal Work
There are a variety of ways to build your team's conversational capacity. However, the first step as a coach is to reflect on and further develop your own conversational capacity. Luckily, your own work environment provides multiple opportunities to practice!

1. *Reflect on your own tendencies.* When you are in meetings, do you tend toward minimizing or winning behaviors, especially when the topics become more challenging? What is the context? Who is in the room? What are your triggers? Try to stay focused on yourself; you will naturally want to apply the framework to others and highlight their tendencies and behaviors rather than your own. ☺
2. *Practice the skills yourself—one skill at a time.* Start in low stakes situations with people you trust and/or in conversations about less challenging topics. As you grow more comfortable with each skill, begin to test them more broadly.
3. *Document your progress.* Keep a journal to track instances when you feel triggered. What was your initial reaction? What were you thinking at the time? How did you respond? How might you have responded differently in hindsight?
4. *Enlist a practice partner.* Ask a colleague to help you prepare for a potentially difficult conversation. Have them help you think through what you want to say and how to say it. Role play the conversation to help you anticipate how the other person might react.
5. *Seek feedback from the team.* Get feedback from your team at the end of meetings. You can also share which skill(s) you are working on and have them help you stayed focused if they notice you veering toward a particular tendency.

Teamwork
We highly recommend that you introduce the concept of conversational capacity to your team and invest the time and energy to build the team's skills. It will pay off in both the quality of the team's learning as well as its outcomes.

1. *Recognize hierarchy.* According to Weber, the most common factor that kills a team's conversational capacity is hierarchy. If a leader is in the room, the other participants tend to defer to his/her comments and thinking. As a coach, it is important to acknowledge the power dynamics in the room and intentionally create opportunities for everyone to participate in the conversation. Also, if you are the leader yourself, be cognizant of creating safe spaces for others to contribute.
2. *Visual reminders.* Have a copy of the ladder of inference or conversational capacity skills posted in the room or as part of your agenda, so team members can use it as a reminder and/or reference during discussions.
3. *Appoint a conversational capacity facilitator for meetings.* Have this person focus primarily on the team's conversational capacity during a meeting or discussion. They can either actively facilitate the conversation or observe and then debrief his/her observations with the team at the end of the conversation.

4. *Establish code of conversational conduct that you hold people accountable to.* Add conversational norms to the operating norms for your team. These may cover conduct both during meetings and beyond (see pp. 175-176 in *Conversational Capacity* for sample norms).
5. *Acknowledge effective conversational capacity.* Recognize team members who exhibit good use of one the conversational capacity skills. Be specific about what you noticed so that others can also learn from the experience.

Managing Conflict

People most commonly view conflict as negative and something to be avoided. While some types of conflict are unproductive, healthy conflict—where two or more ladders of inference are shared and explored by a team—leads to more learning. According to Boudett and City in their book *Meeting Wise*, "You want the kind of heat and disagreement in a meeting that sheds light and makes ideas better. Some of the most illuminating moments we've experienced in meetings have come from differences of opinion, perspective, or ideas that people have been comfortable and courageous enough to share" (pg. 108). However, they also note that "many groups, particularly in education with its pervasive 'culture of nice,' are uncomfortable with conflict and thus have meetings with little heat and thus little light" (pg. 108).

Encouraging healthy conflict lies at the heart of conversational capacity. As mentioned earlier, encouraging team members to practice and develop their conversational capacity skills and establishing a conversational capacity code of conduct will support the type of conflict that promotes light and new learning.

1. *Set the expectation.* Actively encourage the team to put different ideas and opinions on the table at the beginning of the meeting.
2. *Maintain safety.* When you notice the conversation heating up, remind the team about norms that keep the conversation focused on the ideas and not the people.
3. *Role play.* If the team is having a hard time generating different perspectives, role playing is often an effective strategy for infusing the conversation with new ideas.

However, as a coach, you also want to avoid generating heat that gets too hot and leads to fire, which can cause irreparable damage to the team. You will notice this when conversations become overly negative or comments begin sounding more like personal attacks. Given that these situations will arise occasionally, it is important to understand your own triggers and comfort level with conflict. When managing unhealthy conflict, Elena Aguilar in *The Art of Coaching Teams* offers the following suggestions (p. 256-261):

1. *Ground yourself.* Acknowledge what you are feeling and take a deep breath.
2. *Return to the team's norms.* Share the impact on the team when a norm isn't adhered to.
3. *Identify the conflict or the impasse.* Being able to quickly read and assess the situation in order to determine the best response is critical. Ask yourself where this negativity is coming from. Is it the larger culture in which the team exists? If there is widespread dysfunction in the organization, it is likely to spill over into your conversations. Do they simply not have the right or enough information? Are there unresolved issues between members of the team? Is someone simply having a bad day?

4. *Decide to address the conflict now or later.* Given your assessment of the conflict, decide whether to address it in the moment with the whole team or if primarily concerns two or three members and needs to be addressed to later.
5. *Let it go.* If you try to address the conflict successfully or unsuccessfully in the moment, the best strategy sometimes is to just let it go, redirect the team, and move on.

Facilitating Conversations about Equity

As mentioned earlier, conversations about complex or difficult topics can spur tense and defensive conversations. This is because they usually challenge the tacit and explicit beliefs that form the top rungs of our ladders and shape how we see and understand the world, which can feel uncomfortable and unsettling. This is particularly true when talking about equity. Given the systemic nature of the inequalities that exist, whether based on race, gender, sexual orientation, perceived ability, it is often difficult to see or acknowledge the biases we all carry. As a result, conversations about equity can quickly become heated and raise strong emotions such as anger, guilt, shame, and denial.

As a coach, it is important to recognize that wrestling with one's biases and beliefs around equity issues is a lifelong process. As such, your primarily goal during conversations about equity is to "effectively hold and facilitate a space for others to do so" (Aguilar, pg. 255). This obviously assumes that you also need to do your own wrestling to identify and manage your own emotions around these topics so that you can help others do the same. Furthermore, establishing team norms and agreements that help support psychological safety is critical as well as engaging teams in activities that build authentic relationships. While these activities will help create a base foundation to support tough conversations about race, they will not always make them easier. As Aguilar notes, "There is no 'right way' to have these conversations…but we have to do it anyway" (pg. 255). We highly suggest that you explore other resources for engaging in conversations about equity since it often lies at the heart of the many systemic issues we see in education.

References

Aguilar, E. (2016). The Art of Coaching Teams: Building Resilient Communities That Transform Schools. San Francisco: Jossey-Bass.
Argyris, C. (1982). "The Executive Mind and Double-Loop Learning." *Organizational Dynamics*. Autumn.
Boudett, K.P. and City, E.A. (2014). *Meeting Wise: Making the Most of Collaborative Time for Educators*. Cambridge, MA: Harvard Education Press.
Weber, C. (2013). *Conversational capacity; The secret to building successful teams that perform with the pressure is on*. NY, NY: McGraw Hill Education.

Additional Resources

Diangelo, R. (2018). *White Fragility*. Boston: Beacon Press.
National Equity Project. Various resources. https://nationalequityproject.org/resources
Senge, P. (1990). *The fifth discipline: The art and practice of the learning organization*. NY, NY: Currency Doubleday. See in particular chapter 12: Team learning.

Coaching Stances

One of the key roles of improvement coaches is to support the team to develop their collective improvement capability. Doing so is a complex practice, requiring coaches to be able to assess a team's learning and determine how to support the team to move forward.

The Skills of Coaching

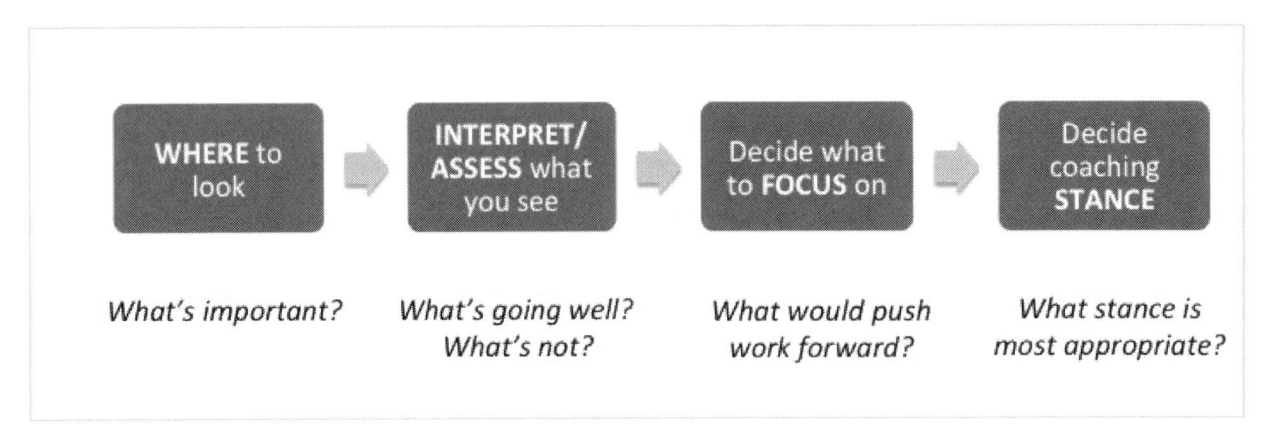

WHERE to look	→	INTERPRET/ ASSESS what you see	→	Decide what to FOCUS on	→	Decide coaching STANCE
What's important?		What's going well? What's not?		What would push work forward?		What stance is most appropriate?

As improvement coaches plan conversations with teams and individuals, they can choose between several different stances to take. The choice of a stance has important implications for how team members relate to each other and the coach. The coach moves flexibly but purposefully between these stances often taking multiple different stances during a single conversation with the team.

Coaching Stances

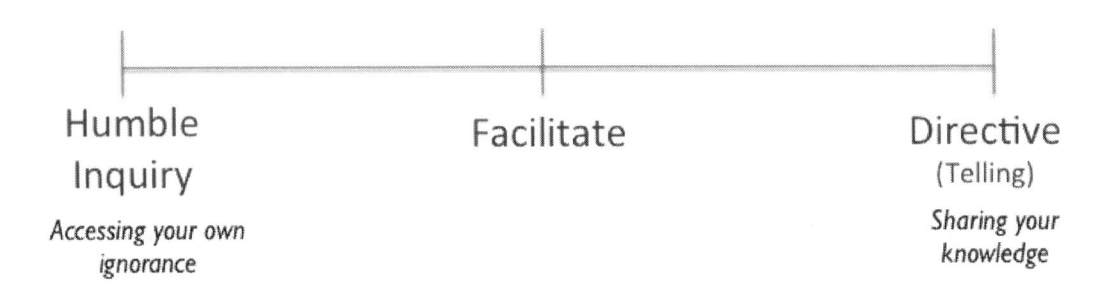

Humble Inquiry	Facilitate	Directive (Telling)
Accessing your own ignorance		Sharing your knowledge

As coaches plan for conversations with their teams, it can be useful to plan out the specific questions that the coach will use with the team. Different kinds of questions imply different stances on the part of the coach. One common challenge that coaches face is attempting to take a more open inquiry approach and inadvertently asking questions that are in fact more facilitative. Edgar Schein, refers to a completely open approach as "humble inquiry." He differentiates humble inquiry from other forms of inquiry. These categories can be useful in reviewing questions before using them with a team.

Different Forms of Inquiry

Humble Inquiry	Diagnostic Inquiry	Confrontational Inquiry	Process-Oriented Inquiry
Does not influence the content of what the other person has to say, nor the form in which it was said "I want to access my ignorance." Maximize curiosity and minimize bias and preconceptions.	The inquirer gets curious about part of the conversation and starts to focus the conversation there. Inquirer steers the other's mental process, often to make them more self-aware of feelings, causes, actions or connections.	Insert your own ideas in the form of a question. May be still based on curiosity or interest but now it is in connection with your own interests. Inquirer is taking charge of the process and content of the conversation.	Shifts the conversation to a meta conversation about the conversation itself.

Source: Humble Inquiry; The Gentle Art of Asking Instead of Telling

3. Organizing Improvement Journeys

A key role of leaders and coaches of improvement is helping teams structure their improvement journey. Improvement teams are unique in that they are organized to learn their way into improved outcomes. To structure their learning, they have a variety of tools and methods at their disposal. In this section readers will be exposed first to the five major phases of the improvement journey.

1) Understand the current system
2) Focus collective efforts
3) Generate ideas for change
4) Learn in practice
5) Sustain and spread

Each phase is guided by key questions, with several phases guided directly by one of the three questions of the model for improvement.[7] A purpose for each phase is described as well as core activities. Guidance for each activity is provided. Coaches can use these activities as a checklist with teams they facilitate. Throughout the phases and activities various tools are recommended for use.[8] These suggestions should not be rigorously adhered to or even seen as complete but should serve instead as a guide for consideration by coaches and teams engaged with that phase and activity associated with their improvement journey.

Suggestions for future reading

- *Managing to Learn* by Jim Shook

---

[7] See Section 1: The Model for Improvement for greater detail.
[8] See chapters in Sections 5 and 6 for specific guidance on the use of various tools for improvement.

Organizing the Improvement Journey

Improvement science offers a wide range of tools and methods to help structure learning in practice to improve. It can be tempting, especially in the early stages of learning improvement science, to seek out a prescriptive step-by-step guide of what to do. Unfortunately, such guides do not work universally because the problems and opportunities improvement teams encounter are unique, requiring flexibility to discover what works in practice. Asking good learning questions at the right time and applying the appropriate methods to answer them are what drive meaningful learning and improvement.

Improvement Journey Overview

The *Improvement Journey Map* below is intended to provide teams with a broad overview of the phases of a learning journey as well as underscore the flexible thinking that lies at the heart of improvement science.

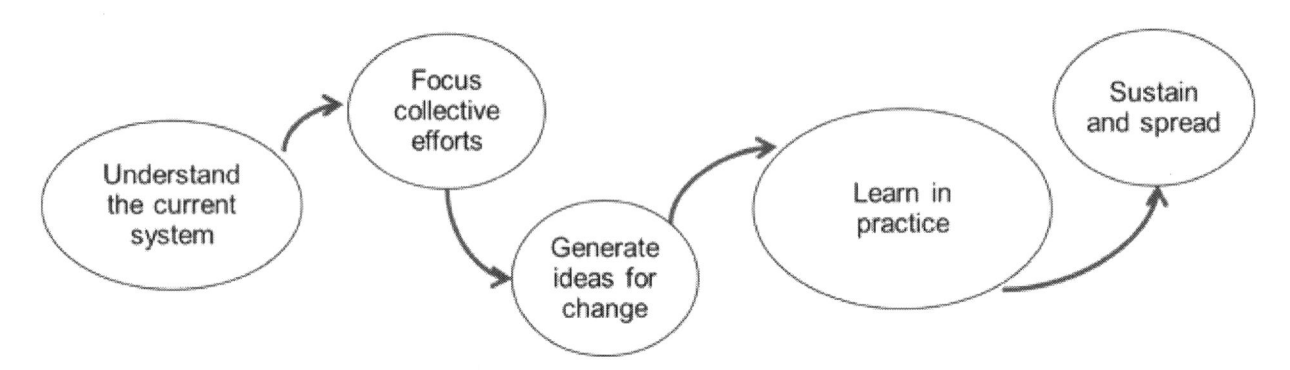

Figure 3.1 Improvement Journey Map depicting the general phases of a learning journey.

Each oval represents a major phase in the improvement journey; most journeys begin with teams trying to understand the current system and end when the work transitions from discovering solutions to sustaining or spreading them within or beyond the original system of interest. The dark black arrows indicate the general flow from phase to phase.

While these phases represent the general flow of most improvement projects, the reality that teams experience on a day-to-day basis is usually non-linear. Teams often need to return to previous phases or jump ahead to other phases to sustain momentum and direct their learning. The map below captures the complexity and non-linear flow of most improvement work using the gray arrows looping back and forth. A key responsibility of an improvement coach is to help improvement teams move from start to finish within the given time frame and resources allocated for the work while staying open to the natural twists and turns that are the hallmark of all improvement journeys.

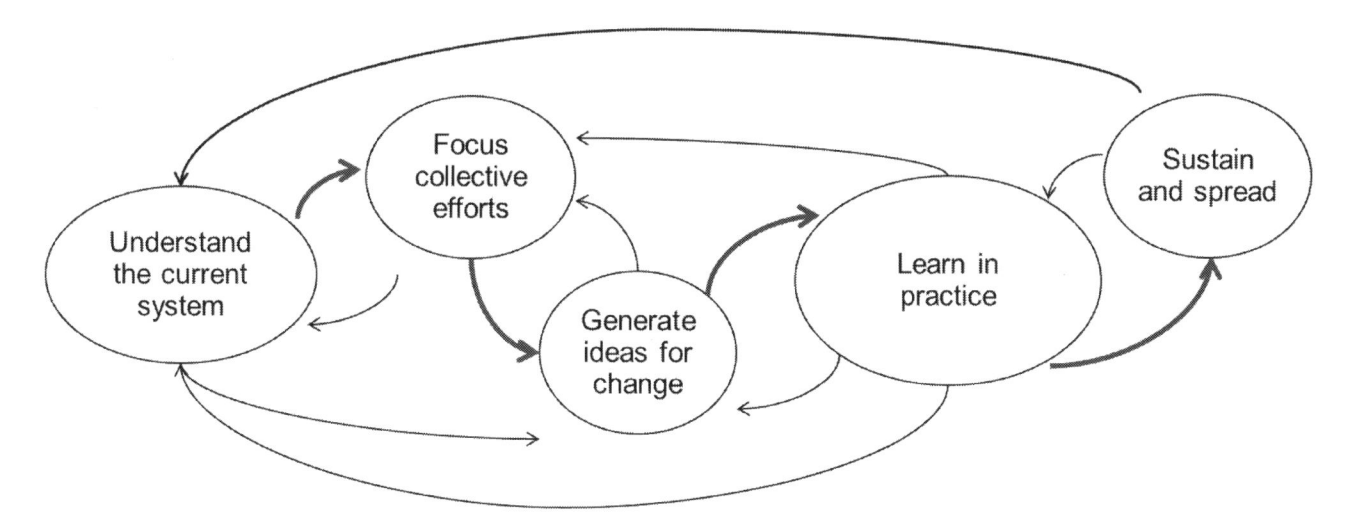

Figure 3.2 Improvement Journey Map depicting the micro non-linear movement improvement projects often experience while progressing their efforts over time.

To appreciate the non-linearity and complexity of what improvement teams experience, we offer the following example. An improvement team is testing a change idea using a PDSA cycle. At the macro level, they are in the "learn in practice" phase. At the end of the cycle the team discovers that the change idea is not producing the predicted and desired impact. They need to understand why because the results of their PDSA cycle are inconsistent with their theory of how to improve their system. A next step, at the micro level, could be for the team to return for a moment to the phase "understanding the current system," to answer the question, "How is our system producing our current outcomes?" to learn what might be causing the failure of the change idea.

In this situation, the improvement coach's responsibility is to move the team back to "understanding the current system," facilitating the team to apply the appropriate tools to uncover why the specific change idea failed in practice. For example, did the team have incomplete knowledge about the user experience, the steps in the process, or how long something might take? The performance of a process or the nature of the idea and the system will influence what the next learning question will be. What this micro move is not, is a return to the phase for understanding the current system from a macro perspective. The team is still squarely in the phase of "learning in practice" and their brief return to an earlier phase is designed to help keep the momentum going.

Using the Improvement Journey Map

A key challenge coaches face when working with improvement teams is helping them appreciate the need for a roadmap to guide the work while also applying the flexible thinking that allows for discovery. Teams will need to pivot as new information is uncovered but also maintain focus on the overall improvement journey. This will require teams to distinguish between learning that will help them move forward versus that which might take them in distracting and tangential directions. Starting with the macro perspective (using figure 3.1 above) with teams before introducing the concept of micro moves (using figure 3.2 above) to further their learning as they progress is one way that coaches can achieve this balance.

Organizing the Work

Mapping out your improvement journey before you begin will help you anticipate when you will likely need move from phase to phase give the time frame allocated for your project. An Improvement Journey Plan template can be found in the Appendix on pg. 248.

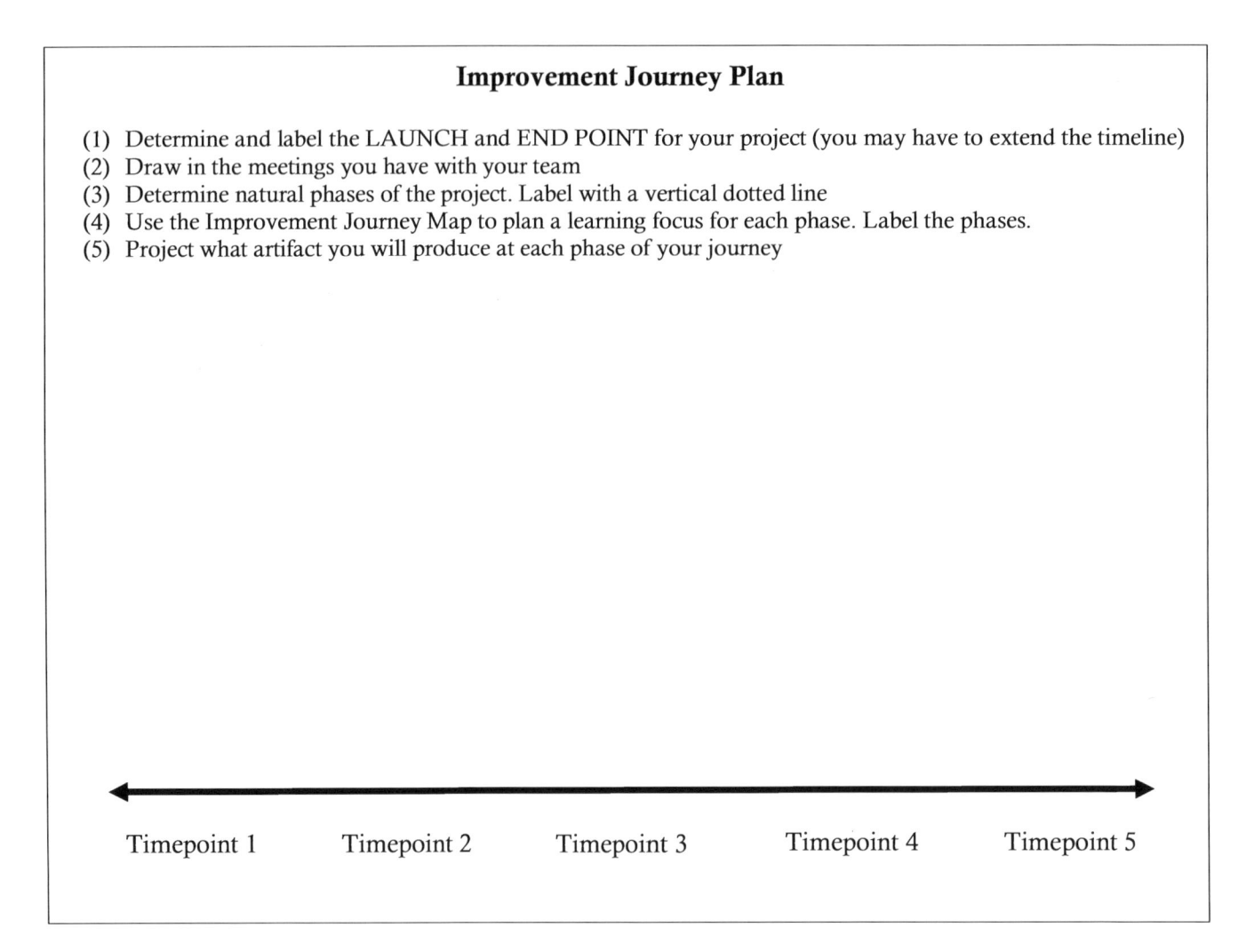

Improvement Journey Plan

(1) Determine and label the LAUNCH and END POINT for your project (you may have to extend the timeline)
(2) Draw in the meetings you have with your team
(3) Determine natural phases of the project. Label with a vertical dotted line
(4) Use the Improvement Journey Map to plan a learning focus for each phase. Label the phases.
(5) Project what artifact you will produce at each phase of your journey

⟵———————————————————————————⟶

Timepoint 1   Timepoint 2   Timepoint 3   Timepoint 4   Timepoint 5

Understanding the Current System

Guiding Questions

- What are **our** current outcomes?
- What is the current design of **our** system?
- How is the design of **our** system producing **our** outcomes?

Purpose
- Develop a shared understanding of what is currently happening
- See the system from multiple perspectives
- Identify key levers for change

Core Activities

Determine the participatory process

Seeing the system requires a diverse set of participants with different windows into the system. How to engage them, elicit their perspectives and build a shared understanding of the system is an important step in the process.

Define the problem or opportunity

Identifying a shared and clear anchor from which to see into the system — whether it be a gap in performance, or a key leverage point — will help focus and guide the team's investigation.

Generate learning questions

Given the complexity of most systems, developing a set of learning questions that reflect the team's initial wonderings will also help focus and guide the team's investigation.

Select method(s)

Different types of learning questions often necessitate different types of methods of investigation. Generally, they fall into three broad buckets: 1) leveraging data, 2) understanding the user's perspective, and 3) depicting work practices. Selecting the appropriate method or tool will help generate the most learning for the team.

Related tools and methods

- Empathy methods: Interviews, observations
- Data collection strategies: Exit slips, surveys
- Process-mapping

Investigate

Apply the appropriate method to answer the learning question and regroup as a team to share learning. Typically, investigations occur in iterative cycles with each round of investigation leading to the next learning question(s) as your understanding of the system deepens.

Analyze to identify key levers

While your investigations require divergent thinking and will generate a great deal of information, analysis requires convergent thinking to identify important themes and key levers in your system that may be the focus of your improvement work moving forward.

Related tools and methods

- Data visualizations: Pareto, run charts, etc.
- Headlining
- Say-Think-Do-Feel
- Fishbone diagram

Summarize Systems Analysis

Different types of learning questions often necessitate different types of methods of investigation. Generally, they fall into three broad buckets: 1) leveraging data, 2) understanding the user's perspective, and 3) depicting work practices. Selecting the appropriate method or tool will help generate the most learning for the team.

Related tools and methods

- Empathy methods: Interviews, observations
- Data collection strategies: Exit slips, surveys
- Process-mapping

Investigate continued...

Apply the appropriate method to answer the learning question and regroup as a team to share learning. Typically, investigations occur in iterative cycles with each round of investigation leading to the next learning question(s) as your understanding of the system deepens.

Analyze to identify key levers continued...

While your investigations require divergent thinking and will generate a great deal of information, analysis requires convergent thinking to identify important themes and key levers in your system that may be the focus of your improvement work moving forward.

Related tools and methods

- Data visualizations: Pareto, run charts, etc.
- Headlining
- Say-Think-Do-Feel
- Fishbone diagram

Summarize Systems Analysis continued...

After each iteration of investigation and analysis, the team should succinctly summarize its current understanding of the system, highlighting key learnings about the gap in performance and causes of the problem. This will help the team determine the focus of the next iteration or the direction for the next phase of the improvement journey.

Organizing the work

Given the complexity of this phase, it is important that you have a clear strategy for organizing the work. The K-W-L (What we Know-What we Want to Know-What we Learned), Learning Plan, and A3 Storyboard are all helpful ways in which to track your learning questions, methods, and findings. Templates for these organizers can be found in Appendix C starting on page 273.

K-W-L Template

OUR IMPROVEMENT PROBLEM

What we **KNOW** about current performance	What we **WONDER** about current performance	What we **LEARNED**

✪ Priority questions

Investigation Summary

Title/Team: _____   Date/Version: _____

Team:

Important background on my local context:

DESCRIBE current performance (Charts, graphs, quotes, observations, visualizations that describe what is currently happening)

ANALYZE: Why does this problem or need exist? (charts, graphs, visualizations that explain the gap)

GAP

GOAL or TARGET (what would success look like?)

Learning Plan Template

Title/Team: _____

Iteration 1: {dates} Driving Question(s):	Iteration 2: {dates} Driving Question(s):	Iteration 3: {dates} Driving Question(s):
Perspectives Needed:	Perspectives Needed:	Perspectives Needed:
Activities:	Activities:	Activities:

70

Focus Collective Efforts

Guiding Questions

- What specifically are **we** trying to accomplish?

Purpose

- Create a shared sense of purpose and direction for improvement work
- Establish the boundaries and develop the scope of work

Core Activities

Revisit team structure

The improvement team needs to be made up of the people who can work together to actively test ideas in practice. Selecting a specific direction for the improvement work often necessitates changing the configuration of the improvement team from that of the previous phase.

Review system analysis & choose a focus

Review what is known about the system that is producing the current outcomes and determine where to focus the improvement work. Teams should consider the leverage points uncovered in the systems analysis and where they have the will, ideas, and ability to execute improvement work.

Related tools and methods

- Pareto
- Shewhart control chart

Create a shared vision/narrative

Provide opportunities for team members to connect to the purpose of the improvement work. Create a clear and persuasive case to motivate the need for change.

Related tools and methods

- Narrative

Craft an aim statement

Create an initial aim statement that captures the team's answer to "what are we trying to accomplish?" Create clear definitions of what, where and by when improvement is expected.

Related tools and methods

- Aim statement

Select key measures

Identify at least one or two key measures that will provide useful feedback on the improvement work. Attention should be paid to identifying outcome measures that provide feedback on the progress towards the aim and process measures that can be collected more regularly.

Related tools and methods

- Measurement tree

Create an initial theory of improvement

Improvement teams benefit from having an anchoring document to organize their ideas for change. For teams choosing to focus on multiple systems' components at once, it can be useful to use a driver diagram. For teams focusing on a single process, a high-level process map can be useful.

Related tools and methods

- Driver diagram
- Process map

Summarize in a team charter

Team agreements can be recorded in a team charter. The charter can take the form of a document, slide deck, or storyboard, and is regularly updated to capture the team's learning.

Related tools and methods

- Charter

Organizing the Work

The charter is a key document that helps define the focus of the improvement project and can be displayed in a variety of ways (document, slide deck, on a white board). Various charter templates can be found in Appendix C on pg. 276-280.

Charter Board Template

Team:
Members, norms, routines

What specifically are we trying to accomplish?	How will we know that a change is an improvement? *Performance measures, graphs*	What changes can we make that will result in improvement? *Driver Diagram, process map, process list, initial change ideas*

Charter Form

What are we trying to accomplish?
Problem to be addressed (Broadly defines the WHAT? Provides any necessary background information and introduces the problem that the team is formed around. Two to three sentences)

Reason for the improvement work (Defines the WHY? Makes a powerful case to all stakeholders about why improvement is needed. Four to five sentences)

Aim statement and expected outcomes (How good? For whom? By when? One to three sentences)

How do we know a change is an improvement?
(Identify appropriate measures, outcome and process measures are specified at a minimum; very brief description of how often data will be collected, not necessarily how. Four to five sentences)

What changes can we make that will lead to improvement?
(Initial changes, ideas for PDSA cycles, constraints/barriers identified and brief ideas on how to address them. Four to five sentences)

Team Information
Who is on the team and what knowledge/skills do they bring?

Charter Slide Deck Template

Slide	Content
1	Improvement Team
2	Problem and Motivation
3	Aim Statement
4	Family of Measures
5	Initial Driver Diagram or Process Map

Types of Improvement Projects

While each improvement journey is unique, it can be helpful in planning an improvement journey to distinguish between these three typical types of improvement projects:

Process Improvement

An existing service/routine/daily practice or process within your system you plan to continue providing, whose performance is not at the desired level

Design

A desired service/routine/daily practice or process for your system, that does not exist yet, but that you believe could be a valuable addition

Spread within or beyond your organization/system

Having created/improved an excellent service there is a desire to replicate the service/performance throughout your system or in other systems

Generate Change Ideas

Guiding Question

What changes might **we** introduce?

Purpose

- Make your theory of change explicit
- Develop specific, actionable ideas for change to test

Core Activities

Revisit aim and key drivers

It is important that the change ideas generated are tied to the team's aim and key drivers, reflecting the team's theory of change.

Elicit potential ideas for change from team

Create space for team members to share their own ideas for change. If you have the right team configuration, then members will usually have the professional and/or content knowledge to identify potential change ideas since the focus will likely be on their own work processes.

Assess and prioritize ideas for change

Review ideas for change elicited from the team or identified through other methods and assess and prioritize them for testing using criteria such as feasibility of execution, potential impact based on empirical evidence, potential for scalability etc.

Related tools and methods

- PICK Chart
- Matrix Diagram

Select and use methods for identifying new ideas for change

If the team is unable to identify potential ideas for change, there are other methods they can use to identify new ideas. These include scanning the literature, harvesting ideas from "bright spots" (places that have solved the problem or made significant movement toward the aim), using creative thinking techniques, such as Edward de Bono's Six Thinking Hats.

Summarize ideas for change to test as part of theory

Add ideas for change selected by the team for testing to the team's anchoring document or theory of improvement (e.g., driver diagram, high-level process map).

Select and use methods for identifying new ideas for change continued...

Related tools and methods

- Logical thinking
- Learning from others (benchmarking, bright spotting)
- Creative thinking
- Change concepts
- Scanning research
- Expert convenings

Test Ideas in Practice

Guiding Questions

How can **we** test our ideas in practice?
How will **we** know if a change is an improvement?

Purpose

- Learn about the utility, functionality, and impact of change ideas

Core Activities

Revisit theory and determine testing strategy

Identify which change ideas to start with and how to sequence learning across the theory. You may strategically decide to select a focus in common or use a divide and conquer approach.

Related tools and methods

- Driver diagram
- Process map

Determine testing, data, and consolidation routines

Schedule team meetings. Agree upon frequency for data collection and testing cycles as well as methods for documentation. Identify moments when the team can step back and consolidate what was learned.

Related tools and methods

- Improvement routines

Collect, annotate, and review data

Team members should be collecting, entering, and reviewing data as often as is appropriate, annotating charts with key learning.

Related tools and methods

- Data conversation protocol

Learning cycles

Team members use iterative learning cycles to learn their way into improved practices. These learning cycles need to be documented. Coaches often work with teams either collectively or individually to build inquiry skills and routines.

Related tools and methods

- PDSA (Plan-Do-Study-Act)

Sharing learning

Team members need regular opportunities to share what they are learning. Teams benefit from having shared online workspaces and frequent huddles to create a rhythm for the improvement work.

Related tools and methods

- Team meeting protocol

Consolidation of learning

Periodically, teams benefit from consolidation moments where they review data and their learning cycles. This learning is used to revise their theory and decide where to focus next.

Related tools and methods

- Driver diagram
- Process map
- PDSA tree

Summarize

It is important for teams to document the key learnings along the improvement journey. This can be done in a storyboard or charter that gets updated after each consolidation meeting or in preparation for an improvement review.

Organizing the work

Establishing reliable improvement routines during this phase is critical to making progress. These routines are highly intertwined so mapping out a plan for their execution will help your team maintain momentum during this phase.[9]

IMPROVEMENT ROUTINES

1) **TEAM MTGS/HUDDLES:** Identify how frequently you would like to meet as a team. If you can identify dates/times now, even better. Team meetings are usually for longer conversations (data conversations, consolidating learning from learning cycles. Huddles are no more than 30 min and usually used to maintain testing momentum (share learning from learning cycles, articulate next steps, trouble-shoot issues that arise during testing, etc.).
2) **LEARNING CYCLES:** Identify how frequently you will run learning cycles—how many PDSAs can your team run each week given what you're testing? Write down the number for each week. Ideally, you will run a <u>minimum</u> of one PDSA per week.
3) **DATA COLLECTION:** Identify how frequently you will collect data--daily? weekly? monthly?
4) **CONSOLIDATE LEARNING:** Identify when you would like to pause and consolidate what you have learned so far. Again, this will likely happen during a team meeting. Plan on consolidating once before LS5 and and once before the Improvement Reviews.
5) **DATA CONVERSATION:** Identify when you would like to review data with your team. Some teams like to review their data and consolidate learning at the same time; others like to review their data more frequently and allocate some time during huddles to do this.

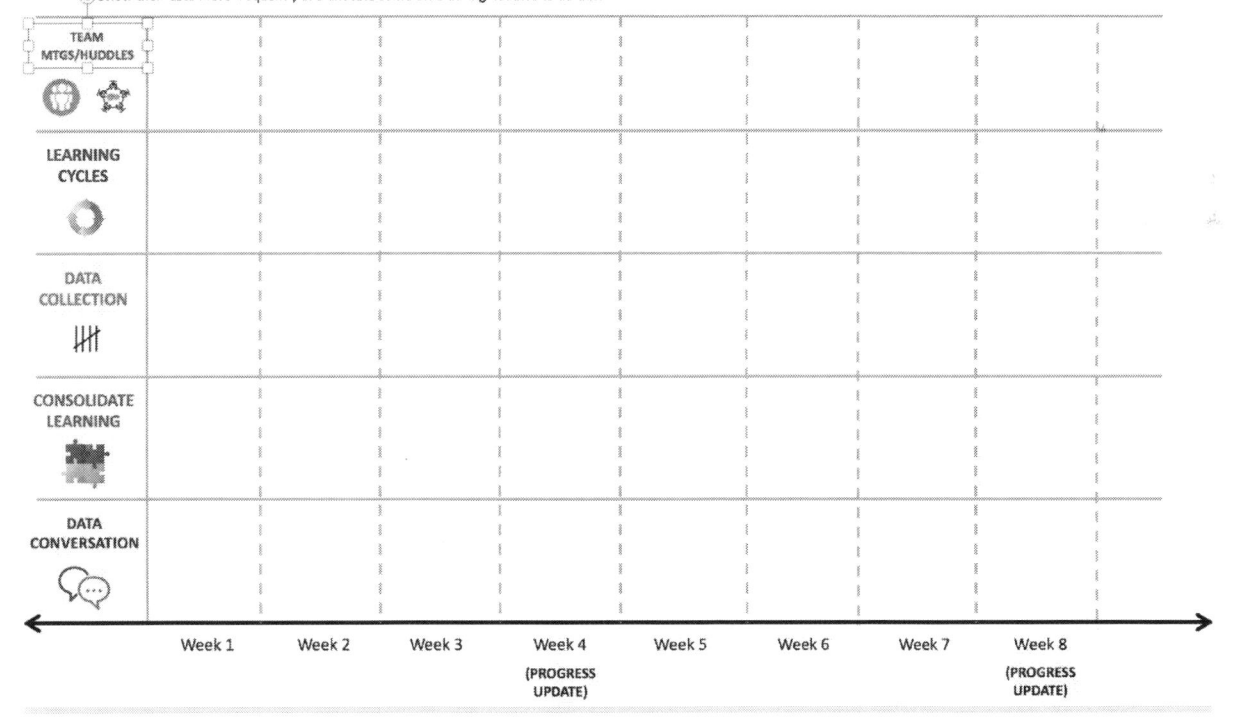

	Week 1	Week 2	Week 3	Week 4 (PROGRESS UPDATE)	Week 5	Week 6	Week 7	Week 8 (PROGRESS UPDATE)
TEAM MTGS/HUDDLES								
LEARNING CYCLES								
DATA COLLECTION								
CONSOLIDATE LEARNING								
DATA CONVERSATION								

---

[9] See Appendix C: Improvement Routines for a template useful when working with improvement teams.

Sustain and Spread

Guiding Question

How do **we** get changes to work reliably across an increasingly diverse set of contexts?

Purpose

- Embed changes in the system to ensure sustained improvement
- Consolidate "proven" changes worthy of spread
- Create conditions for change ideas to spread

Core Activities

Assess the evidence, group readiness, and cost if failure for the change idea/theory to be implemented

Transitioning to implementation requires teams to decide if a single idea or an entire set of ideas should be made permanent in the system. Teams will need to discuss if there is enough evidence to support implementation of a change and if the organization is ready to accept it and can tolerate a failure should it occur.

Related tools and methods

- Run chart
- Shewhart control chart

Engage in implementation activities

Teams need to consider at least five activities when implementing an idea or set of ideas to ensure their sustainability. These include: the creation of standard work where appropriate, changes to documentation such as job descriptions, necessary training for desired practices, updates to the measurement system to track the progress of implementation, and allocation of resources to ensure continuation of the practice.

Related tools and methods

- Implementation checklist

Identify opportunity for spread and/or scale

Improvement teams need to identify and scope opportunities to spread their learning or best practices, either to other areas of the organization or to other organizations with a similar purpose. Teams will need to decide where the change will be most beneficial and if there the will exists to adopt the new practices.

Documentation of key practices

For others to adopt the team's change ideas requires a clear description of the ideas themselves, how they work in practice, and a set of measures to track progress as they try them out in their own contexts.

Related tools and methods

- Change Package

Select method(s) for spread and/or scale

Spreading across an organization or beyond is a difficult task. Different spread and scaling opportunities require different approaches. Teams will need to select methods based on the context of where spread is planned and the specific skills they bring to the process. There are a variety of spread methodologies, which are listed to the side.

Related tools and methods

- Natural diffusion
- Breakthrough Series Collaborative model
- Extension agents
- Wedge and Spread
- Campaign model
- Social Movement Theory/Grassroots Organizing
- Innovation Competition (X-prize, SXSW hackathon)

Telling your Improvement Story

Improvement teams benefit from regular opportunities to tell their emerging improvement story. In this section you will find templates to guide the construction of an improvement story.

Improvement Story Arc

WHY? WHO?
- The Problem
- User Quotes
- Current Performance
- Community/Team

STARTING THEORY
- Baseline performance
- Orientation to current learning
  - How fits DD
  - 3 Questions

KEY LEARNING & EVIDENCE OF IMPROVEMENT
- Learning from testing
- Learning from data
- Development of improvement practices
- Evidence of change
- Key challenges

ENDING THEORY & NEXT UP
- Updates to what know
  - Driver diagram
  - Standard practices
- What we will do next

Template for teams

Data

WHY? WHO?

The Problem (User Quotes, Current Performance etc)

The Community/Team

Data

STARTING THEORY

Baseline performance

Orientation to current learning (How fits DD, 3Q)

Data

KEY LEARNING & EVIDENCE OF IMPROVEMENT

Learning from testing
Learning from data
Development of improvement practices
Evidence of change
Key challenges

ENDING THEORY & NEXT UP

Updates to what know (Driver diagram, standard practices etc)
What we will do next

4. Assessing Team Progress

To track progress and help guide the selection of next steps, it can be helpful to have ways to assess progress. In this section you will find a *Project Progress Score Rubric* that assesses a team's progress toward their aim and a *Coaching Rubric for Teams* that helps coaches diagnose problems and decide where to focus with a team.

Project Progress Score Rubric

Version 7/29/21

Apply these criteria to your improvement project. Select the definition that best describes the progress of your project. Please note that assessments are progressive. For example, all elements of a score 3.0 must be satisfied before rating your project with an assessment of a 3.5 or higher. Evidence for your assessment should be documented in a regular report or other knowledge management tool for your project

Project Progress Score	Operational Definition of Project Progress Score
0.5 INTENT TO PARTICIPATE	A general focus area has been identified but a specific project has not been selected nor the team formed.
1.0 TEAM ESTABLISHED	Team has been identified, but no work has been accomplished. The team has chosen a specific area to investigate.
1.5 PLANNING HAS BEGUN	Organization of the project structure has begun (i.e., meetings are scheduled, required resources and support are identified, tools/materials are gathered etc.)
2.0 ACTIVITY BUT NO TESTS	Initial learning has begun. May include investigation about the problem, collection of baseline data, creation of team charter, development of initial theory of improvement, etc.
2.5 TESTS BUT NO IMPROVEMENT	Initial testing cycles have begun. Some measures have been established to track progress. Data displays have been created.
3.0 MODEST IMPROVEMENT	Completed tests of changes have produced meaningful learning relevant to the theory of improvement identified in the team's charter. Anecdotal evidence of improvement exists.
3.5 IMPROVEMENT	Testing continues and additional improvement in project measures towards goals is seen.
4.0 SIGNIFICANT IMPROVEMENT	Expected results are achieved for the identified population or subsystem. Support for implementation has begun (training, documentation of practices, establishment of standard work routines, etc.).
4.5 SUSTAINABLE IMPROVEMENT	Data on key measures indicate sustainability of the improvement. (i.e., 9-12 data points over time at the new level of performance.)
5.0 OUTSTANDING SUSTAINABLE RESULTS	Project goals and expected results have been accomplished. Organizational changes have been made to accommodate new practices and make the changes permanent.

Source: Adapted from API Improvement Advisor Project Assessment Scale

Guidance on what to expect when using the Project Progress Score

The Project Progress Score above is meant for self-assessment by teams with their coaches. The pace of movement from score to the other will depend on the complexity of the improvement project, the dynamics of the improvement team and the resources (time, money, people, etc.) allocated for the improvement journey. Most teams will experience movement from 0.5 to 2.5 relatively quickly but then may experience a prolonged period of seeming stagnation as their use of PDSA cycles picks up in earnest and learning about what changes work, where for who, and under what conditions takes place. It is common for teams to stay at a score of 2.5 or 3.0 for a "longer" period of time before they can demonstrate change in their outcome measure and achieve "3.5 Improvement." Movement to a 4.0 may occur soon thereafter but then progress may slow again as the criteria for Sustainable Improvement and Outstanding Sustained Results become harder to achieve, requiring significant amounts of time to unfold.

Project Progress is not linear. As such the Project progress score should be used for monitoring, discussion and decision making inside the team but not for judgement or accountability associated with the learning journey. It is always important for leaders and coaches of improvement to remember these are learning journeys, generation of desired outcomes has not previously occurred, and complete knowledge of how to achieve does not exist (otherwise there would be no need for the improvement journey, the work would already be done).

Team Rubric

Each of the following components critically impacts the likelihood of success for improvement efforts. Reflect with your improvement team on the extent to which each component is present. Use your ratings to determine how to best enhance the learning of your team.

	1 Red Flag	2 Potential Barrier	3 Adequate	4 Accelerator
LEADERSHIP SUPPORT	‣ Improvement work not connected to organizational priorities ‣ Insufficient allocation of time and/or resources			‣ Direct tie to organizational priorities; sustained focus ‣ Appropriate time & resources ‣ Regular leader check-ins & barriers removed
CONVERSATIONAL CAPACITY	‣ 1-2 people dominate ‣ Disconnected, stilted, safe or defensive talk			‣ Equitable talk ‣ Actively build on and challenge each other's assumptions
RHYTHM OF LEARNING	‣ Inconsistent participation of team members ‣ Infrequent, inconsistent, and one-off activities			‣ Active participation of team members ‣ Efficient and frequent data, testing, and meeting routines
QUALITY OF CHANGE IDEAS	‣ Weak change ideas			‣ Evidence-based change ideas ‣ Change ideas target high-leverage problems
PRODUCTIVE INQUIRY	‣ Rote, mechanistic use of PDSAs ‣ No documentation of learning			‣ Strategic use of PDSAs that produce relevant learning ‣ Reliable documentation ‣ Updating of common theory based on learning
USE OF DATA	‣ Little or no use of quantitative or qualitative data			‣ Regular and efficient use of data to guide learning
EQUITY FOCUS	‣ Silences about inequities ‣ Blaming			‣ Explicit equity focus ‣ Locate inequities in the system and take responsibility

Guidance on using the Coaching Rubric for Teams

Coaches of improvement teams have a unique perspective on how those teams are functioning, what behaviors are contributing to their success and what dysfunctions might be getting in their way. The Coaching Rubric for Teams aims to assist coaches in reflecting on some key elements of team function. It is recommended that coaches use this tool on a periodic basis (monthly or quarterly) to check in with themselves about the dynamics of the teams they coach. Each element of the tool focuses on an aspect of team function that is critical to team success. For example, if a coach, when reflecting on their team, notes a low score on the Rhythm of Learning, that might prompt them to focus their efforts on moving the team toward a more regular meeting pattern or might prompt them to speak one on one with team members to understand their lack of consistent participation. Is the explanation motivational, or is it connected to the burden of other work the system is placing on them? In reflecting the coach can decide what is the best move to make in pushing the team forward toward success.

Like the Project Progress Score, the Coaching Rubric for Teams is not meant to judge a team. It should not be connected to an accountability mechanism. Rather it is meant as a helpful guide for coaches as they coach.

5. Improvement Methods and Tools I

In this section you will find a brief overview of the tools we use most frequently with front-line improvement teams. We separate out the tools for using data in improvement in Section 6—not because the tools are separate, but because we find that we often want to page through these reference pages separately.

As you coach various teams you will build out your own improvement toolkit. Most important is to stay focused on the questions you want to answer and pick the tool that best meets the team's needs. Keeping in mind the phase of the improvement journey, the team is in can be an immense help in selecting which tool to use next.

We have linked each method and tool here to both the phases of the improvement journey as well as to the key lenses for improvement presented in Section 1: The System of Profound Knowledge and the Six Principles for Educational Improvement. This should help coaches of improvement connect the various tools of improvement to the underlying theories of how to improve systems. When a particular tool does not work to produce the learning a team needs, coaches can revisit the theories presented in Section 1 to see if there is a source of knowledge not examined or a lens associated with systems improvement that has not yet been considered.

Suggestions for future reading

- *The Improvement Guide* by Langley, Moen, Nolan, Nolan, Norman, and Provost
- *Learning to Improve* by Bryk, Gomez, Grunow, and LeMahieu

Empathy Interviews

(Adapted from The Chalkboard Project)

> Understand the current system | Generate ideas for change

Conceptual Links

- System of Profound Knowledge: Understanding Variation, Theory of Knowledge
- Six Principles: Attend to variability

Purpose

The stories that people tell and the things that people say they do are strong indicators of their deeply held beliefs about the world. Listening is a powerful way to understand individuals. Empathy interviews are designed to elicit stories and uncover hidden needs through deep listening and asking smart follow-up questions. Empathy interviews should not be confused with traditional interviews which ask for opinions and feedback on narrow topics. Rather, empathy interviews use a semi-structured protocol but follow the themes and topics that the interviewees bring up through their stories.

How to Conduct Empathy Interviews

Before the Interview

- **Be clear about purpose.** Are you collecting stories to identify or refine a problem of practice? Or to understand the root causes more deeply? Or to identify the specific needs of those most impacted by the problem we seek to address? In other words, how will you use the data and not just admire it?
- **Write interview questions.** Empathy interviews use a semi-structured approach which means you begin an interview with a pre-established series of questions, but you also have the freedom to ask follow-up questions and go deeper when possible. Your protocol should:
    - Ask open-ended questions. Host a conversation that builds upon stories rather than asking binary questions that are answered with one word like yes/no. Use question stems such as…
        - Tell me about a time when…
        - Tell me about the last time you…
        - What are the best/worst parts about…?
        - Can you help me understand more about…?
    - Ask about specific examples. Do not ask interviewees to report what they "usually" do. Rather, ask them to specifically "tell me about a time when…"
    - Do not ask for the solutions. Interviewers should stick to concrete examination of what is currently happening and how the interviewees feel, not "what should we do?"
    - Create conversation starters. Pictures, prototypes, or other objects can help elicit responses during interviews.
    - Minimize the number of questions. Usually, you only have 10-15 minutes to talk to a person, so 4-6 good, open-ended questions will be sufficient.

- **Deal with data logistics.** Who is going to collect data? When? From whom? How will you ensure that those historically underserved are represented in the sample? How will data be recorded?
- **Decide on the number of interviews.** There is not a magic number of interviews to conduct. Think about how to have a diverse sample, including those historically underserved. Consider your resources, the size of the interview team, and the purpose of interviews. Often, four interviews can yield as many insights as 40. However, because the data collection experience itself is powerful, make sure there are enough interviews for everyone on your team.
- **Train your team.** Model an empathy interview and then practice together. Make sure everyone conducting the interviews is familiar with the guidelines, the questions, and expectations for notetaking. Role play an interview.
- **Find a partner.** Conducting interviews in pairs allows one person to take notes while the other person remains focused on listening and asking follow-up questions. When it is not feasible to conduct interviews in pairs, plan your note-taking method carefully.
- **Attend to your own bias.** Be sure to reflect on how your identity and role might affect how and what individuals share with you. Maintain an awareness of your biases and challenge them to see the community more authentically. Ask yourself how systemic oppression and/or privilege might affect your empathy interviews.

During Interviews
- **Make the person you are talking to feel comfortable.** Provide the purpose of the interview and promise their answers will remain anonymous. Start with a light, positive, personal connection. Take the posture of humility.
- **Encourage stories.** Stories reveal how interviewees think about the world. Ask questions that elicit stories; not questions that can be answered on a survey.
- **Go deeper.** Use prompts like these to learn more:
    - Why? (Then ask why again). Why? Why did you say/do/think that?
    - Really? Why was that? What do you think would change that?
    - Tell me more. Can you say more about that?
    - What were you feeling then? Why?
- **Be neutral.** Do not imply your question has a right answer.
- **Look for inconsistencies.** Sometimes what people say is different from what they do (e.g., I love my professional learning community, but I never go to its monthly meetings). These inconsistencies often reveal interesting insights. Consider ending interviews with one or more of these questions:
    - What should I have asked you?
    - Did I miss anything?
    - What else do you want to share?
- **Do not suggest answers to your questions.** Even if they pause before answering, do not help them by suggesting an answer.
- **Capture what you hear.** Capture as much as possible, including quotes. Use recordings only as a last resort and with permission.

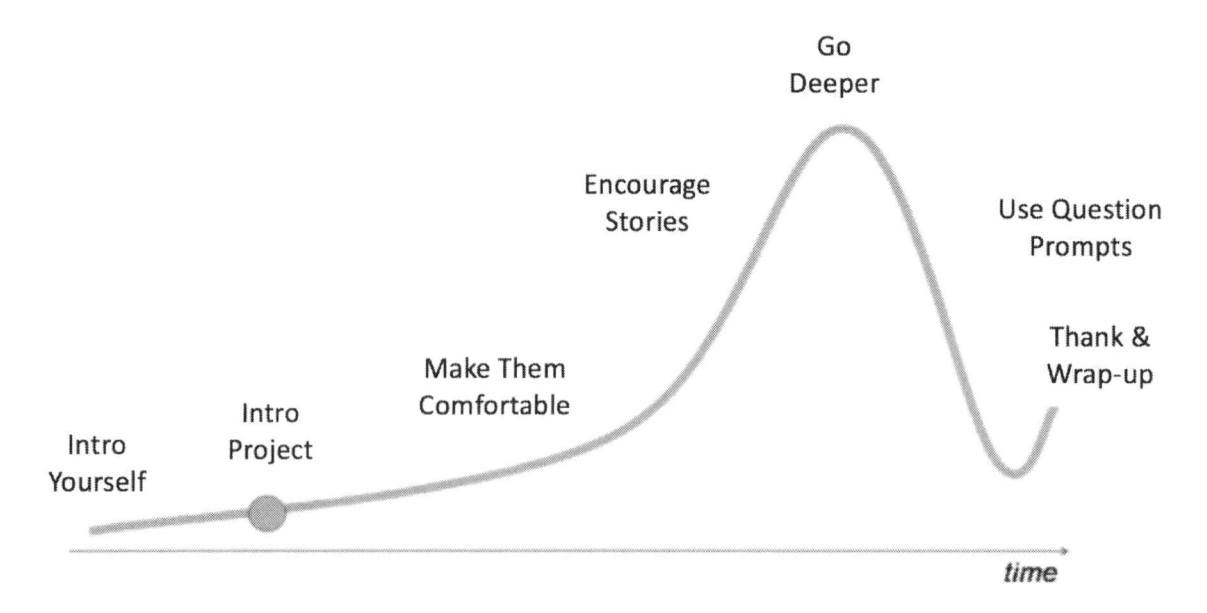

Image adapted from the Luma Institute

After Interviews
- **Prepare data for analysis.** Remove any identifiable information, number the interviews, and print out the number of copies you need.
- **Bring a team together to analyze results.** Involve people with diverse perspectives in the analysis of empathy data. Depending on amount of data and team size, allow anywhere from 30 to 90 minutes.
- **Debrief the process.** What was the experience like for people? What worked well? What would you do differently next time?

How to Use Empathy Interviews

Always be prepared to uncover something quite different than you expected during analysis. Three protocols are summarized below. You should revise or expand each protocol to meet your need.

Headlines
Use this analysis when you want a descriptive summary of the data you have collected.
1. As a whole group, model how headlines are created: One person shares an interview while other members capture headlines and/or representative quotes on post-it notes. These should be descriptive in nature; they should not contain inferences, opinions, or solutions. For example, "One time the morning meeting was so pointless I made my grocery list" or, "Doctors very bored by irrelevant topics presented during grand rounds." One interview might result in one to six post-it notes.
2. Once the group understands the process, break into smaller groups or pairs to complete analysis of the data set (the size and configuration depends on the size of your data set, team size, and amount of time you have). Continue to generate post-it notes with headlines.
3. Once finished, saturate a wall space with the post-it notes and then organize the post-its into groups of related themes. Note: You may hit data saturation before you finish the full data set. That means that all the main themes have already emerged. It is okay to stop the headline activity if you agree you've reach data saturation.
4. Label the groupings with descriptive sentences ("e.g., Feeling safe is more than just physical safety" rather than just "Safety").

5. Discuss and apply what you have learned.

Possible extensions:
- As you are creating headlines, keep a side poster of tensions, surprises, and/or contradictions.
- Create a list of insights as you move through each interview

Empathy Map
Use this analysis when you want to understand human needs or clarify the problem you are trying to solve from the perspective of those most impacted by the problem. An empathy map serves to synthesize key pieces of what you learned about your interviewee. It is important to keep them at the center and try to see things from their point of view.

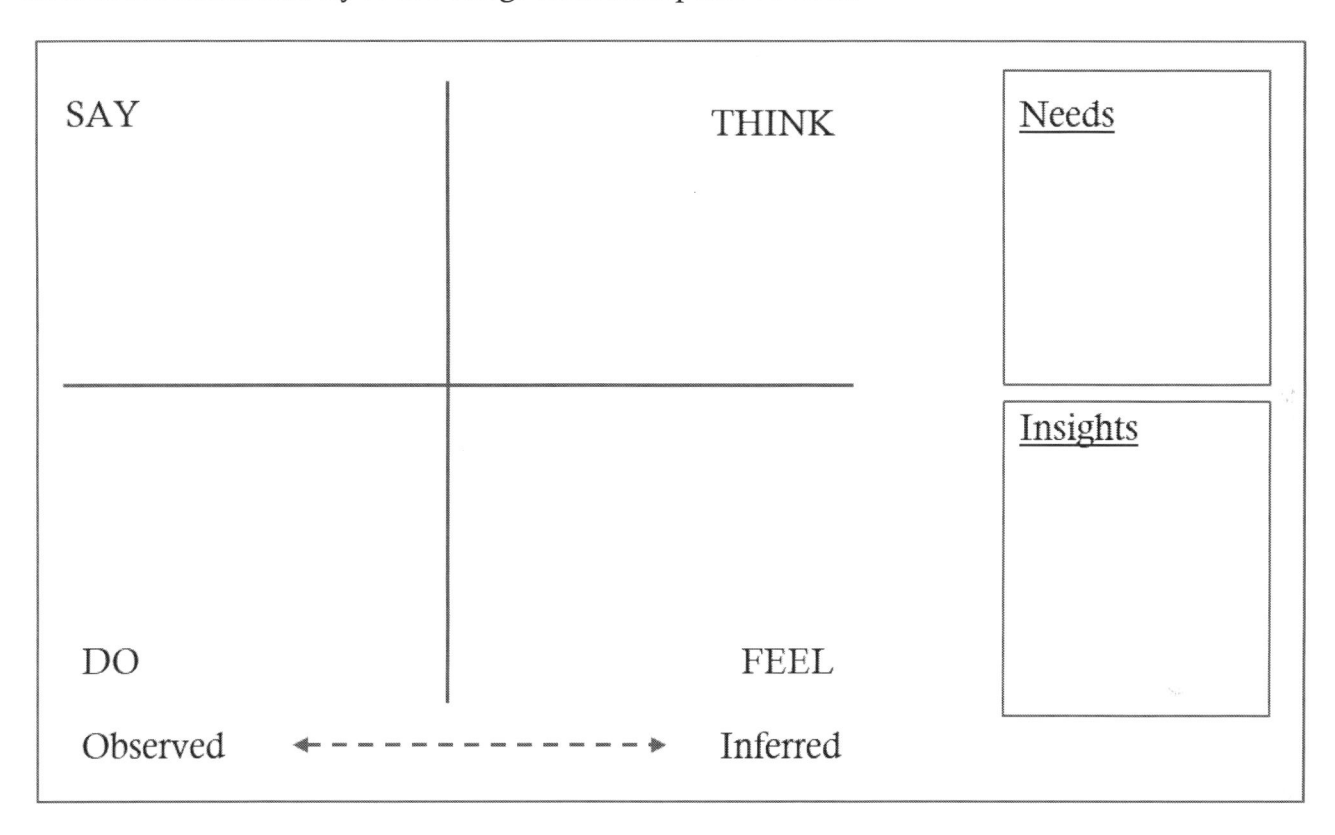

```
┌─────────────────────────────────────────────┬──────────────┐
│                      │                      │   Needs      │
│   SAY                │   THINK              │              │
│                      │                      │              │
│                      │                      │              │
│                      │                      │              │
│──────────────────────┼──────────────────────├──────────────┤
│                      │                      │   Insights   │
│                      │                      │              │
│   DO                 │   FEEL               │              │
│                      │                      │              │
│  Observed  ◄ - - - - - - - - ► Inferred     │              │
└─────────────────────────────────────────────┴──────────────┘
```

- Create a four-quadrant layout on paper or a whiteboard.
- Populate the map by taking note of the following four traits of your user as you review your notes, audio, and video from your inquiry:
    - **Say:** What are some quotes and defining words your user said?
    - **Do:** What actions and behaviors did you notice?
    - **Think:** What might your user be thinking? What does this tell you about his or her beliefs?
    - **Feel:** What emotions might your subject be feeling? (*Note that thoughts/beliefs and feelings/emotions cannot be observed directly. They must be inferred by paying careful attention to various clues. Pay attention to body language, tone, and choice of words.*)
- Write down needs on the side of your Empathy Map. "Needs" are human emotional or physical necessities. Remember: Needs are verbs (activities and desires with which your user could use help), not nouns (solutions). Identify needs directly out of the interviewees

traits you noted, or from contradictions between two traits — such as a disconnect between what she says and what she does.
- Write down potential insights on the side of your Empathy Map. An "Insight" is a remarkable realization that you could leverage to better respond to user's need. Insights often grow from contradictions between two attributes (either within a quadrant or from two different quadrants) or from asking yourself "Why?" when you notice strange behavior. One way to identify the seeds of insights is to capture "tensions" and "contradictions" as you work.

Point of View Analysis

Use this analysis when you have interviewed only one or a few people and want to go straight from human-perspective to brainstorming change ideas.
- Share all the data from an interview with a team and then generate one need statement which is human + need + insight. For example, the need statement is, "A seven-year-old hates doing homework because it takes forever to finish." The next step is to turn this into a Point of View Question, which always starts with How Might We. "How might we create a way for this student to do his or her homework more efficiently?" The HMW statement leads directly into a brainstorm of change ideas.

Empathy Observations

(Adapted from The Chalkboard Project and the Luma Institute)

Conceptual Links

- System of Profound Knowledge: Understanding Variation, Theory of Knowledge
- Six Principles: Attend to variability

Purpose

Empathy observations allow you to watch what people do and how they interact with their environment. Observations give you clues about what they think and feel and help you learn about what they need.

Empathy observations are very different than traditional observations in schools that involve administrators observing teachers as part of the evaluation system. Instead, empathy observations are often open-ended, allowing the observer to capture descriptions and insights that might otherwise be missed. It is about finding a new perspective, from a different angle. This story highlights the power of an observation:

> *It was the day class lists and teacher assignments were posted in front of the school, the week before school started. This was a favorite day for Joan [the principal], since she loved welcoming back the students and families and was always filled with possibilities for the new year. This year, though, Joan decided to just observe. She parked her car across the street and watched. Sure, there was some excitement and happiness to be observed, but she also saw a different side to the day. She noticed the kids who feigned excitement in front of their friends while looking at the list, but then walked away with their heads down, fighting back tears. She noticed parents getting on their cell phones, having agitated conversations as they left school. Maybe the day wasn't as great as she had perceived it to be. Could there be a better way?*
>
> —*Design Thinking for School Leaders*, page 25-26

How to Conduct an Empathy Observation

- **Decide who you are observing and why.** These answers might be specific (I want to understand how newcomer parents are treated their first time in the front office) or they can remain very broad (hallway behavior).
- **Be a learner.**
    - Approach problems as a novice. Question everything, even those things you think you know.
    - Maintain awareness of your biases.
    - Let yourself learn. Be truly curious by assuming a posture of wonder and curiosity, especially in circumstances that seem either familiar or uncomfortable.
    - Observe without judgment.
- **Think like a traveler.** Pay attention to every detail and be acutely aware of your surroundings. Find something new in the mundane.

- **Capture your learnings.** It is crucial to record exactly what you see and hear. It's easy to interpret what's in front of you before you've fully understood it, so be sure you're taking down concrete details and quotes alongside your impressions.

Fly-on-the-Wall Observations
This is an approach to conducting field research in an unobtrusive manner, where the observer does not ask questions or interfere in the process in any way.
  Conducting a Fly-on-the Wall Observation:
  - Identify a subject area to study.
  - Jot down some questions or areas that you want to focus on to guide your investigation.
  - Consider which people and activities to watch.
  - Choose a location to visit.
  - Obtain the necessary access and permission(s).
  - Prepare materials for capturing what you see.
  - Go out and observe.
  - Record your findings in videos, photos, and notes.

  Helpful hints:
  - Make every effort to blend into the background.
  - Take on the role of an objective bystander.
  - Look at the situation from several vantage points.

Context Inquiry
This an approach to _interviewing_ and _observing_ people in their own environment.
  Conducting a Context Inquiry:
  - Identify a _location and the people_ to be involved.
  - Prepare your questions and recording equipment.
  - Go to the site.
  - Introduce yourself and the purpose. Obtain consent.
  - Ask the participants to do tasks in a normal way.
  - Observe their actions in an unobtrusive manner.
  - Interject questions at opportune moments.
  - Record your findings in videos, photos, and notes.
  - Thank each participant.

  Helpful hints:
  - Ask people to do activities, not just give you a tour.
  - Use more than one researcher to get multiple views.
  - Stay focused on your goals, yet open to discovery.

Shadowing
This is an empathy interview that involves picking a person and following them throughout a process. The point of shadowing is to learn about the experience from the start to the end of a process for a user. For example, an observer can choose a patient's experience throughout the day once they are admitted to a hospital. Alternatively, an observer interested in classroom culture can follow a student throughout the day to better understand their experience. Shadowing can be especially useful to understand the experience of user's when there are multiple "hand-offs" involved in their experience of a system.

Do-It-Yourself Immersion
This is an empathy activity in which the observer goes through the process that the "user" is required to complete. For example, when leaders at the Carnegie Foundation were seeking to learn more about the experiences of community college students being placed into developmental math, they took the placement test that is required of incoming students. The experience illuminated the ways in which the test conditions could potentially heighten the anxiety of students and allowed the observers the opportunity to better learn the experiences that result in students being placed into developmental mathematics.

Journey Map

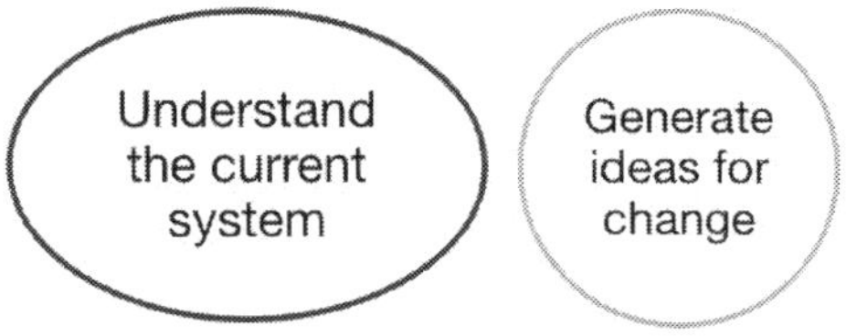

(Adapted in part from the Carnegie Foundation and CORE Districts)

(Understand the current system) (Generate ideas for change)

A **journey map** is a visualization of a user's specific experience, creating a process map from the user's perspective. You can think of it like an annotated timeline. They can be used to observe how a user crosses institutional boundaries, which otherwise cannot be seen through snapshots in time (e.g. a student's day throughout multiple classes or their college application process). Journey maps can help teams better understand users' lives by identifying moments that elicit strong emotional reactions. They are often created after conducting both empathy interviews (see page 84) and observations (see page 89).

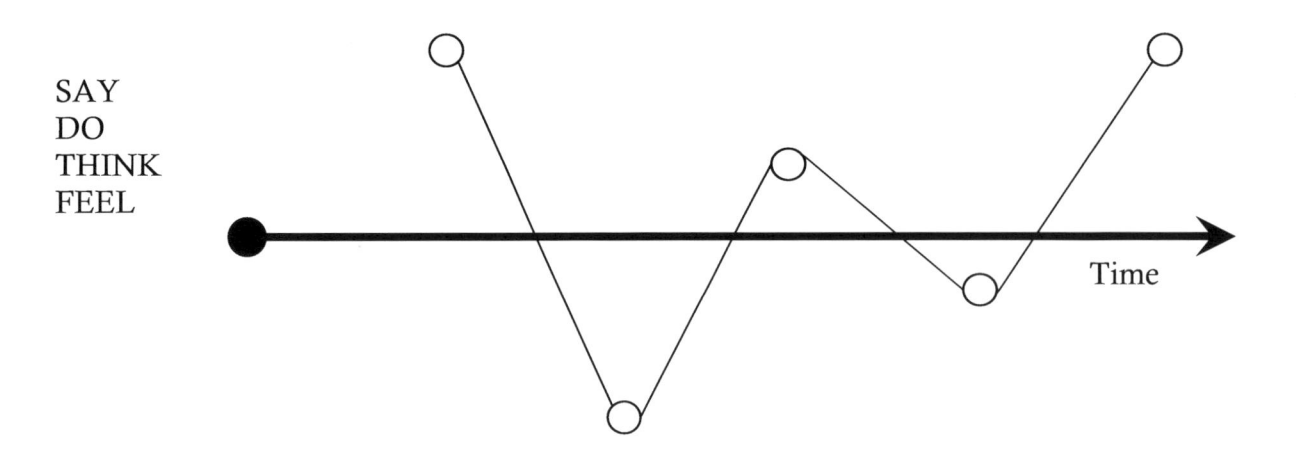

SAY
DO
THINK
FEEL

Time

Constructing a Journey Map

- Choose the user you want to learn more about and identify your learning goal. How will this help provide insight to the problem you are trying to solve?
- Choose the "journey" or experience you want to map and learn more about; determine where the journey begins and ends.
- Conduct an empathy interview and observation.
- Identify the key phases of your user's journey based on your interview and/or observation.
- Map them onto a timeline.
- Add details to each phase by including similar traits as those described in the empathy map above. What do people say and do and how do they think and feel at different points along their journey? You can also add your own categories like emotional highs and lows, key decision points, or key interactions with others.
- Feel free to play with the display of the timeline. For example, you can think of the display as a graph with time on the x-axis and emotion on the y-axis. Or you can create a matrix that has the traits listed above as the rows and the key phases of the journey as the columns.

Sample Journey Map Template:

Description of the user:		Description of the "journey" or experience:	
	Beginning	Middle	End
Description of activities/steps			
Actors or institutions involved in each activity/step			
Emotional high?			
Neutral?			
Emotional low?			
Potential opportunities for improvement			

Process Map

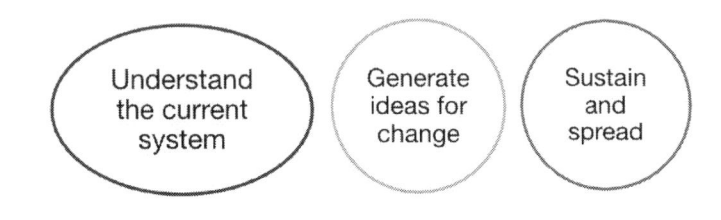

Other Names: Flow Chart/Diagram, Value Steam Map, Swim Lane Diagram, Process Chart

- Understand the current system
- Generate ideas for change
- Sustain and spread

Conceptual Links

- System of Profound Knowledge: Appreciation of a System, Theory of Knowledge
- Six Principles: See the System

Purpose

Process mapping is an activity many improvement teams find especially useful for at least two purposes:
- To visualize and build shared understanding of each step and decision point in the daily workflow for an individual, team, or organization. During the preliminary stages of the improvement journey, process maps can help teams discover what their work really is: what order it happens in, where the bottlenecks are, how long things take, and who does what. In doing so, teams often uncover places in the process where improvement is needed or are inspired about what changes could be made to improve the daily work of the system.
- To capture an intended idealized design for what daily work might look like in a future state of the system, especially for teams facing a problem of process design or redesign.

Elements of a process map

Process maps usually follow a defined nomenclature, or set of symbols,[10] which make it easy for people from different systems to read and understand the flow of work being described (see figure below).

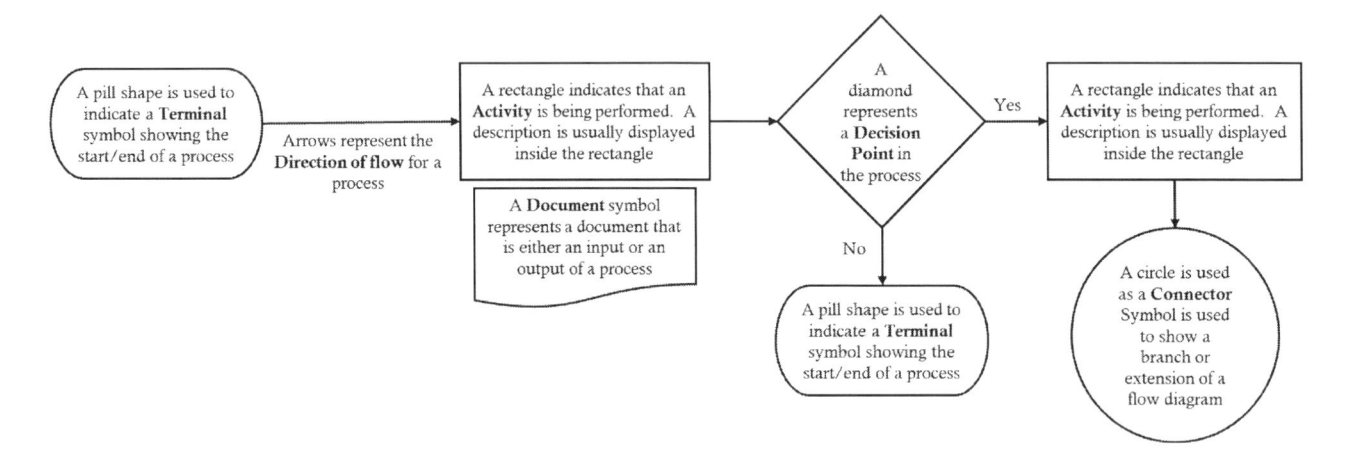

- A pill shape is used to indicate a **Terminal** symbol showing the start/end of a process
- Arrows represent the **Direction of flow** for a process
- A rectangle indicates that an **Activity** is being performed. A description is usually displayed inside the rectangle
- A **Document** symbol represents a document that is either an input or an output of a process
- A diamond represents a **Decision Point** in the process
- Yes → A rectangle indicates that an **Activity** is being performed. A description is usually displayed inside the rectangle
- No → A pill shape is used to indicate a **Terminal** symbol showing the start/end of a process
- A circle is used as a **Connector** Symbol is used to show a branch or extension of a flow diagram

---

[10] While the symbols presented are the most frequently used when creating a process map, some teams will find it helpful to replace some symbols with others of their choosing. These might include clipart or may involve more specialized symbols as in the case of Value Stream Mapping. For a more complete treatment on the symbols used for more formal value stream maps see Manos T., *Value Stream Mapping: An Introduction*. Quality Progress. 2006. 6:64-69. In some instances, teams might abandon formal nomenclature for the ease of simple rectangles and arrows only.

How to construct a process map — two mechanisms

Social Process

Most teams will lean toward the use of a social process in the creation of a process map. This entails gathering the various participants in a process: workers, designers, managers, participants, etc., and asking them to create a process map based on their collective understanding of what happens when the work of the process is accomplished. Frequently there will be some confusion, debate, and negotiations as to what the steps are, when they occur, and who is responsible for them. The social process can thus clarify to everyone involved what the work of the process really is. The inherent weakness in this form of process mapping is that it relies on the reconstructive memory of the workers/participants. In some instances, this will mean that important steps or deviations are forgotten as people create the "regular or standard way" excluding decision points for the minority of circumstances when such things occur.

Empirical Process

Use of an empirical process to create a process map can take longer than a social process, but may be more accurate, revealing important variations in the process under study as well as details about the process participants might overlook or forget during a social construction. An empirical process involves a person following the work of the process from start to finish, mapping each step and each decision point as the work unfolds (e.g., following a patient from the time they arrive in the emergency room to the time of discharge, noting each of their experiences along the way). In order to be complete, comprehending each decision point or variation, a team using an empirical process will likely find it helpful to follow the process several times in order to observe the elements of a process which occur following each decision point in the process under study. Because of this, the empirical process generally takes longer to complete but is often the most accurate way to create an understanding of the current state. When faced with a process design problem, this mechanism is generally not suitable until a team reaches the simulation or testing phases of a process they desire to implement, as prior to that, there is no process to observe in practice.

Steps for construct a process map

1. **Define boundaries** (the beginning and end of the process)
2. **Determine the type of diagram**
3. **Visually represent the steps in the process** (using either the social or empirical process)
   - Use the basic symbols and use action words for the major activities. Follow the flow of decision points to completion before returning to alternate paths.
4. **Review the diagram and add important information.**
   - Review for missing steps, specificity, clear language, and ensure that all the end points or connection points are accounted for. Note any missing knowledge that requires follow up.
5. **Analyze the process.** Review the process with a focus on how the process may be improved.
   - Defining what constitutes a quality process can help to focus the analysis (e.g. equitable, effective, efficient). Key questions for analyzing processes are listed below. In some cases, teams may use a process failure analysis to record their analysis and start to generate change ideas (see Process Failure Analysis, page 98).

6. **Improve the process.** The model for improvement can be used to test improvements to the process. The process map should then be updated to reflect changes and learning.

Process Analysis

The following categories and questions can guide team's analyses of processes:

- Time: How long does the process take? How long for each step? How long between steps?
- Space: Where did/does each step take place?
- Human Resources: Who performs each step? Who ultimately has responsibility for performance of each step?
- Geography: In cases where people or products are changing location, how far is the journey between steps?
- Financial Resources: What is the cost of each step? For whom is there a cost (the system, the participant, etc.)?
- Number of Steps: How many steps are in the process? Are any unnecessary?
- Order: Are the steps ideally placed in their order? Or is there a better, more efficient, more reliable order they might be completed in?
- Transfers: How many transfers occur in the process? Understanding that transfer points represent opportunities for errors to be introduced to a process or system.
- Delays: At which step(s) do delays occur in the process?
- Bottlenecks: Can you identify known bottlenecks in the process where the work of the process cannot proceed efficiently for some reason?

Variations

So far, we have been describing **simple process maps** that describe a single flow of steps, generally from left to right. In addition, the following diagrams can also be useful:

- **Swim Lane Diagram:** When using a swim lane diagram, the focus is on understanding who is performing or participating in each step (as in the example below) or where the steps are occurring. Each "lane" is designated with either the name of a person, their role, or where each step is performed/takes place. In this way, part of the detailed analysis is depicted through the diagram.
- **Top-Down Process Map:** This version of a process map takes high level view. Rather than detailing all the steps in a process it instead reduces the detail of the map a level to show only 5 or 6 "major steps" which can represent the process from start to finish.
- **Value-Stream Mapping:** Also known as VSM, this type of process map is very popular within specific disciplines like Lean and Six Sigma. It is used to not just map a process but to depict those steps which add value to the product or service in meeting a customer need. VSM has it's own more complicated nomenclature and is most often used in manufacturing environments.[11]

Below is an example of the intervention pathway for families with students who have become chronically absent from school or who display serious behavioral offenses requiring referral to a

---

[11] A good introductory reference for readers is "Value Stream Mapping – an Introduction" authored by Tony Manos and published in June 2006 issue of Quality Progress.

district attorney's office.[12] The pathway is first depicted using a simple process map and then is reconfigured to demonstrate other types of process maps teams might find helpful in documenting or communicating their process.

---

[12] This example is courtesy of the Helping Families Initiative, www.h-f-i.org. HFI is an organization focused on reducing chronic absenteeism in schools, and thus early criminal behavior, in the state of Alabama. It is housed with Volunteers of America South Eastern region.

Simple Process Map

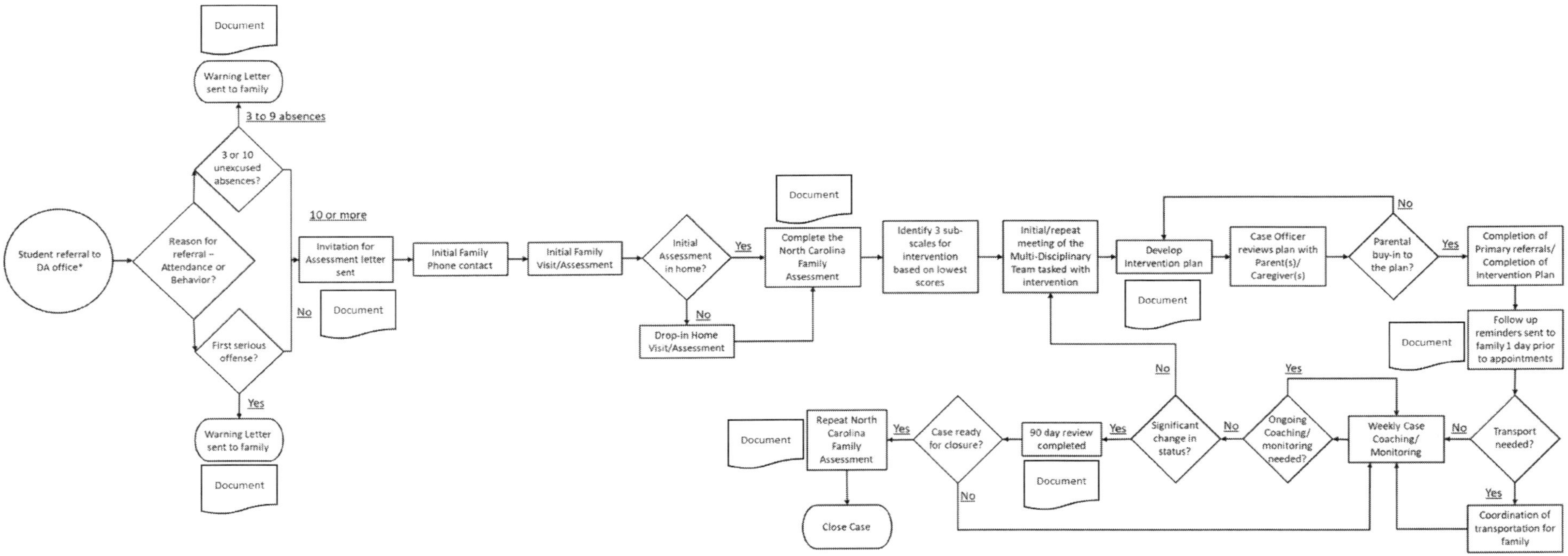

Swim Lane Diagram

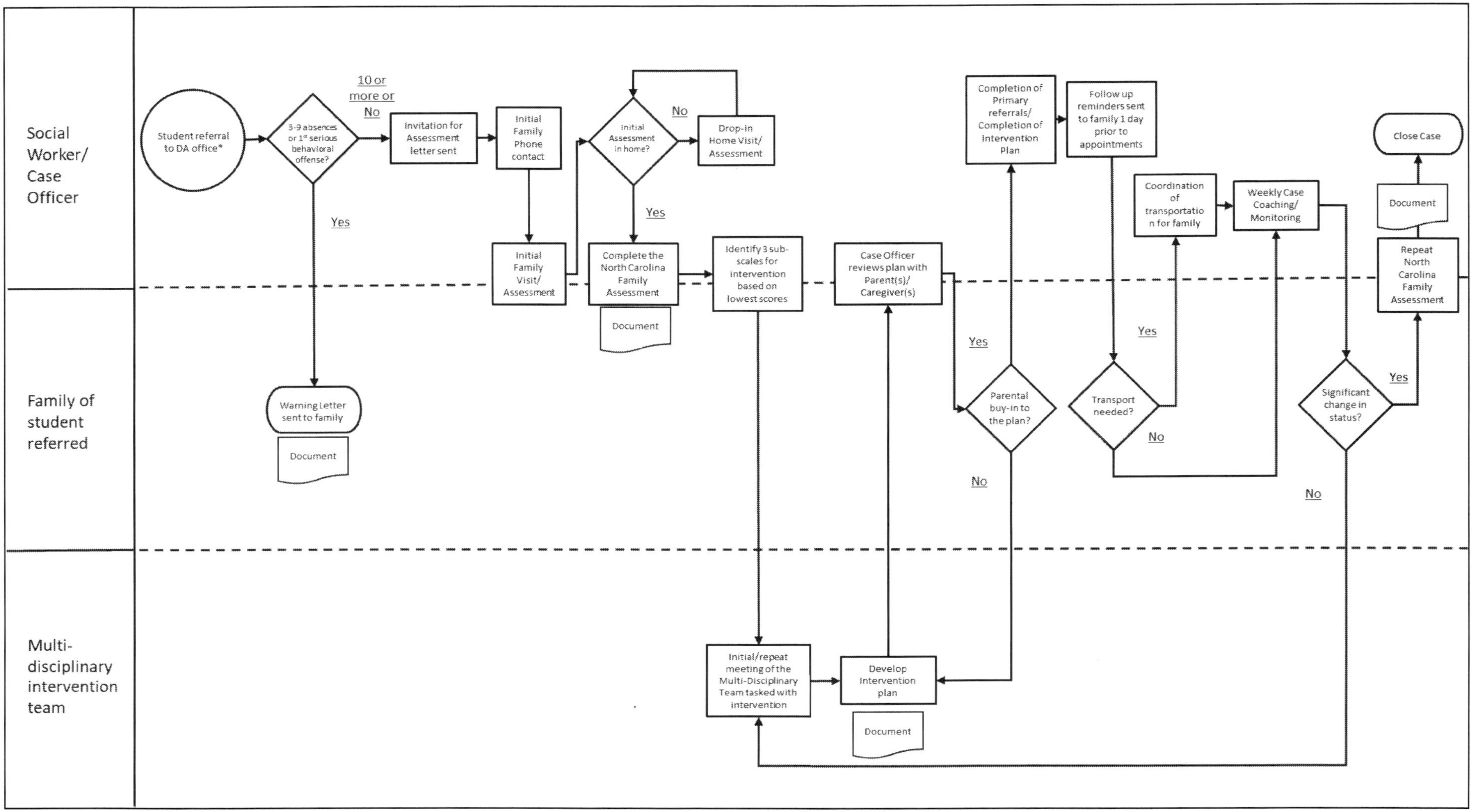

Process Failure Analysis

Conceptual Links:

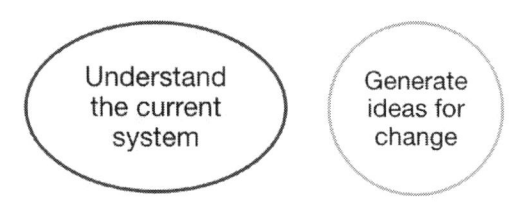

- System of Profound Knowledge: Systems Thinking, Theory of Knowledge
- Six principles: See the system that produces the current outcomes

Purpose

A **process failure analysis** is a systematic method to identify process problems/breakdowns that may result in the inability to achieve desired outcomes consistently and connect mitigating change ideas to those failure modes.

When to use a process failure analysis

Improvement teams will find this visualization helpful when answering the process analysis questions for a process map, they have developed.

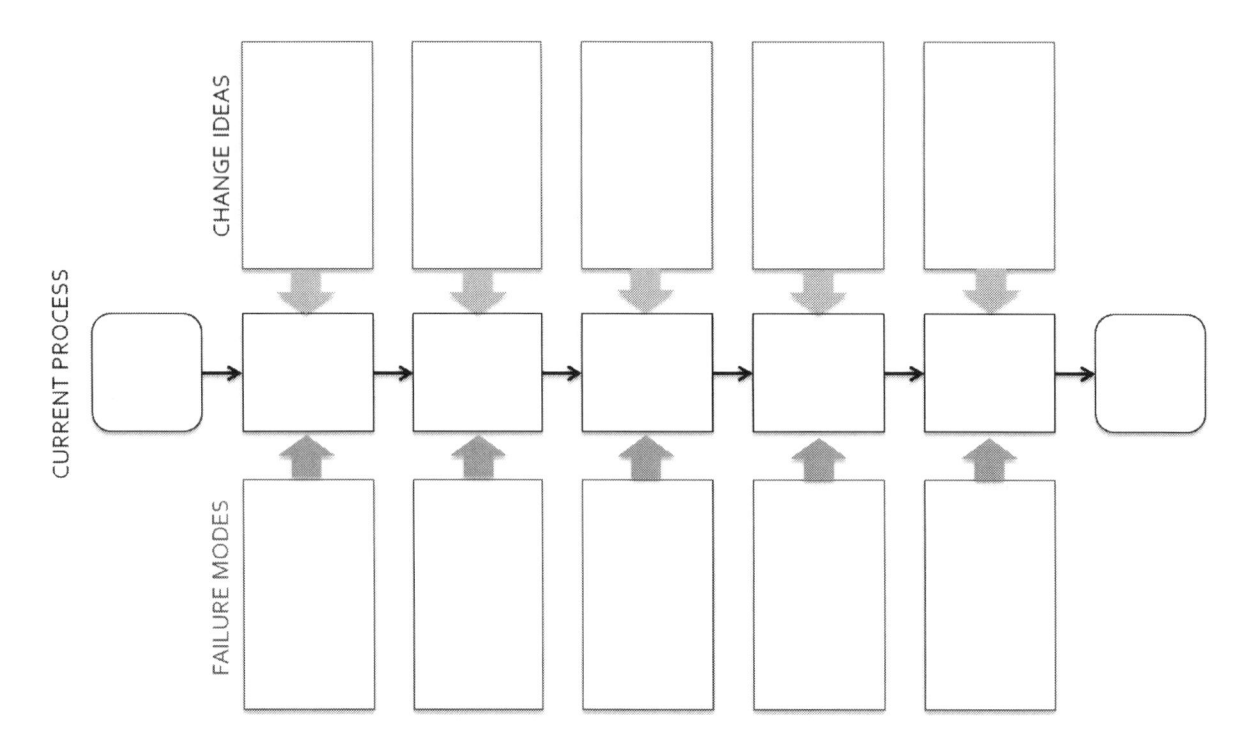

Elements of a process failure analysis

There are three component parts for the process failure analysis tool:

- The process that will be analyzed is drawn in the middle of the map. It is useful to use a high-level process map rather than a detailed version when using this method.
- Process breakdowns are located below each process step
- Change idea to address these breakdowns are listed above each problem step

How to create and use a process failure analysis

1. Create a high-level process map
2. Identify possible causes of failures for each high-level process and document these in the boxes below the process maps steps
   a. Ideally you would collect data to identify the frequency of each cause.
   b. Ideally you would rate how critical each possible failure is regarding the effect on the desired outcome of the process.
3. Generate change ideas for the high priority breakdowns documenting these in the boxes above the process map steps

Process failure analysis example

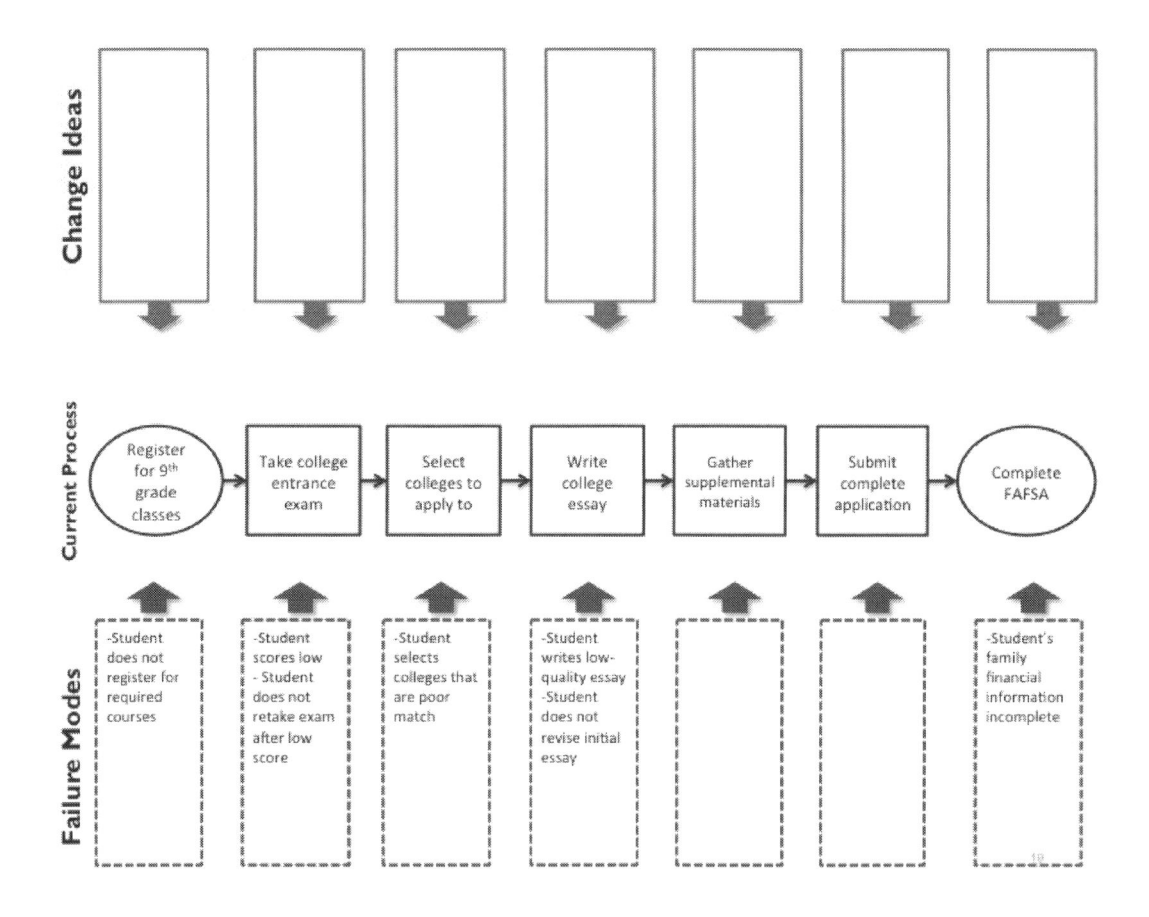

Change Ideas (empty boxes)

Current Process: Register for 9th grade classes → Take college entrance exam → Select colleges to apply to → Write college essay → Gather supplemental materials → Submit complete application → Complete FAFSA

Failure Modes:
- Student does not register for required courses
- Student scores low; Student does not retake exam after low score
- Student selects colleges that are poor match
- Student writes low-quality essay; Student does not revise initial essay
- (empty)
- (empty)
- Student's family financial information incomplete

References

This tool is an adaptation from the simplified FMEA described and in use by Cincinnati Children's Hospital and Medical Center.

Force Field Analysis

Other Names: Force Field Diagram

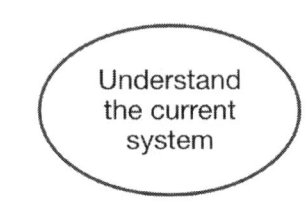

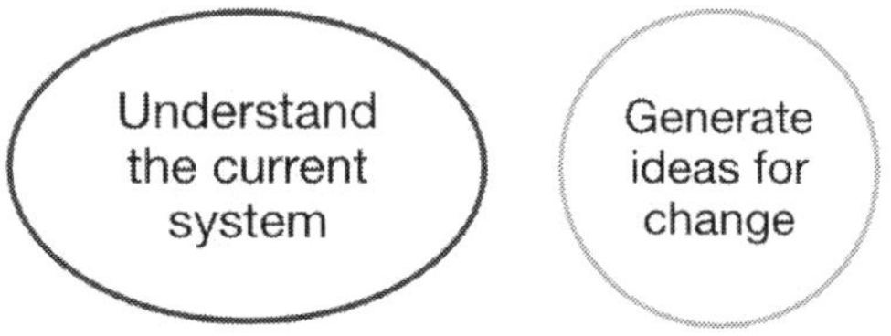

Conceptual Links:

- System of Profound Knowledge: Appreciation of the System, Theory of Knowledge, Psychology
- 6 Principles: See the system that produces the current outcomes

Purpose

Force field analyses are used to visually summarize and build collective understanding of the forces within systems which are creating a current equilibrium (status quo) regarding either an outcome of interest or an identified problem of practice. Their purpose is to assist with the exploration on individual and shared perceptions of forces working on/in the system and to build a consensus understanding about what people do and why they do it. In doing so they provide guidance and opportunity to individuals and teams on which forces to act on (reducing restraints or reinforcing drivers for positive change). They are useful in assisting teams to "unfreeze" the current state by understanding the current state and where it might be useful to act on it.

When to use force field analysis

Force field analyses can be used for multiple reasons:

- Teams may choose to produce this visualization when there is a need to create a common understanding of the "field" in which they work.[13]
- When there is a desire for improvement and a team needs to examine the current forces, which might drive or restrain the environment toward the desired performance.
- When a team has identified a problem of practice (poor performance) within their environment and there is a need to examine the current forces reinforcing (driving) the problem and the current forces preventing (restraining) the problem from growing.

Elements of a force field analysis

Force Field Analysis are most often depicted vertically, and they include five key elements:

- A description of the desired performance. Usually written across the top of the page.
- The center line or line of equilibrium. This line, drawn vertically down the page represents the quasi-stationary equilibrium of the system as it currently exists regarding the desired performance described.
- Driving forces — existing forces acting on the current system which are supportive or are pushing performance toward the desired performance described. These are typically written to the left of the center line.

---

[13] Field is a term coined by the Gestalt Psychologist Kurt Lewin and refers to the environment (or system) in which a person or group find themselves. Lewin recognized the field to be comprised of individual and shared perceptions (interpretations) of the environment.

- Restraining forces — existing forces acting on the current system which are antagonistic or working against the desired performance described. These are typically written to the right of the center line.
- Arrow lines are drawn between each force and the center line. The length of arrow lines is traditionally an indicator of the perceived strength of the force described. Longer arrow lines indicate perceived stronger forces while shorter arrow lines indicate perceived weaker forces.

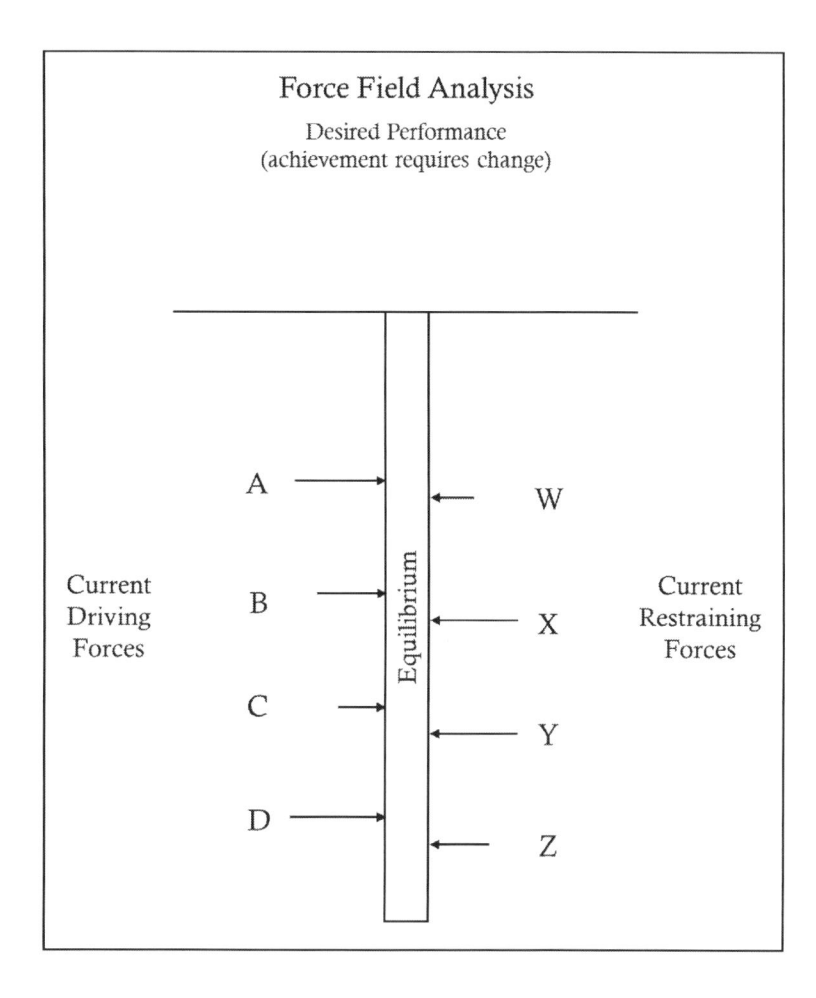

Force Field Analysis

Desired Performance
(achievement requires change)

Current Driving Forces: A, B, C, D (arrows pointing right toward Equilibrium line)

Current Restraining Forces: W, X, Y, Z (arrows pointing left toward Equilibrium line)

How to perform a force field analysis

Format the diagram:

1. Identify the desired outcome for the system or process. Write this on the top of the page (see example).[14]
2. Draw a line from the desired outcome vertically down the page. This represents the current state of equilibrium.
3. Label the quadrants (Left = Current Driving Forces, Right = Current Restraining Forces).

Developing a shared understanding of the current forces creating equilibrium in the system:

---

[14] An alternative approach orients the diagram vertically. See Variations section at the end of this chapter for an example on the vertical orientation.

4. Brainstorm a list of driving forces which are a part of the current system, and which are pushing the system toward the desired outcome. List these in the quadrant labeled Current Driving Forces.
5. Brainstorm a list of restraining forces which are a part of the current system, and which are pushing the system away from the desired outcome (i.e., working to maintain the status quo). List these in the quadrant labeled Current Restraining Forces.
6. Draw an arrow from each force to the center line. Vary the length of arrow based on the degree of belief that the force named is very strong (long arrow) or weak (shorter arrow). Use consensus where possible to make this decision.[15]

How to use a force field analysis in practice

Lewin argued for a three-step model to change – unfreezing, changing, and refreezing. The Force Field Analysis serves as a tool to assist in the unfreezing and changing stages.

Steps for use in practice:

1. Create a force field diagram in partnership with multiple participants from the environment/system focused on the current forces creating the perceived equilibrium.
2. Build a consensus understanding of the system by negotiating the strength and types of forces.
3. Prioritize forces to reduce or promote. Note: Lewin emphasized reducing or eliminating restraining forces.
4. Develop change ideas to either reduce restraining forces or promote driving forces.
5. Employ a learning method, like PDSA cycles, to try change ideas in practice and learn if they have the effect of reducing restraining forces or promoting driving forces.

---

[15] A variation on the use of arrow length is to assign a numerical value to the strength of names forces. See the section Variations at the end of this chapter for more detail.

Example of a force field analysis

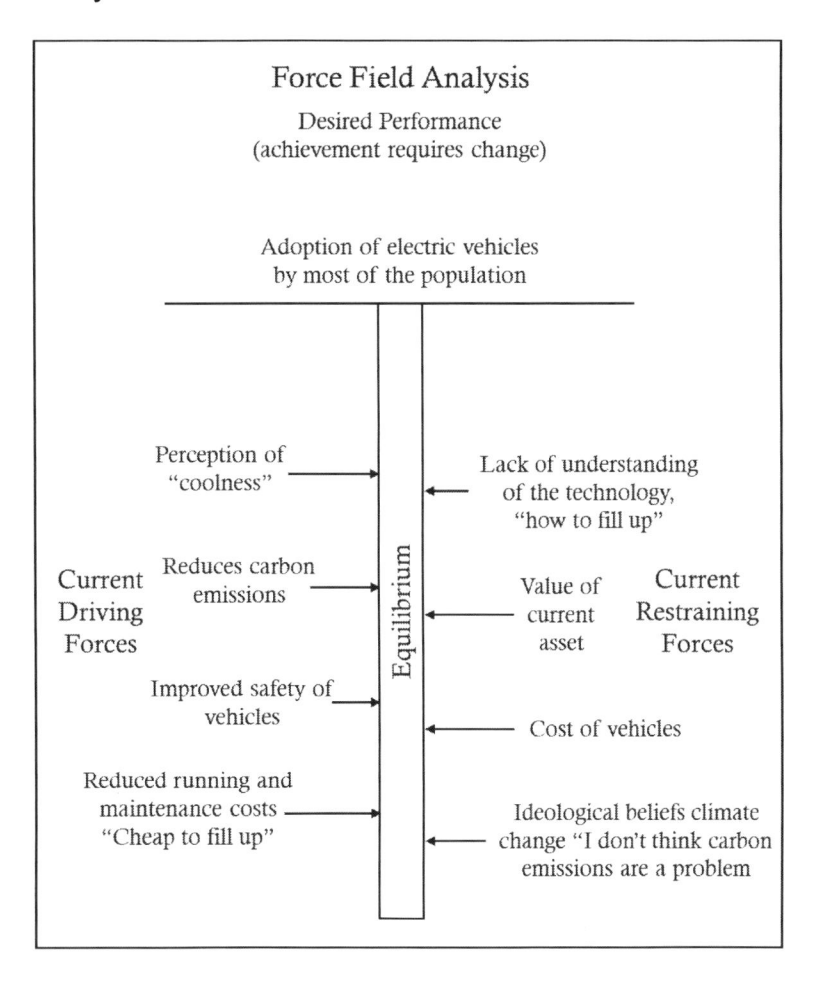

```
                    Force Field Analysis
                    Desired Performance
                 (achievement requires change)


                  Adoption of electric vehicles
                    by most of the population
              ─────────────────────────────────


            Perception of              Lack of understanding
             "coolness"      →    ←       of the technology,
                                            "how to fill up"

  Current    Reduces carbon                          Current
  Driving      emissions     →    ←    Value of    Restraining
  Forces                                current       Forces
                                         asset

           Improved safety of
               vehicles      →    ←    Cost of vehicles

          Reduced running and
          maintenance costs          Ideological beliefs climate
           "Cheap to fill up" →  ←   change "I don't think carbon
                                       emissions are a problem
```

Lewin argued most systems have an easier time experiencing change when restraining forces are removed or reduced. This allows driving forces to have a greater impact on moving the system in the direction of interest. In the example above, it may be more impactful to give people the opportunity to test drive the vehicles including practice at a charging station or provide a premium petrol-powered trade-in to promote carbon reductions or gains in safety in advertising to consumers.

Coaching Notes

Below are some common challenges teams face in building and using force field diagrams and include some thoughts on how to direct teams:

1. Some teams may have a propensity to want to focus on reinforcing driving forces depicted by the diagram. The challenge they face when doing so is that the driving force may cause a "reaction" from the system which will reinforce opposing or restraining forces. This is often seen in systems and can be described as a balancing loop. Lewin recommended teams focus on reducing or weakening the restraining forces. This is akin to weakening or eliminating balancing loops from the system.

2. When constructing a force field diagram for the first time, teams will be brainstorming a variety of forces. Sometimes people on the team will want to identify a force as both a driving force and restraining force. Coaches will need to probe this statement. Ask why a force is a driving force? Why is it a restraining force? Dig deeper into the underlying elements people are really thinking of

when they declare it to fall into both camps. Help them to identify these elements as unique forces that apply one way or the other but not both and code them as such. An example might be, "Leadership is both a driving and restraining force." Coaches might ask, "In what ways is leadership a driving force, in what ways is it a restraining force?" As team members unpack the behaviors or actions of leaders in support or against a performance change, these elements can then be added to the diagram.

History

Force Field Analysis was developed in the late 1940s by the psychologist Kurt Lewin. Lewin argued that social systems reach a steady but dynamic state akin to an equilibrium. This state is created by both driving and restraining forces which act on the field (or shared environment) of a particular group, shaping their beliefs and actions. *Driving forces* push the dynamics of the system in the direction of change while *restraining forces* push back preventing the system from moving in the direction of change. The forces can act at the individual level, the group level, and at the system level to influence the behavior of the people within the system. For Lewin the forces are motivational (referring to psychological motivators) but may refer to structures, processes, or importantly, norms the group holds for what constitutes acceptable behavior in the shared environment. Force Field Analysis emerged to visually describe the driving and restraining forces that would need to change to disrupt the current system. Lewin argued it is often more important to reduce restraining forces than it is to promote driving forces to achieve a desired change for a system.

Lewin also postulated a Three Step Model of Change: 1) Unfreezing 2) Changing 3) Refreezing. Unfreezing involved identifying the forces that create current equilibrium and Force Field Analysis was a tool designed to facilitate this step. Lewin believed the completion of steps 2 and 3 could only be accomplished using experiential learning once the unfreezing had occurred. His language for achieving this movement was Action Research. In the context of Improvement Science, we would promote the use of the Model for Improvement and specifically PDSA cycles to move from understanding forces, to changing and "refreezing" the system.

Variations

Vertical vs Horizontal Orientation
Various sources depict Force Field Analysis in different ways. The more commonly seen diagrams are draw with a vertical orientation, but some authors will create diagrams which are oriented horizontally. In the case of horizontally organized diagrams, it is traditional to place the description of desired performance on the right-hand side of the page and to place the driving forces at the top of the page, the restraining forces at the bottom of the page. See example below.

```
        Force Field Analysis with a Horizontal Orientation

            Current Driving Forces          Desired Performance
                                            (achievement requires
                                                   change)
         A      B      C      D
         ↓      ↓      ↓      ↓
        ┌──────────────────────────┐
        │        Equilibrium       │
        └──────────────────────────┘
         ↑      ↑      ↑      ↑
         W      X      Y      Z

          Current Restraining Forces
```

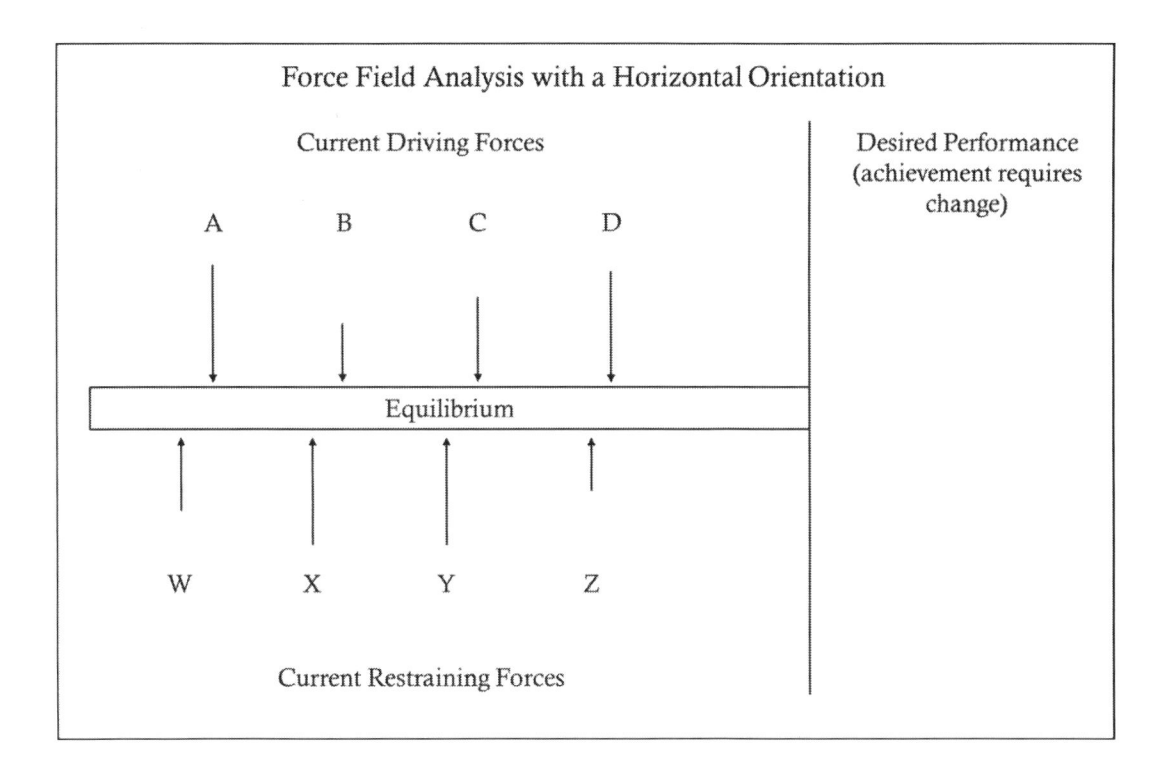

Strength of Force

With most Force Field Analysis, the length of arrows depicts the perceived strength of the force described. Some teams will find this confusing or imprecise. One variation that exists is to assign a numerical value between 1 (weak force) and 5 (strong force) as an indication of the strength of the force described. These values are typically listed to either side of the force descriptions for easy reference. When numbers are used, arrow length may or may not also be varied to illustrate strength. See example below.

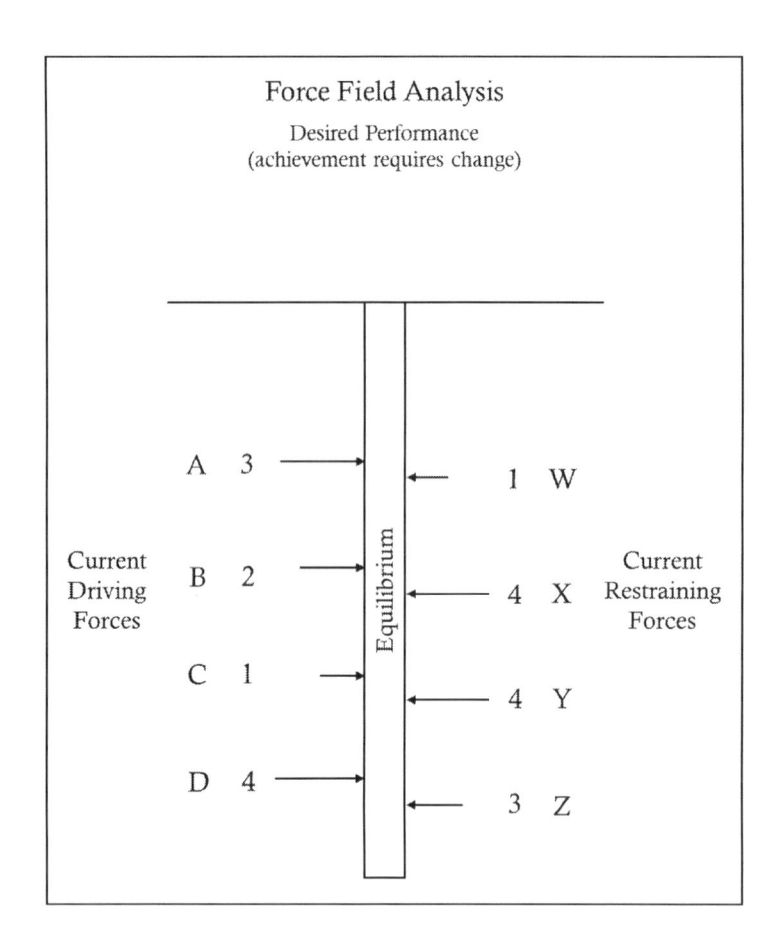

```
                    Force Field Analysis
                    Desired Performance
                  (achievement requires change)


                                    │
                                    │
              A   3  ──────▶  │  ◀──  1   W
                                    │
   Current                          │              Current
   Driving    B   2  ──────▶  │  ◀──  4   X      Restraining
   Forces                           │              Forces
                                    │ Equilibrium
              C   1  ──▶      │  ◀──  4   Y
                                    │
              D   4  ──────▶  │
                                    │  ◀──  3   Z
                                    │
```

Outcome or Problem Focus

In some instances, rather than focusing attention on desired performance it is useful for a team to instead focus their efforts on an identified problem within their environment or system. In these cases, the portion of the chart describing the desired performance is changed to a description of the problem.

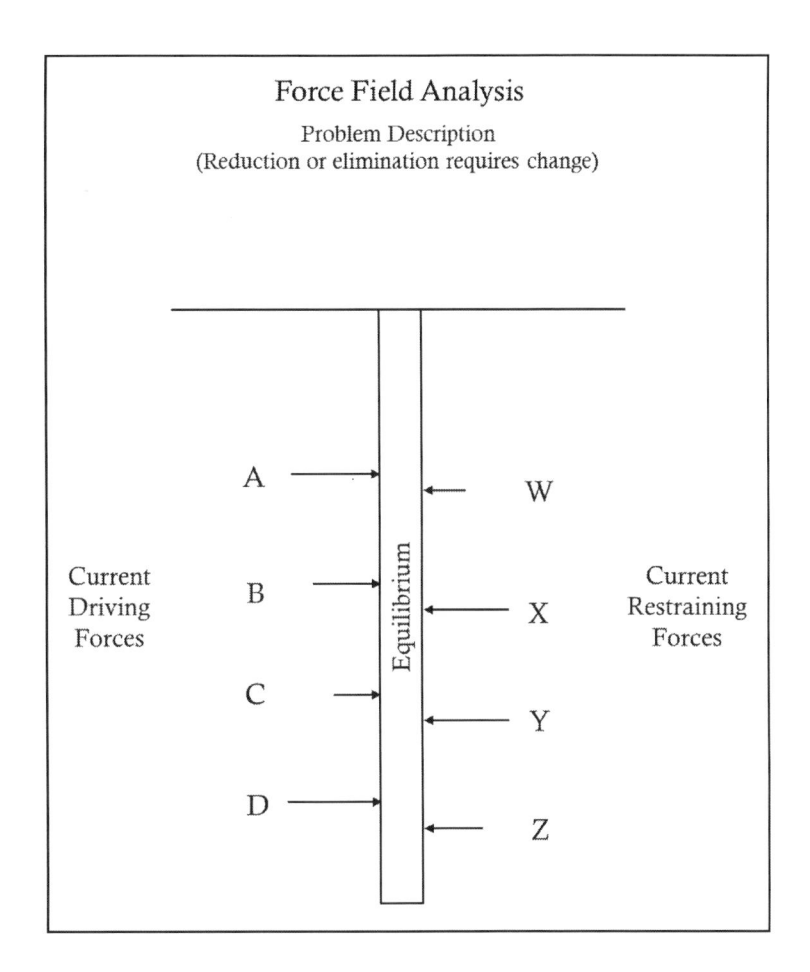

```
                    Force Field Analysis
                     Problem Description
              (Reduction or elimination requires change)


                                                    
                    A  ─→    │  ←─  W
                             │
    Current         B  ─→    │E ←─  X          Current
    Driving                  │q                Restraining
    Forces                   │u                Forces
                    C  ─→    │i ←─  Y
                             │l
                             │i
                    D  ─→    │b ←─  Z
                             │r
                             │i
                             │u
                             │m
```

Integration of potential forces with current forces

Some teams may find it helpful to add potential forces (both driving and restraining) to their diagram. These potential forces represent predicted forces the team perceives will act on the system as the team works to introduce changes that will "unfreeze" the status quo. As the change journey unfolds these are force the team believes they are likely to encounter. Some will be supportive of the change effort while others will work against it. Examples of potential restraining forces might predict reactions individuals might have once asked to behave in different ways.

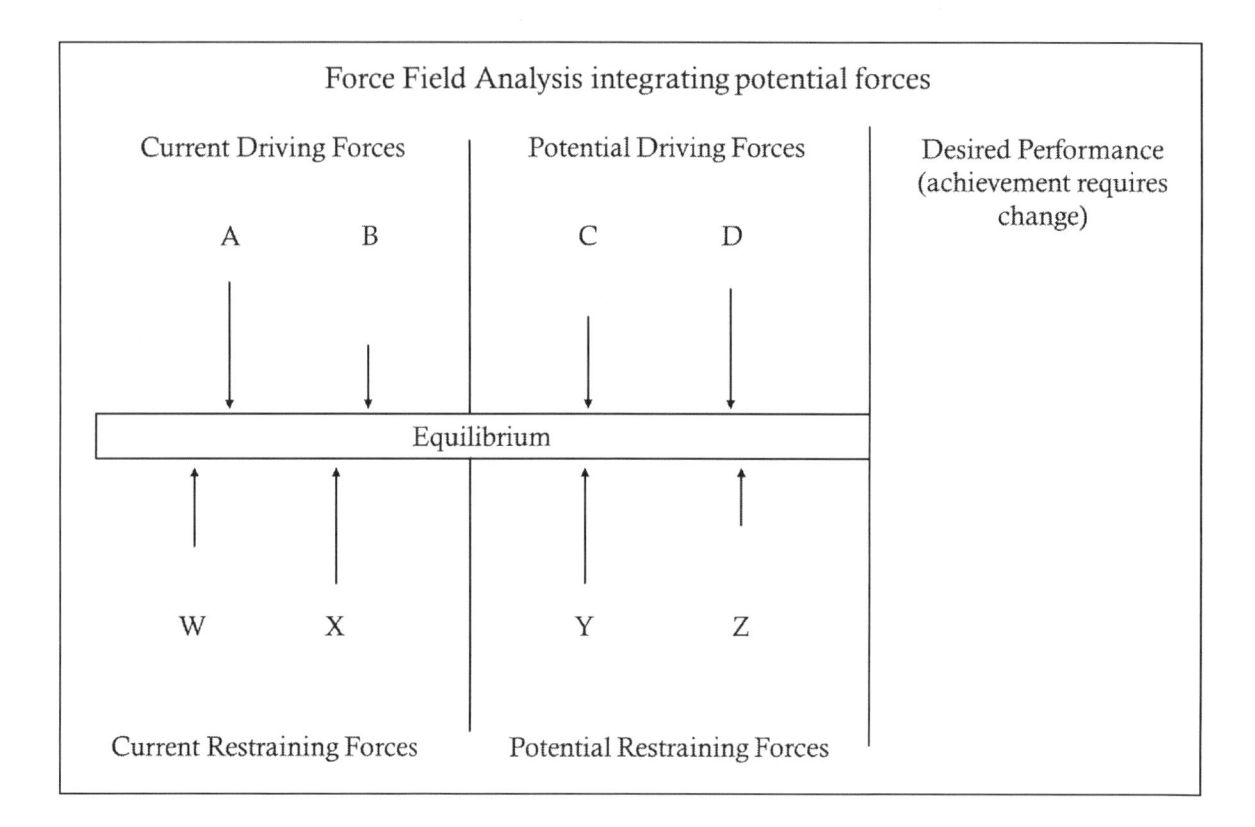

```
           Force Field Analysis integrating potential forces

  Current Driving Forces      Potential Driving Forces    Desired Performance
                                                          (achievement requires
                                                                 change)
      A        B                  C         D
      |        |                  |         |
      ↓        ↓                  ↓         ↓
   ┌─────────────────────────────────────────────┐
   │              Equilibrium                    │
   └─────────────────────────────────────────────┘
      ↑        ↑                  ↑         ↑
      |        |                  |         |
      W        X                  Y         Z

  Current Restraining Forces   Potential Restraining Forces
```

Subgrouping Forces
Some teams find it helpful to subgroup their forces into categories. This may make it easier to talk through the diagram or brainstorm mechanisms for promoting or reducing the effect of certain types of forces working on the system. Some subgroups of forces teams might use include:

- Individual forces — forces which act on individuals working within the system and are specific to their psychology or to their work.
- Group forces — forces which act on the group or organization as a whole and relate the organizational culture which influences behavior patterns. These might be forces related to communication norms for example.
- System forces — forces which act to empower or constrain behaviors within the system. These can range from process designs to policies and procedures.

Special Considerations

1. When using force field analysis to build an understanding of current problems (rather than forces impacting a desired outcome) the focus shifts from reducing restraining forces, to reducing driving forces, as now the driving forces are responsible for the creation of the perceived problem the system is experiencing and the diagram is exploring.
2. Some authors argue for the use of force field analysis alongside cause and effect analysis. They combine the two tools and describe the process as CEFFA (Cause and Effect Force Field Analysis). When used this way, in partnership with cause and effect diagrams, the Force Field Analysis serves a tool for digging deep into individual causes which are discovered and prioritized using the Cause and Effect Diagram. This is a way to explore all the forces at work related to a single cause. As a result, a single Cause and Effect Diagram may yield several Force Field Diagrams, each building an understanding of the complex forces working on the system.

References

Associates in Process Improvement. The Improvement Handbook. Austin: Associates in Process Improvement. 2007

Burnes, Bernard; Cooke, Bill (October 2013). "Kurt Lewin's field theory: a review and re-evaluation". International Journal of Management Reviews. 15 (4): 408–425. doi:10.1111/j.1468-2370.2012.00348.x.

Dent, Eric B., Goldberg, Susan G., Challenging "Resistance to Change". The Journal of Applied Behavioral Science. Vol. 35. No. 1. March 1999. Pp. 25-41

Lewin, Kurt (June 1947). "Frontiers in Group Dynamics: Concept, Method and Reality in Social Science; Social Equilibria and Social Change". Human Relations. 1: 5–41. doi:10.1177/001872674700100103.

Stratton, Donald A. Solving Problems with CEFFA: Combining cause and effect diagrams with force field analysis gives employees a powerful tool for identifying problems and solving them. Quality Progress. April 1986. Pp. 65-70

Tague, Nancy R. The Quality Toolbox. (2nd Edition) Milwaukee: American Society for Quality, Quality Press. 2015

Cause and Effect Diagrams

Other Names: Ishikawa Diagram, Fishbone Diagram, Causal System Analysis

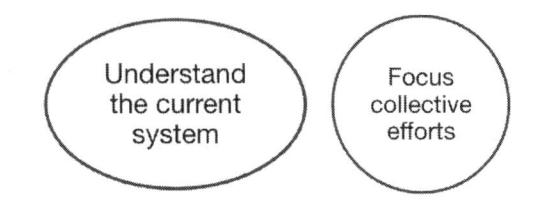

Conceptual Links:

System of Profound Knowledge: Appreciation of the System, Theory of Knowledge
6 Principles: See the system that produces the current outcomes, Use disciplined inquiry to drive improvement

Purpose

The cause and effect diagram, created by Japanese engineer Kaoru Ishikawa in 1943, is a tool useful in discovering, organizing, and/or summarizing knowledge about causes contributing to an observed effect or problem. The diagram helps teams and communities to visualize their shared assumptions about the multi-faceted set of causes presumed to be influencing the outcome. Improvement teams often find this tool particularly useful during the early stages of the improvement journey to come to a shared definition of the problem and guide decisions of where to focus their change efforts.

When to use a cause and effect diagram

- **To identify categories of causal factors where deeper investigation would be useful.** Generating a cause and effect diagram can be helpful to surface the multi-faceted cause categories that stakeholders believe are influencing identified problem. These proposed causes then structure an investigation into the problem in which these causes are explored and data (qualitative and quantitative) is gathered. The cause and effect diagram is often paired with a Pareto analysis, where teams formally collect data on the frequency of each causes in practice to determine where change efforts could be most productively focused.

- **To summarize a groups' understanding of a problem after an investigation into the system.** Alternatively, the cause and effect diagram can be used to summarize a team's understanding of the problem *after* conducting an investigation. In this case, team members conduct a more open-ended investigation into what is currently happening disciplined by learning questions and utilizing methods such as empathy interviews, describing current work practices and analyzing or collecting data. The cause and effect diagram are used to visualize and communicate the complexity of causes believed to be causing the effect. In either case, the cause and effect diagram should be treated as a live document, to be updated as discoveries are made.

Elements of a cause and effect diagram

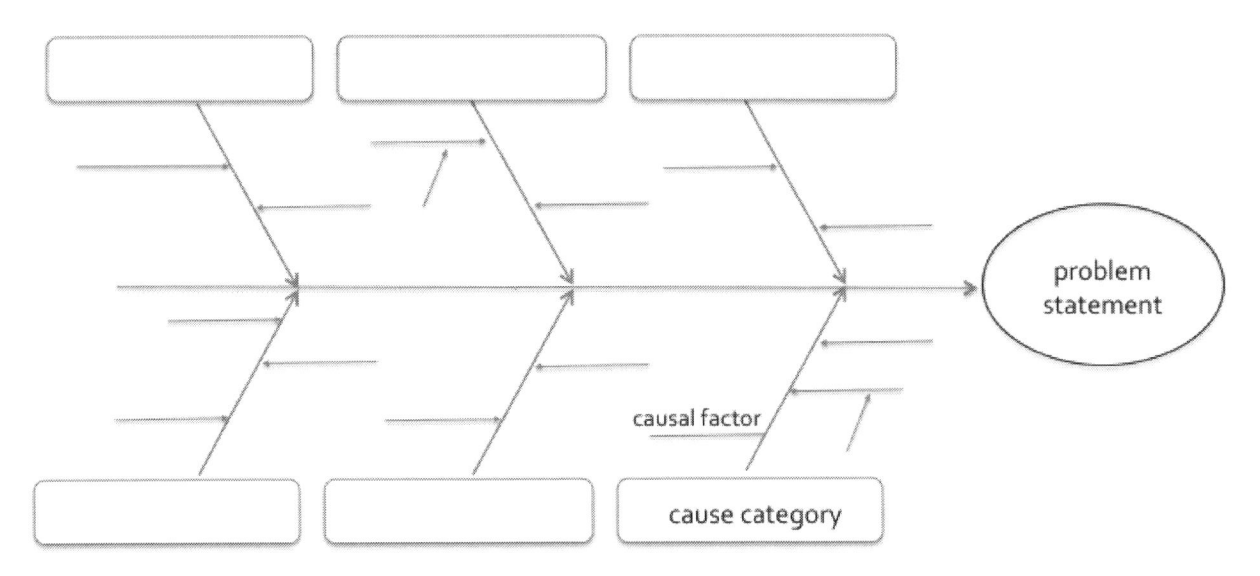

How to construct an initial cause and effect diagram

1. Choose the effect (or problem) to be studied.
2. Create an operational definition of the problem. Record the resulting problem statement in the "head" of the fishbone diagram. In developing a problem statement, it is useful to have a defined outcome or measure that demonstrates the unwanted variation or gap in performance of the process or system.
3. Gather the team members and/or other key stakeholders with diverse perspectives on the problem. Ideally, these team members have already engaged in investigation activities and bring that evidence to the gathering.
4. Have each team member individually record their hypotheses about the main contributing causes based on their perspective and/or the evidence they gathered.
5. Share out proposed causes. Group causes into categories and continue working together to achieve agreement that most known or knowable/discoverable causes are described. The groups can either be general categories or the pre-existing categories used in a dispersion analysis—materials, methods, equipment, measurement, environment, and people (see below for more). Where necessary, nest secondary or tertiary levels within primary causes as they arise.
6. Determine a method and process for deepening the understanding of the problem using evidence (quantitative or qualitative).

Tip: It is important to create a collective, visual representation of the proposed causes in real time as the conversation progresses. It is helpful to assign a facilitator who creates the visual creation at the front of the room as the team co-creates through discussion and ideation.

Dispersion Analysis

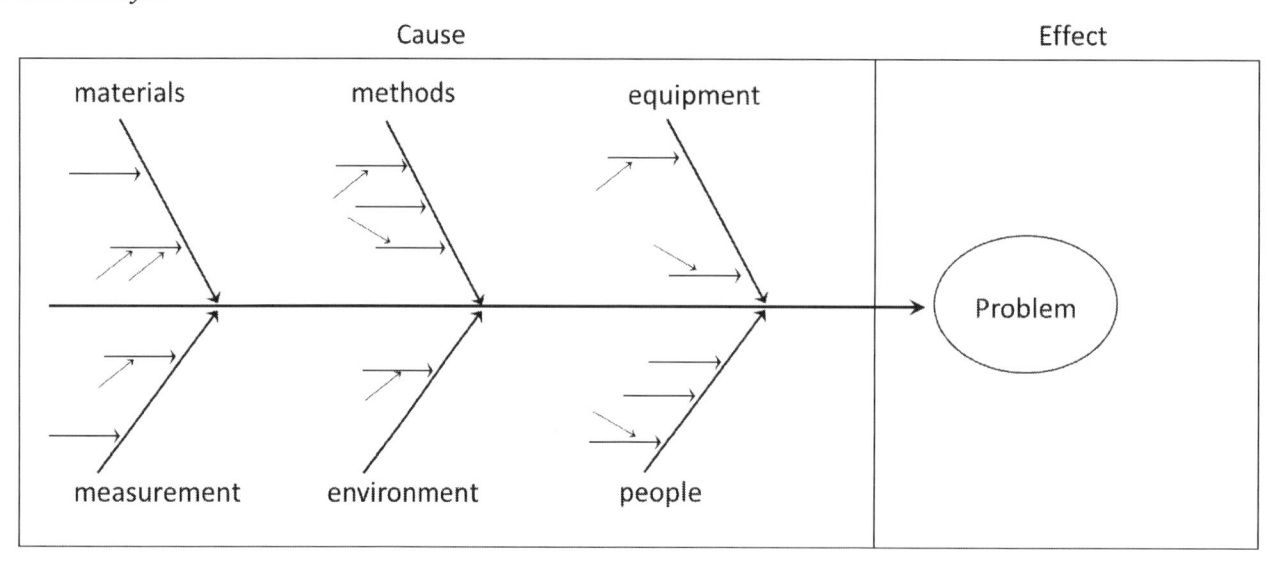

[Fishbone/Ishikawa diagram with categories: materials, methods, equipment (top) and measurement, environment, people (bottom), with arrows pointing to "Problem" under "Effect"; "Cause" labels the left side.]

The dispersion analysis is the most common type used outside the education field. When using a dispersion analysis, the possible causes are grouped according to categories generated by the team studying the system of interest. Categories may vary from diagram to diagram, but those depicted in the figure above are a common starting point for teams when considering what possible causes of variation exist in the system. These are categories that seem to be general enough to apply in many process situations across a variety of industries. They include:

- **Materials** — Raw materials or inputs for a process or system. In manufacturing it might be incoming supplies, in healthcare, the instruments, or pharmaceuticals, in education usable materials like curricular materials.
- **Methods** — The day-to-day work of the system. Often this is described as the process or process steps that make up what happens as the system does what it does to produce a defined or desired output.
- **Equipment** —Physical objects within the system that are used in the day-to-day work. In manufacturing it may be machines, in healthcare it could be beds, x-ray or fMRI scanners and in education it might refer to the desks, paper, pencils, whiteboards, tablets, or other things used regularly in the administrative or pedagogical process.
- **Measurement** — When looking at variation in practice, or outcome, measurement is often an important category for understanding variation. How measures are defined (inclusion/exclusion criteria), how the data is collected, the process for data entry, data analysis and data feedback all have the potential to influence variation. If how data is treated varies from place to place, ward to ward, or classroom to classroom, then its quality can be variable which in turn can introduce variation into the outcome observed
- **Environment** — The physical environment of the place. How the structure(s) is/are designed, built, their age, their fitness for purpose, especially as purposes evolve or change. However, this category can also refer to the social environment. Teams sometimes find it useful to describe elements of the local organizational culture which contribute to variation in the outcomes observed.
- **People** — Individuals who may be participating in the system in different ways (workers, teachers, physicians, patients, students, parents, community members, etc.). As a category it

can refer to variation between people (i.e., gender, socio economic status, age, etc.), or it can refer to variation in knowledge, skills, or abilities within the system under study.

How to use a cause and effect diagram

1. Use the identified causes to create a check sheet for the system producing the problem or the outcome of interest (for more on Check Sheets see page 164)
2. Collect data on the frequency with which causes are observed in practice. This is an empirical process, requiring the team to return to the process or system of interest and observe the work of the system in practice, noting/counting the causes as they are observed
3. Visualize the frequency of causes using a Pareto chart to help inform where to target improvement efforts (for more on Pareto Charts see page 164)
4. If revealed, focus efforts on the vital few causes which emerge most frequently, or which subject matter expertise suggests may be very important for improving the system (see special considerations, below)

It is not uncommon for teams to experience flashes of insight into how they might improve the system simply by making the cause and effect diagram. Facilitators are encouraged to nurture ideas as they arise. If the ideas are for how to improve the system, rather than what a cause of variation in the system is, then facilitators can keep a separate list for these change ideas which can then be added to a team's theory of practice improvement (i.e., their driver diagram).

Coaching notes:

- *Misconception.* Often teams misapply the cause and effect diagram in practice. After creating the diagram, the next logical step is to prioritize which causes are the most important to address for improvement in practice. Teams often fall into the trap of discussing or voting which causes they will prioritize. While this may seem like a good way to draw upon experiential knowledge of the system, it is actually prone to several types of cognitive biases that individuals experience like the recency bias, the primacy bias, hindsight bias among others. Because of this, voting is not recommended as an effective prioritization mechanism when using this tool.
- *Defining the problem.* The definition of the problem has a profound influence on the ensuing analysis. Defining the problem broadly can make the resulting investigation too general and narrow definitions cut off meaningful explorations. The definition of the problem will be deeply influenced by who does the defining. It is important to ensure multiple perspectives—most notably the user perspective—are included in developing the definitions of the problem. It is also critical to maintain a systems perspective in the definition, with blame placed on the design of the system as opposed to attributing blame to the individuals where the symptoms of the problem are manifesting. Look out for and prepare to call out definitions of the problem with a deficit orientation (e.g. families that do not care, bad teachers, uneducated patients, unmotivated students, people who don't speak English).

Special considerations when using cause and effect diagrams

- Sometimes the most frequently occurring causes of variation in a system are not, from a subject matter perspective, the most important causes to be addressed by the improvement journey. An example from healthcare illustrates this perspective: An improvement team is tasked with reducing severe harm from medication errors in a hospital. After reviewing the frequency of medication errors, they note the most frequent error observed is a prescribing error associated with ibuprofen (a common over the counter medication used for mild pain relief and inflammation reduction). One of the least frequently observed medication errors was administering a wrong dose of insulin (an important regulator of blood sugar in diabetic patients which when under or overdosed can lead to severe outcomes for patients, including death). While the team could dramatically reduce the frequency of medication errors by focusing on ibuprofen, subject matter expertise suggests they would be better off eliminating insulin related errors if they want to reduce severe harm in the hospital from medication-related errors.

- While the creation of cause and effect diagrams can seem straightforward, their use in practice requires an important consideration. When observing a process or system and counting the occurrence of causes, it is very important to first establish that the process or system is performing in a stable way. Stable can be defined by the absence of special cause variation from the system. Special causes are causes which are temporary, do not affect everyone, do not happen everywhere, and their correction is reactionary in nature. By contrast, stable systems display only common cause variation. Common causes do apply to the system all the time, in every place or to everyone. If an improvement team creates a cause and effect diagram, observes the causes in practice and then fundamentally changes the system based on those causes when the system is unstable, then there exists a strong possibility the changes made will not improve the performance of the system, and may in fact worsen its performance over time. (For more on this issue see the chapter on Shewhart's Theory of Common and Special Cause variation and the associated management errors that accompany these differing types of variation.)

Variation

Process Classification Analysis
Visually similar (see below), the process classification analysis differs from the dispersion analysis in how it describes the possible causes of variation in the observed outcome. The process classification analysis is used only when a team is considering the observed outcome for a single process. In this case, each arm of the diagram is categorized as a step in the process under study.

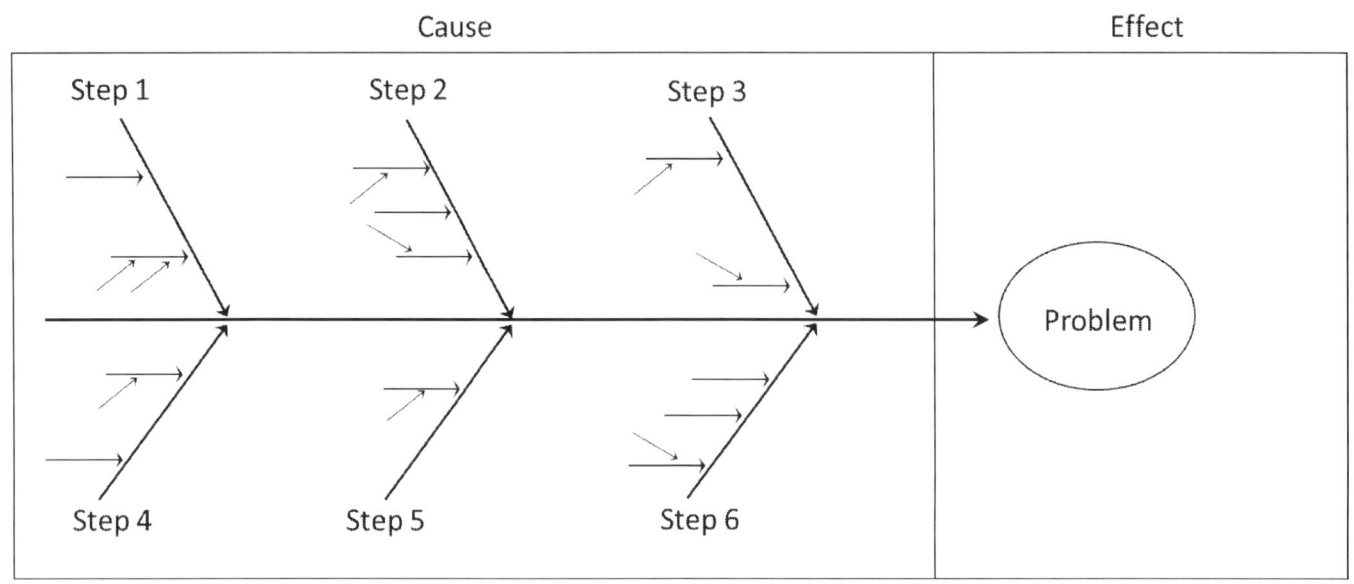

When using the process classification analysis teams categorize possible causes of variation in outcome according to when and where they occur in the process. Categories like equipment, methods, and environment are all grouped into the process step where they are used or accessed. As a result, this form of cause and effect diagram has a much more linear feel when being created by teams.

Aim Statements

Focus collective efforts

Conceptual Links

- System of Profound Knowledge: Theory-based learning, Psychology of Change
- Carnegie 6 Principles: Be Problem Focused and User Centered

Purpose

The aim statement answers the first essential question of improvement: *What specifically are we trying to accomplish?* Sharing a common definition of success is important for teams generally and improvement teams specifically.

Aim statements:

- Clearly define success for the improvement effort
- Focus change efforts strategically
- Motivate collective action

When to use

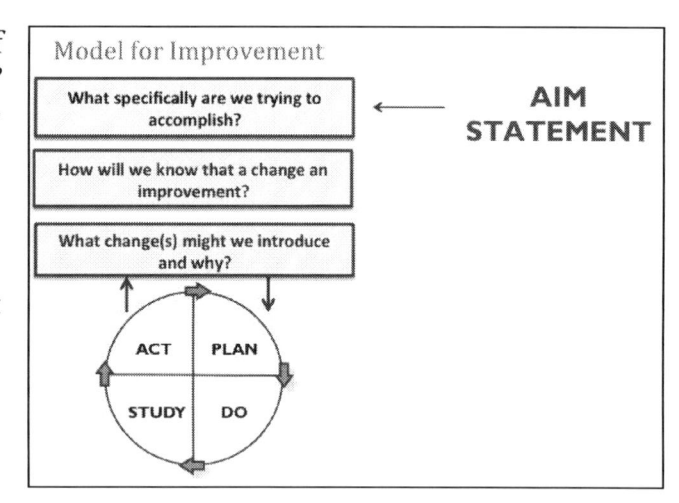

All improvement efforts should be disciplined by a clearly articulated aim statement. Improvement teams often first invest in activities, or a phase of work dedicated to investigating the problem before deciding where to focus and creating their aim statement. This helps the team come together around a joint understanding of what is currently happening and increases the likelihood that the aim is focused on a high-leverage aspect of the system. Committing to a common aim generally marks the launch of a phase of work dedicated to testing change ideas in practice. Teams regularly return to the aim statement to discipline change efforts, make decisions about the direction of the improvement work, and further define their common purpose.

Elements

Aim statements **clearly define success** for the improvement effort by specifying:

- *What will be improved?* (Clear, operational definitions of all key terms)
- *How much?* (Measurable, specific numerical goals)
- *By when?* (Timeframe)
- *Where? For whom?* (Target population)

Crafting an aim statement requires translating the purpose that brought the team together into operational terms that can be used to drive collective work. Getting really specific often requires the team to hash out conflicting, often implicit assumptions about what is meant by "improving" or "getting better." The table below provides some examples of nonspecific improvement goals translated into improvement aims.

Vague improvement goal	Aim statement
Improve the number of community college students who successfully complete college level math.	By July 2013, Exemplar College will increase the percent of developmental math students who achieve college math credit within one year of continuous enrollment from 5% to 50%.
Improve the quality of feedback and support for new teachers.	Improve the quality and feedback and support for new teachers in 15 schools by June 2010.
Increase the number of students who graduate college ready.	By June 2018, increase the percent of district students who attend a post-secondary learning institution from 45% to 65%.

Clearly define success for the improvement effort
Crafting an aim statement involves providing clear and shared definitions of terms like "successfully complete," "quality of feedback" and "college ready" to discipline assessments of whether the changes they are making are indeed an improvement. Key in defining these terms is identifying *outcomes measures* that can be used to assess progress towards the aim.[16] Often more than one outcome measure is used to assess progress to retain attention on multiple dimensions of what constitutes success. Whenever possible, teams should begin with outcome measures that are already collected to provide baseline comparisons and provide immediate data to guide the improvement effort. Discussions about which outcome measures will be used can help teams clarify what constitutes success.

Setting aims requires an understanding of the current performance on each of the measures and a prediction of how much improvement could be expected through redesigning the system. They should create tension, require, and inspire a reimagining of the current system, and represent a meaningful accomplishment for the team. In the words of the *Billions Institute,* aims should "walk the line between electrifying and electrocuting."[17]

In contrast to an accountability effort, failing to meet the performance target in the aim statement does not necessarily indicate that the improvement effort was not successful. In some cases, the change efforts of improvement teams result in improved performance but nonetheless fall short of the established target in the aim. This simply means that the team's current theory of improvement and/or understanding of the current system are incomplete. The improvement team should celebrate the improvement that was achieved and revisit their current understandings and assumptions to identify where more learning is needed.

Focus change efforts strategically
In answering *by when, where, and for whom*, improvement teams are required to make choices about where to focus limited improvement resources. A key consideration in crafting an aim statement is selecting an appropriate *scope* given the timeframe and available resources.

The table below displays three different aim statements of varying scopes, all initiated from a desire to increase college attendance rates. The improvement aim on the left represents a larger impact but also

---

[16] See Section 6: The Measurement Tree for more on outcome measures

[17] In a presentation at the Carnegie Foundation Summit 2018. For more on the Billions Institute see: http://www.billionsinstitute.com/

implies a more complex improvement effort that requires more resources to initiate, manage, and sustain. The improvement aim on the right in contrast focuses on only one high-leverage cause of low college-going rates and confines the improvement activity to a single site. As a result, the aim could be achieved through the work of a single improvement team at that site. Improvement teams should consider the resources they have to dedicate to an improvement effort in selecting an appropriate scope.

Large	Midsize	Small
By July 2018, increase the percent of students who attend a post-secondary learning institution from 45% to 65% across the 20 high schools in the county.	By June 2018, increase the percent of Lookatme School District students who attend a post-secondary learning institution from 45% to 65%.	By June 2018, increase the percent of Lookatme School District Seniors with a completed FAFSA from 35% to 80%.

Examples of Aim Statements with Different Scope

Motivate collective action
With all the technical considerations of aim statements, it can become easy to lose the motivational aspect of an aim statement. Therefore, the aim statement must also represent an accomplishment that is **compelling** and be collectively owned by the team. This has implications for the wording of the aim statement and the social process in which the aim is defined.

The specific aim for an improvement team develops over time. In most cases, the leadership of the organization identifies improvement priorities for the organization and improvement teams are commissioned around these priorities.[18] The improvement team members should have a role in defining the specific aim that will drive the work in negotiation with the initiating leaders. This ensures that the focus of improvement is aligned with organizational priorities while enabling the team members to frame the goal in ways that connect to their personal motivations and perspectives.

The wording of the aim statement is also important in compelling collective action; it should capture the impact on the "users" of the improvement work and use words that help the team stay focused on the inspiration of the improvement work. For example, in reworking their original aim statement the Carnegie Math Pathways chose an expression of their aim statement that utilized more compelling language over technical specificity: By July 2013 we will reclaim the mathematical lives of 10,000 community college students.

Aim statements are the central component of an improvement team's *charter*, which communicates the shared purpose, goals, and agreements of the team. The charter often contains a motivation for the improvement work, key findings from understanding the problem, and measures to guide the improvement work. The aim statement should be considered in this larger context as a mechanism for creating and communicating the clearly defined, compelling focus for the team.

Equity Goals
Many organizations and teams invest in improvement as a mechanism for pursuing the equity mission of an organization. Key in an equity mission is the recognition of inequitable outcomes for different user groups, and a commitment to using resources to ameliorate these gaps. Aim statements can be used to explicitly draw attention to equity gaps. In particular, specifying the *for whom* part of an aim statement identifies the expected beneficiaries of the improvement work. Here the specific "user group" is identified.

---

[18] See Section 2: Stage 1: Commission an Improvement Team

For example, senior leaders at High Tech High set out to increase the percent of their graduating students who enrolled in a post-secondary education. In their investigation of the problem, they learned that the boys of color in their institution had particularly low college going rates. This result ran counter to their organizational values and mission, and they set an aim statement to explicitly address this gap.

> By June 2018, increase the percent of boys of color[19] at High Tech High who attend a post-secondary institution from 55% to 90%.
>
> VS.
>
> By June 2018, increase the percent of Lookatme School District students who attend a post-secondary learning institution from 45%-65%.

Organizations and teams dedicated to close equity gaps, do not always choose to call out those gaps in their aim statement. These teams may carefully choose focus areas and sites based on their equity goals and intend to focus on a specific subgroup of students but prefer to frame the articulation of their aim statements in overall performance goals.

It is important to remember that answering the question, "What, specifically, are we are trying to accomplish?" and crafting an aim statement always represents a choice. Teams and organizations need to put a stake in the ground about where they will focus their necessarily limited energies and resources. This choice can be informed by an understanding of the problem, but also represents the values and aspirations of the team in terms of what kind of future they want to create.

How to craft an aim statement

When it comes time to craft an aim statement as a team, the general challenge is to go from a broad sense of collective purpose to an appropriately scoped and well-defined common goal. This requires a facilitated process. Various challenges will naturally arise in making these collective decisions which may require additional activities.

(1) Create a sentence (or two) that captures the team's current answer to: What are we trying to accomplish? (Without much attention to specificity). Write it on the board.
   a. Appropriate scope?
(2) Add specificity:
   a. Define key terms
   b. Identify measures
   c. Set targets based on baseline data
(3) Settle on and record a final (for now) articulation of the aim
(4) Creating a compelling narrative and charter that motivates the specific focus selected by your team.

---

[19] African American, Latino and Native American

Coaching Notes

Challenge	Coaching Moves
Lack of ownership or agency for the aim	➢ Go-round of why this aim is important to me/ my role. ➢ Constellation exercise to surface and discuss disagreements. ➢ Directly state that it seems that they are not excited about the aim and have them discuss. ➢ Record a less specific, narrowed answer to the question "what are we trying to accomplish?" that captures what is important to everyone (see below). ➢ Split into workstreams with two different aims.

Aim is too large in scope	➢ Introduce the idea of long-term goals or outcomes (sometimes called big dot goals) and how aims for projects can serve as milestones on the way to achieving those outcomes. Write down the big dot goal where everyone can see it and, in a way, they are excited about.
	➢ Emphasize the time frame: "What might you achieve during this school year that would feel like progress?"
	➢ Prompt a discussion about starting points?
	    o Are there any sites, departments, or groups of people that you could set a goal for?
	    o Can you bite a piece off this huge, aspirational goal?
	➢ Create a visualization that maps out all the different parts that are contributing to the aim. Use dot-voting to identify high leverage processes or low hanging fruit.
	➢ Continue to try to understand the problem.

Aim is vague and/or conceptual	➢ Facilitate a conversation that tries to get people to describe what they want to happen, compared to what is happening now (recording answers on the board)
	    o What are you hoping to see change?
	    o Who is the user? How would things be different for that user? What do they say now? What would they say when you are if you are successful?
	    o What data would indicate that you made progress on your goal?
	➢ Switch to asking: What is the problem you are trying to solve?
	➢ Suggest one or two possible statements that could capture "what are we trying to accomplish?" and have them choose and adapt one for their purpose.

Aim is unlikely to lead to the outcome they want	➢ Zoom back out to the team's big dot goal or the why behind their aim statement. Echo back the theory to them… "So, we think that if we improve _____ we will get to _____?" and/or directly state your belief and rationale about that theory. ➢ Zoom back out to the team's big dot goal. Map out other parts of the system that impact the goal. Go back to the team's original aim and ask, "Is this the highest leverage area to work?" (or directly assert that you do not believe that this is the highest leverage area to work). ➢ Directly state that you think we need to learn more about the problem we are working on before setting an aim. Engage the team in reading a relevant research article, talking to someone else who has worked on a similar problem or understanding the problem.
Wrong team to	➢ Describe how changes are tested in improvement science. Ask who would be testing changes and explore their possible involvement on the team.

| work on the aim | ➢ Divide into workstreams. |

History

The use of aim statements was popularized with the emergence of the Model for Improvement in the *Improvement Guide*. A key contribution of the authors was the use of three essential improvement questions to help connect local inquiry efforts (structured through PDSAs) with the strategic goals of the organization. The authors introduced aim statements as the answer to the first improvement question.

An aim statement bears a close resemblance to popularly used goal statements, targets, and SMART goals. However, the authors purposefully choose to introduce the language of "aim statement" to signal a new way of thinking when answering the question: *What specifically we are trying to accomplish?* In practice, organizations' SMART goals often strive for small, incremental improvements that can be achieved without making any fundamental changes to how work is organized. In some cases, this comes from goals being set in an accountability framework that does not inspire risk taking. In contrast, an improvement science approach purposefully sets aim statements to require fundamental changes or reinventions of the current system to produce a new level of performance.

References:

Langley, G., Moen, R., Nolan, K., Nolan, T., Norman, C., and Provost, L. *The Improvement Guide: a practical approach to enhancing organizational performance.* 2nd Edition. San Francisco: Jossey-Bass, 2009.

Theory of Practice Improvement: Driver Diagram

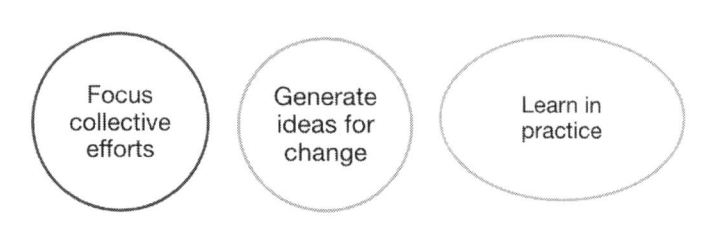

Focus collective efforts — *Generate ideas for change* — *Learn in practice*

Conceptual Links

- System of Profound Knowledge: Theory of Knowledge, Appreciation of the System
- 6 Principles: Disciplined inquiry

Purpose

Driver diagrams have three purposes:
1. To develop a **shared theory of improvement** that visualizes the complex dynamic nature of the targeted system and the changes that are hypothesized to improve it.
2. To **communicate visually** the improvement team's work to external stakeholders.
3. To act as a **knowledge management tool** for teams working to improve systems. As will be stated further below, driver diagrams can and should evolve as learning takes place during the improvement journey. Often teams will have multiple versions with the latest being the most up-to-date understanding of how best to accomplish progress toward their articulated aim.

When to use a driver diagram

There are four time periods when teams find use of the driver diagram valuable:

- **Chartering** — During the early stage of an improvement journey, the creation of an initial theory of improvement is a critical step to develop will and interest in the work.

- **Prioritization, direction, and measurement** — Once an initial theory is visualized using a driver diagram, teams may choose to use the tool during meetings to decide where to start introducing changes to the system or to inform what measures will be needed to help the team determine whether a change is an improvement.[1] Some teams will opt for work through primary and secondary drivers (add the associated change ideas) sequentially, building knowledge bit by bit. Others will take a divide and conquer approach, assigning specific ideas or drivers to various subgroups on the team. In either case, the driver diagram helps teams to stay clear on who is doing what. It is not uncommon for teams to annotate their driver diagrams with specific responsibilities for the pursuit of learning or with specific timelines as to when they would like to try different ideas in practice. In addition, teams may uncover new areas of interest or need when they begin running PDSA cycles on their change ideas or when they begin to apply other tools like process maps or cause and effect diagrams to their work. The driver diagram then acts as a sounding board for the team. When they uncover some new area of interest they can ask, "Does this fit into our theory of what is needed to improve X outcome for the system?" Sometimes the answer is yes and an update to the diagram is needed. Other times the answer is no, and the team needs to recognize the importance of the finding but set it aside to be addressed at a later time or by a different project. Teams often refer to this as placing something in a "parking lot" for later.

- **Consolidation** — At regular intervals improvement teams should pause in their work to reconsider their driver diagram, ensuring it reflects the learning they have achieved regarding what it takes to

---

[1] See Section 6: The Measurement Tree for more information on this topic

improve the system or to achieve the outcome of interest.[2] In this text we refer to this as the Consolidation Routine.[3] This involves the team reviewing their learning, primarily from the application of PDSA cycles, but also from the use of other tools and then changing the diagram to reflect the learning. Many teams find it useful to update their driver diagram monthly or quarterly in this way.

- **Publication** — At the end of many improvement journeys, teams are often asked to present on the nature and progress of their improvement effort. Their driver diagram can act as a clear, single visualization of their progress to date. Some teams go so far as to stack various iterations in an animated fashion when displaying their driver diagram, so audiences can note the learning, all the work the team has done, and the evolution of the theory over time. In addition, there may also be a desire or need to publish the work accomplished. Final driver diagrams are very useful elements of change packages (published packages on specific topics that other teams may use as a starting place for their pursuit of improvement). They are also useful in communicating the work in peer reviewed publications, through presentations (academic conferences, board meetings, etc.), to funders, or in final evaluative reports.

Elements of a driver diagram

(1) Aim Statement or Outcome of Interest

The aim statement typically articulates the following: the outcome(s) of the system desired to be improved; the intended magnitude of the improvement (with a direct link to an outcome measure of interest); and a timeframe for completion.[4]

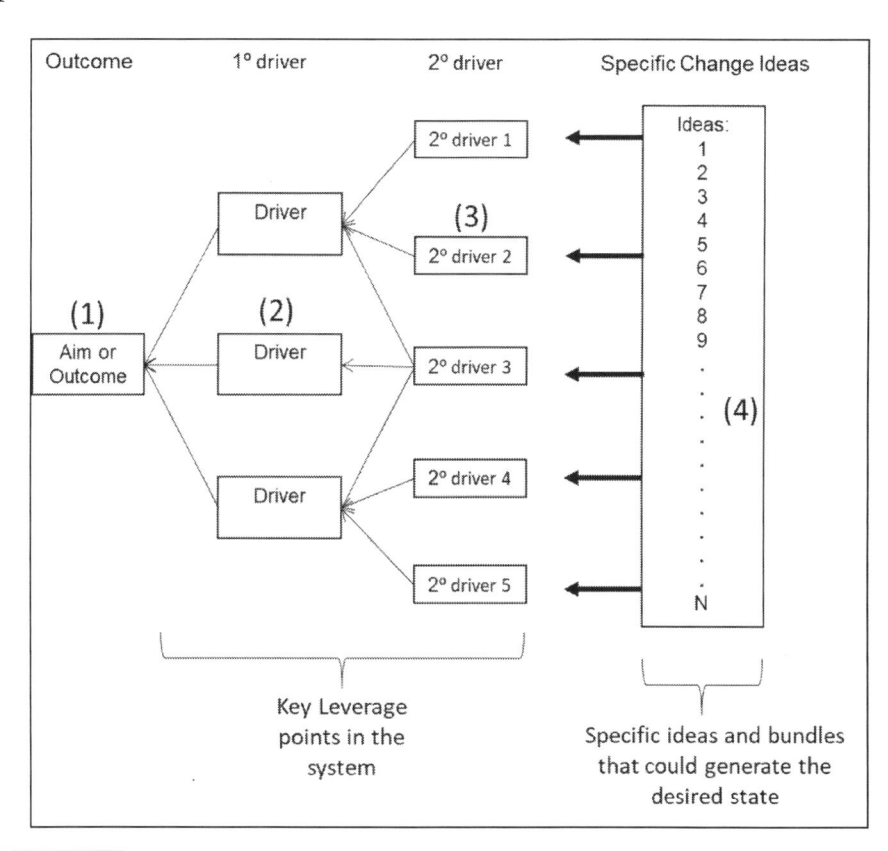

---

[2] See Section 2: Stage 3 Engaging in Collective Improvement Work for more information on Consolidation of Learning

[3] See Section 2: Stage 3 Engaging in Collective Improvement Work for more information on Consolidation of Learning

[4] See Section 5: Aim Statements for more information on developing and writing aim statements

(2) Primary Drivers

Primary drivers are high level elements within the system that are believed to need to change to accomplish the aim. They can be thought of as "what" needs to change in the system. Primary drivers can be comprised of structures, processes, or operating norms found in the system (see side note below on general notes that apply to both primary and secondary drivers).

(3) Secondary Drivers

Secondary drivers are more actionable approaches, places, or opportunities within the system where a change can occur. They can be thought of as "where" in the system a change can be applied. Sometimes they are referred to as the actionable moment in time when something can be changed or done differently to change the performance of a process step, process, or the system as a whole. Like primary drivers, secondary drivers are also comprised of structures, processes and operating norms found in the system.

> Side note
> - **Structures** may include the physical design of a space or product, technological elements (i.e., equipment), the overarching architecture of software, the departments and other groupings in the organization, and/or organizational policies. Management systems such as financial, administrative, improvement, and leadership structures, are also often included.
> - **Processes** refer to the workflow of the system, how things are accomplished, what steps are taken, and in what order. In some organizations, processes are named, and most employees can say which processes they work in and for which steps they are responsible. In other organizations, processes are vaguer concepts that must be studied and mapped to improve them. It is worth noting that these are often where the greatest improvements can be made given existing resource constraints.
> - **Operating norms** include both written and unwritten rules that govern the behavior of members of the system. These norms reflect the organizational psychology of the system and are therefore critical elements when considering the introduction of change to any status quo.

(4) Change Ideas

Change ideas are tangible and specific in nature. They can be thought of as "how" the system will be changed. They represent very specific actions to be taken on the system.

How to create a driver diagram

The development of a driver diagram is usually accomplished after some pre-cursor work has been done to understand the current state of the system. Information and learning gathered from an initial investigation (which can include scanning literature, speaking with experts and frontline staff, data analysis, process mapping, or empathy exercises) is then leveraged by a team to identify drivers and change ideas in the system. Its construction is a social one, involving negotiation and dialogue by various stakeholders and team members. Achieving a version 1.0 of the tool will likely be iterative and require some back and forth before a team feels comfortable proceeding with a consensus theory of improvement.

There are two common ways teams pursue the creation of the first iteration of a driver diagram. Readers are encouraged to use either one, depending on their context and the needs of their team.

Creating a driver diagram from aim to change ideas

1) Develop and articulate an aim statement[5]
2) Identify the primary drivers and place them on the visualization
3) Identify the secondary drivers that have strong influence over the primary drivers, place them on the visualization, and connect the important links between secondary and primary drivers[6]
4) List change ideas (gathered from: scanning, creativity methods, logical thinking, etc.)
5) Place these on the visualization, along with links to the secondary drivers they are intended to influence in the direction of interest[7]

Creating a driver diagram by grouping change ideas

1) Develop and articulate an aim statement
2) List change ideas (gathered from: scanning, creativity methods, logical thinking, etc.)
3) Conduct an affinity protocol on the generated change ideas to look for commonalities in what they are addressing in the current design of the system
4) Based on the affinity protocol generate secondary drivers and place them on the driver diagram visualization
5) Determine what primary drivers represent, are influenced by, or are connected to the secondary drivers identified
6) Place primary drivers on the driver diagram visualization
7) Connect change ideas to secondary drivers to primary drivers to the aim statement

---

[5] See Chapter Five: Aim Statements for more depth on how to develop an aim statement
[6] It is fair to say that in complex systems all processes, structures and operating norms have influence on the whole system, however linking all secondary drivers to all primary drivers creates both a mess on the page and does not do justice to the fact that some structures, processes, and operating norms exert more influence on some parts of the system than on others. A driver diagram seeks to show only those connections that are considered to be both important and useful, so as not to distract the team using the tool. It should be noted there are times when a secondary driver is theorized to have a strong effect on more than one primary driver and so may display multiple connections.
[7] As with secondary drivers, it is possible a team will theorize a single change idea having effect on multiple secondary drivers. In those instances, connections to all drivers effected is encouraged.

Coaching Notes

There are predictable pitfalls teams experience when developing and using the tool in practice.

Common Mistake	Coaching Move
Teams may describe the primary and secondary drivers like aim statements, using measures and goals.	Coaches should try to help teams describe the driver simply as a noun, meaning a process, structure, or norm that can move in any direction.
Teams may describe secondary measures at too high of a level. For example: an entire training or recruitment system, rather than some aspect of it	Coaches should test each secondary driver by asking, "Could we take direct action on this?" Whether the driver is a process, structure or norm, teams should be able to do something different at the moment it manifests in the system.
Teams might be too vague in the description of a change idea, describing it conceptually or at a high level.	Coaches should encourage teams to describe change ideas as the specific action to be taken (i.e., use tool "a" rather than "b", rearrange steps 2 and 3, introduce X, etc.). Change ideas should represent directly different ways of doing something
Teams often connect change ideas to drivers or drivers to aims that do not seem to influence each other.	Coaches should "test the logic" with teams, asking questions like "If you do this, make this change, where do you expect to see a change in the system and why do you think that is the case?"

History

For decades, the Tree Diagram has been a staple tool used by improvement practitioners to improve the quality of products or services. The driver diagram is an extension on the use of this tool. While tree diagrams can be used to explicate problems, diagram opportunities, or plan interventions, the driver diagram arose to fulfill a very specific need for theory building in the pursuit of quality improvement.

Interviews with Lloyd Provost (Associates in Process Improvement) and Uma Kotagal (Cincinnati Children's Hospital) credit the creation of the driver diagram to Tom Nolan (Associates in Process Improvement). In use for many years at Cincinnati Children's Hospital, where it is referred to as Key Driver Diagram (KDD), the driver diagram was first created to help leadership understand the theory of improvement being pursued for multiple projects by multiple teams throughout the hospital.

As use of the tool spread to other healthcare organizations, Bennett and Provost noted wide variation in how teams articulated theories of improvement using the tool. To clarify and codify how the tool works and standardize its application, they published "What's your Theory? Driver Diagram serves as a tool for building and testing theories for improvement" in Quality Progress in July 2015.

Variation

Nested Driver Diagrams: There may be times when the theory being developed is quite complex, which would require the addition of a tertiary level in the driver diagram. This adaptation is not recommended for practical reasons: the diagram is intended as a clear and simple visual depiction of theory, so if it includes too many drivers or associated changes, its utility may be compromised. In such circumstances, teams may instead make driver diagrams that nest one to another, each with only primary and secondary drivers.

In this circumstance, it will be important to develop an aim statement related to the primary driver that is being developed into its own driver diagram (see illustration below). This should be undertaken only when the achievement of the primary aim is complex enough that multiple teams are needed to address the complexity inherent in the system.

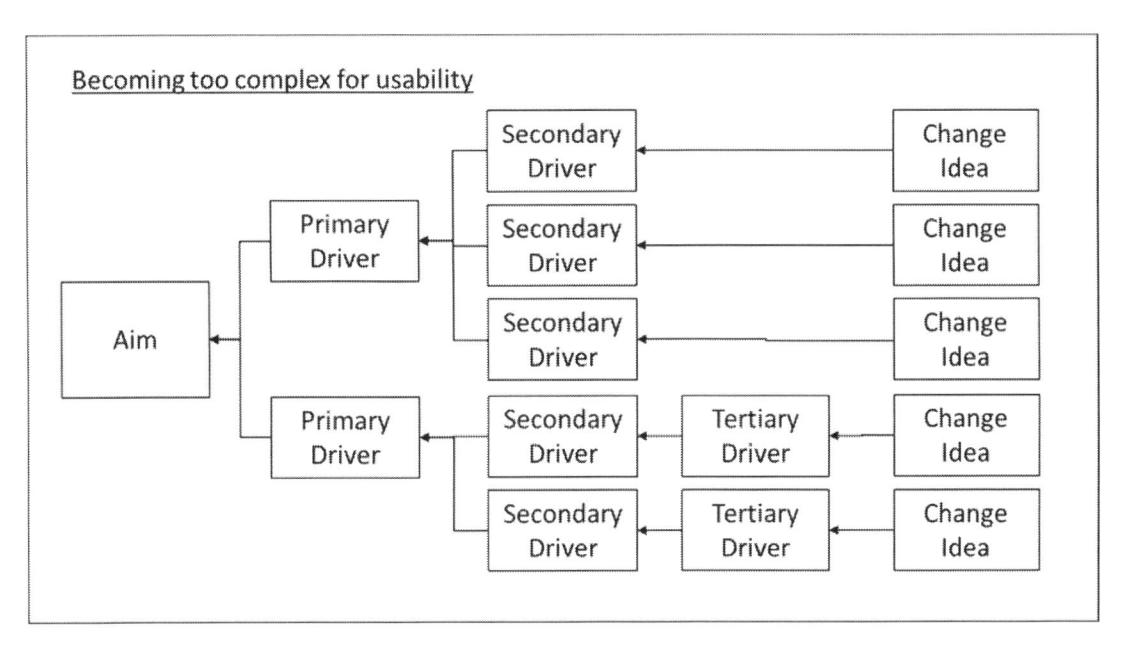

Becoming too complex for usability

[Diagram: Aim → two Primary Drivers; first Primary Driver connects to three Secondary Drivers each leading to a Change Idea; second Primary Driver connects to two Secondary Drivers, each leading to a Tertiary Driver and then a Change Idea.]

Consider breaking up the driver diagram into more manageable chunks and nesting them to see their contribution toward longer term, more complex aims the system is pursuing.

137

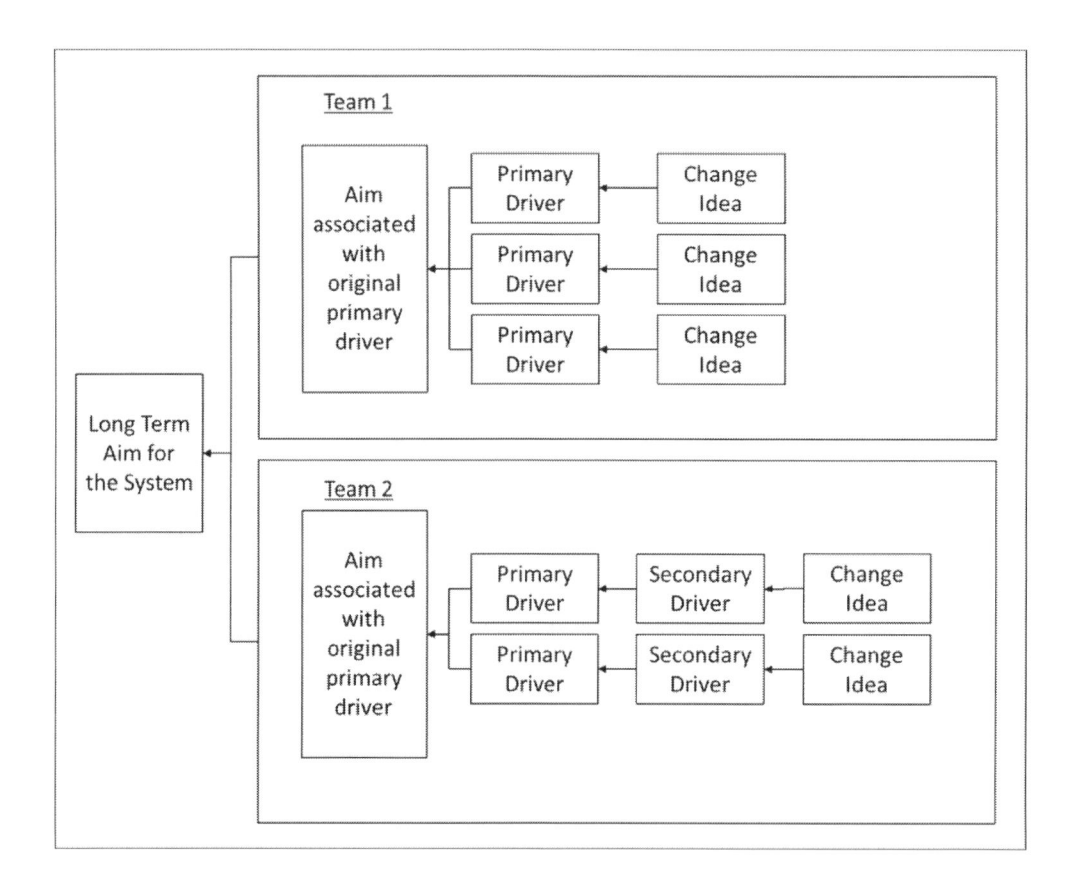

Another instance for creating nested driver diagrams is when we can identify subsystems as primary drivers that are distinct from each other (weak ties) and clear improvement aims for these are apparent.

Importantly, we should not move to a nested driver diagram approach when we have poorly specified drivers at the primary and secondary levels, and so think we need further levels to achieve actionable moments in our system of interest. Rather we should work to improve the clarity of the drivers prior to moving forward with a nested diagram.

Special Considerations

1) **Change Concepts**: Change concepts are abstractions of specific ideas, representing their underlying concepts (see figure below). For example, the specific idea of a calendar invitation used commonly with Outlook or Gmail, can be abstracted to the concept of "Use reminders." Some teams using driver diagrams find it very helpful to codify the underlying concepts[8], so that when a specific change idea they hypothesize will work in practice fails, they can fall back to the concept and creatively generate other specific actions from it that can act as alternative ideas to the one that failed. The concept might be the right one, but the specific action originally hypothesized may not be.

    Example: A clinic was struggling with the problem of patients not showing up for appointments. This was leaving some patients frustrated, as they could not secure appointments when they wanted them. It was also frustrating the staff, as they often found they had gaps during the day when they could be seeing patients in need but could not do so because of a no-show. After conducting some empathy journey maps with patients, they learned a key issue for their patient population was transportation to the clinic. Patients suggested a van could come to their location to

---

[8] Using the 72 Change Concepts presented in *The Improvement Guide* (Langley et al)

pick them up. After considering this idea and simulating it using a PDSA cycle, the clinic realized it was too difficult to coordinate multiple locations and times to provide their own van service. However, they had identified an underlying concept related to providing a van service: use affordances (concept 62 in *The Improvement Guide*, make the right thing the easy thing to do). They decided to abandon the idea of a van service and then focus on developing ideas for testing using the change concept. Working forward from "use affordances" they thought of perhaps providing bus passes to some patients. For other patients who all live in a collective location, they thought of trialing a mobile clinic to make it easy for patients to attend their appointments. These two ideas are now incorporated into their driver diagram and the original idea of providing a van transportation service has been deleted from their driver diagram.

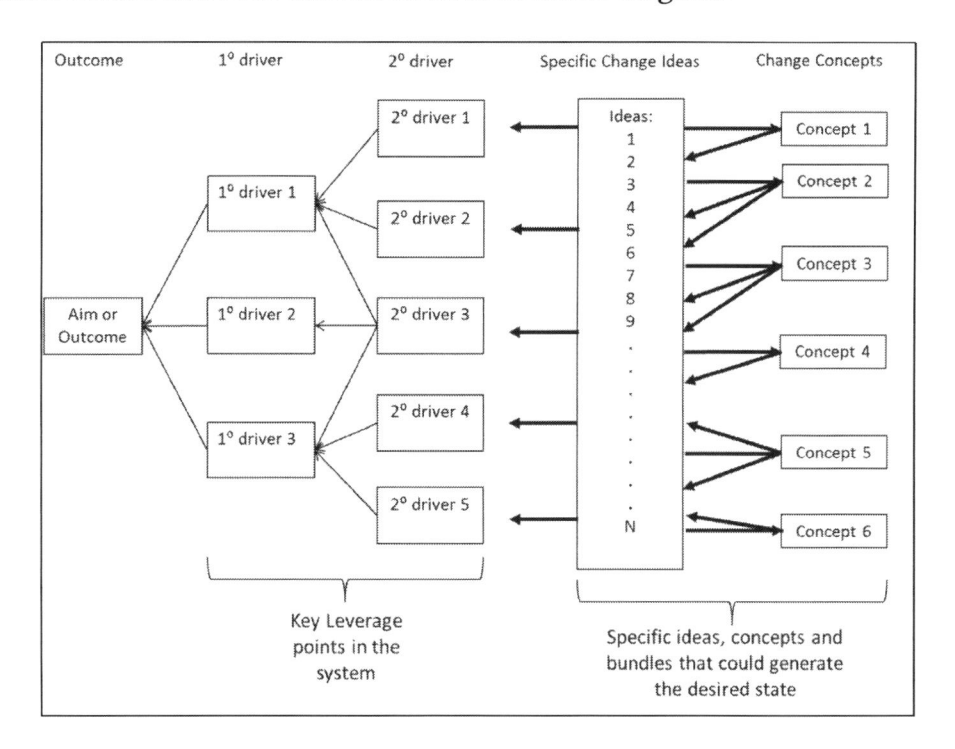

2) **Primary vs. Secondary Drivers**: Not every driver diagram needs both primary and secondary drivers. In some instances, the link between aim, driver, and change ideas can be made using just primary drivers. However, in more complex systems, secondary drivers serve the purpose of more fully exploring and illustrating the complexity that both exists and needs to be addressed to achieve the outcome of interest.

References

- Langley G, Moen R, Nolan K, Nolan T, Norman C and Provost L. *The Improvement Guide: A Practical Approach to Enhancing Organizational Performance*, Jossey-Bass, 2009
- Bennett B, Provost L. "What's Your Theory?" *Quality Progress*, July 2015, pp. 36-43.
- Associates in Process Improvement. *The Improvement Handbook*. Austin: Associates in Process Improvement. 2007

Scanning

Conceptual Links

- System of Profound Knowledge: Theory of Knowledge

Purpose

The goal of a scan is to review current academic and practical knowledge relevant to the problem you are trying to address.

How to Conduct a Scan

These are the key activities of the scan phase:
1. *Read literature.* Scholarly journals and books on the topic are the primary sources of literature. Take notes on key points while reading and share them with teammates during regular meetings to synthesize emerging ideas.
2. *Interview experts from the field.* Experts include scholars and practitioners who are knowledgeable about the topic at hand. It is critical that the scan include both researcher and practitioner perspectives. Approach interviews with an open mind. It can be helpful to articulate your ideas ahead of time about what topics will be most useful but be willing to hear things you were not expecting, and for the conversation to go in unanticipated directions. Note any surprises. (A semi-structured interview protocol is often a good bet. It helps guide your subject through important topics while remaining open to new information and directions.)
3. *Interview "out-of-field" experts.* Innovation depends on bringing ideas together in new ways. Professionals from outside fields who have grappled with issues related to those your cycle is designed to address can be a great source of inspiration. Find out what these "out-of-field" experts think about a topic, and how they address the same problem in their field. Listen for what can be adapted to your field, and what lessons can be learned from their experiences.

  - *Example of "out-of-field" experts:* For a project about improving the performance feedback process for teachers, the team interviewed attending physicians about their process for giving feedback to residents.

Coaching Notes

- **Where to begin reading?** A recent literature review can be a great place to begin the scan. The right literature review will summarize some essential understandings in the field and point you to some of the key texts and experts on the topic.
- **Encourage scheduling interviews ASAP.** The logistics of scheduling can take time, so schedule interviews early.
- **Have a "go-to" expert.** If there is an expert who is particularly helpful and interested in the work, solicit his or her help at key points during your investigation to test your ideas and emergent understandings.

Further Reading

- Park and Takahashi (2013). **90-Day Cycle Handbook.**

Plan-Do-Study-Act Cycles

Learn in practice

Other Names: Inquiry cycle, learning cycle

Conceptual Links:

- System of Profound Knowledge: Theory of Knowledge
- 6 principles: Disciplined Inquiry

Purpose

Improvement in organizations requires making changes in highly complex social and operational environments. The Plan-Do-Study-Act (PDSA) cycle structures learning from trying out changes in practice to determine (a) which changes are useful (as well as which are not) and (b) how changes need to be adapted to local environments. Used in conjunction with the Model for Improvement, PDSA cycles are a key method for structuring disciplined inquiry in an improvement science approach with the final goal of generating practical knowledge about how to improve outcomes across contexts.[1]

The PDSA is purposefully a flexible and general methodology that can be used to test different kinds of changes and structure learning at different stages of the improvement journey. PDSA cycles are typically used to:

(1) Learn about the feasibility of a change idea in practice. Discover the user-response, resources required to execute a change idea, and/or potential side effects
(2) Learn whether one or more changes will lead to the desired improvement in a specific context
(3) Learn how to adapt a change to a new context
(4) Give individuals a chance to experience a change to minimize resistance in implementation.
(5) Learn how to embed a change or set of changes in an organization so improvements are sustained.

When to use a PDSA cycle

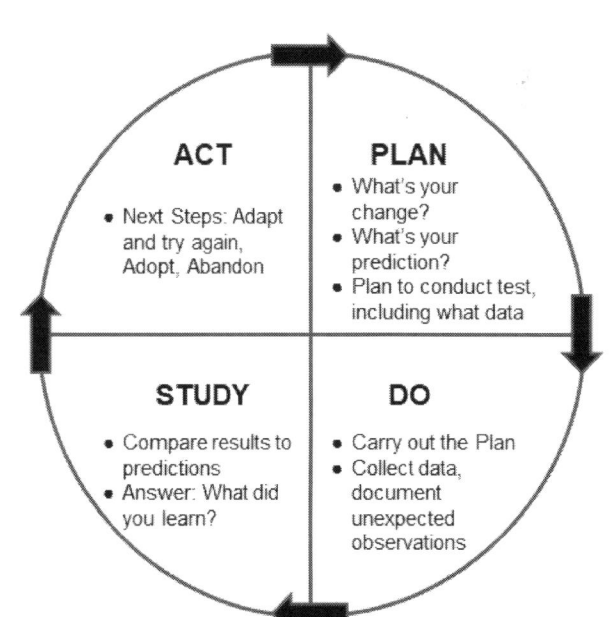

PDSA cycles are used to test change ideas in practice. Typically, teams engage in PDSA cycles after they have created a **charter** for their improvement work and identified or developed specific **change ideas** to try.

When possible, it is recommended that teams use a sequence of iterative PDSA cycles to guide learning instead of trying to pack all the learning into a single cycle. This trial-and-error approach enables teams to get started faster and take advantage of multiple opportunities to learn from trying ideas in practice. In the early stages, teams often — but not always — use small scale PDSAs to learn which change ideas seem promising and to iterate on the specific

PLAN
- What's your change?
- What's your prediction?
- Plan to conduct test, including what data

DO
- Carry out the Plan
- Collect data, document unexpected observations

STUDY
- Compare results to predictions
- Answer: What did you learn?

ACT
- Next Steps: Adapt and try again, Adopt, Abandon

---

[1] See Section 1: The Model for Improvement for a more complete explanation of the Model for Improvement, the three questions (What are we trying to accomplish? What change can we make that will result in improvement? How will we know a change is an improvement?) and the connection to PDSA cycles.

design of the change idea. In the later stages of an improvement effort, some changes are tested on a larger scale to learn how to adapt change ideas to different contexts and finally to learn how to make changes permanent.[2]

Elements of a PDSA cycle

PDSA cycles are structured as a four-stage experiment that follows the scientific method.

Change Idea

Before beginning a PDSA cycle, teams must develop or identify a specific **change idea** they want to test. A change idea is defined as a "specific intervention or work practice that represents an alteration in how work is done" (Langley et al). Change ideas can be aimed at an individual practice, a process step, a process, or the system. Improvement teams generate change ideas through (a) analyzing current practice, (b) engaging in creativity or design exercises, or (c) adapting known practices. Particularly for equity improvement projects, it is critical to engage the user perspective in co-developing the ideas for change.

In order for change ideas to be testable it is important to move past vague, conceptual descriptions of a change (i.e., "have a conversation") to a clear specification of the details of the proposed new work practice (i.e., "speak to the new teacher for 15 minutes at 9am on Monday using a structured protocol"). Creating artifacts like prototypes, process maps, and protocols are useful for working out the specific details of change ideas so they can be effectively tested in practice.

Plan

In the PLAN stage, teams clearly articulate the hypothesis underlying their change idea(s) and design an experiment to test that hypothesis. This begins by identifying the appropriate scale for testing the **change idea** and clearly articulating a **learning goal** for the cycle (see above section for different learning goals).

The heart of the PLAN section is the clear articulation of the hypothesis behind the change idea through making and recording **predictions**. In stating a prediction of what the team thinks will happen, the team is putting a stake in the ground, saying to themselves "based on what we know about how this system/process/interaction functions, we expect that in making this change we will get this result." Predictions are useful for surfacing the assumptions of different team members, preventing hindsight bias, and determining what data needs to be collected. Teams will return to these predictions in the STUDY portion of the PDSA to determine whether their initial hypotheses were confirmed or need to be revised. Most PDSA cycles have multiple predictions. PDSA templates often include a place for **learning questions** as a scaffold for generating predictions (predictions have within them an implied question). Teams' learning questions and predictions include hypotheses about: (a) how the change(s) will be actually implemented in context (i.e., time it will take, modifications that will be made etc.), (b) the results of the change (impact and/or user perception) and (c) the unintended consequences of the change.

As the team makes predictions, they must also **identify data** that can be used to evaluate these predictions. Particularly in the early stages of an improvement project, PDSA measures are different from the overall project measures, tailored specifically to the learning questions of the team and the scale in which they are working. One particularly critical form of data is learning how the change was experienced from the user perspective. In mature projects, when teams are implementing changes across the scale of interest, project measures can be useful in evaluating some of the team's predictions. Even then, teams often supplement these measures with additional input related to the learning goal of the PDSA cycle.[3]

---

[2] See Section 5: PDSA Ramps for information on testing change ideas under multiples conditions and at different scales.

[3] See Section 6: The Measurement Tree for more information on a family of measures, including PDSA level measures.

Finally, it is critical that teams take time to attend to the **logistical details** of running the test. This includes working out who will carry out the work of the cycle, creating data collection sheets to ensure the appropriate data can be easily recorded, and scheduling a time to debrief what was learned.

Do

In the DO phase, teams carry out the plan and collect data. In addition to collecting the data identified to evaluate the team's predictions, teams should capture notes from their open-ended observations of what happened in practice. In some cases, the most important learning from a PDSA cycle will come through these observations revealing unexpected consequences, unforeseen events, or unexpected ways in which the change idea interacts with other elements of the system.

Study

The STUDY stage of the PDSA cycle occurs when teams gather to review the data collected during the DO stage of the cycle. During this phase, teams are engaged in a dialogue intended to answer their learning questions, drawing on the data and observations collected to assess whether their predictions were true in practice. Differences between the team's predictions and the empirical result create an opportunity for learning. The gap between the expected outcome and the actual outcome can be equated to a gap in knowledge about how and why a system functions as it does.

In the STUDY phase, teams evaluate each of their predictions using the data they collected. They then summarize their learning, indicating how their initial hypotheses were confirmed, changed, or unaddressed by their mini experiment. Teams in the STUDY stage may debate the information they have collected, though they will ultimately need to come to consensus as to what the information means and how to use it to move forward their improvement journey.

Act

In the ACT phase of the PDSA cycle, teams determine what to do next. There are often four choices open to a team coming out of the STUDY stage: (1) **adopt** the change idea in practice as is, (2) **adapt** the change idea is some way based on the learning of the cycle, (3) **abandon** the change idea because the learning revealed the idea to not be helpful in practice. In addition, teams may (4) **decide to scale up** the change idea to new contexts to learn how the change idea works across contexts. Practically speaking, improvement teams often complete the STUDY and ACT section of a PDSA in the same team meeting, often in conjunction with the PLAN section of the next PDSA.

How to run a PDSA cycle:

① Identify the **change idea** you want to test
② PLAN the experiment
- Identify a learning goal
- Determine the scale and opportunity to test
- Identify learning questions
- Make predictions
- Create a data collection sheet
- Prepare to test the change idea

③ DO the experiment
- Carry out the plan
- Collect data and record surprises
- Understand the user experience

④ STUDY the results
- Compare results to predictions
- Reflect on the initial hypothesis

⑤ ACT on the results and determine the next step

⑥ PLAN the next PDSA

The discipline of using PDSA cycles can be difficult to master in practice. However, their use can be eased and accelerated through coaching, repeated practice with the tool and by using a template as a guide. Several templates are appended here which teams can consider using.[4] It is recommended that teams chose a template that makes sense to them. It should be noted though; some of the simpler looking forms are often best leveraged by more experienced teams. Teams new to the PDSA cycle often can benefit from the specificity contained in the longer forms. While they can seem cumbersome at first, they can often help a team to avoid the pitfalls of running through PDSA cycles without learning much about the system under study.

Example: Small-scale test

The following example comes from Lawrence Morales, who was trying to increase the number of students in his community college course who turned in their weekly quiz corrections. Lawrence used small scale testing to sort through several ideas he had. Through this process he discovered changes that seemed to have promise, larger scale PDSAs could also be used to test the impact of implementing the change ideas for an entire semester and trying out the ideas in more classrooms.

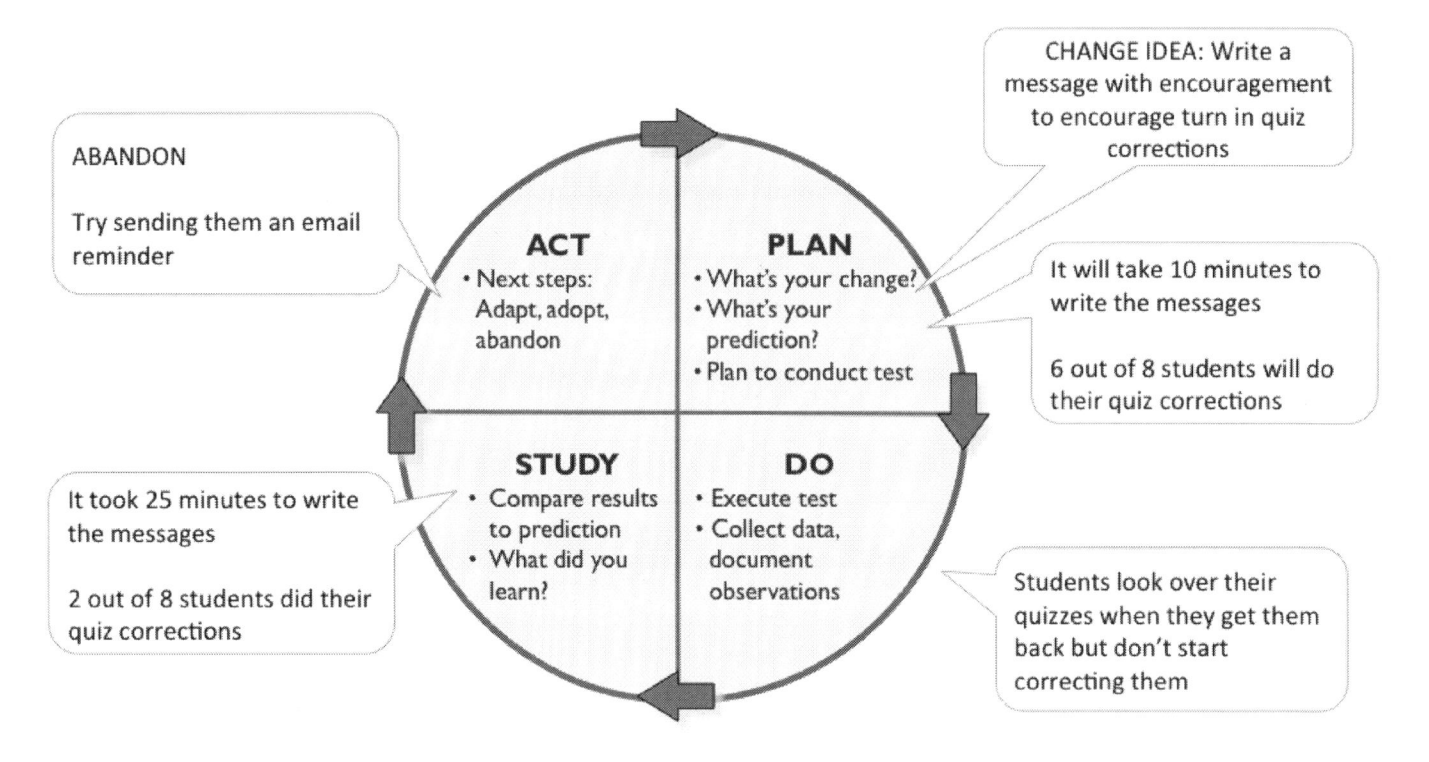

PLAN
- What's your change?
- What's your prediction?
- Plan to conduct test

CHANGE IDEA: Write a message with encouragement to encourage turn in quiz corrections

It will take 10 minutes to write the messages

6 out of 8 students will do their quiz corrections

DO
- Execute test
- Collect data, document observations

Students look over their quizzes when they get them back but don't start correcting them

STUDY
- Compare results to prediction
- What did you learn?

It took 25 minutes to write the messages

2 out of 8 students did their quiz corrections

ACT
- Next steps: Adapt, adopt, abandon

ABANDON

Try sending them an email reminder

The above illustration is a simplified version of the PDSA that Lawrence ran, and is used to show the logic of PDSA testing. In reality, teams use a PDSA form to help structure the planning and execution of their experiment. Teams and individuals are encouraged to choose a form that works for them, keeping the attention on the logic of the experiment, not the filling in of a form.

---

[4] See Appendix A: Improvement Tools – Reference Sheets, Templates and Checklists: PDSA Template 1, 2 and 3.

How to use in practice

Establishing a team rhythm and routine for engaging in PDSA cycles is critical for team learning and requires teams to make decisions regarding (a) which change ideas will be tested, (b) who will document the PDSA, and (c) who will run the experiment(s). The timeframe of a PDSA depends on the specific practice that is being tested and the stage of the improvement journey—small scale tests take less time to execute than tests designed to understand the sustainability of a practice. However, in general improvement teams benefit from establishing a daily or weekly rhythm of engaging in PDSAs.

The specific social structure of testing will purposefully change across the team's improvement journey depending on the perspectives needed, the ability of the team members to individually run PDSAs, the coach's capacity to support concurrent testing, the need for autonomy vs. commonality, and the shifting learning needs of the team. Three common social arrangements for PDSAs are described below.

- **Testing in common.** In some cases, improvement teams will agree on a common change idea for the whole team to test. Typically, teams will design the change idea, complete the PLAN section of a PDSA at a team meeting, and come back together as a team to debrief the STUDY and ACT. Often, an experienced improvement coach facilitates these team meetings and may take the main responsibility of completing the PDSA form. In between the team meetings, the actual experiment, and data collection (DO) is done by each of the team members simultaneously in their separate contexts or by a single team member that is best positioned to run the test and bring back the learning to the team.

- **Individual testing.** Improvement teams can also choose to organize testing by allowing team members to independently select and test change ideas for their specific context. In this case, huddles or team meetings are used to share the learning that arises from the individual PDSAs and provide time for people to select and prepare the next PDSA. In this structure, an improvement coach can use team meetings to build PDSA skills and/or meet individually with team members. When testing is individual, the selection of change ideas should either be disciplined by a common team theory from the onset or result in a common team theory through consolidation of learning from individual tests.[5]

- **Orchestrated testing.** In orchestrated testing, multiple PDSAs are occurring concurrently but the learning goals (and choice of change ideas) for the PDSA are determined by consensus. Orchestrated testing is usually used for more complex PDSAs and mature improvement teams. In a planned experiment for example (see Variations below), team members agree to test different combinations of change ideas to learn which combination is most advantageous. In another form of orchestrated testing, improvement teams or team members may be assigned to different parts of a common driver diagram to ensure learning in all parts of the initial theory.

---

[5] See Section 5: Theory of Practice Improvement: Driver Diagrams for more information on the formation of a common theory which can guide teams as they apply PDSA cycles.

Who is at the table?

The questions asked, hypotheses that are tested, and the conclusions that are drawn will be strongly influenced by the perspectives on the team. Paying attention to the social arrangements of the testing is critically important to maintain an equity focus for the work. The inquiry process should be done *with* the end users and not *on* end users. Particularly if there are no end-users formally on the team, it is critical to engage users both in the co-development of change ideas and in the interpretations during the STUDY section of the PDSA. This can be done by inviting end-users to improvement team meetings and/or purposefully identifying how the user perspective will be integrated during the PLAN section of the PDSA. Engaging directly and transparently with end-users to understand their perspective is often preferable to surveys in creating a co-learning environment.

> **Plus/Delta**
> In Menomonee Falls, teachers use a PLUS/DELTA process to collect data from students on various instructional strategies they are trying. As a regular part of the data collection during the STUDY section, students are asked what they liked about the change idea (PLUS) and what they would change (DELTA). This feedback is incorporated into assessments of the change ideas. The plus/delta practice can easily be integrated to illicit user feedback in a variety of contexts.

Coaching Notes

1) **Keep learning at the heart of the PDSA practice.** It is important to remember that the purpose behind the specific structure of a PDSA cycles is to promote learning. As a result, the first question that should always be asked when debriefing a PDSA cycle is "what did you learn?" Valuable learning often arises through imperfect PDSAs and feedback on improving various elements of the PDSA should only be done to enhance learning. In many organizations, people are not accustomed to being asked to learn as their primary responsibility and so being asked to engage in PDSAs will be initially interpreted through a compliance lens.

2) **Treat disciplined inquiry as a form of expertise that develops over time.** Like other forms of expertise, developing a skilled PDSA practice requires deliberate practice and feedback from a more experienced expert. As a result, improvement coaches should think about how to scaffold the development of PDSA skills over time. In the early stages, novices often benefit from activities or games (such as coin spinning or Mr. Potato Head; for more see www.dmwaustin.com) that demonstrate the utility of making predictions and iterative testing. The coach may initially take on the main responsibility for filling out the PDSA form, focusing the novice primarily on selecting a change idea to test, making predictions, and reflecting on those predictions. Most people require scaffolded practice before they feel comfortable running PDSAs independently. With experience, the logic of running a PDSA becomes less effortful, and people become more skilled at strategically applying PDSAs to maximize learning. In Appendix A, you can find a PDSA checklist which can be used by coaches and individuals to reflect on the core elements of a PDSA to develop facility with the tool over time.[6]

3) **Focus on making predictions and evaluating those predictions.** The main source of learning in a PDSA comes from making hypotheses about change explicit and then testing those hypotheses in practice. As you review and or facilitate a PLAN section it is important to be able to clearly identify the hypothesis in the form of an if/then statement (e.g., if I write growth mindset phrases then students will correct their quizzes). In the STUDY section it is important to explicitly come back to this hypothesis to determine whether what you learned confirms this hypothesis, requires a

---

[6] See Appendix A: Improvement Tools – Reference Sheets, Templates, and Checklists: Reviewing PDSAs for a checklist useful in reviewing the elements and quality of PDSA cycles.

change in hypothesis or does not help to evaluate the hypothesis. Because of confirmation bias, it is easy to miss or dismiss disconfirming evidence during the STUDY. Particularly early on in a PDSA practice it is common for teams not to "close the learning loop" in PDSAs, lacking tight logical connections between the original hypothesis and the conclusions that are drawn from the test. For most people in the social sector, the prediction-based test of change is what most distinguishes this form of inquiry from forms of inquiry they have experienced, and it requires some time to develop.

4) **Attend to the quality of conversations around PDSAs.** Running a PDSA requires unearthing the often-implicit hypotheses behind our ideas for change and reflecting on when these hypotheses need to be revised. This is harder than it sounds and is fundamentally a social process. We often do not know why we believe what we do until we try to explain it to someone else and it can be difficult to identify ways our thinking needs to change without the perspective of others. The real promise of the PDSA as a tool is the creation of a dialogue in which implicit theories become explicit and the subject of a productive, collective debate. This both requires and reinforces a capacity for team dialogue in which team members can be candid about their beliefs and can respectfully challenge each other's assumptions.[7]

5) **Balance a focus on inquiry and content knowledge.** Improvement coaches can bring either a content lens or an improvement lens to coaching teams' PDSA cycles.[8] The content lens prompts coaches to comment on the viability of the change idea itself and, whether it's based on best practice. The inquiry lens in contrast focuses on how well the PDSA cycle is structured to produce learning. Ultimately, actual improvements will require both quality change ideas and high-quality inquiry. However, in each coaching session the coach will need to figure out where to focus to best support the learning of the team and individual team members.

6) **Documentation.** It is not uncommon for team members to struggle with the documentation of PDSA cycles, purporting to doing "PDSAs in their head" without writing them down. This tendency to rely on memory should be avoided for a number of reasons: (a) without clearly recorded predictions, we are all subject to **confirmation bias**, missing important changes in our thinking, and (b) the utility of the learning from a PDSA cycle may not be obvious until several cycles later. The ability to look back across a series of PDSA cycles is critical for teams to be able to consolidate their learning; summarizing what seems to be working, what is not, and how their thinking has changed. To build documentation practices, coaches may (a) take on some of the documentation responsibilities, (b) help teams and team members identify a form and a routine that can fit into the day-to-day of doing work, and (c) build strong norms around documentation.

History

The PDSA cycle is the application of the scientific method in practice. Thus, in the deepest sense, the PDSA has roots back to the birth of modern science and the emphasis on generating knowledge through testing hypotheses through real world observation. Walter A. Shewhart began the move to apply the scientific method to think about organizational practice in 1939. Over the next several of decades, W. Edwards Deming worked with leaders in manufacturing organizations in Japan to shift from thinking of the work of production as linear (design, produce, inspect) to organizing work in continuous improvement

---

[7] See Section 2: Conversational Capacity for more information on how to build effective team dialogue.

[8] See Section 1: System of Profound Knowledge for more information on an "improvement lens" and Section 1: Kinds of Knowledge Needed to Improve for more information on a "content lens."

cycles (design, produce, test, redesign). The early iterations of these cycles were called the Shewhart cycle and the Deming Wheel. In the 1960s, the Japanese executives adopted and evolved the cycles into a management tool, defining the key steps as PLAN-DO-CHECK-ACT. This formulation of PDCA cycles is still in use in some improvement methodologies today.

The first articulation of a Plan-Do-**Study**-Act cycle came from Deming himself, towards the end of his career in 1993. Deming believed the language of STUDY over CHECK better communicated to Western audiences the central purpose of structuring continual learning, a significant shift from the prevalent manage-by-inspection practices of the day. Associates of Process Improvement, students of Deming, further elaborated the PDSA cycle, adding a focus on "building knowledge" by emphasizing predictions in the PLAN section and reflections on those predictions in the STUDY section. They also combined the PDSA cycle with three basic questions to discipline the overall improvement effort forming what they call the Model for Improvement. API's articulation of the Model for Improvement forms the basis of many of the methodologies we present in this Resource Guide. (For a complete history of the PDSA cycle, see *Circling Back,* Moen et al. 2010).

While improvement science is new to many organizations in the social sector, investing in practitioner inquiry is not. The education sector has a history of investing in teacher inquiry as a productive structure for professional learning and collaboration. As a result, many school organizations have already established inquiry practices, sometimes in the form of lesson study, action research, and professional learning communities. Organizations with established inquiry practices would be advised to make thoughtful decisions about whether and how to introduce PDSA cycles, leveraging the inquiry skills and structures that already exist. Some of the notable differences in a PDSA form of inquiry are the (a) use of predictions, (b) use of rapid cycle tests, and (c) use of an aim, measures, and a shared theory of improvement to determine the focus of the inquiry (as opposed to being purely based on individual's interests). Many of these differences arise from the explicit intention in improvement science to generate knowledge: to discover and test clinical practices that can be spread to other parts of the organization. Thus, one of the advantages of the PDSA cycle is its general application. It can be used by different role groups across the organization and can structure small-scale as well as large-scale tests.

Variations

1) **Investigation cycles.** In the above text, we describe PDSAs as a method for testing a change in practice. In *The Improvement Guide,* the authors also describe the use of a PDSA for structuring investigations into the current state of the system where the primary purpose is understanding. For example, teams can use PDSAs to learn how a hiring process breaks down or the primary reasons for student absences. The structure of an investigation PDSA remains the same, with the omission of identifying a change idea to test. Often investigation PDSAs utilize other improvement tools such as process failure analysis or Pareto charts to answer the question at hand.

2) **Planned experiments.** A planned experiment is a more complicated form of a PDSA that enables a group to generate more robust evidence about the effect of a change or set of changes. In a planned experiment, the participants come to agreement on the outcome of interest, the changes that will be tested, and key contextual variables that may influence their impact. Then, an improvement expert designs the experiment, creating well-scripted specifications of what, where, and when different change ideas will be tried. Through the application of experimental design principles, planned experiments can generate robust learning about the impact of changes. Planned experiments are both technically and socially difficult to apply but can yield significant learning, particularly for learning about practices that occur infrequently (i.e., on an annual basis).

Special considerations

As you think about structuring tests to maximize learning, consider this typology of testing designs:
- Observational
- Before and after
- Time series
- Factorial

References

- Langley G, Moen R, Nolan K, Nolan T, Norman C and Provost L. The Improvement Guide: A Practical Approach to Enhancing Organizational Performance, Jossey-Bass, 2009.
- Moen R, Norman C. Circling Back: Clearing up myths about the Deming cycle and seeing how it keeps evolving, Quality Progress. 2010; 43(11):22
- Bryk, A.S., Gomez, L.M., Grunow, A. & LeMahieu, P. (2015). Learning to improve: How America's schools can get better at getting better. Cambridge, MA: Harvard Education Press.
- Ogrinc G, Shojania K. Building Knowledge, Asking Questions, BMJ Qual Saf 2014;23:265–267. doi:10.1136/bmjqs-2013-002703
- Taylor M, McNicholas C, Nicolay C, Darzi A, Bell D, Reed J. Systematic review of the application of the plan-do-study-act method to improve quality in healthcare. BMJ Qual Saf 2014;23:290–8.

PDSA Ramps

(Sustain and spread)

Conceptual Links

- System of Profound Knowledge: Theory of Knowledge, Psychology of Change
- Carnegie 6 Principles: Disciplined Inquiry

Purpose

PDSA ramps are used conceptually by improvement teams to scaffold their learning journey around specific change ideas. During the learning in practice phase of the improvement journey, improvement teams are tasked with running PDSA cycles for the purpose of learning about the utility, efficacy, efficiency, acceptability, reliability, and any number of other criteria that deal with whether a change idea will yield successful improvement for the system. Because the change ideas proposed have never been implemented in the team's local setting before, the use of PDSA cycles, teams on improvement journeys are encouraged to start at a safe-to-fail scale (see chapter on PDSA cycles). PDSA ramps then, represent the progression of learning from safe to fail toward confirmed knowledge that a specific idea will succeed in delivering improvement upon implementation in practice.

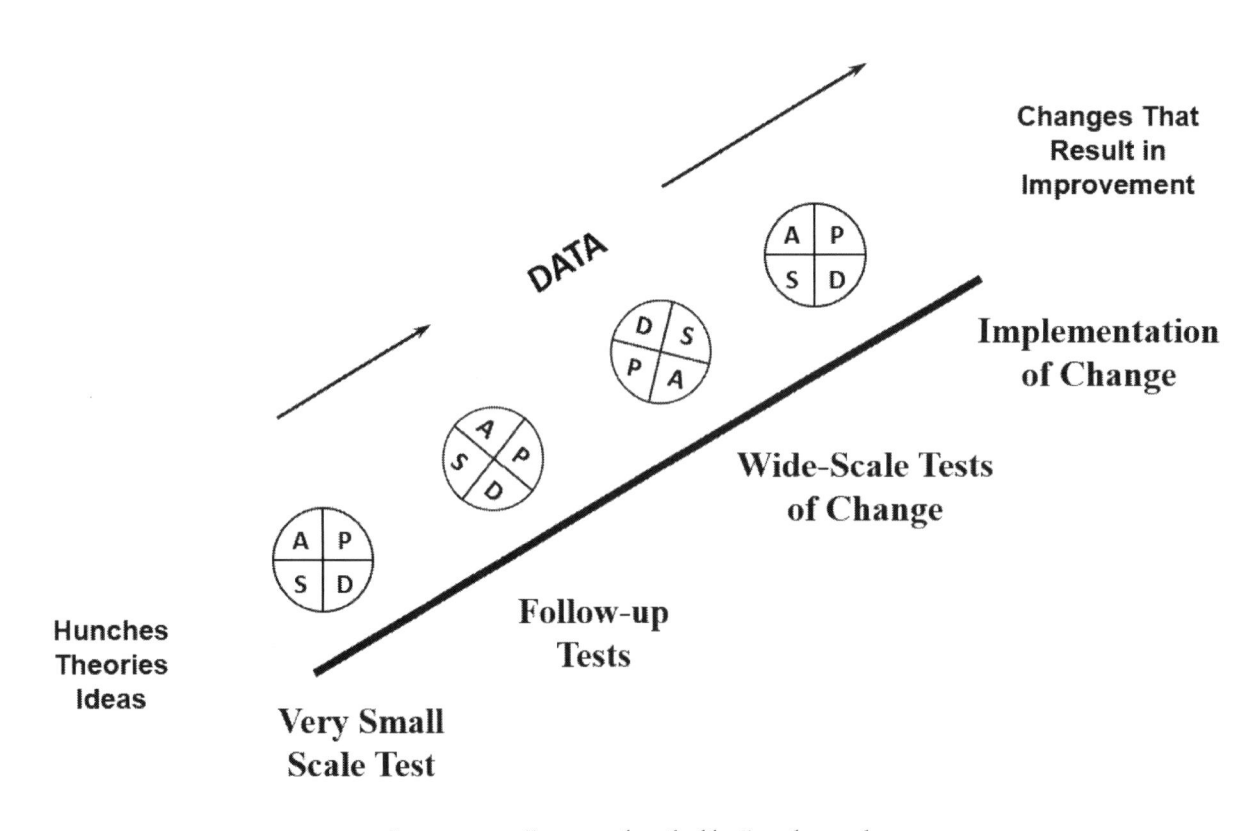

Improvement Ramp as described by Langley et al.

When to use PDSA ramps

Improvement teams will find the use of PDSA ramps useful when planning out their learning journey around specific change ideas. In deciding at what scale to try a change idea in practice (i.e., run a PDSA cycle), improvement teams often find it helpful to consider three aspects of their system: confidence in the evidence a change will lead to an improvement for the system, the cost to the system if the change idea fails to deliver improvement, and the readiness of the staff tasked with change (e.g., workflow, behavior, tool, etc.). The table below adapted from Langley et al. is very useful for deciding on the scale of a PDSA cycle with each of the boxes representing potential points an improvement team may find themselves on their PDSA ramp, considering what is next to keep progressing toward meaningful change.

		Staff Readiness to Make Change		
Current Situation		Resistant	Indifferent	Ready
Low Confidence that change idea will lead to Improvement	Cost of failure large	Very Small Scale Test	Very Small Scale Test	Very Small Scale Test
	Cost of failure small	Very Small Scale Test	Very Small Scale Test	Small Scale Test
High Confidence that change idea will lead to Improvement	Cost of failure large	Very Small Scale Test	Small Scale Test	Large Scale Test
	Cost of failure small	Small Scale Test	Large Scale Test	Implement

Deciding on the Scale of the test of change, adapted from Langley et al.

How to use PDSA ramps

In the chapter on PDSA cycles a key decision is described for the Act step of each cycle. Improvement teams will need to decide what their next step is as they close out the learning from a single learning cycle and the choices presented include: adoption, adaptation, abandonment and/or a decision to scale up a change idea. When teams choose the Adopt or Adapt path, they still have work to do to learn whether the change idea under consideration is ready to be implemented in their system. In the early stages of trying ideas in practice PDSA cycles are usually being run on a small, safe to fail scale. That means the next action is to plan another cycle to either include the adaptation decided upon or test the idea against a wider variety of conditions the system may encounter in practice. This means running another cycle at the same safe to fail scale under different conditions or running it on a slightly larger scale to further increase a team's degree of belief that the change idea really is valuable in practice.

This style of try and try again is often described as an "improvement ramp" and is depicted graphically in the figure above from Langley et al. These authors describe how degree of belief is built on this journey using another figure for illustration, figure 7.1 of their book, *The Improvement Guide* (see figure below). They note that some change ideas can move from development through to implementation in a relatively straightforward way, while others may start strong but when tried under a wide variety of conditions encounter failure and need to be abandoned.

FIGURE 7.1. DEGREE OF BELIEF WHEN MAKING CHANGES TO IMPROVE.

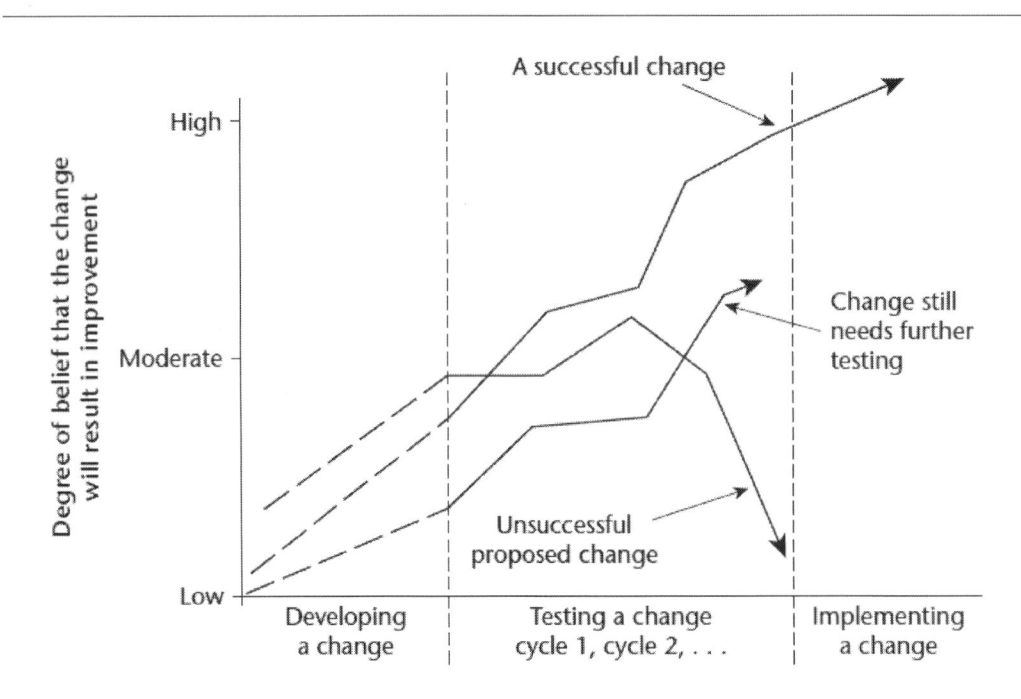

Langley et al on developing degree of belief to the point where a permanent change to a system can be made

While the use of improvement ramps can seem straightforward, in practice teams often struggle; moving ahead only to encounter an unexpected barrier in their system which causes them to backtrack, try an adaptation on a smaller scale, and plot a different path forward for improving a process or the systems outcomes. Ogrinc and Shojania illustrated this concept in a more realistic graphic in their paper on the use of PDSA cycles (see figure below).

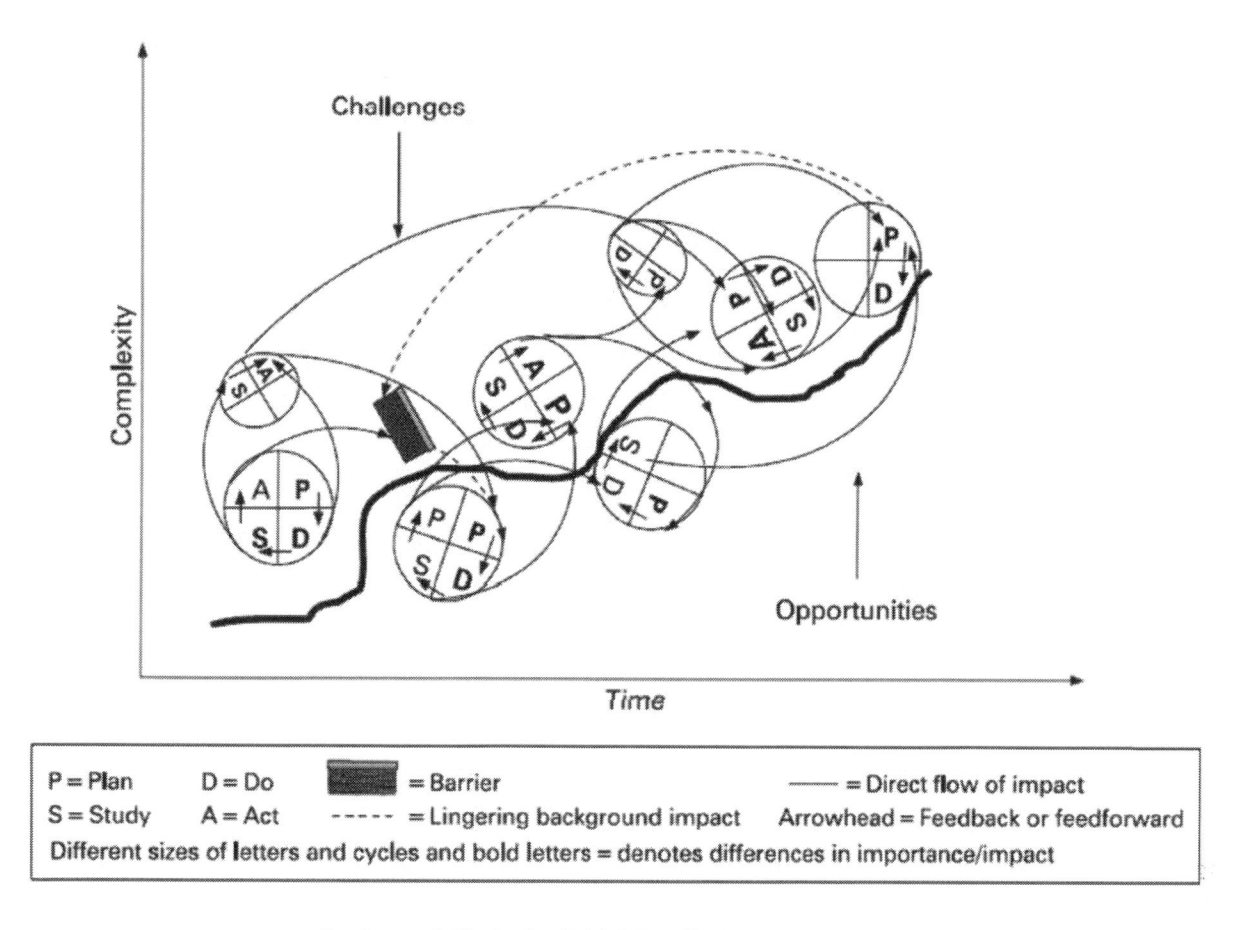

Ogrinc and Shojania, British Medical Journal 2013

Illustrating Improvement Ramps

Many teams find it helpful to visualize their progression up a ramp graphically. It serves to help the team understand their growing degree of belief that the change idea they propose may lead to the improvement they desire. An example of a template for visualizing ramps is shown below and is available in Appendix A.[1]

---

[1] See Appendix A: Improvement Tools – Reference Sheets, Templates and Checklists: Planning PDSA ramps for a PDSA ramp template.

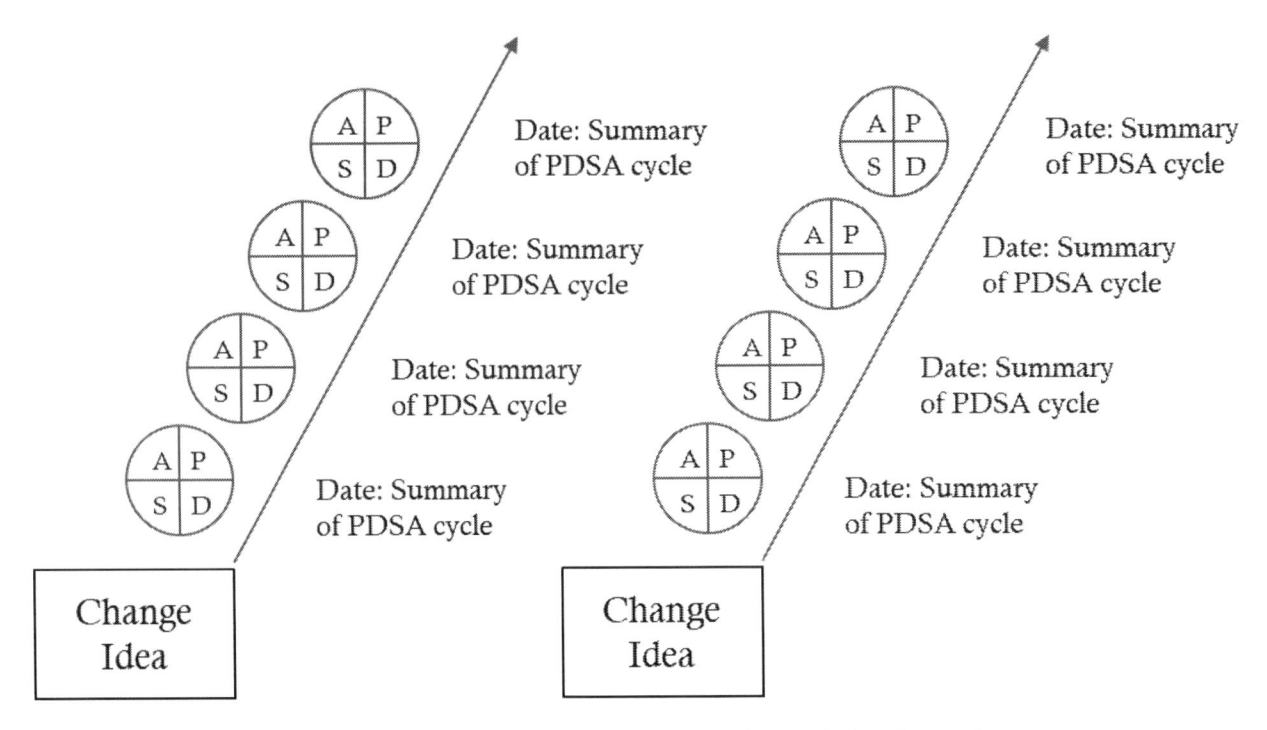

For each cycle summary it is useful to capture: any adaptations tried, who and where the cycle was completed and any lingering questions generated as a result of the cycle.

References

- Langley G, Moen R, Nolan K, Nolan T, Norman C and Provost L. The Improvement Guide: A Practical Approach to Enhancing Organizational Performance, Jossey-Bass, 2009.
- Moen R, Norman C. Circling Back: Clearing up myths about the Deming cycle and seeing how it keeps evolving, Quality Progress. 2010; 43(11):22
- Bryk, A.S., Gomez, L.M., Grunow, A. & LeMahieu, P. (2015). Learning to improve: How America's schools can get better at getting better. Cambridge, MA: Harvard Education Press.
- Ogrinc G, Shojania K. Building Knowledge, Asking Questions, BMJ Qual Saf 2014;23:265–267. doi:10.1136/bmjqs-2013-002703
- Taylor M, McNicholas C, Nicolay C, Darzi A, Bell D, Reed J. Systematic review of the application of the plan-do-study-act method to improve quality in healthcare. BMJ Qual Saf 2014;23:290–8.

Change Packages

(Sustain and spread)

Other Names/Related names: Play book, White paper

Conceptual Links:

System of Profound Knowledge: Theory of Knowledge
6 Principles: See the system that produces the current outcomes

Purpose

"Solutions that deliver results at scale must be simple and sound" is an axiom of large-scale change presented by Bob Sutton and Huggy Rao in their 2016 book, *Scaling Excellence*. Change packages serve to satisfy this axiom, concisely articulating a set of ideas, proven in practice to deliver the results desired by those looking to make an impact at scale.

When to use a change package

Change packages are a starting place. Individuals and organizations looking to produce large scale outcomes find change packages useful during both the planning and execution phases of various scaling strategies (campaigns, networks, collaboratives, use of community organizing, etc.). While a method for introducing change is always critical, so are ideas for what to change and how to change. The change package codifies for improvement teams what works in practice. Change packages distill the best-known evidence as well as the context in which that evidence was generated, providing an accelerated starting point for improvement teams facing the same problem of practice as others who have gone on a similar journey before.

When to create a change package

Improvement teams will find it useful to create a change package toward the end of a learning journey, when there is a desire to codify what has worked in practice to deliver a particular outcome. The change package document captures all their learning, the empirical evidence they have collected about what changes have worked, and how those changes have worked to achieve better outcomes.

Elements of a change package

Introduction
This is a brief statement used to generate interest. The Introduction communicates to the reader/user what the change package will detail and why it might be valuable to them.

Background Information
Described in as much detail as possible, the authoring team recalls the starting conditions of the improvement journey. Starting conditions will vary from place to place, and any context provided can inform subsequent users of the document how much local adaptation might be needed in using the change ideas presented. Because of this emphasis on starting conditions and the context in which improvements occurred this is one of the most important sections of a change package.

Problem Statement
Describe here why the improvement journey was undertaken. Here is the first-place readers will get a sense of what the important measures will be, as the problem is almost always qualified or quantified in some way. In describing the context where the problem is occurring it may also highlight some aspects of the system informing the theory of improvement pursued and ultimately presented later in the document.

Aim (Outcome of Interest)
The aim statement adds to the context of the improvement journey described by providing the direction of interest for readers. It extends the understanding of measurement further by describing the gap in current performance and the specific outcome desired or pursued. It includes the timeline the pursuing team set for themselves to accomplish improvement.[1]

Measurement system
For anyone who is interested in replicating the successes presented in a change package, or achieving success at scale, having knowledge of what was measured is critical. By providing clear descriptions and operational definitions of the outcome, process, process step, and balance measures a team used to understand their system, the authors are able to help subsequent teams answer the question, "How will/did we know a change was an improvement?" If the team was part of a network or led a network, measures of network health can be included here. Measures about how the improvement journey was managed might also be described here (i.e., frequency of meetings, number of learning cycles, frequency of interactions with leadership, etc.).

Theory of Improvement (Driver Diagram)
Remember, the change package represents the culmination of the improvement journey for a team or system. This section is reserved for the consolidated knowledge gained during that journey. It is frequently represented by the most complete, most up-to-date driver diagram representing which change ideas have worked in practice. The purpose of including this element is to highlight for subsequent teams what and where the leverage points are in the system which the change ideas included in the change package helped to move to better performance.[2]

Ideas to change the system (Detailed)
While the driver diagram is a good visual depiction of the overall theory of improvement, it may lack the detail needed by scaling teams to replicate the changes ultimately implemented in practice. Teams want to know the "how." This section provides a place for the innovating team to describe each change idea in detail: what was done, what was learned, and what evidence was generated. In some cases, they will also describe where across the system the idea proved fruitful (i.e., when ideas that worked did not work universally, but did work under specific conditions across a variety of locations).

Ideas to change the system (Evidence for ideas)
While the previous section provides information on what actions were taken to achieve new/improved outcomes, this section exists to display the empirical evidence generated by change ideas which led to a strong degree of belief that their implementation created the observed outcomes.

Teams can include a **visual display of the family of measures here**, using a dashboard, or small multiples with annotation to highlight changes in performance over time or across locations linked to the implementation of different ideas. This section focuses on the process and process step portions of the

---

[1] See Section 5: Aim Statements for more depth on this topic.

[2] See Section 5: Theory of Practice Improvement: Driver Diagram for more on the development and visualization of driver diagrams.

measurement system.[3] In some instances, teams find it helpful to classify ideas into four categories for potential readers:

1. Very strong evidence — generated by the authoring team (a shift or trend on a run or control chart), presence in research literature or in practice elsewhere (with reference).
2. Strong evidence — locally generated evidence by the authoring team only. Often this level of evidence is very good, but ideas may require adaptation elsewhere as context shifts in a scaling effort.
3. Weak evidence — present in the literature but either untried locally by the authoring team, or without demonstrable quantitative evidence of improvement in the local setting.
4. Very weak evidence — belief and anecdote, often a good starting place, based in clinical knowledge/experience but with a word of caution that is yet to be proven at all in practice (either locally or in the literature).

Outcomes Achieved
A change package's warrant or relevance in being propagated at scale depends entirely on whether change in practice has delivered change in outcome. This section is an opportunity for the change package to highlight the evidence of improvement from the innovation phase of the work. This entails the visual display of data in the form of annotated charts (run charts, Shewhart control charts, or other charts/analysis) which clearly communicate improved performance at the outcome level. The results presented in this section move beyond changes at the process level or process step level which may have been included in the evidence for change ideas presented above.

User story (Narrative experience)
The experience of change leading to improvement is not purely quantitative. Generating the will to engage in an improvement journey is a critical factor in determining whether ideas are adopted at scale. This section represents an opportunity to tell the story of change, often from multiple perspectives (leadership, frontline worker, end user, community member, support service personnel, etc.). The improvement team can relay what it was like to take on the work. End users can describe their experience of the process/system before and after the change. It is critical to communicate why the effort expended was necessary to achieve the outcome. Seeing this through the eyes of multiple stakeholders can serve as a demonstration of worth of the journey to change and in the ideas presented.

Team
"Attribution is infinitely divisible."
—Don Berwick, Institute for Healthcare Improvement

It costs nothing to give credit to the team and the users who did the work of innovation. By highlighting their names, and roles in the improvement journey, a change package provides insight on what human resources are necessary to achieve improved outcomes. These are also people with valuable tacit knowledge that subsequent teams may wish to contact for more insights into the change process.

References
References are always powerful sources for more information. Including as many relevant ones as possible for readers can only be of help. These provide value in directing scaling teams to original research, or practice-based knowledge connected back to the ideas for change presented in the document.

Appendices

---

[3] See Section 6: The Measurement Tree to learn more about Outcome, Process, Process Step and Balance measures.

Appendices represent a chance to include specific tools or artifacts produced by a team for others to adapt/adopt. They also provide a chance to offer any extra guidance the innovation team thinks might be valuable to future users of these lessons learned.

How to create a change package

When developing a change package, it is helpful to identify a small group of individuals who can pull together the change package prior to its review by a larger audience.
Its creation is usually accomplished in one of two ways:

A. As a consolidation and synthesis activity at the end of an improvement journey where a single team or network operating on some smaller scale is looking to describe what they have learned about what works in practice to achieve better outcomes or to solve a common problem of practice.

   It is recommended the improvement team who has been tasked with leading the work make a first attempt at developing the change package.

   1) **Gather artifacts** from the life of the project-based improvement journey, including the chartering document[4], aim statement, the family of measures (including operational definitions and actual data collected/visualized), the most current theory of practice improvement (driver diagram), process maps, checklists developed, systems maps, protocols of various sorts, etc.

   2) **Conduct interviews** with various stakeholders who have either participated in the direct work of learning to improve or whose outcomes, environment, system, or processes have been the focus of the improvement work. These interviews will be particularly important when developing the narrative of how the learning occurred and to informing what contextual knowledge is important for understanding the place/system where the improvements were generated. Stakeholders might include frontline workforce, improvement team members, middle managers, senior leaders, individuals from the population or sub-population whose outcomes were targeted for improvement (teachers, students, patients, families, community members, community leaders, etc.).

   3) **Write a first draft** the change package. Note: there are many forms a change package can take visually. The final document might be organized in the order of the elements presented here, or it might combine elements where appropriate, or take on a different visual format. There is flexibility, what is important is ensuring enough context, detail, and evidence is presented so others might reasonably use this work as a starting place for their improvement journey.

   4) **Test your draft change package** with both those who were responsible for developing the change ideas and enacting them in practice and others in the system who experienced the changes in practice. Solicit their feedback on the accuracy, timeline, experience, and narrative of what is described. Every story, like every system, needs multiple perspectives so that its audience gets a full and richly detailed description of what creating the improvement was really like. Revising the narrative to reflect these many perspectives is a helpful part of codifying what worked in practice.

   5) **Revise your change package** based on the feedback received.

---

[4] See Section 3: Focus Collective Efforts for more information on chartering.

B. At the start of a scaling journey when there is a need for a starting theory of practice improvement and the desire is to utilize, to the best of the team's ability, an evidence-based approach to the pursuit of better outcomes.

It is recommended an improvement team start with evidence-based ideas for improvement. Where possible, that means starting an improvement journey building upon the work of others, using their change package as a starting point. This assumes two things: A change package has been created and published and the improvement team starting on the journey is aware of the change package. Often neither of these are true, because many problems we face are novel to our circumstances and because change packages are by their nature most often confined to the grey literature that exists within fields or individual organizations.

When teams are starting a scaling journey and access to a previously published change package is lacking but some knowledge of best practice around the topic of interest is known, the development of change package can and should be undertaken to assist the teams who will be participating in the learning-improvement network. This will give them a starting place for the development and adaption of a theory of practice improvement.

1) Review the literature using a formal scanning process[5] with an eye on two things: gathering knowledge that will help leaders and teams to better understand the problem and the system that is producing it and gathering research-based ideas about how to intervene in the system effectively to produce a different outcome. Gather evidence-based change ideas.

2) Work with one or two subject matter experts to review your findings and to guide your investigations of the literature. Note: steps and one and two may be iterative, one being informed by two and repeated to ensure relevant literature on a topic is reviewed.

3) If possible, convene an expert meeting. The purpose of this meeting is to review your findings from the literature review process and add to your growing body of knowledge of context, ideas for practice improvement, and leverage points that may exist within the system(s) being targeted. The expert meeting is also a place where an improvement team can achieve consensus or gather input on what the Aim should or could be, what measures might be practical, and which will not be. It can also be a place where the improvement can identify potential candidates to advise the work longer term, those who want to stay, close, participate, follow progress, and review the work on a periodic basis.

   This meeting can include 10-15 subject matter experts. Some of these may be academics, others are practitioners and still others might be leaders of the organizations targeting improvement. It is important at expert meetings that we include some frontline workers and some people who experience the system (i.e., students, family members, patients, community members, etc.) as these people are a source of expertise on this system that is very often ignored. Their ideas for change are often aligned to the systemic barriers they see/experience daily and can be very important as starting places for change that is engaging to those being asked to carry out changes to the system.

4) Following an expert meeting, an improvement team will want to draft a change package as a starting place for their scaling work. Steps 3-5 from the change package creation process above

---

[5] See Section 5: Scanning for information on how to conduct a literature scanning process.

can be used at this point: Draft the change package -> Pressure test the change package -> Revise the change package.

How to use a change package in practice

In *Scaling Excellence*, Sutton and Rao argue solutions spread to a larger scale in one of two ways:

1) The ideas evolve to the local context, taking on a life of their own in delivering impact under a variety of different conditions. This often occurs when the outcome is complex, and the systems involved in creating the outcome vary deeply.

2) Sometimes though, the application of the ideas from a change package needs to be more rigid when moving to scale. The specific application of ideas maintains integrity, being implemented more exactly despite the local context they are entering. Such occurrences are not uncommon, especially when basic science is at work (i.e., surgical safety, the treatment of cholera, or the prevention of certain infections). Local adaptation is discouraged because the evidence clearly suggests adaptation would weaken impact toward accomplishing the desired outcome.

Governments, systems, networks, collaboratives, and individual teams when adopting the use of a change package must decide prior to implementation which of these mechanisms makes the most sense for what they are trying to accomplish. The focus from the start is always on successful integration of change ideas into a local context. Pursuing local adaptation of evidenced ideas requires partnership with a method for ongoing learning (i.e., the Model for Improvement). It also requires a structure, a learning system, that can manage the evolution of the theory as new learning is achieved. A more rigid approach might require additional methods (i.e., changes in policy or law, or a focus on reliability of implementation).

Examples

Below is a list of topics for which change packages have been developed. It is not exhaustive but is meant to illustrate the wide range of conditions and issues for which development of a fungible, malleable package of ideas has been developed in the pursuit of better outcomes.

- Chronic absenteeism in schools — High Tech High
- Enrollment and Attendance in Early Childhood Education Centers — Ko Awatea and the New Zealand Ministry of Health
- To Prevent Central Line Associated Bacteremia, A How to Guide — Ko Awatea and the Health Quality and Safety Commission of New Zealand

Coaching Notes

We recommend teams using a change package as a starting place for scaling a known set of solutions (change ideas) partner their scaling effort with capability building around the use of Plan-Do-Study-Act cycles. In every case we have encountered, frontline teams tasked with implementing changes or with trying changes are on a learning journey. They are either learning how to change their local system to accommodate sustainable implementation or they are learning what ideas will work in practice in their environment. In both cases a disciplined approach to the learning process is needed for effective scaling of changes that work.

History

In 1994, Dr. Paul Batalden and Dr. Donald Berwick were frustrated that training and professional development in the use of quality improvement methods and tools was not leading to rapid improvement in patient safety efforts in the USA. In response, they conceived an organized a method for the rapid dissemination on known best practices, the Breakthrough Series Collaborative (BTS). Integral to this network approach to change was the codification of a set of ideas that were empirically shown to be the current best practice in the field of medicine. They described this group of ideas as a change package. These change packages, when partnered with a purposeful network focused on their spread and practical methods for adaptation and adoption (the Model for Improvement), became the core components of the BTS method popularized by the Institute for Healthcare Improvement.

Since the mid-1990s there has been an explosion in the use of BTS Collaboratives focused on improving many different aspects of health and healthcare, and now a diverse number of fields including oral health, social welfare, and education. Even as the BTS method has evolved, the change package has remained an integral component. In most cases, the change package is still the codification of known best practices and serves as the starting point for the dissemination of those practices through the collaborative structure. In some instances, where best practices are still unknown, the Collaborative structure serves as an opportunity to develop a change package that can then be provided to a field in search of how to achieve better outcomes.

Variations

White Paper
A white paper is as a positional paper describing the issuing organization's stance regarding a topic, issue, or solution set. As such, a white paper and a change package might overlap significantly in content. However, white papers can move well beyond what a change package would include. They can serve to help a reader understand an issue from a specific viewpoint or express an ideological position. They may also serve a promotional purpose, promoting a product or service. Originally, white papers were used to express a government position on a law or policy and were open to comment and revision by the public through a democratic process. This way, they are like change packages, both being open to revision as new information and learning is accomplished.

Play Book
A play book is a term that comes from sports. It references the various set plays a team may choose from when facing the opposition. In the business, government, and non-profit sectors, play books are often referenced as documents which define a workflow. Their purpose in use is to "ensure a consistent response to a commonly encountered situation." They may be thought of as standard operating procedures or defined workflows for an organization.

In many ways a play book resides somewhere between a change package and a single or set of change ideas. They are often specific to circumstance; they often do not include partnership with a learning methodology for local adaptation and so do not quite rise to the level of a change package in detail or information. However, they are very pragmatic, describing specific circumstances (i.e., problems of practice) and specific solutions (i.e., change ideas in the form of steps to take, checklists to follow or workflows to adhere to). Play books may be an excellent source of ideas for inclusion in a change package and can be strong references for the development of a change package when a scan of the literature is first undertaken. For individual organizations, a play book might be developed to reflect the specific adaptions developed and adhered to as part of the improvement journey.

References

The Breakthrough Series: IHI's Collaborative Model for Achieving Breakthrough Improvement. IHI Innovation Series white paper. Boston: Institute for Healthcare Improvement; 2003. (Available on www.IHI.org)

Sutton and Rao. Scaling Up Excellence: Getting to more without settling for less. New York: Crown Business. 2014

Bryk A., Gomez L., Grunow A., LeMahieu P. Learning to Improve: How America's Schools Can Get Better at Getting Better. Cambridge, MA. Harvard Education Press, 2015)

McCannon J., Massoud R., Alyesh A. Many Ways to Many. SSIR. October 2016

Bennett and Provost. What's your Theory? Driver diagram serves as tool for building and testing theories for improvement. Quality Progress. July 2015.

Bennett. Branching Out: Use Measurement Trees to determine whether your improvement efforts are paying off. Quality Progress. September 2018

Gerald J. Langley, Ronald D. Moen, Kevin M. Nolan, Thomas W. Nolan, Clifford L. Norman and Lloyd P. Provost, The Improvement Guide: A Practical Approach to Enhancing Organizational Performance, Jossey-Bass, 2009.

6. Improvement Methods and Tools II: Data

Tools for use with data to answer learning questions
Why do individuals, groups or improvement teams gather data from the systems in which they live and work? To learn, to explain why things are the way they are, where things are occurring, what things are influencing outcomes, how things work, why things work or in some cases do not work. These sorts of learning questions are at the heart of all data collection. The various tools presented in this section are designed to help improvement teams answer their learning questions. Each, in its own way, takes raw data and transforms that data into information — into a story describing some aspect of the performance of the system under study. Each tool gives a different glimpse into the variation that exists in the performance of the system, and each visualizes information in a slightly different way.

The selection of which tool to use and when, will depend largely on the learning question posed by an improvement team. Examples might be:

- What set of measures might we use to understand when the changes we are making result in the improvements we desire? A measurement tree to discover, select and display a family of measures
- How could we learn from variation in performance occurring across multiple sites in our network? A small multiples view of performance by site
- Which reasons for failure in performance should we focus on for improvement? A Pareto chart will reveal the frequency and contribution of categorical data
- Where in my system is performance good, where is it bad? And what is the overall picture of performance? An ordered bar chart might be a good choice for seeing the system at a glance.

The visualization of data through the tools presented here can make information about the system more accessible to stakeholders. A single picture of performance can represent collective understanding and serve a focal point for discussion and decision-making. Without such tools, improvement teams may struggle to find consensus, falling back on individual perceptions of why things are the way they are or what the impact of a change on the system really was. Collecting and analyzing data in a visual way to answer a shared learning question will help improvement teams accomplish the learning they need to move their systems forward.

In this section teams will find entries on:

1. The Measurement Tree
2. Visualizing Quantitative Information (including Data Visualization Checklist)
3. Data Visualization Using Small Multiples
4. Order Bar Charts *(look at variation in performance across different subgroups)*
5. Pareto Diagrams *(analyze frequency with which classification data occurs in a process or system)*
6. Run charts *(determine the predictability or stability of a system over time or whether change is happening in the system)*
7. Histograms *(see the distribution of data on a continuous measure)*
8. Box and Whisker Plots *(compare distributions across different subgroups)*

Suggestions for future reading
- *The Health Care Data Guide* by Provost and Murray
- *The Visual Display of Quantitative Information* by Tufte

The Measurement Tree

Other Names: Family of Measures
Conceptual Links
System of Profound Knowledge: Understanding Variation, Appreciation of the System, Theory of Knowledge
Six Principles: Focus on variation in performance, We cannot improve at scale what we cannot measure

Purpose

Measurement for Improvement is about learning, not judgement. The primary purpose in creating a measurement tree is to create a logical structure, consistent with an improvement team's theory of improvement, which links various measures at different levels of the system together. This can provide a set, or family, of measures which can then assist an improvement team in learning about the complex nature of their system as well as help them to detect if and when improvement is occurring in their system at different levels.

When to use a measurement tree

The development of a measurement tree is recommended any time an organization is chartering improvement work within their system. Individual teams will find the act of creating a measurement tree a challenging task. Identifying measures often challenges the team's thinking about what is responsible for the outcomes they see in practice. It may cause them to recognize important gaps in the data normally collected for the management of the system. It may also help a team to appreciate the full complexity of the scope of the undertaking they have launched. This may result in changes to theory, updates in data collection, or a shift in the aim or charter.

All improvement projects should have a family of measures. Many teams will find it helpful to articulate such a family through the visual logic of the measurement tree.

Elements of a measurement tree

There are five measures which comprise a measurement tree: Outcome, Process, Process Step, Balance and PDSA level measures. Each are described in some detail below.

Measurement Tree

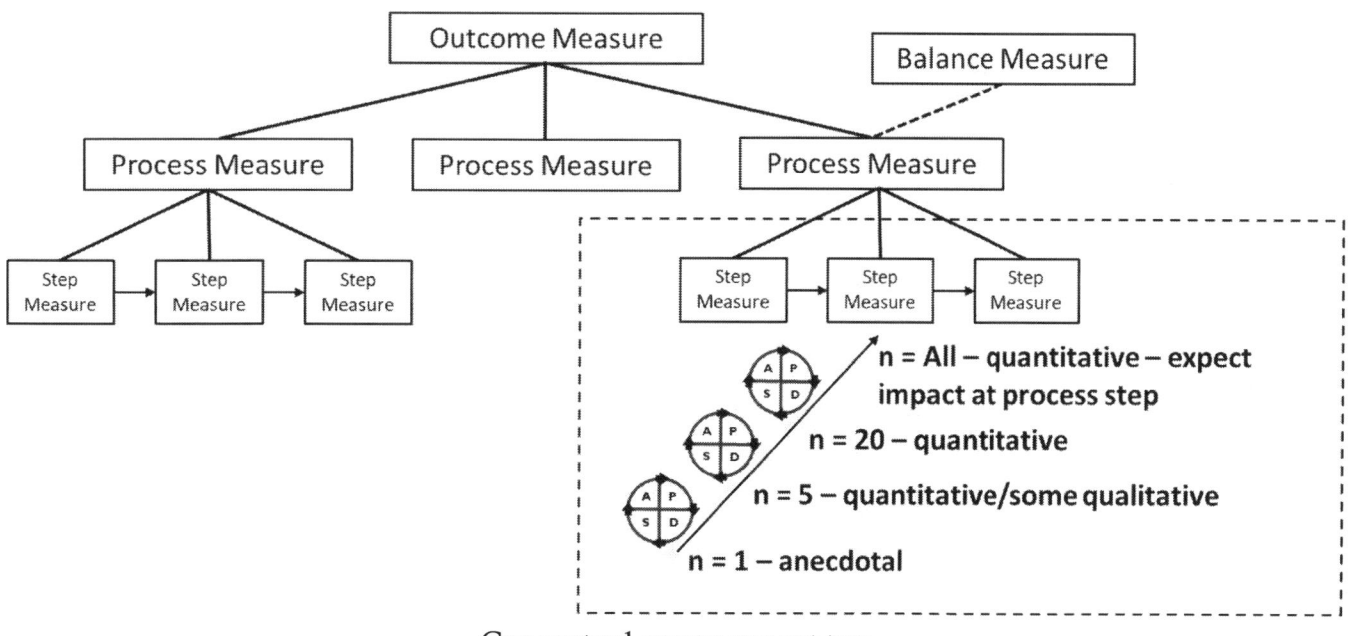

Conceptual measurement tree

1) Outcome Measure(s)

The outcome measurement represents the primary focus of the measurement tree. It measures the purpose of the improvement work that has been undertaken and serves as the improvement team's motivating force. This is the measurement a team uses to understand whether it has achieved its outcome. It measures the quality of the service, product, or result that is meaningful to the team's community, student body, client base, or workforce. Outcome measures are directly related to the aim statement and are included specifically in the aim statement set forth by a team.

Teams developing a measurement tree for an improvement project will need specificity in the aim statement around the measure of interest in order to effectively proceed on the improvement journey. Possible places for identifying outcome measures are through data currently used for accountability that address the purpose for the system. Sometimes this data can be repurposed for improvement. Other places to look for data are in broader definitions of quality outcomes for the system and may include data previously overlooked such as data which reflects the perspective of various stakeholders in the system: user perspective data, employee perspective data, business perspective data, or operational perspective data.

2) Process Measure(s)

Process measures represent the data a team can collect to understand the performance of a system's day-to-day work. While outcome measurements often lag in time, process measurements are more readily available because they are directly connected to concrete work processes happening regularly. The availability of data for process performance can vary from daily to weekly to monthly.

Process measurements in the measurement tree are deeply influenced by subject matter expertise and the theory crafted by the team aiming to achieve a new outcome. Teams readily identify them through connections to their theory of improvement. In cases where a driver diagram is used to depict theory, these measurements often are connected to the primary and secondary drivers (structures, processes or operating norms) identified as key leverage points in the system.

3) Process Step Measure(s)

   Processes are often complicated. They are made of many steps—small actions taken in sequence—that lead, little by little, to the production or completion of a service or product. These steps are where process step measures are identified for inclusion on a measurement tree.

   Process steps happen every day in systems. They represent the work of individuals and teams: from teaching a class to administering a budget to intervening on behalf of a client or family. These steps are the places in the system where applying a change idea can result in improved performance. While process measures are connected to the day-to-day work of a system, process step measures are linked to the individual steps that make up the day-to-day processes. An example of a Process broken down into steps that could be measured could be a process for Screening (patients, students, individuals, etc.). Steps that could be measured include registration, administration of a screening test/tool, and provision of counseling post administration of the screening tool/test on next steps, and referral.

   Generating process step measures is accomplished for most teams by first mapping the processes identified through their theory. A process map allows teams to see the various steps in the processes they theorize need change. Teams can then dialogue about which steps to measure, what data to collect on a step and what tools exist or need to be created to help them collect the data.

4) Balance Measure(s)

   Another component of the measurement tree is a balance measurement. Balance measurements are used by improvement teams to see whether the improvement work is having an unintended consequence in the system. These measures may be outcome measures other than the outcome targeted for improvement or process measures the team is not currently focused on but theorize may be influenced by the improvement work through "knock on" effects through the system.

   Balance measures may also importantly help teams by showing that improvements observed in an outcome are not related to a secular trend in the performance of the system. Secular trends being general overall movements in outcome unrelated to the work of the improvement team. They can be caused by unknown factors from the environment within which the system exists or may be related to long term effects of policy applications within the system of interest.

   Teams can identify balance measures by looking to outcomes or processes important to the system but not under study by the improvement team. Returning to the stakeholder perspectives (user perspective data, employee perspective data, business perspective data, or operational perspective data) of parts of the system not currently targeted is a good first step.

5) PDSA Level Measure(s)

   Measurements developed for PDSA cycles, or rapid learning cycles, comprise the final component of the measurement tree. These measurements are used to answer specific learning questions put forth by teams when testing a change idea in practice. They often are used as part of a single cycle of learning at a small level—with one client, in one huddle, in one school for a month, or across several locations for a week. They exist to build an improvement team's knowledge and confidence about what might work to improve the system.

   PDSA measurements are harder to describe conceptually because often they exist for just a single cycle. They provide the information necessary to propel a team forward in its learning and help it know when and whether to move trialing of change ideas to a more diverse set of conditions or a larger scale.

These measurements are crafted uniquely for the cycle at hand and can be operationally defined qualitatively or quantitatively, depending on the learning needs of the cycle. Though teams may collect data on these measurements for only a short time or in an ad-hoc way (not incorporate them into the permanent data collection microsystem of the organization), they are incredibly important on the improvement journey.

PDSA measures are often articulated conceptually on the measurement tree. This is because PDSA measures will be selected at the time of the development of the PDSA. See the discussion on these measures above for a reminder on why these can be difficult to define conceptually. Generally, teams can readily identify these in the moment with coaching during the Planning phase of a PDSA cycle.

Data collection tools, such as check sheets, recording forms, surveys, and empathy maps, frequently serve the function of data collection for single PDSA cycles. Often, the data from these cycles build sequentially, helping the team tasked with improvement to learn what ideas improve the process or system in practice.

Some of these data collection tools and the data they collect are used for several cycles while the degree of belief a team has in the utility of an idea increases. Some become important enough to be elevated to process step measurements (and thus formalized into the system). Some are used just long enough to confirm the utility of an idea before being discarded.
A ramp of sequential cycles is included in the conceptual view of the measurement tree to highlight their contribution. Early on, learning may be anecdotal or purely qualitative, but as cycles progress and a change idea is trialed on a larger segment of the process, quantitative impact is noted.

How to make a measurement tree

The creation of a measurement tree is fundamentally a social process, influenced by subject matter expertise, the initial theory of improvement, the experience of individuals working within the system, and any constraints the system may extend on data collection, time, or resource allocation. Teams may find they need several iterations on the tree before they feel comfortable with a depiction, they believe adequately describes the logic of measurement within their project or system.

While a measurement tree may fully define the family of measures for a team, in practice it is not uncommon for the measurement tree to depict a full enumeration of all the measures that are possible (consider the example on four-year college going below). Collecting and analyzing data on all the logical links and for every possible measure is not practically feasible nor is it advisable, as improvement is a resource intensive activity with measurement for improvement being just one piece of the improvement journey.

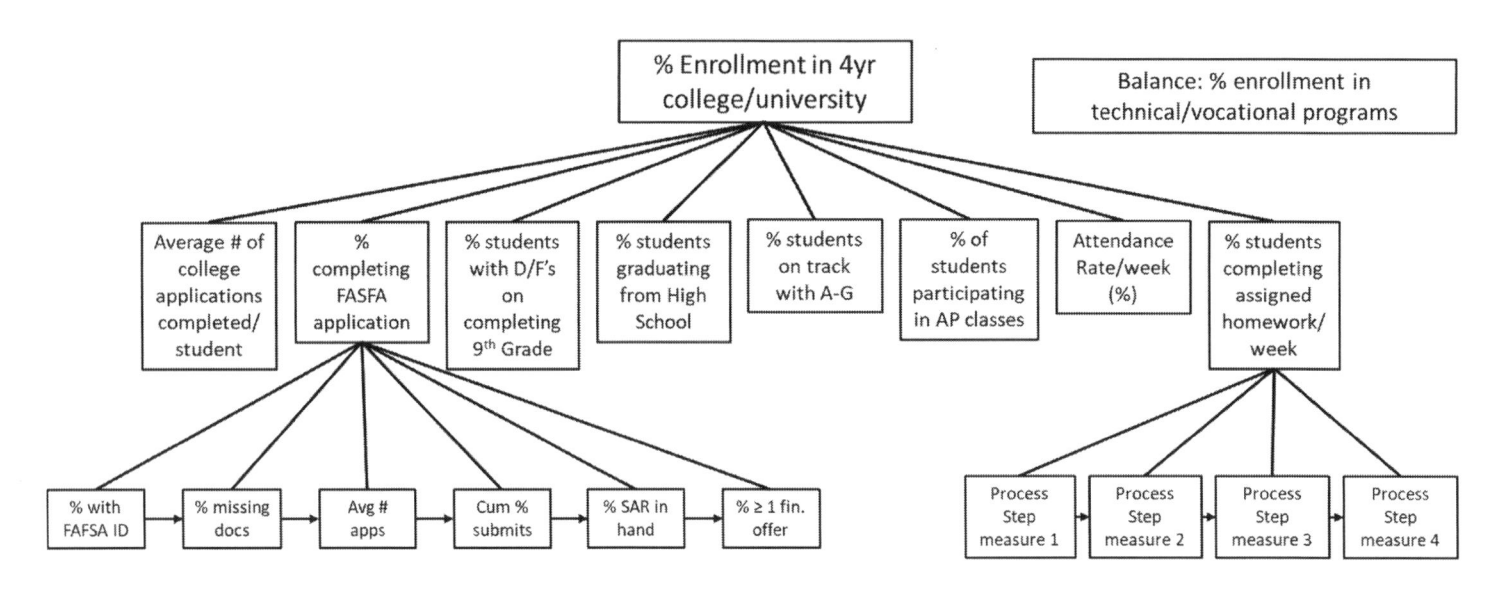

```
                         ┌─────────────────┐                                    ┌──────────────────────┐
                         │ % Enrollment in │                                    │ Balance: % enrollment│
                         │      4yr        │                                    │ in technical/        │
                         │college/university│                                   │ vocational programs  │
                         └─────────────────┘                                    └──────────────────────┘
```

(Measurement tree diagram with the following nodes branching from "% Enrollment in 4yr college/university":)

- Average # of college applications completed/student
- % completing FASFA application
- % students with D/F's on completing 9th Grade
- % students graduating from High School
- % students on track with A-G
- % of students participating in AP classes
- Attendance Rate/week (%)
- % students completing assigned homework/week

(Sub-nodes under "% completing FASFA application":)
% with FAFSA ID → % missing docs → Avg # apps → Cum % submits → % SAR in hand → % ≥ 1 fin. offer

(Sub-nodes under "% students completing assigned homework/week":)
Process Step measure 1 → Process Step measure 2 → Process Step measure 3 → Process Step measure 4

Improvement Teams will often want to select a subset of measures from their measurement tree which reflect two important considerations:

Consideration 1: The measures selected are directly tied to the work of the team. In many instances improvement teams are launched as part of a broader network of improvement focused on a common outcome, identified as important for many locations, or teams. In this case a team might choose measures based on their local conditions, where they have identified failure points in the system, or where their leadership has directed the improvement to begin.

Consideration 2: The measures selected serve as indicators for what may be happening throughout the system under improvement. In some sense, the measures chosen are acting as "the canary in the coal mine," allowing teams a strong degree of belief that when those measures change for the better, improvement really is happening in the system. Identifying these measures can be done objectively. For example, research literature might suggest measures which are very important to track during an improvement journey. They may be selected based on relationships (i.e., a scatter plot developed for two measures shows a strong relationship between the two such that tracking one, yields a high degree of belief about what is happening with the performance of another). Selection might also be more subjective, based on the experiences/beliefs of team members or of subject matter experts consulted for the work.

How to use a measurement tree in practice

Once a measurement tree has been created and scoped, teams will need to translate the selected measures into data displayed in graphical form. Once a team has decided on a family of measures, it is critical those measures now be put to work for improvement. "Because improvements are made over time, in order to facilitate learning and communication, measures should be displayed on run charts or Shewhart charts." (Provost and Murray). As stated, Provost and Murray recommend that selected measures be charted in graphical format. This allows for careful annotation, linking when measures are made in time. It also allows teams to visually assess their progress, understanding at a glance when a change is an improvement and when it is not.

Coaching notes

1) If a team has a poorly articulated aim statement that does not include specific measurement, then the development of an outcome measure is likely to be difficult for them. A coach should push an improvement team to further refine their aim statement until a specific outcome measure can be identified.
2) A common error teams make when crafting a measurement tree, or any family of measurements, is to write out their measurements as an aspirational statement, such as, "Increase student enrollment by X%." This language is closer to that of an aim or goal statement and is not the measurement of interest. It does, however, contain the measurement of interest: student enrollment as a percentage.

It is important for improvement teams to understand that measurements in and of themselves have no directionality and are simply a reflection (adding a voice) of the system's performance. Measurements depict the data that allow a team to understand, empirically, whether a process step, process or outcome is changing, either toward or away from the team's aspirations. Change in performance often is ascertained through a run chart or Shewhart control chart. Coaches should take a hand in guiding teams away from aspirational language and toward specific identification of the measures identified in those statements.

History

In 1966 Avedis Donabedian, a noted physician and professor at the University of Michigan School of Public Health, set forth a model for evaluating medical care. His now famous model suggested that outcomes for systems are driven by the processes (the work of the system) that comprise the system and the structure (the contextual environment of the system) in which those processes operate. This first link between process, structure, and outcome inspired a great deal of thinking about how to apply measurement in the context of improvement.

Langley et al (1996), as well as Provost and Murray (2009) would go on to further this thinking by defining three important types of measures necessary for improvement journeys: Outcome, Process, and Balance measures. Taken together the authors suggest improvement journeys benefit from developing a family of measures that can assist improvement teams in answering the question "How will you know that a change is an improvement?" while recognizing the complex dynamic nature of systems.

In 2018, Bennett published work on the use of the Measurement tree, furthering the work of Langley et al. In his article he specifically adds two previously undiscussed measures, process step and PDSA measures, to the trio of outcome, process, and balance measures. He also connects these measures visually based on the logic suggested by Donabedian, Langley et al, as well as Provost and Murray.

Variations

In some industries, such as education, healthcare, and social welfare, it's useful to distinguish between lagging outcome measurements, which can only be collected infrequently, and leading outcome measurements, which are highly correlated to the lagging measurements and available for collection more frequently.

An example from the education field helps illustrate this phenomenon:

- Lagging outcome measurement: The percentage of new teachers retained each year. This measurement can be collected only once per year (at the end of a school year when retention rates are calculated and reported at the school and district levels).
- Leading outcome measurement: The percentage of new teachers reporting a feeling of burnout. This measurement could be ascertained by surveying new teachers in a school or across a district every six weeks during the academic year.

This measurement might be chosen because measurements of burnout are highly correlated with retention. A leading outcome measurement indicating high levels of burnout early in the year can serve as motivation for leaders to intervene before teachers choose to exit the workforce.

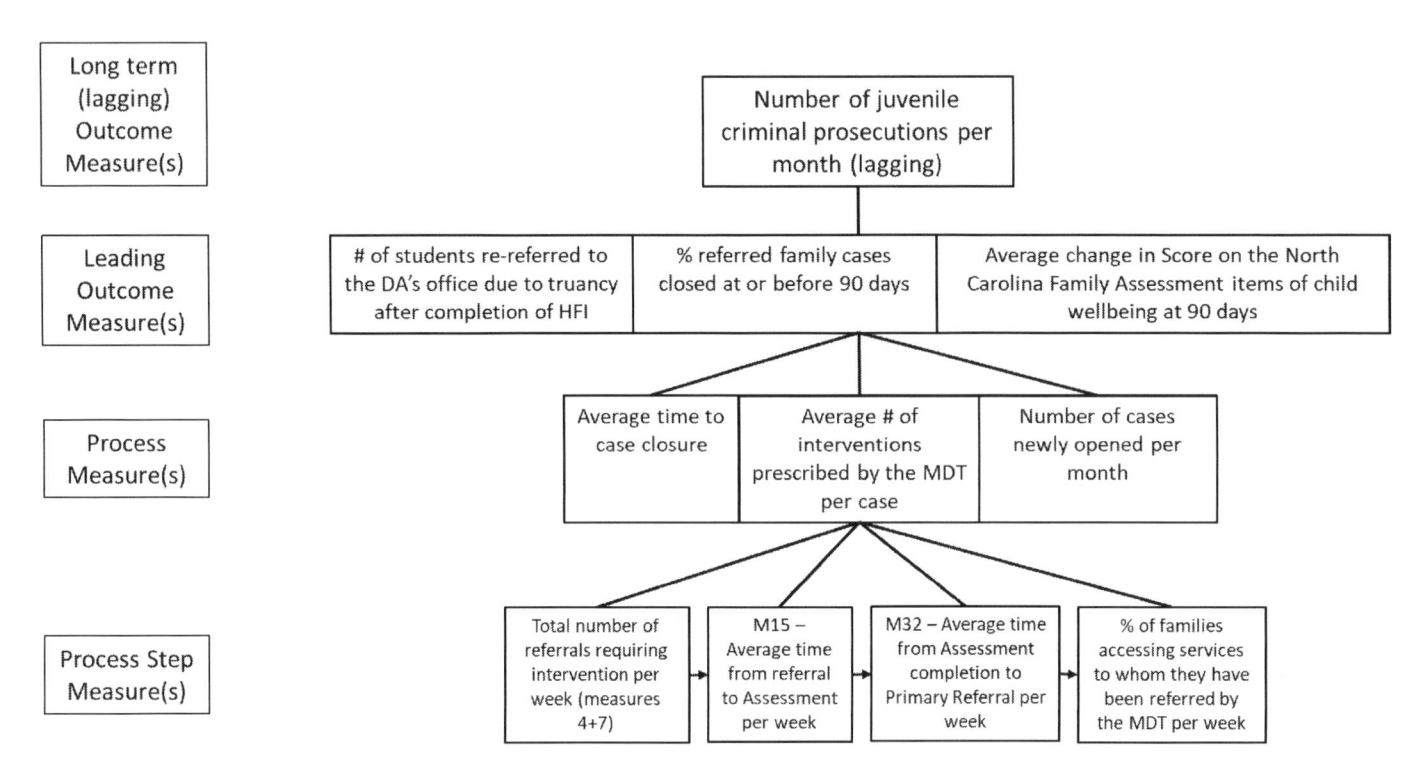

Another example of Leading and Lagging Measures

References
Bennett, Brandon. Branching Out: Use measurement trees to determine whether your improvement efforts are paying off. Quality Progress. September 2018
Donabedian, Avedis. Evaluating the quality of medical care. Milbank Memorial Fund Quarterly. 1966, 44: 166-206
Langley G, Moen R, Nolan K, Nolan T, Norman C and Provost L. The Improvement Guide: A Practical Approach to Enhancing Organizational Performance, Jossey-Bass, 2009
Provost L, Murray S. The Health Care Data Guide: Learning Data for Improvement. San Francisco: Jossey-Bass, Publication, 2011

Visualizing Quantitative Information

Conceptual Links
- System of Profound Knowledge: Understanding Variation
- 6 Principles: Focus on variation in performance; We cannot improve at scale what we cannot measure

Purpose

There are many reasons why an individual or team might choose to visualize their quantitative information. Five are listed below:
1) To create a visual display of information which maximizes learning
2) To describe what a data set says
3) To explore or investigate a topic or answer a question
4) To summarize data in some digestible way
5) To motivate and entertain consumers of information

Improvement teams often benefit from the visualization of the data they collect, finding greater meaning and encouraging greater participation in the work of improvement by creating a transparent window into the performance of the system they are trying to improve.

When to use visualizations with quantitative information

Improvement teams will benefit from using graphic displays of data, to assist the creation of useful information under these conditions:
1) When the improvement team have data that is not already in a visual form. This occurs frequently when the data improvement teams are accessing are collected through observation or sampling and reflect measurements, counts, classifications or rankings of some kind.
2) When the improvement team have tabular data. It is nearly always the case that in the presence of a large data set, it is easier to learn from a picture of the data, a graphic display, rather than trying to decipher meaning from a large table of numbers.

An illustration of the second instance comes to us in the form of Anscombe's Quartet, a famous illustration of the power of data visualization first published by Francis Anscombe in 1973. Anscombe notes that several commonly used summary statistics describe each data set in the same way, making them appear to be "equal" in tabular form, however, visualization of the data displays a very different story, showing very different performance for each of the four data sets.

	1		2		3		4	
	X	Y	X	Y	X	Y	X	Y
	10.0	8.04	10.0	9.14	10.0	7.46	8.0	6.58
	8.0	6.95	8.0	8.14	8.0	6.77	8.0	5.76
	13.0	7.58	13.0	8.74	13.0	12.74	8.0	7.71
	9.0	8.81	9.0	8.77	9.0	7.11	8.0	8.84
	11.0	8.33	11.0	9.26	11.0	7.81	8.0	8.47
	14.0	9.96	14.0	8.10	14.0	8.84	8.0	7.04
	6.0	7.24	6.0	6.13	6.0	6.08	8.0	5.25
	4.0	4.26	4.0	3.10	4.0	5.39	19.0	12.50
	12.0	10.84	12.0	9.13	12.0	8.15	8.0	5.56
	7.0	4.82	7.0	7.26	7.0	6.42	8.0	7.91
	5.0	5.68	5.0	4.74	5.0	5.73	8.0	6.89
N	11	11	11	11	11	11	11	11
Mean	9.0	7.5	9.0	7.5	9.0	7.5	9.0	7.5
Standard Deviation	3.3	2.0	3.3	2.0	3.3	2.0	3.3	2.0
Correlation coefficient	0.82		0.82		0.82		0.82	
Regression: Intercept/Slope	3.00	0.50	3.00	0.50	3.00	0.50	3.00	0.50
Standard Error of Slope		0.118		0.118		0.118		0.118
t=	4.24		4.24		4.24		4.24	
Sum of Squares X-x̄	110.0		110.0		110.0		110.0	
Regression Sum of Squares	27.50		27.50		27.50		27.50	
Residual Sum of Squares Y		13.75		13.75		13.75		13.75
$r^2=$	0.67		0.67		0.67		0.67	

Anscombe's Quartet, 1973

Elements of good quantitative visualizations

There are three basic structures for showing data: the sentence, the table, and the graphic. In this section we are primarily concerned with addressing characteristics of good visualizations associated with the graphical display of quantitative information.[1]

In chapter 1 of *The Visual Display of Quantitative Information*, Edward Tufte summarizes what graphical displays should do:

- Show the data
- Induce the viewer to think about the substance rather than about methodology, graphic design, the technology or graphic production, or something else
- Avoid distorting what the data have to say
- Present many numbers in a small space
- Make large data sets coherent
- Encourage the eye to compare different pieces of data
- Reveal the data at several levels of detail, from a broad overview to the fine structure
- Serve a reasonably clear purpose: description, exploration, tabulation, or decoration
- Be closely integrated with the statistical and verbal descriptions of a data set

Tufte further elaborates, noting graphics should tell the truth about the data they depict, should be clear, detailed, and well labeled. They should have integrity, never misleading the reader, with any numbers shown being directly proportional to the numeric quantities represented.

Graphical display of quantitative information should seek to communicate the most amount of information using the least ink possible.

Common types of quantitative visualization

There are five main types of graphics associated with the visual display of quantitative information. Each can be used for the purposes described above:

1) Graphics displaying data over time, also known as time-series data displays. These include simple line graphs, run charts, and Shewhart control charts
2) Graphics displaying the distribution of data, showing the shape, and spread of the data. These include histograms, Pareto charts, stem-and-leaf plots, among others.
3) Graphics displaying the relationship existing between data or characteristics of a system. These include scatter plots, response plots, and line plots.
4) Graphics displaying the location of data in a system. These include data maps, maps of physical layout (i.e., spaghetti diagrams), as well as various infographics.
5) Graphics displaying data for multiple measures. These include radar charts (also known as spider diagrams), as well as other formats like Chernoff faces.

---

[1] It should be noted though that in some circumstances, as when a team is dealing with smaller amounts of data, or a small number of descriptive statistics, a sentence or table can be better than a graphic for communicating meaning.

One common variation on the use of these charts is in plotting them as small multiples to illustrate variation in performance across a variety of sites, locations, individuals, or other category of interest.[2]

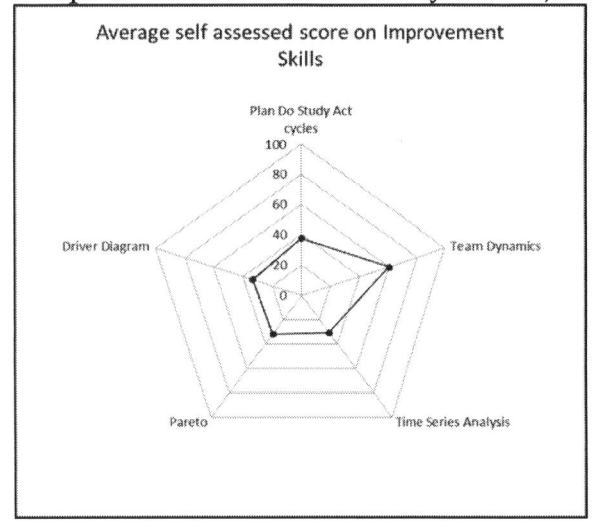

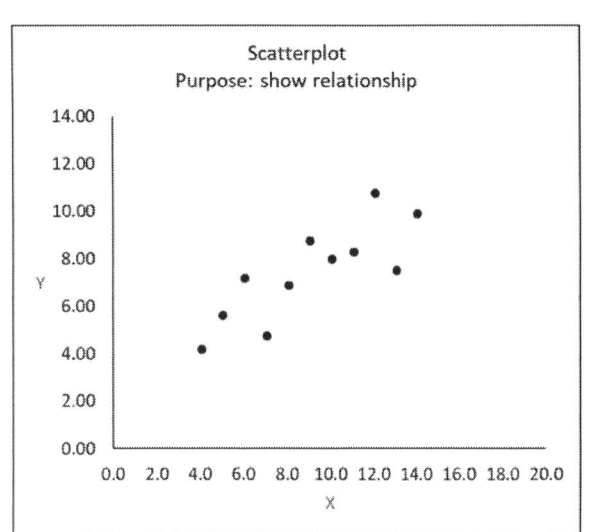

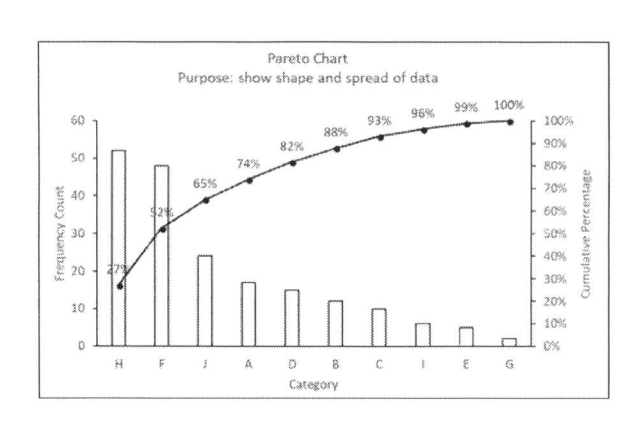

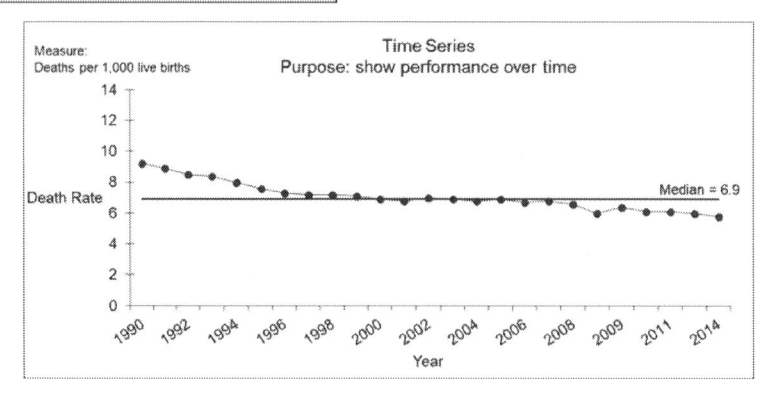

How to develop a good graphical display of quantitative information

Developing clear and concise graphical displays should be the goal of improvement teams using graphics to communicate information and learning. How to do well, remains a difficult question to answer. Once again, Edward Tufte suggests some principles individuals and teams can use to enhance their production of good graphics:

---

[2] See Section 6: Data Visualization Using Small Multiples to learn more about the use of small multiples.

- Have a properly chosen format and design — choose the right chart type for the data in hand and purpose for data visualization
- Use words, numbers and drawing together — label and annotate each graphic to better tell the story
- Reflect a balance, a proportion, a sense of relevant scale — maintain the integrity of the data, never distorting the display to fit a particular narrative, rather allow the data to tell its own story
- Display an accessible complexity of detail — use table for small amounts of data, never overly large data sets
- Often have a narrative quality, a story to tell about the data — integrate a learning question the graphic is intended to answer, integrate words and/or qualitative experiences that illustrate the quantitative depiction, etc.
- Are drawn in a professional manner, with the technical details of production done with care — 80-90% or more of the ink presented on the chart should assist the narrative, communicating information to the reader
- Avoid content-free decoration, including chart junk — extraneous ink in the form of dimension, color, line thickness or other embellishments that do not add information to the graphic being produced

Coaching Notes

1) Watch out for scaling issues on charts produced by the team's you coach. Some common guidelines for two common data displays can help:

    a. Bar charts are read vertically. They should begin at zero on the vertical axis (y-axis). If there is a compelling reason to not start at zero, then an annotation or break in the bar should be included as a visual queue to the reader that the bars presented do not reach down to zero as would normally be inferred.

Bar Chart

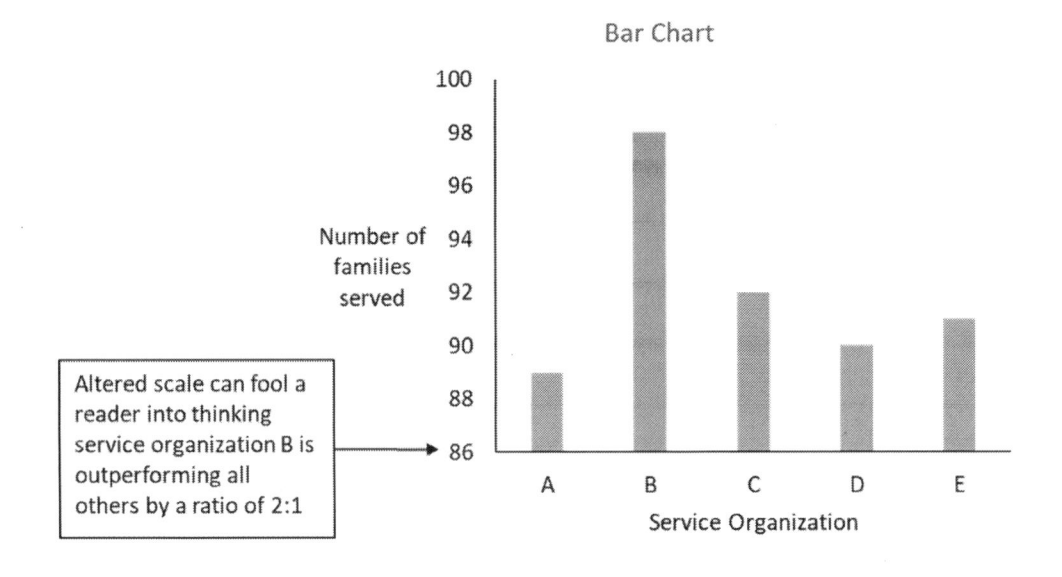

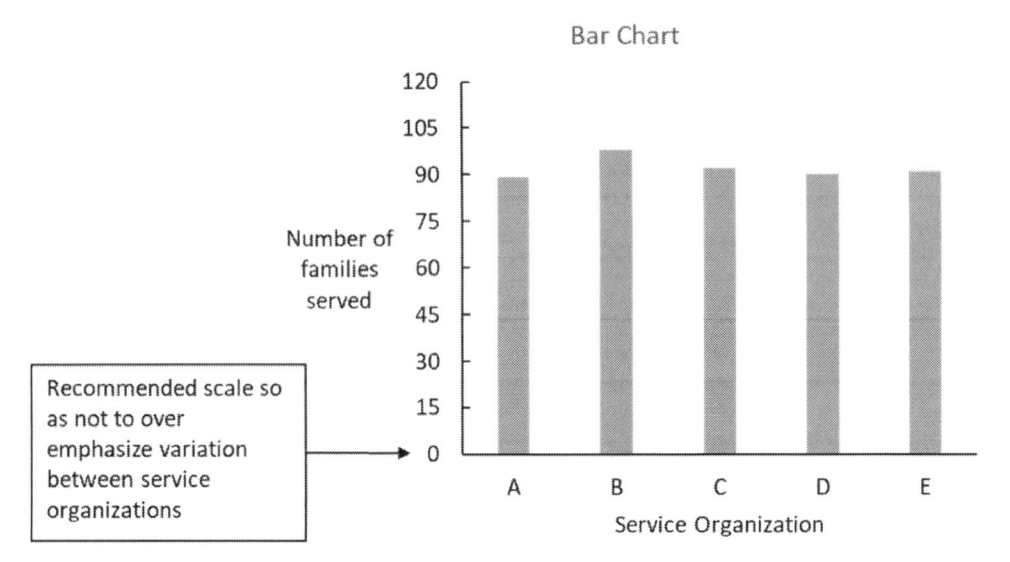

Number of families served

Altered scale can fool a reader into thinking service organization B is outperforming all others by a ratio of 2:1 →

Bar Chart

Number of families served

Recommended scale so as not to over emphasize variation between service organizations →

b. Line charts are read horizontally from right to left. When developing line charts (i.e., simple line graphs, time series charts, run charts, Shewhart control charts) approximately 1/3 of the space below the data line should be white space, approximately 1/3 of the space should be allocated to the data line and approximately 1/3 of the space above the data line should be white space. This guideline helps prevent the exaggeration of scale when depicting the data.

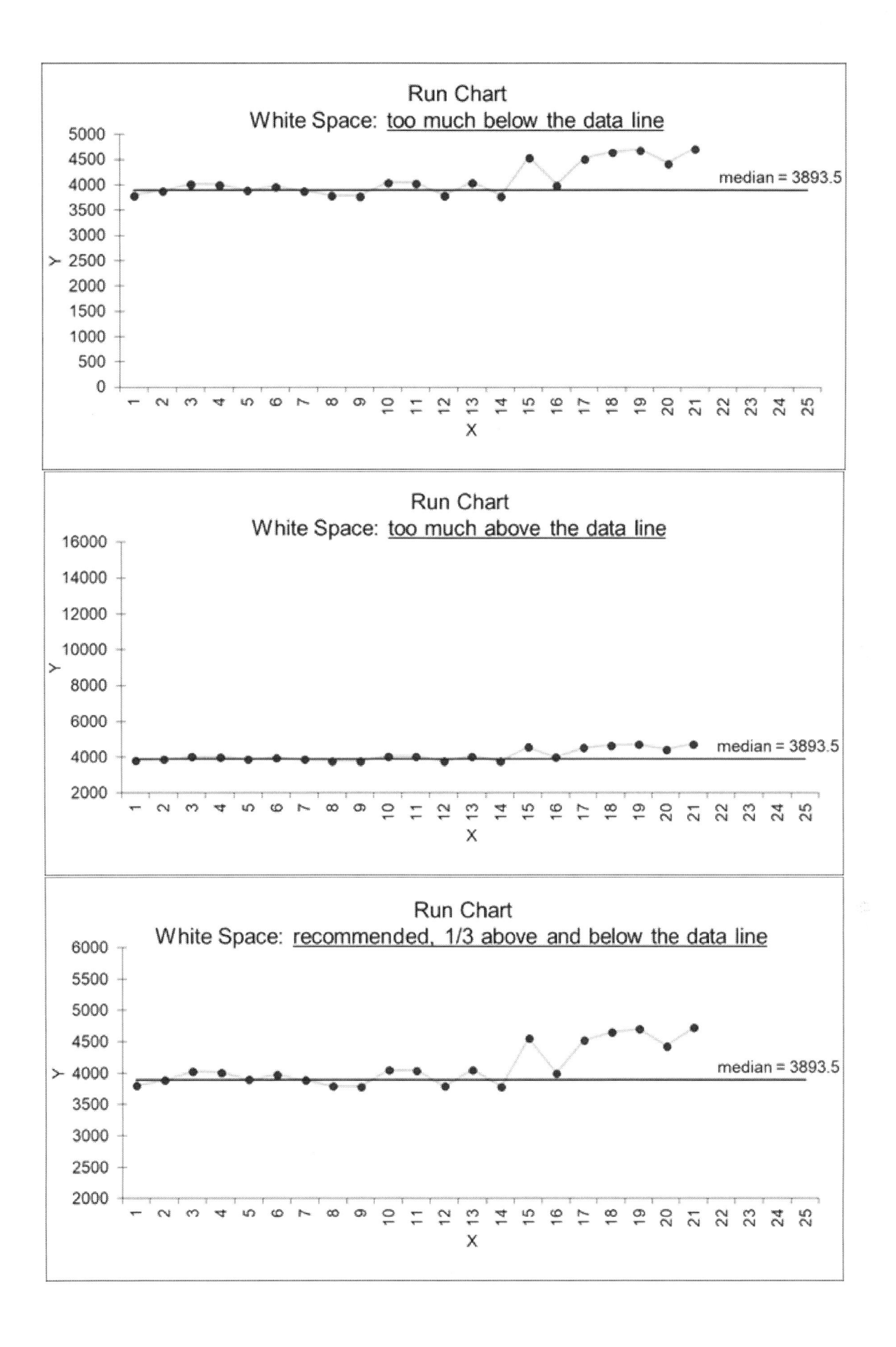

Run Chart
White Space: <u>too much below the data line</u>

median = 3893.5

Run Chart
White Space: <u>too much above the data line</u>

median = 3893.5

Run Chart
White Space: <u>recommended, 1/3 above and below the data line</u>

median = 3893.5

2) Whenever possible coach teams to present scatterplots as square. While the x and y-axis will depict different continuous variables with different scales, it is most helpful visually to keep the shape of the chart square, so readers can more easily ascertain relationships which may exist in the data, even without formal analysis (i.e., strong positive, strong negative, moderate positive, moderate negative, nonlinear, or no relationship).

3) Ensure teams are incorporating careful and concise annotations on their graphics to help explain when and what occurred during their improvement work. This will anticipate and reduce questions from readers and clarify for readers exactly what happened. Annotations act as a guide for interpretation, preventing unfounded inference into the graphic displayed.

History

Visualization of data has existed in some form or another since human beings first started drawing on the walls of caves more than 40,000 years ago. Modern application for statistical purposes though picks up in the 1700s with William Playfair and Johann Heinrich Lambert. Playfair is credited with popularizing the use of several important tools: the bar chart (though earlier depictions exist in 15th century literature), line graphs, area charts, and pie charts. Many important statistical thinkers and graphic artists have built upon his work including Joseph Minard in the 1800s, Karl Pearson spanning the 19th and 20th century, Mary Eleanor Spear in the 1950s, John Tukey in the 1960s, Francis Anscombe in the 1970s, and Edward Tufte in the 1980s. Tufte deserves special mention as he more than any other codified rules and recommendations for helping make meaning from visualized quantitative information. He also popularized visualization through seminars over 30 years. Today graphic artists and statisticians alike reference his materials when producing graphic displays of data for consumption by specific and general audiences.

Special considerations in visualizing quantitative information

There are several considerations when developing graphic displays of quantitative information. Attending to the three presented here will assist any improvement team in helping the data they have to tell a compelling story to various readers.

1) Add text to graphics to improve the narrative design. Use annotations in partnership with data values to better explain what is happening on the chart to the reader. Words are a powerful way of communicating information and the integration of just a few of them on a quantitative graphic can enhance and clarify the story being told by the data.

2) Avoid the use of visually distracting elements from your graphical design. Specifically, watch out for these three:

   a. Have you ever seen a drawing or a piece of artwork that is static but appears to move (i.e., spins, or vibrates in some way)? This is referred to as the moiré effect, and it is deeply distracting for readers trying to interpret graphic displays of data. It is caused by an interaction of the design with the natural movements of the eye. Avoid cross-hatching patterns, most often used to color bar charts to prevent this.

   Also, be wary when working in three dimensions to avoid the Necker Illusion. This occurs commonly when drawing a cube of rectangle in three dimensions and to the visual system it is unclear (i.e., can flip back and forth) which edge is protruding toward the reader and which is receding away from them.

    b. On many graphical displays (i.e., line charts, bar charts, scatterplots, etc.) grid lines are an unnecessary distraction and should be removed from the visualization. They do not add information to the graphic and in some instances can act as a distraction from the plotted values, which are the real voice of the story.

    c. Many statistical programs come with many options for the decoration of the graphic displays they can create. These include the option to apply things like: cross-hatching, various colors to the data values or their backgrounds, three dimensions, different shapes (i.e., triangle rather than rectangle bars on bar charts), the addition of data tables, the ability to embellish or change fonts, line thicknesses, addition of data labels and on and on. The use of these elements should be carefully considered and assessed to ensure they add information the reader needs. If they do not, then they are purely cosmetic and likely a distraction. If the data can be displayed in a simpler way, then it should be. For example, on most line graphs, the individual data points depicted on the line chart demonstrate the data values. In most cases a data table or individual data labels is redundant and not needed.

3) If possible, communicate more of the story by combining two or more types of data into the same graphic. This can be done simply by displaying multiple measures on a single graphic as in the case of a family of measures (i.e., all the project measures, each with its own chart, displayed side by side as a single graphic) or using small multiples (i.e., displaying multiple iterations of the same measure together but for multiple institutions, locations, individuals or others). In more complex graphics, consider combining a data map with a time series, showing the change over time and across a location map.

References and Further Reading

- Anscombe, Francis J. "Graphs in Statistical Analysis." *American Statistician*. 27. February 1973
- Tufte, Edward R. *The Visual Display of Quantitative Information (2nd Edition)*. Connecticut: Graphic Press. 2001
- Tufte, Edward R. *Envisioning Information*. Connecticut. Graphic Press. 1990
- Associates in Process Improvement. *The Improvement Handbook*. Austin: Associates in Process Improvement. 2007
- "Paid Maternal Leave: Almost Everywhere." *The New York Times*. New York, New York. 17 February 2013

Data Visualization Checklist

☐ Clear title
☐ Axes are clearly labeled
☐ Scale is appropriate (and not deceptive)
☐ Appropriate display for the data presented
☐ Annotations are present (where they should be) and helpful
☐ Display allows for easy visual comparisons
☐ Interpretation integrates appropriate subject matter knowledge

Edward Tufte: The Friendly Data Graphic

<u>Friendly</u>	<u>Unfriendly</u>
Words are spelled out, mysterious and elaborate encoding avoided	Abbreviations abound, requiring the viewer to sort through text to decode abbreviations
Words run from left to right, the usual direction for reading occidental languages	Words run vertically, particularly along the Y-axis; words run in several directions
Little messages help explain data	Graphic is cryptic, requires repeated references to scattered text
Elaborately encoded shadings, cross-hatching, and colors are avoided; instead, labels are placed on the graphic itself; no legend is required	Obscure codings require going back and forth between legend and graphic
Graphic attracts viewer, provokes curiosity	Graphic is repellent, filled with chart junk
Colors, if used, are chosen so that the color-deficient and color-blind (5 to 10 percent of viewers) can make sense of the graphic (blue can be distinguished from other colors by most color-deficient people)	Design insensitive to color-deficient viewers; red and green used for essential contrasts
Type is clear, precise, modest; lettering may be done by hand	Type is clotted, overbearing
Type is upper-and-lower case, with serifs	Type is all capitals, sans serif

Data Visualization Using Small Multiples

Other Names: Grid Chart, Panel Chart

Conceptual Links
- System of Profound Knowledge: Understanding Variation, Appreciation of the System
- 6 Principles: Focus on variation in performance, We cannot improve at scale what we cannot measure

Purpose

"At the heart of quantitative reasoning is a single question: Compared to what?"
—Edward Tufte

In research studies, the answer is, compared to a control group(s), with accountability frameworks it is in relation to some set standard generated by leadership, or one to another. In improvement science the answer is almost always in comparison to ourselves, or our system, at a previous point in time.

Small multiples serve the purpose of forcing visual comparisons across groupings of data. They allow comparison at a glance and benefit from our visual ability to notice variation. Small multiples emphasize what Tufte refers to as "changes in the data, not changes in the data frames."

When to use small multiples

The main instance when we would choose to use small multiples is when we would like to show large quantities of multivariate data. This often occurs when improvement efforts are focused on change across multiple sites or locations, across many individuals or when there is a need to stratify or disaggregate data in some way. Such displays allow readers to see important sources, or locations, of variation with ease, learning from them and using the learning to further direct the improvement effort.

Elements of small multiples

Small multiples are comprised of:

- A series of graphics (charts, pictures, data maps, etc.)
- Displaying the same combination of variables for each graphic (i.e., if a chart, the x and y axis for each panel are the same variable and are scaled the same)
- Indexed by changes in a third variable of interest (i.e., time, location, site, individual, gender, ethnicity, etc.). Meaning each panel represents a different location, or time, or is denominated by another variable but retains the same measure(s) of interest for the purpose of comparison

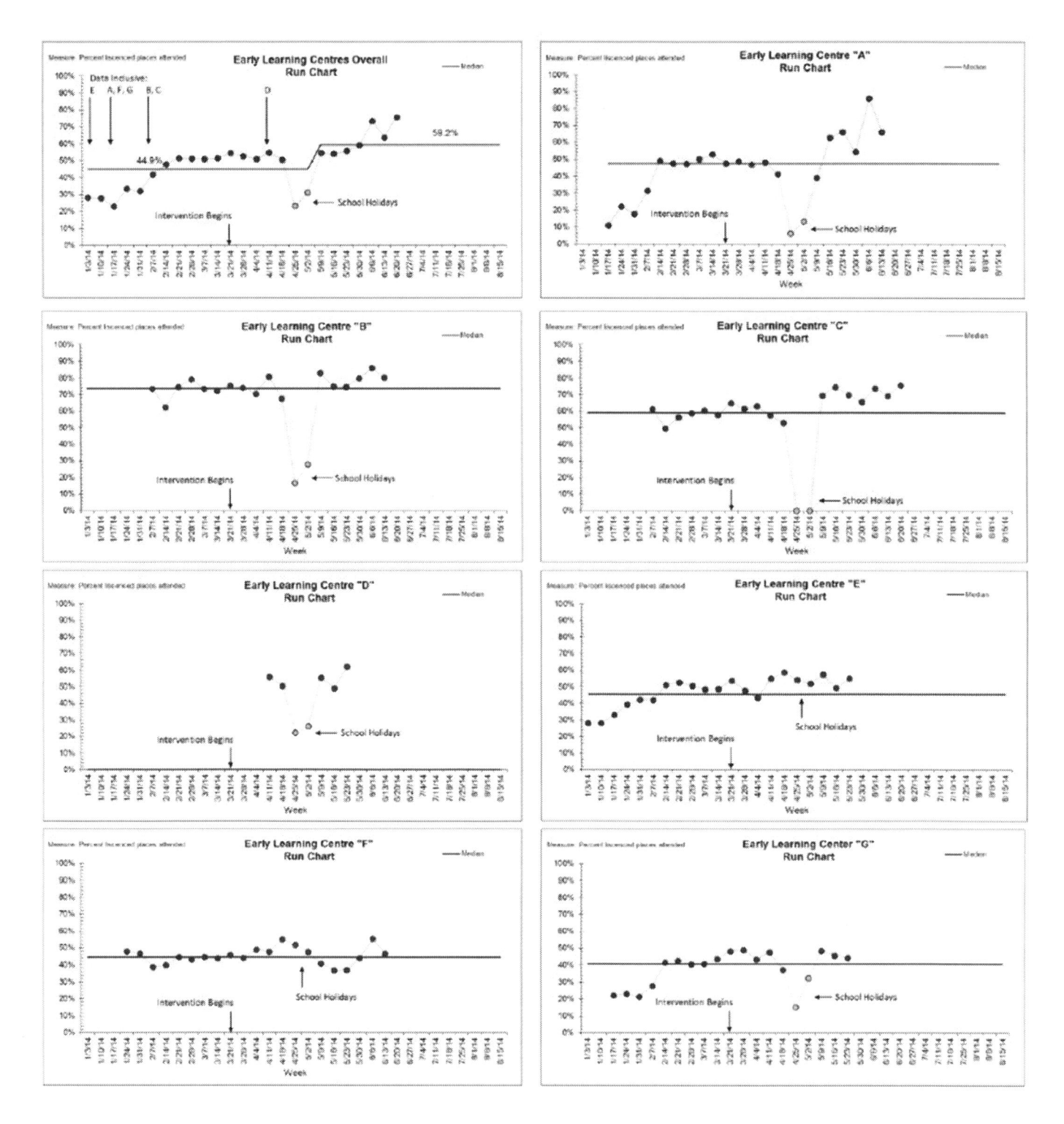

In the example above, there are eight graphics. Seven of these Run charts display the performance of percent attendance at seven early childhood education centers participating in a network focused on improving attendance for local children. The eighth graph (upper left-hand corner) displays the aggregate performance of the seven centers participating in network. At a glance, readers can see a great many things: the network as a whole has seen improvement, the improvement is largely attributable to four centers (A, B, C and E), center D struggled with data collection, centers F and G have largely seen no change in performance. Careful annotation, also assist the reader to make sense of the graphs, showing when the improvement network began, and when school holidays occurred which might have influenced attendance.

How to make small multiples

1) Develop a graphic for a measure of interest using at least two variables (in the example above the variables are percent attending and time). Do this for each variation in a third variable of interest (in the example above the third variable of interest is early education center location).
2) Standardize the format for each graphic created. If this a line chart, bar chart or scatter plot then the x and y axis for each graphic should be standardized to the same scales. If the graphic is radar plot, then the scale of each chart should be the same. If the chart is a data map, drawing or picture, then the frame should be standardized to be the same for each graphic.
3) Arrange the graphics produced into a grid pattern, where in each graphic is the same size and shape. This will allow for quick and easy visual comparisons across the standardized frames you have created for the data you are displaying.

How to use small multiples in practice

Improvement teams and coaches leading improvement networks (i.e., Network Improvement Communities, Break Through Series Collaboratives, Collaborative Learning Networks, Collaborative Improvement and Innovation Networks, etc.) will find utility in using small multiples to display the data of the network. It is an easy way, as previously stated, for leaders, participants, or other stakeholders to quickly see the performance of the network, make comparisons and engage in learning conversations as a result. Individual organizations (i.e., schools, school districts, hospitals, non-governmental organizations, etc.) will find small multiples helpful in visualizing the performance of important metrics across departments, wards, individuals, and all sorts of other denominators of the system.

Improvement teams can use small multiples to:

- Accomplish rapid analysis and learning from their data
- Act as a focal point for important data conversations
- Assist in the targeting of deeper learning, the targeting of improvement work, or for the celebration of accomplishments within the system.

History

As with other visualizations of data, it is difficult to pin an exact date on when the use of small multiples was first employed. Known early examples exist from the 1600s and persist into the present day. With the advent of computers and powerful data visualization software, the use of small multiples is easier now than it has ever been, allowing teams to take advantage of this special form of data visualization.

Variations on small multiples

There are many different variations on the conceptual use of small multiples. Iterations most used in improvement science include the production of small multiples using:
- Run charts
- Shewhart control charts
- Pareto charts
- Histograms
- Scatterplots

Special Considerations with using small multiples

Special consideration should be given to ensuring the readability of a graphic using small multiples. As previously stated, small multiples work by allowing rapid visual comparisons of the data presented. For this to occur, each panel in the series must share a common frame (i.e., same scale for x and y axis). If they do not, then a reader could very easily misinterpret the data being presented. Data that cannot adhere to this rule due to quantity or frequency should be left off the small multiples view and treated in another way. Alternatively, it can be included with obvious annotations to direct readers to the important differences occurring in the data.

References and Further Reading

- Tufte, Edward R. *The Visual Display of Quantitative Information (2nd Edition)*. Connecticut: Graphic Press. 2001
- Tufte, Edward R. *Envisioning Information*. Connecticut. Graphic Press. 1990
- Tyler, J., Davies, M., Bennett, B. "Increasing early childhood education enrolment and attendance rates in South Auckland, New Zealand." *NZ International Research in Early Childhood Education Journal*. Volume 21. No. 1. 2018

Ordered Bar Chart

Conceptual Links

- System of Profound Knowledge: Understanding Variation
- 6 Principles: Focus on Variation in Performance

Purpose

Ordered bar charts exist as a visual tool for rapid sense making of the comparison of categorical data. It is not uncommon that an improvement team will want to compare data from across locations, individuals, classrooms, wards, or some other category of interest. The ordered bar chart allows such comparisons to be done visually, while minimizing the amount of effort an individual consuming the data needs to interpret the information they are seeing.

When to use ordered bar charts

Order bar charts should be used when graphing categorical data.[1] Improvement teams will find the use of ordered bar charts especially useful early in their improvement journey. It is not uncommon for many teams to have access to categorical data that can be plotted using an ordered bar chart at the start of their improvement journey.

Elements of an ordered bar chart

Like a bar chart the ordered bar chart has some standard elements that are visually distinctive. Ordered bar charts always have two distinct axes. The x axis displays the labels of the categories being plotted on the chart. The y axis plots the statistic of interest. The numerical scale might be a frequency count, a percentage, a monetary amount, time, or one of many other measures a team takes an interest in. Most importantly an ordered bar chart is distinguishable in that it orders the categories based on the data from least to greatest (as in the example below) or from greatest to least.

---

[1] An important note on the use of ordered bar charts is that they are not a good choice for use when the data being plotted are not categorical. If continuous or numerical data is being graphed, then a histogram is the better choice for plotting a chart.

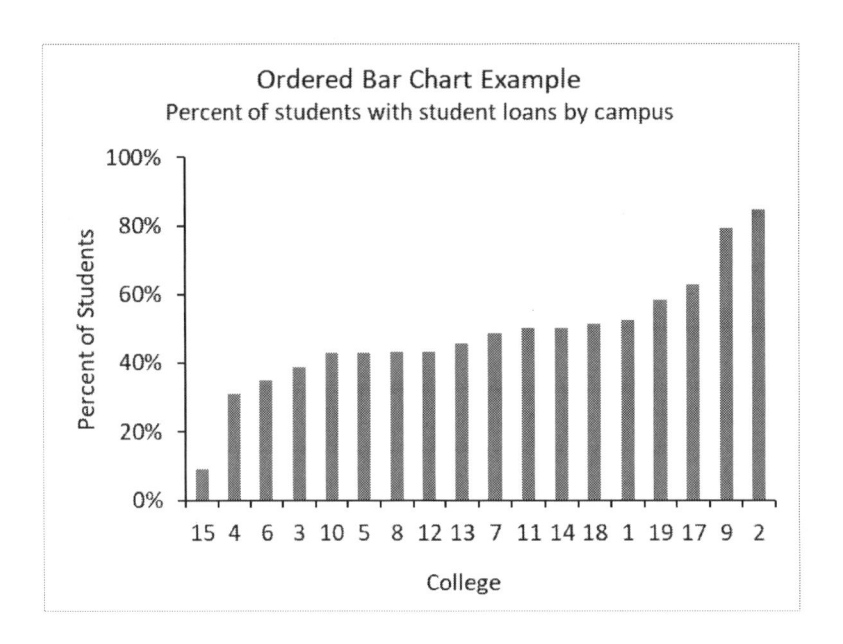

Ordered Bar Chart Example
Percent of students with student loans by campus

How to create an ordered bar chart

1) Identify a learning question(s)
2) Identify what information is needed to answer the learning question
3) List possible variables that could be useful in stratifying the data collected[2]
4) Develop any important operational definitions to clarify the investigation
5) Identify the duration and location for the collection of data
6) Devise a form for collecting the data
7) Collect the data (minimum of 30 occurrences)[3]
8) Draw the vertical and horizontal axes
9) Determine the highest value that needs to be displayed on the chart to assist in the scaling of the chart.
   Tip: The scale should be slightly larger than the range of the data to be plotted
10) Place categorical labels on the chart
11) Draw the bars in order of magnitude from greatest to least or least to greatest. Always start the bar chart from the value zero.

How to use an ordered bar chart in practice

Improvement teams often find an ordered bar chart is a good place to start their investigation into a systems performance. It is not uncommon for organizations to have aggregate data on performance across all their locations (i.e., schools in a district, or hospitals in a network) and to only look at the data collected either in aggregate form or at each location individually. What is missing for them is the ability to see all of their data at a glance. In making this simple visualization teams often find insight into where they should be asking clarifying questions or trying to learn about promising practices that could be replicated across the broader system.

---

[2] These could be category types in the case of a Pareto chart but also a team might list possible rational sub-groups for further investigating the data once it is collected. See discussion on Macro to Micro analysis in the special considerations section below.

[3] With categorical data sample size is an important consideration and having less than 30 occurrences across the categories of interest may result in a wrong finding by the team investigating as chance alone might skew the data.

Another time when teams find an ordered bar chart helpful is in communicating performance of the system to a diverse group of stakeholders. If an organization has the capability, a control chart would be a better choice for learning from comparative data across the system, but this is not always possible. It is also true that control charts are harder to speak to and so teams presenting data may find this tool is more fit for purpose when dialoguing about the performance of the system, even if deep learning using a control chart has already occurred.

History

It is not entirely clear when the first ordered bar chart was created. However, early references to the use of bar charts are known. The earliest comes from a publication by the 14th century philosopher Nicole Oresme on his *Latitude of Forms*. However, as bar charts are commonly used and visualized today, most scholars point to the work of William Playfair circa 1780. They have long been used as a tool for quality improvement, with Pareto charts being the most notable use of ordered bar charts.

Variations of ordered bar charts

Ordered bar charts are generally displayed vertically but some individuals/teams may choose to orient them horizontally. There is no right or wrong regarding this choice. What is always important is the individual or team making the chart is doing so with their audience in mind, understanding that the choice of orientation may be easier or harder to consume by the users of the data analysis. The example below shows the same data in both a vertical and horizontal format.

Ordered bar chart oriented vertically

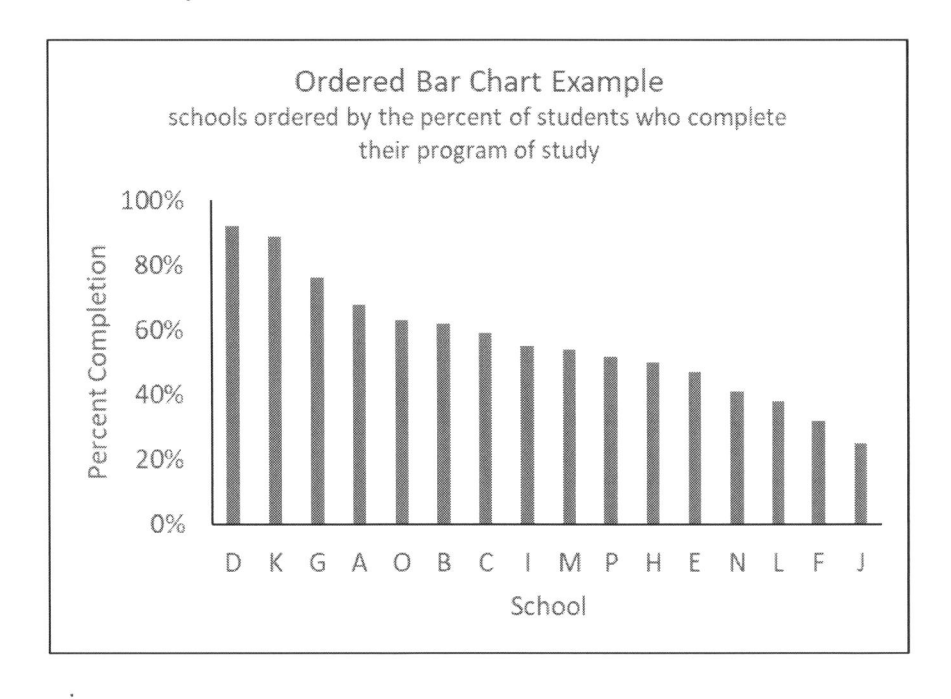

Ordered bar chart oriented horizontally

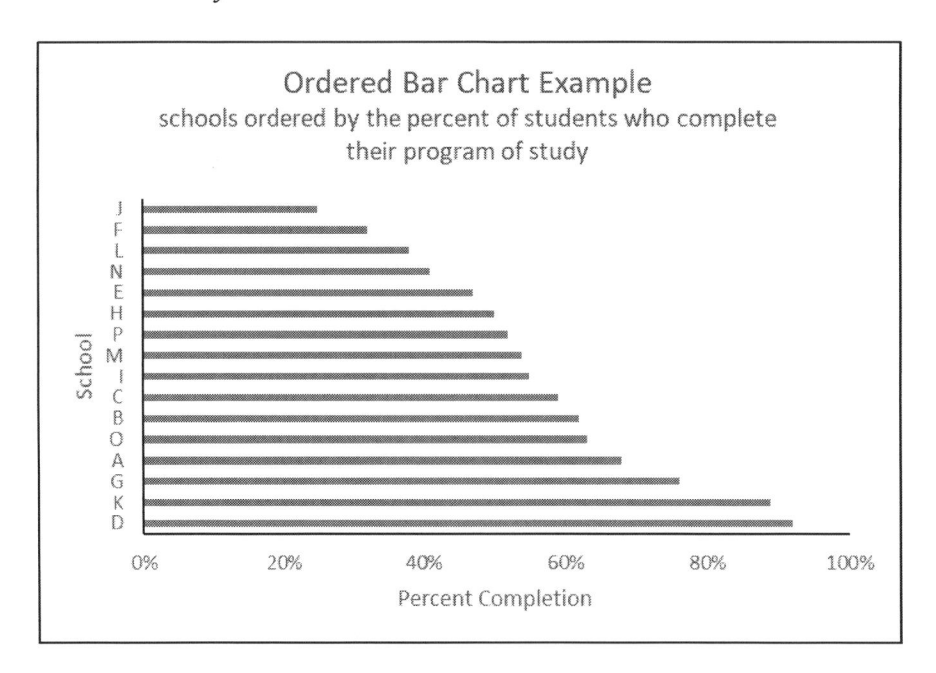

Another common usage of the ordered bar chart is the Pareto chart. A Pareto analysis is a special type of ordered bar chart that focuses on the frequency of categorical data as it relates to understanding the performance of the system. See the chapter on Pareto Analysis for a full treatment on this specific application of ordered bar charts.

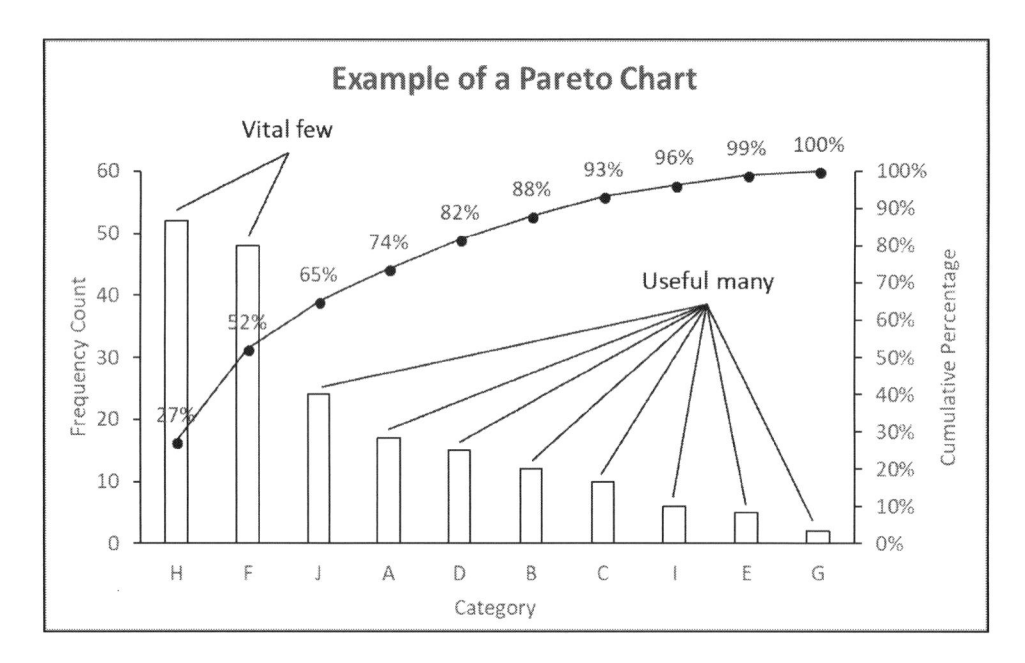

Special considerations when using ordered bar charts

When developing an ordered bar chart there are important considerations to be aware of and to apply in practice. Each of these is described and, in some circumstances, further study is recommended.

1) Improvement Teams should be very careful about applying ordered bar charts to an unstable system.[4] During periods of instability what can or should be generally expected from the performance of the system may be obscured or skewed by the presence of a factor that is not always at work on the system. Before creating an ordered bar chart on a given outcome, it is recommended teams first develop a Shewhart control chart to assess for stability. If the chart indicates a stable state for the process or system, then proceeding with the creation of an ordered bar chart is recommended. If the system is unstable, a better choice of analysis would be the ordered Shewhart control chart (i.e., using a funnel plot in partnership with control chart limits), which will indicate where in the system instability is present.

2) When scaling an ordered bar chart, it is important to avoid confusing the consumer of the data whenever possible. Scaling the chart starting at zero, or whatever the minimum numerical value is for the statistic of interest will assist in preventing misinterpretations of the chart.

3) Because the data being plotted is always categorical when using an ordered bar chart, it is important that there is space between each of the bars that are plotted. This is a visual que to consumers the data is indeed categorical. With continuous or numerical data, such as is plotted on a histogram, this is not the case as the continuous nature of the scale is emphasized by not having any space between bars plotted.

4) A final consideration when using ordered bar charts concerns their use with percentage data. Anytime percentage data is being graphed it is a good idea to indicate somewhere on the chart, the sample size for each bar (especially if they vary widely, >25%). Alternatively, if the denominator size for each bar is relatively consistent (i.e., within 25%) then annotating the chart with an average sample size per bar is a good practice.

References and Further Reading

- Tufte, Edward R. *The Visual Display of Quantitative Information (2nd Edition)*. Connecticut: Graphic Press. 2001
- Tague, Nancy R. *The Quality Toolbox (2nd Edition)*. Milwaukee: American Society for Quality, Quality Press. 2015
- Associates in Process Improvement. *The Improvement Handbook*. Austin: Associates in Process Improvement. 2007

---

[4] For a fuller treatment on assessing for stability the authors recommend multiple references explaining Shewhart's Theory of Common and Special Cause variation with the branch of statistics known as Statistical Process Control Methods. References include Economic Control of Quality of Manufactured Product by Walter Shewhart, The New Economics for Industry, Government and Education by W. Edwards Deming and The Health Care Data Guide: Learning from Data for Improvement by Lloyd Provost and Sandra Murray, among many others.

Pareto Analysis

Other Names: Pareto diagram, Pareto chart

Conceptual Links

- System of Profound Knowledge: Understanding Variation, Systems Thinking
- 6 Principles: Make the work problem specific and user centered, Focus on variation in the process

Purpose

Pareto analysis is a useful tool for analyzing and visualizing the frequency with which classification data occurs in a process or system. Classifying various defects, problems, locations or other categories by frequency or magnitude of occurrence assists teams to understand where in the system improvement efforts might be most useful. As a result, improvement teams find this tool particularly helpful for focusing their efforts.

When to use Pareto analysis

Improvement teams will find Pareto analysis useful during several stages of the improvement journey. In the early stage of investigating the problem, or diagnosis, a Pareto analysis can be especially useful for uncovering where in a process or system breakdowns are occurring.

Example: A school district has noted that many of its students are graduating high school without the requisite requirements for entering a four-year university. The students are considered "off-track". In an effort to address this problem the district has commissioned an improvement team. The team might perform a Pareto analysis to better understand which classes (category) and with what frequency students are missing. This might point them in the direction of where in the system students are getting "off-track" and may even spark some creative ideas about how to correct the problem for the system in the future. Another moment when a team might find a Pareto chart useful is in assessing the frequency of interventions that are occurring in the system.

Example: A non-profit organization working to end homelessness in their city is wanting to understand the frequency of various interventions (services) they are providing to the people they work with. Having this knowledge might better help them plan for their future budget, hire the appropriate work force, or even advocate at a local level for various governmental involvement (i.e., creation of more affordable housing, a rise in the minimum wage, etc.).

Perhaps the most useful reason teams might find to use a Pareto analysis is in the communication of important learning accomplished by the analysis. With leaders, workers, or other stakeholders, the Pareto chart can be a succinct way of displaying data. It can clearly illustrate to people what the vital few categories are that may be a part of an improvement journey.

Elements of a Pareto chart

A Pareto chart can be thought of as one type of ordered bar chart. It always has at least two axes. The x-axis, or horizontal axis, is labeled using the categories or classifications of the data collected. In the example below this is illustrated using the letters A-J. The primary y-axis (left side of the chart), or primary vertical axis, is commonly labeled using the frequency count of the categories described[1]. In the example below this is illustrated by the numbers 0-60. Sometimes a secondary y-axis (right side of the chart) is added and is always labeled using cumulative percentage. This secondary axis displays a line graph showing the cumulative percentage contribution to the frequency of the categorical data on the x-axis. The frequency of occurrence of each category controls the order in which the data is plotted on the chart, with the data being plotted from greatest frequency of occurrence to least frequently occurring, with the most frequently occurring data being plotted on the left side of the chart.

Joseph Juran referred to the most commonly occurring categories as the "vital few" and all other categories as the "useful many." It is in identification of the vital few that Pareto analysis reveals important areas of focus and further learning for improvement teams.

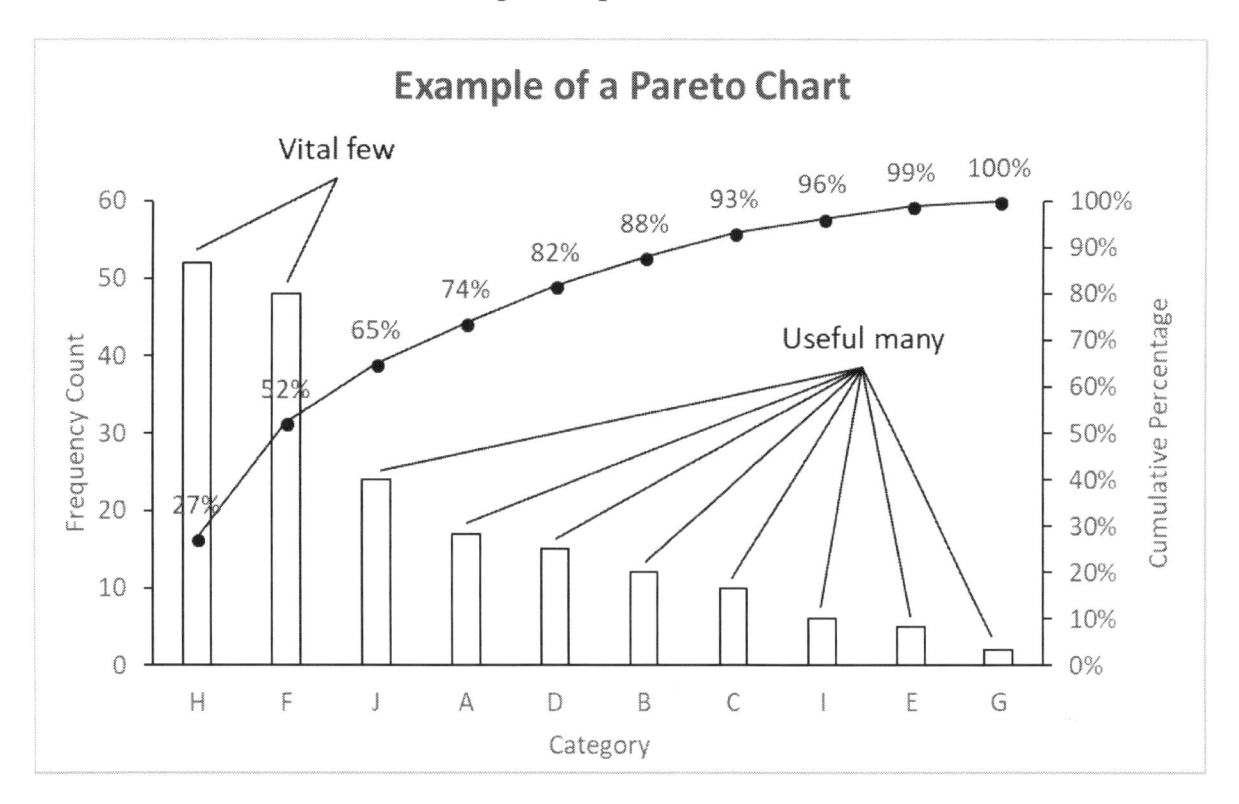

Example of a Pareto Chart

While it is not uncommon for Pareto charts to reflect the "80/20 rule", they do not always subscribe to this principle. As in the example above, categories H, F, J, A, and D are all needed to achieve 80% of occurrences. What is important from the perspective of quality improvement is the ability to identify which occurrences are the "vital few". In the example above these are categories H and F, together representing just 52% of occurrences.

How to conduct a Pareto analysis[2]

1) Identify a learning question(s)
2) Identify what information is needed to answer the learning question

---

[1] Other variations of Pareto charts are described in greater detail later in the chapter. Variations include monetary value, time and percent contribution in addition to frequency count when describing the primary (vertical) y-axis.

[2] Note: Various software packages can calculate and graph Pareto charts. Microsoft Excel can perform and graph Pareto charts using the Data Analysis ToolPak, an optional add-in that can be enabled within the program. Most statistical software packages also include this functionality. However, it is up to the person creating the chart to ensure the chart displays the correct scaling, and interpretation before making the chart available for consumption by various users.

3) List possible variables that could be useful in stratifying the data collected[3]
4) Develop any important operational definitions to clarify the investigation
5) Identify the duration and location for the collection of data
6) Devise a simple check sheet for collecting the data
7) Collect the data (minimum of 30 occurrences)
8) Draw the vertical and horizontal axes
9) Order the categories by most frequently occurring on the left to least frequently occurring on the right
10) Plot the bars using the vertical axis to scale
11) Label the graph (title, axis, data labels, categories, relevant annotations)

Optional steps if using a secondary (vertical) y-axis
12) Calculate the percent contribution of each category to the whole
13) Calculate the cumulative percent of categories moving from left to right on the graph
14) Plot the secondary axis and line graph using the cumulative percent numbers at each category

How to use a Pareto analysis in practice

Teams choosing a Pareto analysis have many good reasons to do so. One of the challenges most improvement teams face is the prioritization of the improvement work needed by the systems they serve. Teams at the start of an improvement journey will find using the tool in this way can help them to scope the work they are chartering for improvement. At other times they will find a powerful tool for digging deeper into the failures they are observing in the system.

Pareto Analysis is used most effectively by teams to reveal important sources of variation that might otherwise remain hidden in aggregate sources of data. Any time a team believes there might be unknown sources of variation, have access to data which could reveal those sources and have a concise learning question for which Pareto analysis is an appropriate way to address the question then it is a good choice for the team.

History

One of the original Seven Quality Tools, the Pareto chart was introduced to the field of Quality Improvement in the late 1930s, by Joseph Juran (Juran, 1951). Juran developed the Pareto chart and named it for Vilfredo Pareto, an Italian economist and professor (University of Laussane) whose work he used to inspire this type of analysis.

In 1896, Vilfredo Pareto published Cours d'Économie Politique which included his findings from a study of the distribution of wealth in 19th century England and his law of income distribution. What he uncovered in his study of England and other countries through time has become known as the Pareto Principle, Pareto Law or 80/20 rule. It states that 80% of the wealth will be owned by 20% of the population. Further, the curve of wealth ownership will follow a power law distribution with 10% of people owning 65% of the wealth and 5% owning 50% (Koch, 1997). Juran found that a broader application of this rule to frequencies of categorical data proved very useful in practice when investigating

---

[3] These could be category types in the case of a Pareto chart but also a team might list possible rational sub-groups for further investigating the data once it is collected. See discussion on Macro to Micro analysis in the special considerations section below.

where in systems failures or defects were occurring and could help focus the direction of improvement as a result.

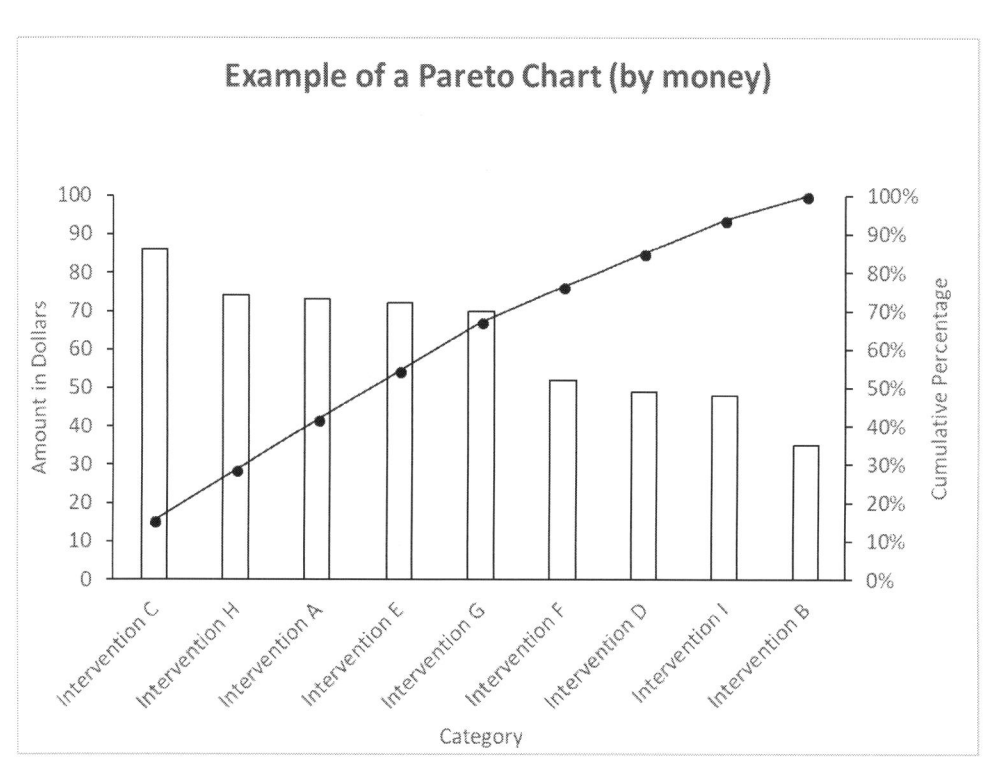

Variations

The most common usage of Pareto analysis is in counting the frequency with which various categories occur in a process or system. Other variations on the tool exist. Modifications can be made to use the tool with time data, monetary data and percent contribution data. Teams may find these variations useful when investigating their systems. Some examples of Pareto charts showing these variations are shown below.

Time data

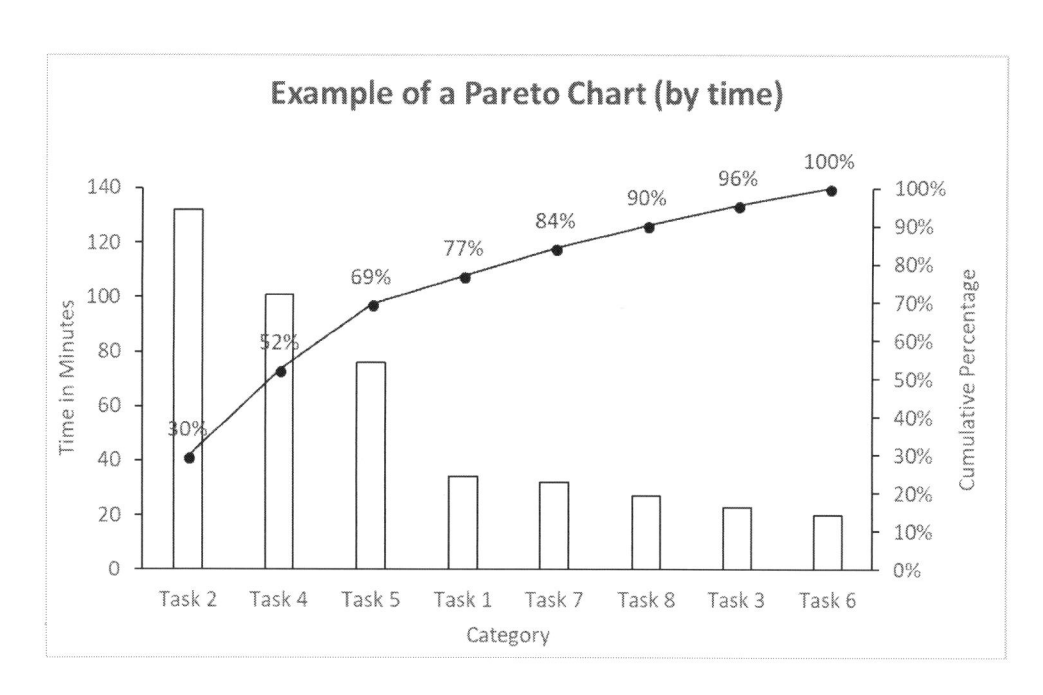

Monetary Data

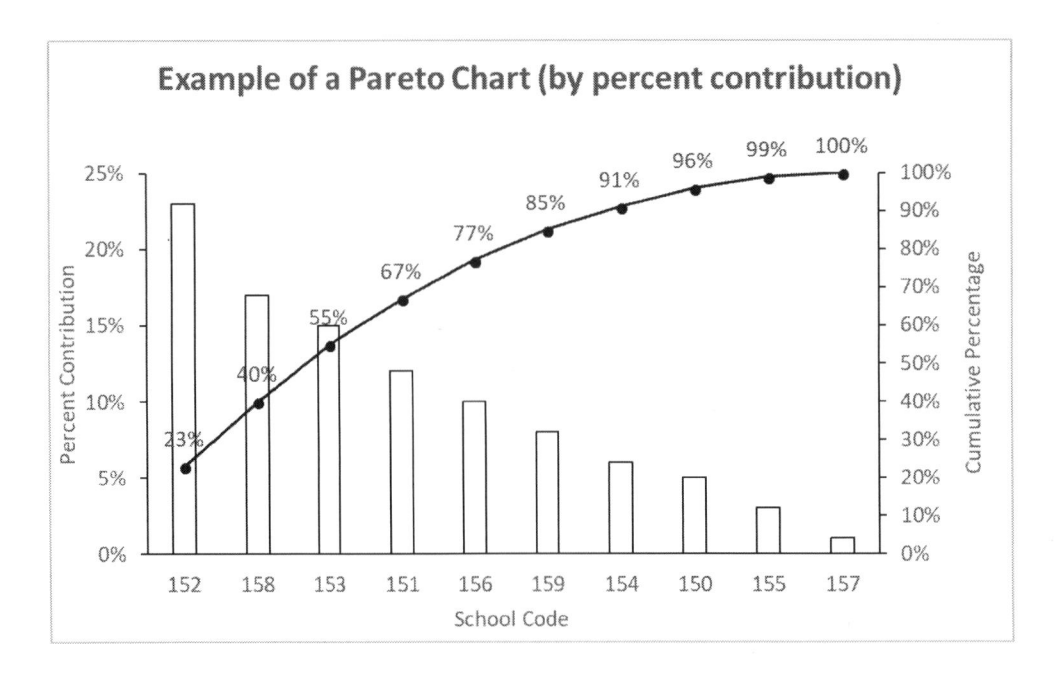

Percent Contribution

Example of a Pareto Chart (by percent contribution)

[Pareto chart showing Percent Contribution (left axis) and Cumulative Percentage (right axis) by School Code. Bars for schools 152, 158, 153, 151, 156, 159, 154, 150, 155, 157 with cumulative percentages: 23%, 40%, 55%, 67%, 77%, 85%, 91%, 96%, 99%, 100%.]

Special considerations with the use of Pareto analysis

When conducting a Pareto analysis there are several important considerations to be aware of and to possibly apply in practice. Each of these is described and, in some circumstances, further study is recommended.

1) Pareto analysis only rarely identifies specific causes of defects, errors, or other categories under investigation. In most circumstances it is a mistake to describe a Pareto chart using causal language. Under most conditions the cause of an observed outcome is multifactorial in nature. Determining the interrelationships of those factors can only be carried out by more robust analyses. In quality improvement other tools (Shewhart control charts, scatter plots, and planned experiments) are often used to assist causal investigations.

    Careful use of language is recommended. In each instance of presented data on a Pareto chart be clear to have clear operational definitions of the categories presented to avoid any confusion.

2) The minimum number of observations of occurrences necessary to create a Pareto analysis is 30, as stated previously in the steps for conducting a Pareto analysis. With less than 30 occurrences it is possible the analysis will not reveal the observable truth of which categories represent the vital few and which the useful many. This can be due to the random chance of occurrences in the system under study. With less than 30 observations it is possible the most frequently occurring categories simply have not occurred by chance alone.

3) Improvement teams, at times, may find it useful to further subdivide or stratify the data they have collected for a Pareto analysis. For example, a school may want to create a Pareto analysis describing the reasons given for why students were absent from school. They may also want to further subdivide that analysis based on other factors they deem relevant for understanding their circumstance (i.e., subdivide by neighborhood or street, socio-economic status, ethnicity, grade level, etc.). In this way they may gain deeper detail about school absences and may uncover important sources of variation to target for learning or action during the improvement journey.

When visualizing the Pareto analysis, teams using further stratification may choose to develop some small multiples or aside by side view of the data. Alternatively, they may create stacked bars within the original analysis to demonstrate important learning. Another way they might visualize the data is to place bars side by side on the Pareto chart, with each category subdivided by the factor of interest.

4) Like the idea of stratification when using Pareto analysis, is the technique of narrowing the focus of investigation using a Macro to Micro approach. In this circumstance a team might perform a Pareto analysis and then select the most commonly occurring category from that analysis to explore further. Using alternative categories, they may perform a second Pareto analysis on just the most frequently occurring category from the first analysis. This second analysis may yield a single category worth digger deeper into, and so a third analysis might be performed on it.

From our example in special consideration 3: A team might learn the most common reason for school absence in the month of February given is illness. The team might then want to answer the question, "what type of illness is most commonly affecting our students?" Revisiting the data, they may perform a secondary Pareto analysis on type of illness learning for their students, the flu was the most frequent type of illness occurring. They may then generate a question, "For our students getting the flu, what quintile economically do they fall into?" A final Pareto analysis might reveal the majority of students contracting the flu fall into the bottom two quintiles. With this learning they might generate new questions, "Why do these students contract the flu?" or they might start the journey of intervention through an immunization program onsite targeting students in the bottom two quintiles. This type of Macro to Micro investigation can be a powerful mechanism for uncovering important sources of hidden variation in the system under study.

5) Improvement Teams should be very careful about applying Pareto analysis to unstable systems[4]. During periods of instability what can or should be generally expected from the performance of the system may be obscured or skewed by the presence of a factor that is not always at work on the system. Before performing a Pareto analysis on a given outcome, teams should first develop a Shewhart control chart to assess stability. If the chart indicates a stable state for the process or system, then proceeding with the Pareto analysis is recommended.

If there are observed periods of special cause indicated by the control chart, then it is recommended that the team remove data from the Pareto analysis collected during the period of instability. In this case stratifying the data and conducting two Pareto analyses is recommended. Creating one Pareto chart during the time of stability and the other during the time of special cause variation. This will prevent the data collected from the time of instability from masking or obscuring the data normally occurring during times of stability. A team can then take appropriate action on their findings (i.e., focusing efforts in the right place at the right time based on an objective view of performance).

6) One unique use of Pareto analysis is referred to as comparative Pareto analysis. This type of analysis is used when a team would like to examine and compare, side by side, two differing data sets using the same categories. This may occur in comparing the same data at two different points

---

[4] For a fuller treatment on assessing for stability the authors recommend multiple references explaining Shewhart's Theory of Common and Special Cause variation with the branch of statistics known as Statistical Process Control Methods. References include Economic Control of Quality of Manufactured Product by Walter Shewhart, The New Economics for Industry, Government and Education by W. Edwards Deming and The Health Care Data Guide: Learning from Data for Improvement by Lloyd Provost and Sandra Murray, among many others.

in time, such as before and after an intervention is put in place or it may occur for two different variables using the same categories at a single moment in time.

When developing a comparative Pareto analysis, the primary x and y axis should be held constant. The chart with the larger y-axis generally is used to benchmark the scale to be applied to both charts (however, if the charts have drastically different frequencies the y-axis may be adjusted for each individual graph). Importantly, for the x axis, the categories are held constant, so that it is possible for one of the two charts to "break" the rule of having the categorical data in descending order. This is allowed because the point of using the tool in this way is comparison of categories across variables.

An example below illustrates the use of comparative Pareto analysis. In this case data from the United States Department of Education is examined. On the left is a depiction of the number of children attending public schools in the year 2012. The category of race is used to develop the Pareto chart, and the data is order from greatest to least as would be expected. In the chart on the right, categories are held constant in their positions and the frequency of school expulsions is depicted. By looking at the two charts side by side it is immediately apparent students being expelled from school are not being expelled in an equitable way. If they were the two charts would both be ordered from greatest to least with each race displaying a frequency of expulsion equal to its representation in the total population of students. Instead the observation is Black and African American students are expelled at much higher rates than should be expected based on their representation in the population. In fact, they are being expelled from schools at a rate four times that of their Non-Hispanic White peers. This represents a deep inequity in the system of education in the United States that is recognized but that the country has yet failed to address.

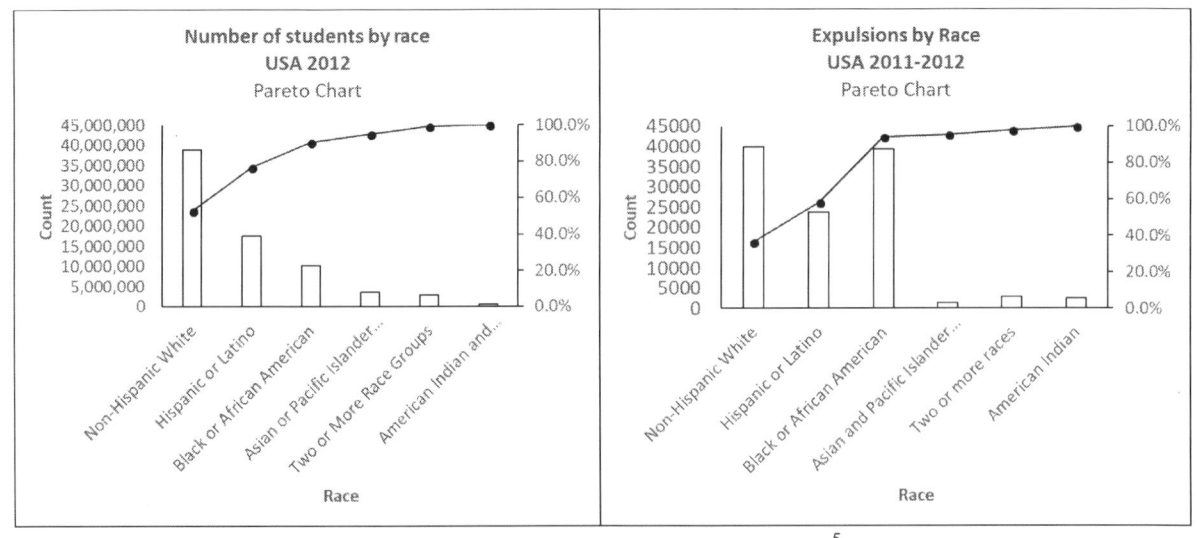

Source: United States Department of Education[5]

7) Another consideration in the use of Pareto analysis is in the development of weighted Pareto charts. These can be created when there are more opportunities for one category to occur than another. Remember the example from above of ibuprofen and insulin: In this case a weighted Pareto analysis may be appropriate as ibuprofen is prescribed and dispensed with much greater

---

[5] **Data Source:** U.S. Department of Education. Civil rights data collection: 2011-12 and 2013-14 Discipline Estimations by Discipline Type. Available at: https://ocrdata.ed.gov/StateNationalEstimations

frequency than insulin. To see them equivalently on the same Pareto chart, considering their area of opportunity (frequency of dispensing) would be very important.

To effectively develop a weighted Pareto chart the data collected must be transformed in some way. Assigning of weights can be done by multiplying the value for each category by the weight assigned to the category. Usually, the weight is determined using a measure of importance, cost, or the area of opportunity. In the case of cost (money) or area of opportunity calculating the weighted value of each category can be fairly straight forward. However, other attributes, such as importance, may be more qualitative in nature. To calculate a weighted value, it is recommended that the teamwork with a subject matter expert to develop an importance scale that can then be applied to each category. A simple formula for calculating weighted scores is presented below:

$$\text{Weighted Score} = \text{Frequency} \times \text{Weight}$$

Example:

Category	Frequency Count	Weight (importance)	Weighted Score
Ibuprofen	55	1	55
Insulin	2	100	200

In the example above a wrong dose for insulin is weighted as 100 times more important than a wrong dose of ibuprofen. Though insulin wrong dosing is infrequent when compared with ibuprofen wrong dosing, it is weighted score is larger.

8) Categorical importance is the final consideration when using Pareto analysis. While some categories will emerge as the vital few from the perspective of frequency of occurrence, they may not be the most important categories to attend to or prevent in the future. Pareto analysis should always be partnered with subject matter expertise for precisely this reason. Teams using Pareto should be careful to examine their analysis with a subject matter expert prior to acting on the system.

For example, a hospital improvement team might discover through Pareto analysis that the most commonly occurring medication error they observe is related to wrong dosing of ibuprofen. While this is a very important finding, there might be a lesser occurring or rarely occurring error that is more important: wrong dosing of insulin. Without a subject matter expert looking at the data, the team might act on ibuprofen and fail to act on insulin errors which often have profound and tragic consequences.

References and Further Reading

- Juran, Joseph M. Quality Control Handbook. (3rd Edition) New York: McGraw Hill. 1979
- Koch, Richard J. The 80/20 Principle. (3rd Edition) New York: Double Day Publishing. 2008
- Tague, Nancy R. The Quality Toolbox. (2nd Edition) Milwaukee: American Society for Quality, Quality Press. 2015
- Associates in Process Improvement. The Improvement Handbook. Austin: Associates in Process Improvement. 2007
- Ishikawa, Koru. Guide to Quality Control. Japan: Asian Productivity Organization. 1976

The Run Chart

Other Names: Run sequence plot

Conceptual Links:

- System of Profound Knowledge: Understanding Variation
- 6 Principles: Focus on variation in performance, We cannot improve at scale what we cannot measure

Purpose

Ott defined the purpose of the run chart as:

1) To test the hypothesis that the data represent random variation from stable sources.
2) To infer the nature of the source(s) responsible for any non-randomness (from the data pattern), that is, to infer previously unsuspected hypotheses.

And while his language is highly technical, when translated, the concept is simple and clear: The run chart exists to help people to understand whether the data presented displays random variation or non-random variation. In the case of the latter, the visualization of the data assists people to hypothesize why the data presented may be displaying non-random variation. It causes teams to look at their data and ask the question, "Why are we seeing what we are seeing?"

There are three reasons why teams use run charts:

1) To build and understanding of variation in the performance of a measure.
2) To detect when a change is occurring in the performance of a measure (presence of non-random variation).
3) To assist in the management of a process or system by creating a window into the regular performance of a measure.

When to use a run chart

Teams should consider displaying their data on a run chart when:

- They are collecting time series or sequentially ordered data of some type, and
- They have at least one data point collected

In addition to these, improvement teams often find value in using run charts when:

- They have a need to display their data to make performance visible (i.e., not in tabular format, rather graphical format) for themselves and various other stakeholders.
- There is a need to assess whether a change made to the system has resulted in a change in performance. Most teams will want to be able to detect when the changes they are making result in the improvement they expect or desire.
- There is a desire to determine whether a performance change has been sustained by the process or system (i.e., in the case of sustained shift in performance that indicates a new level of performance that would be predicted into the future).

Elements of a run chart

The run chart is primarily a visual tool used to assist in the analysis and interpretation of time series and/or sequentially collected data. Run charts can be distinguished from more simple line graphs by the presence of a medial line. Important characteristics that ease the reading and interpretation of run charts are:

- X-axis (horizontal axis) – is ordered sequentially, most often by time (i.e., shift, day, week, month, etc.)
- Y-axis (vertical axis) – plots the measure of interest
- Data points – data points are emphasized on the run chart, with the line connecting them being optional or displayed minimally.[53]
- After 10 sub-groups (data points) are plotted, a run chart plots the median value of data points. Often teams extend a baseline median value into the future as a point of comparison to assist in the detection of changes in performance.[54]
- Labeling – Run charts should be well labeled, including: a label to describe the x-axis, a label to describe the measure of interest displayed on the y-axis, a chart title that clearly and concisely communicates to readers what this chart is created to display, as well as what type of chart it is (i.e., a run chart).
- Annotations – Run charts, like most other visual displays of data, benefit greatly through the addition of words, annotations of specific events, changes, or efforts made to/on the system. For run charts this is especially important as linking a change made in practice (whether policy, process, or behavioral) to a change in performance at a specific moment in time can greatly increase a team's degree of belief that the change made resulted in the performance observed.[55]

---

[53] The presence of a line connecting data points suggests performance between connected data points. As a visual cue, it suggests that performance did not vary greatly during the time between data points. For many measures, because data is sampled, rather than fully enumerative, it is not possible to say this is true. As a result, the line connecting data points can be deceptive (i.e., a large spike in performance in either direction could have occurred between samples and gone unnoticed). For this reason, teams may choose to deemphasize the line by keeping it to a minimal thickness in comparison to the data points (where the actual information collected is contained) but maintaining it to ease the eye across the chart for readers. Other teams may choose to exclude it completely.

[54] See section on How to Use Run Charts in Practice below for more guidance on how to do this.

[55] This is important during the trying of ideas in practice (i.e., running of PDSA cycles) as well as when communicating the story of improvement. Note: not all changes to the system result in immediate change to the performance of the run chart, as is the case in the example, change in performance sometimes lags as changes to the system take time to accumulate or generate impact.

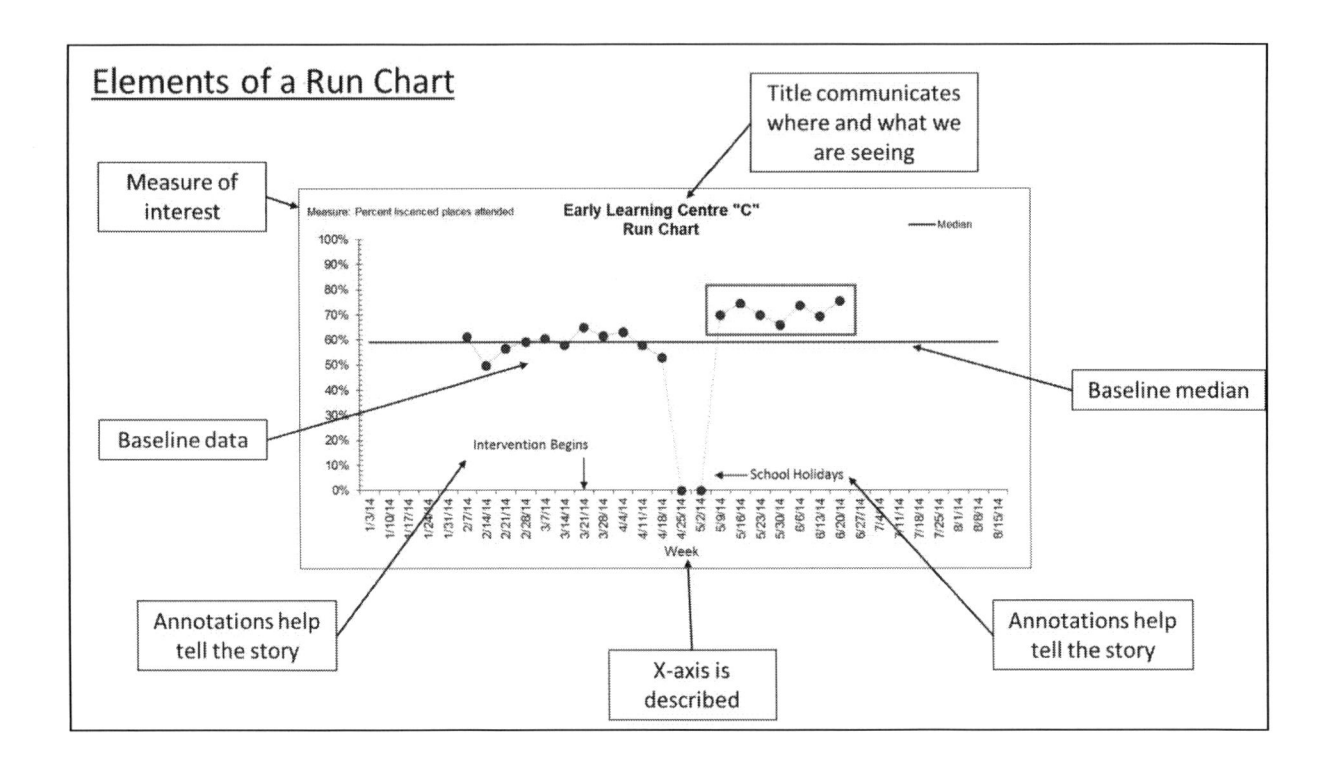

Elements of a Run Chart

- Measure of interest
- Title communicates where and what we are seeing
- Baseline data
- Baseline median
- Annotations help tell the story
- X-axis is described
- Annotations help tell the story

Early Learning Centre "C" Run Chart — Measure: Percent liscenced places attended; Intervention Begins; School Holidays

How to create a run chart

Seven steps for constructing a run chart:

1) Development of a run chart should only be undertaken when an improvement team has a learning question which is best answered by time series or sequentially collected data. Examples of learning questions include:
   a. How many families are we serving per day (or week, or month)?
   b. How many times do I reinforce positive behaviors in my classroom per class?
   c. How many PDSA cycles are we as a network completing each week?
   d. What is the average patient satisfaction score per week?
   e. What percent of my city's homeless population can be considered chronically homeless, measured monthly?

2) Develop the scale for the x-axis (horizontal axis). This will largely depend on the frequency with which the improvement team collects data, or the frequency with which an improvement team would like the data to be summarized; an improvement team might collect data daily but wishes to look at a weekly summary statistic of performance. An example might be daily attendance summarizes as average daily attendance per week and plotted weekly on a run chart. The subgroups chosen will almost always be a measure of time (day, week, month, etc.) or the sequence with which data was collected (i.e., event 1, event 2, event 3, etc.).

3) Develop the scale for the y-axis (vertical axis). The scale of the Y-axis will depend on the data collected but good visual display of information practices should be adhered to: approximately one third of the space of the chart above and below the plotted data points should be left as white space to avoid distorting the interpretation of the data, when graphing percent data the y-axis should, in most cases start at 0% and should not ever exceed 100% (in some cases where most data values fall

near an extreme (0% or 100%) it acceptable to modify the y-axis to meet good visual display recommendations).[56]

4) Plot the data values (points) for each subgroup for which data was collected. If preferred, add a data line to connect the data points displayed.

5) Calculate and place a median on the run chart. In most cases this should be done only when 10 or more data points have been collected and plotted on the run chart. It is also recommended whenever possible the improvement team creating the chart plot, freeze and extend a baseline median to use as a prediction and point of comparison for data collected during the improvement phase of the work.[57]

6) Label the run chart effectively, including labels for the title, x-axis, and y-axis, median.

7) Annotate the run chart with any additional information that might help to tell the story of performance, change and/or improvement. Adding words to run charts (all charts in general) is a recommended practice to assist in telling the performance story.

It should be noted that many software programs can now make run charts at the click of a button. While this can ease the burden of their creation there are some cautions that improvement teams should be aware of:

- Ensure the run chart is scaled appropriately
- Ensure the median reflects the baseline performance, rather than all the data. It is not uncommon for software programs to update the median with the addition of new data points collected and plotted on the run chart. With a constantly updated, or evolving median, it can be difficult for teams to "see" a performance change, as the data indicating a performance change will also be influencing the calculation of the median being plotted.[58]
- In using software to quickly generate run charts improvement teams will still need to engage in careful labeling and annotation of the charts they produce to ensure they are read accurately and retain clarity.

How to use a run chart in practice

The primary reason improvement teams choose to use run charts is to answer one of the three fundamental questions asked during an improvement journey, "How will we know that a change is an improvement?"[59] To answer the question effectively two types of knowledge are necessary. One type of knowledge assisting improvement teams is knowledge of the system and has a pragmatic consideration. This type of knowledge looks at the performance of a measure (changing or unchanged) and asks/answers whether the performance is "good," "meaningful," "important," or "significant" in some way to leadership or other stakeholders on the system.

---

[56] See Section 6: Visualizing Quantitative Information.
[57] See section on How to Use Run Charts in Practice below for more information on using medians effectively to predict future performance and ascertain when changes in performance occur.
[58] See the section on How to Use Run Charts in Practice below for more information on using medians to understand when a change in performance of a measure has occurred.
[59] The two other question from the Model for Improvement being: "What are we trying to accomplish?" and "What changes can we make that will result in improvement?"

The other type of knowledge is statistical knowledge. Applying statistical knowledge to run charts helps us to answer the question, "Is the observed variation in the data presented purely random or does it display non-random variation in performance?" If the answer is, "the chart displays non-random variation," then a change in performance of some type is detected. If the chart displays only random variation, then the assumption is there is no detectable change in performance using this tool. There are four rules improvement teams can apply to run charts to help them discover the presence or absence of non-random variation.

Four rules for detecting non-random variation on a run chart

1) Shift Rule
2) Trend Rule
3) Run Rule
4) Astronomical Values

Rule One: Shift

The presence of a shift in the data is the first circumstance in which there is the detection of non-random variation. This is referred to as the Shift rule as there has been a shift in the performance of the measure either above or below the median value of the data presented. This occurs when six or more consecutive data values fall above the median or below the median (see examples below). The probability of six data values falling consecutively above, or below, the median is 0.015. It is a very rare occurrence.[60]

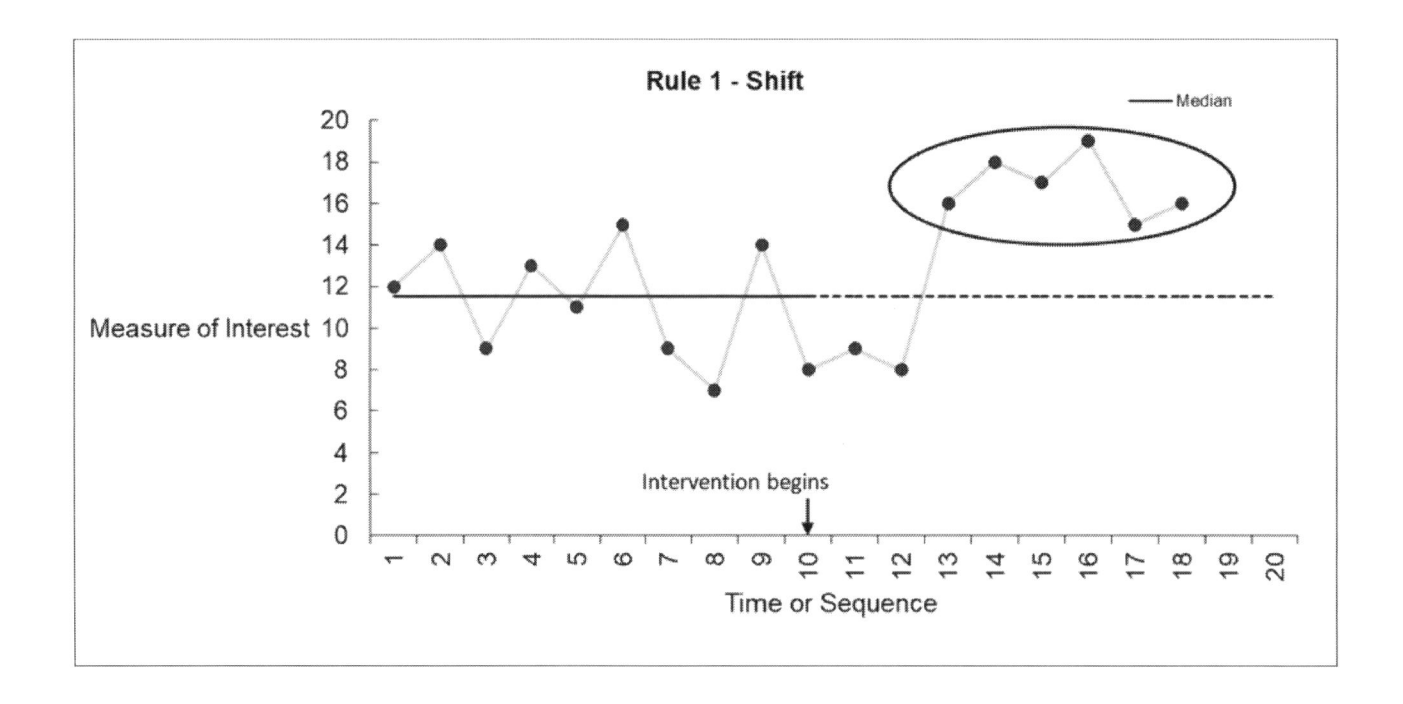

---

[60] See Ott, as well as Provost and Murray for more on calculating the probability of occurrence of the rules presented here.

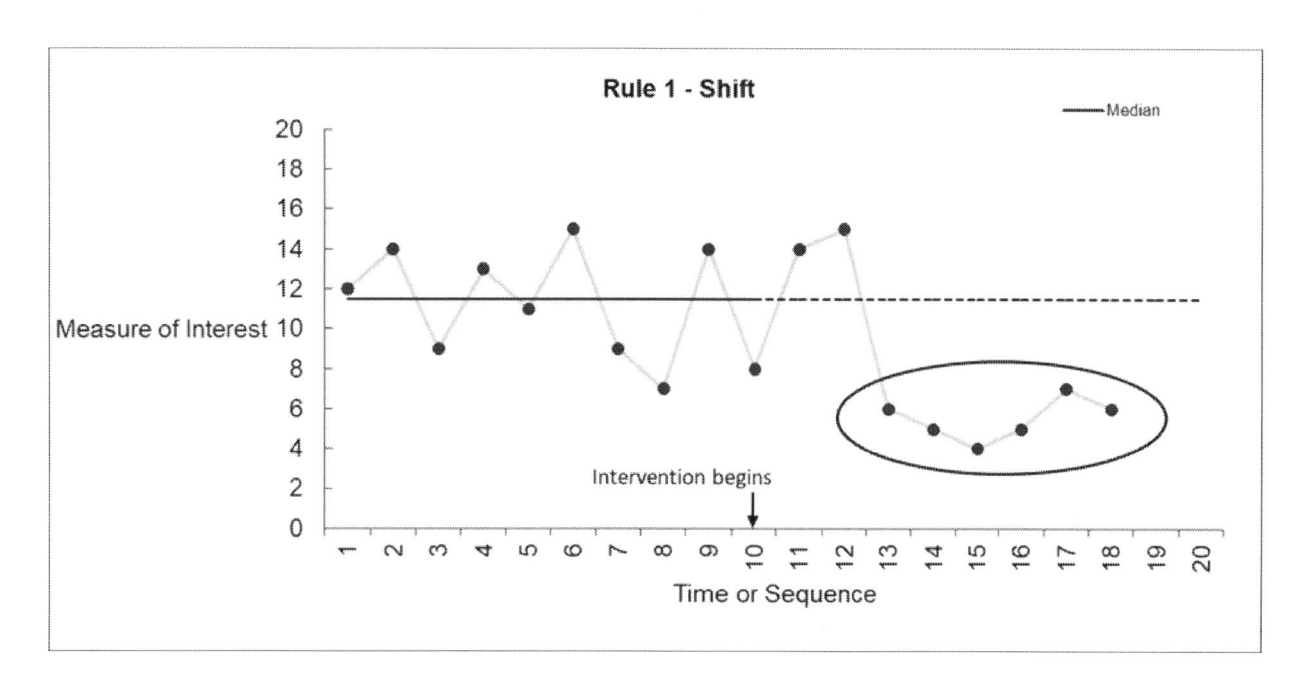

[Chart: Rule 1 - Shift, showing data points over time 1-20 with intervention beginning at point 10, and six consecutive points below the median circled after intervention]

A shift can occur during the baseline data collection period (see below) or during the intervention period (see examples above). Most improvement teams will be looking for (hoping for) a shift in the performance of their outcome measure, and so this rule takes on special significance for teams looking to demonstrate the changes they have made, have resulted in improvement to the process or system under study. Importantly, shifts can be sustained or not sustained. Achievement of six consecutive data points above or below the median indicates a shift, but a shift is not considered sustained until 10 or more data points are achieved.[61]

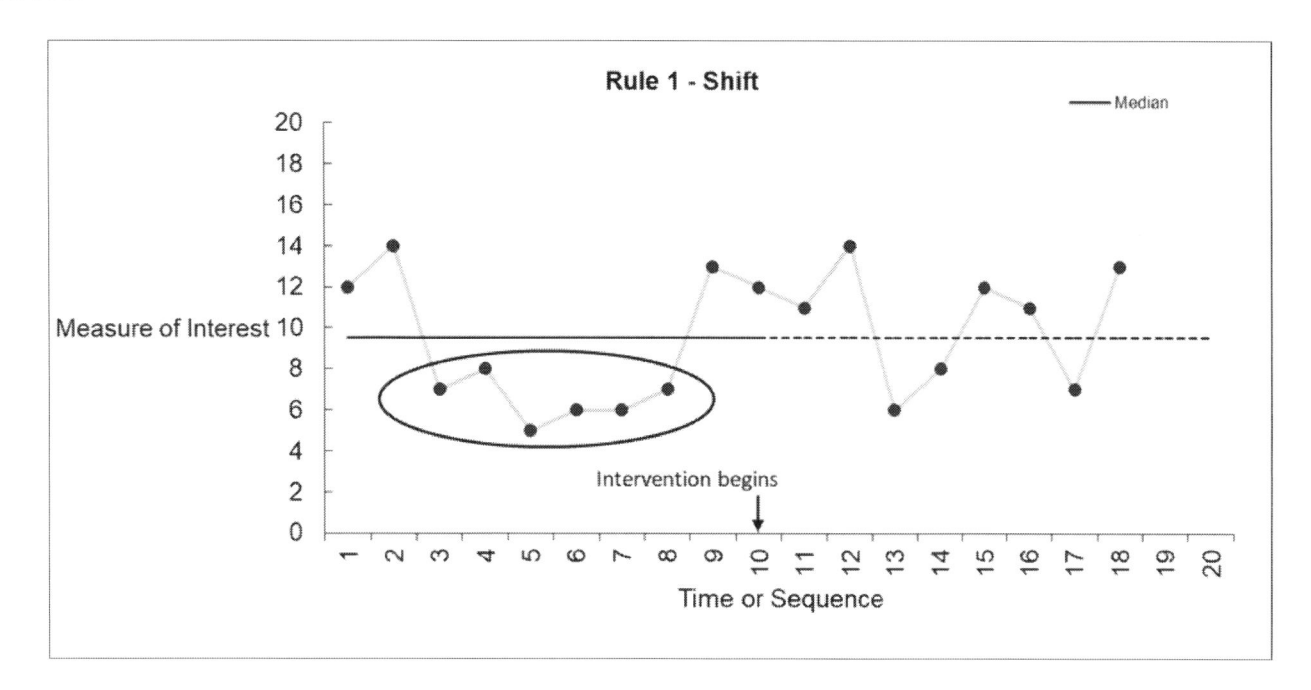

[Chart: Rule 1 - Shift, showing data points over time 1-20 with intervention beginning at point 10, and six consecutive points below the median circled during the baseline period]

---

[61] Note that 10 data points is the recommendation given by Ott, as well as Provost and Murray, for the calculation of a useful median. There is some debate as to when sustainability occurs in the performance of a measure displaying a shift and the application of subject matter knowledge should be included in the discussion. For example: 10 data points in a measure captured daily may feel less sustained than a measure captured weekly or even one captured monthly. The nature, frequency and volume of data collected should be considered in a conversation about sustainability.

In some circumstances, data points can fall directly on the median. In these cases, the data points falling directly on the median do not count toward the presence of a shift, nor do they count against the presence of a shift (they do not break a shift). They should be ignored and the count of data for a shift should continue after them. See the example below for a visual picture of this phenomenon.

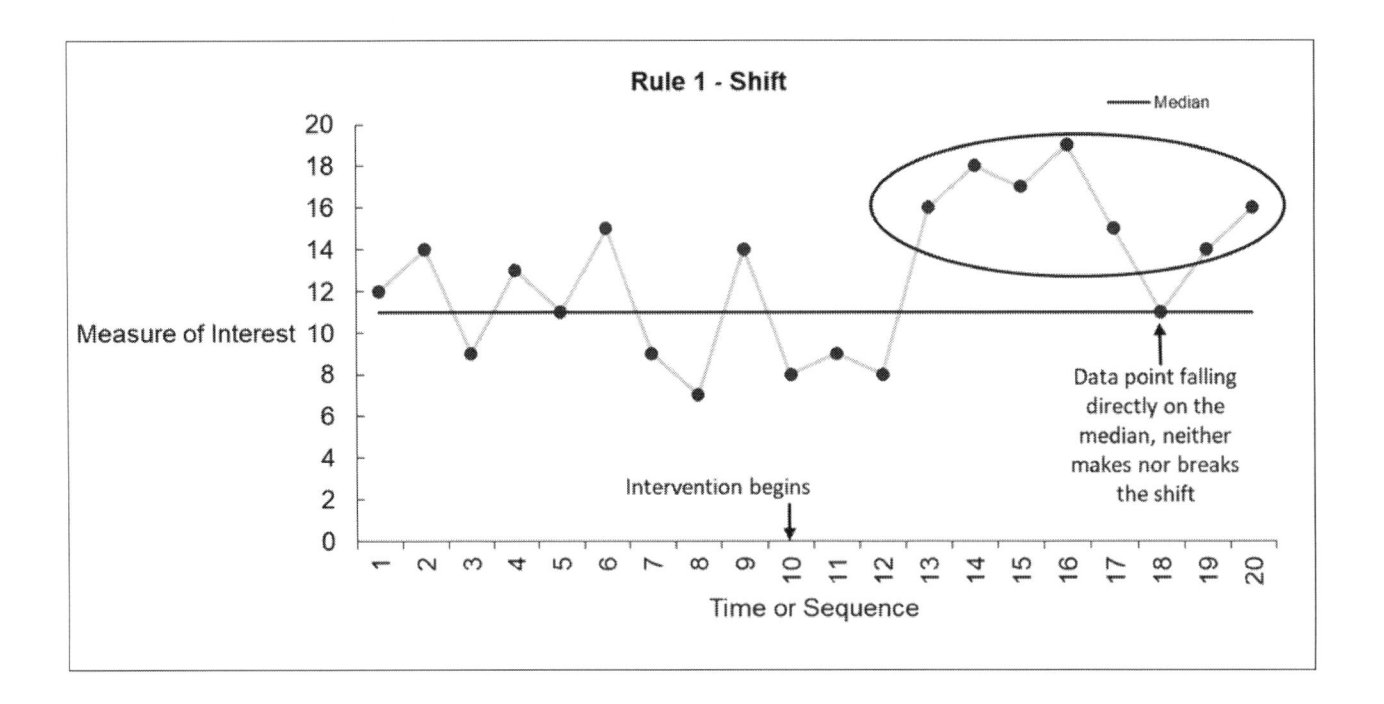

Rule 1 - Shift

(Chart showing Measure of Interest over Time or Sequence 1–20, with median line at 11, intervention begins around point 10, and a circled shift of points above the median from points 13–20; annotation indicates "Data point falling directly on the median, neither makes nor breaks the shift")

Rule Two: Trend

The presence of a trend in the data is the second circumstance in which there is the detection of non-random variation. This is referred to as the Trend rule and occurs when five or more consecutive data values are all increasing or all decreasing (see examples below). The trend rule does not depend on the presence of a median as a point of comparison and the occurrence of five or more consecutive values running up or down is estimated at less 0.05.[62]

---

[62] This probability can change based on the total number of subgroups plotted, see Ott for more information on calculating this probability. "It is easy to see and remember that a run up of length six or seven is quite unusual for sets of data even as large as k=200. Even a run of five may warrant investigating," Ott, 1975.

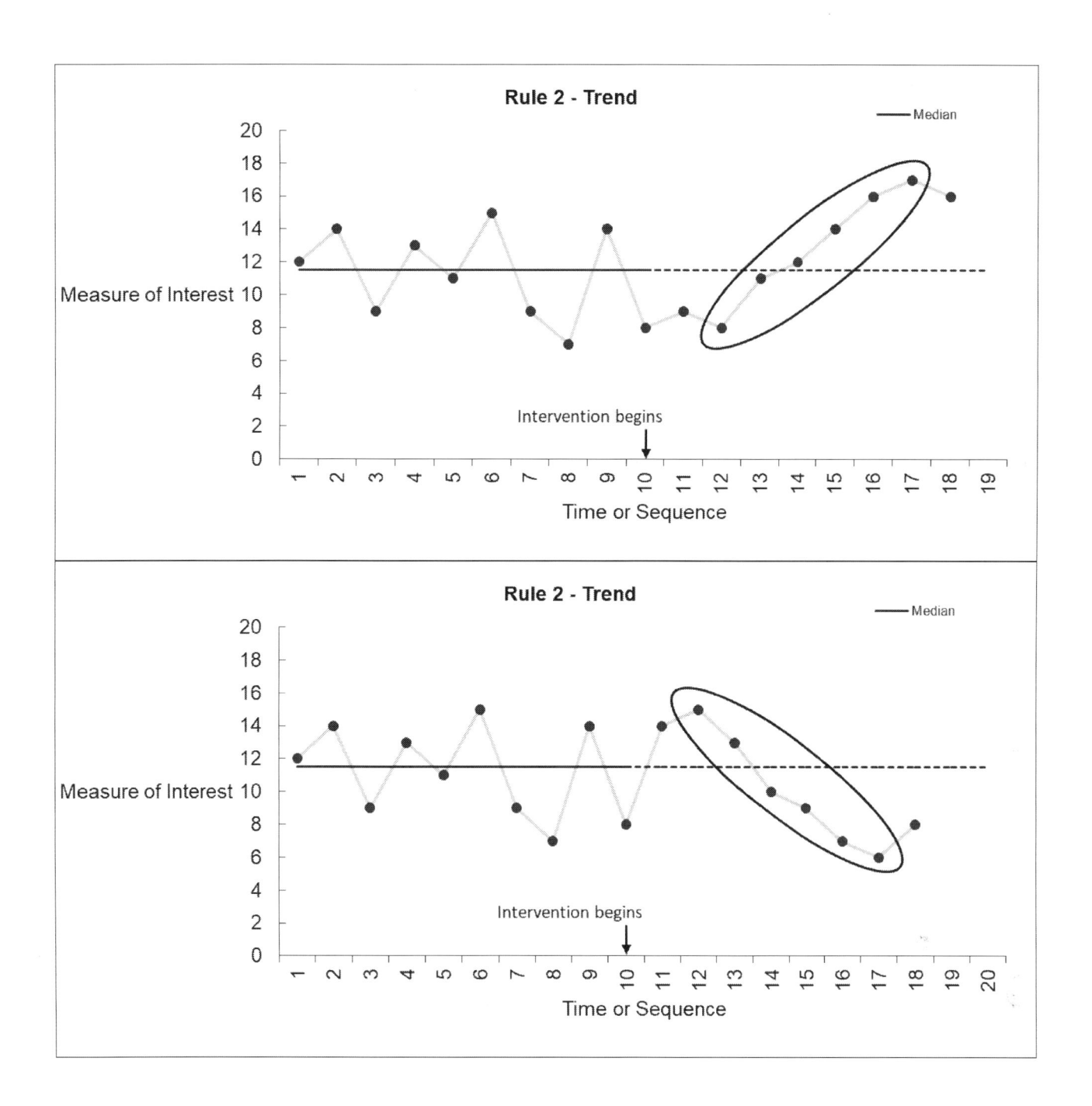

In some circumstances it is possible for two or more consecutive values to have exactly the same value. In these cases, the data points, having the same value, falling consecutively neither make nor break the trend. The first of these data points can count toward the trend but subsequent data points of exactly the same value should be ignored. The count toward a trend picks up after these data points as is illustrated below. In this case the first three data points are a part of the trend, the fourth data point of equal value to the third is ignored, and fifth, sixth and seventh data points continue in the making of the trend.

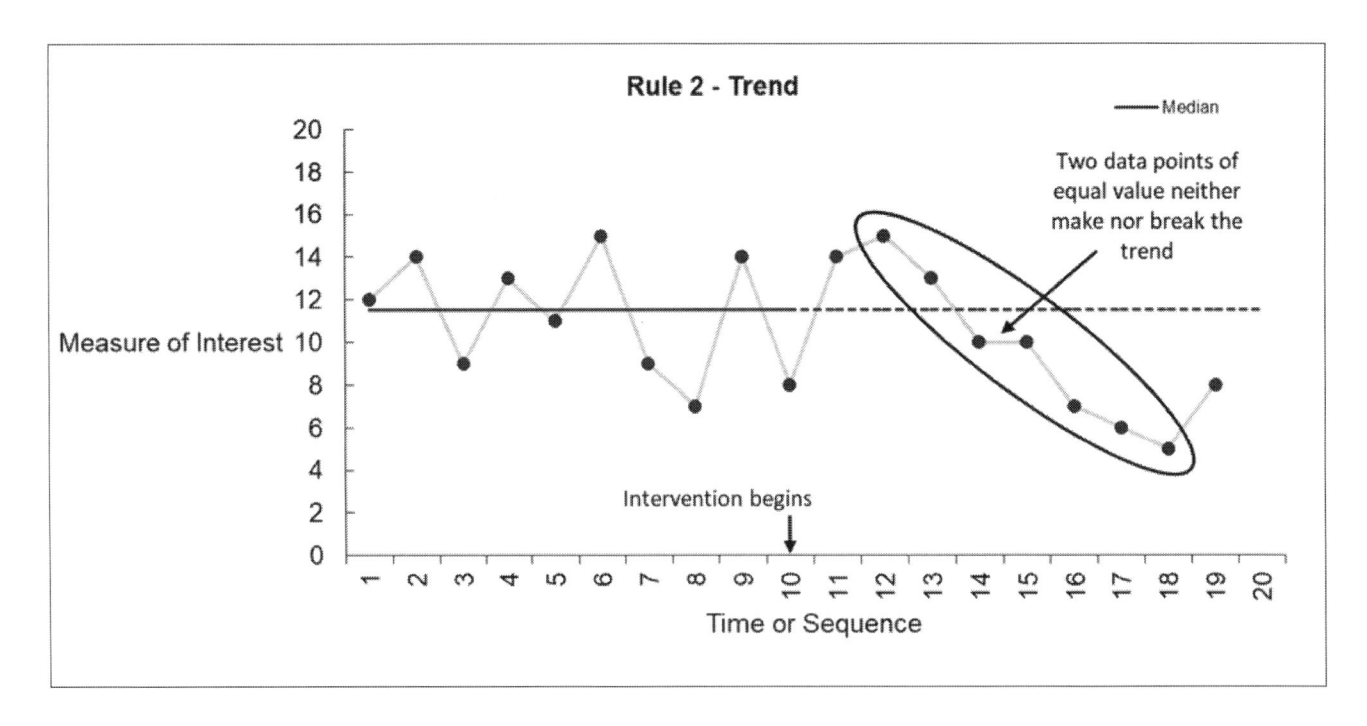

Rule Three: Too many or too few runs

The presence of too many or too few runs about the median in the presented data is the third circumstance in which there is the detection of non-random variation. This is referred to as the Run rule. To effectively use this rule teams, need two things, knowledge of what a run is and given the number of data points, knowledge of how many runs might be expected given a random distribution of the data about the median.

A run is defined as consecutive data points on one single side of the median. Each time the data line crosses the median, or each time a data point falls on the opposite side of the median as compared to the previous data point, a new run is begun. If a data point falls exactly on the median, that point does not break the run, meaning it does not start a new run nor is it included in the data point count for an existing run. It is ignored. In the example below each of the runs is encircled.

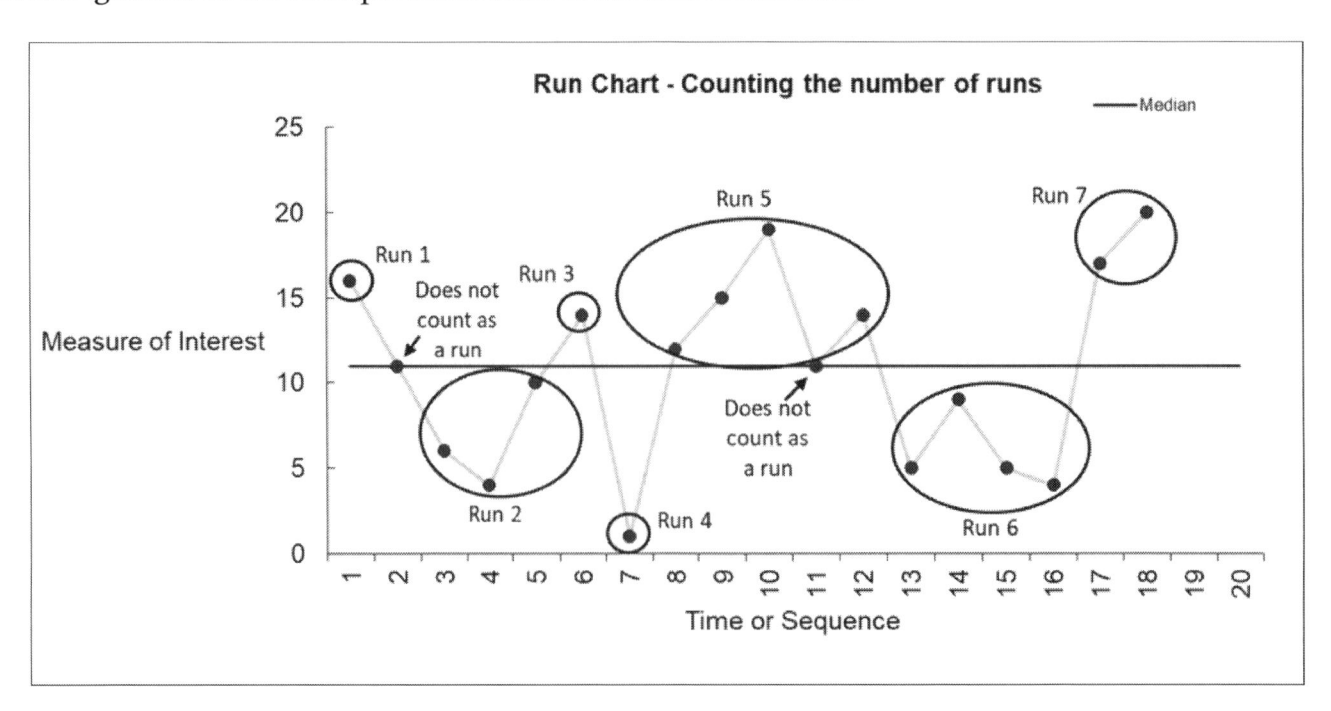

With knowledge of what a run is, it is rather easy for an individual or improvement team to count the total number of runs present on a given chart. "We usually count the number (of runs) directly from the figure once the once the median line has been drawn," Ott, 1975.

To understand if a team is seeing more than the expected number of runs or less than the expected number of runs it is useful to use the table below. The first column describes the total number of data points displayed, in the second column is the minimum number of runs needed to describe the presence of only random variation, while the third column displays the maximum number of runs allowed to describe the presence of random variation.[63]

Total count of number of data points displayed on the run chart (excluding any data points falling exactly on the median)	Minimum number of runs needed for random variation (if there are fewer than this number, non-random variation is detected)	Maximum number of runs allowed for random variation (if there are more than this number, non-random variation is detected)
10	3	9
11	3	10
12	3	11
13	4	11
14	4	12
15	5	12
16	5	13
17	5	13
18	6	14
19	6	15
20	6	16
21	7	16
22	7	17
23	7	17
24	8	18
25	8	18
26	9	19
27	10	19
28	10	20
29	10	20
30	11	21

Values described by Swed and Eisenhart, 1943, summarized by both Ott, 1975 and Provost and Murray, 2011

Examples of too many and too few runs are provided below. Too many runs are sometimes referred to as a sawtooth pattern and often is an indication the data should be stratified in some way. For example, the data being plotted may be coming from two different shifts. Too few runs are also not uncommon when

---

[63] Swed and Eisenhart calculated these probabilities at multiple levels. Those shown in the table here reflect a probability on each side of 0.05. There is a chance the total number of runs may not achieve the minimum or exceed the maximum by chance alone, but the chances of that are small, set at the 0.05 level.

the data follows a predictable pattern in performance. For example, discharges from a hospital generally follow this pattern, with far fewer discharges happening on weekends than happen on weekdays.

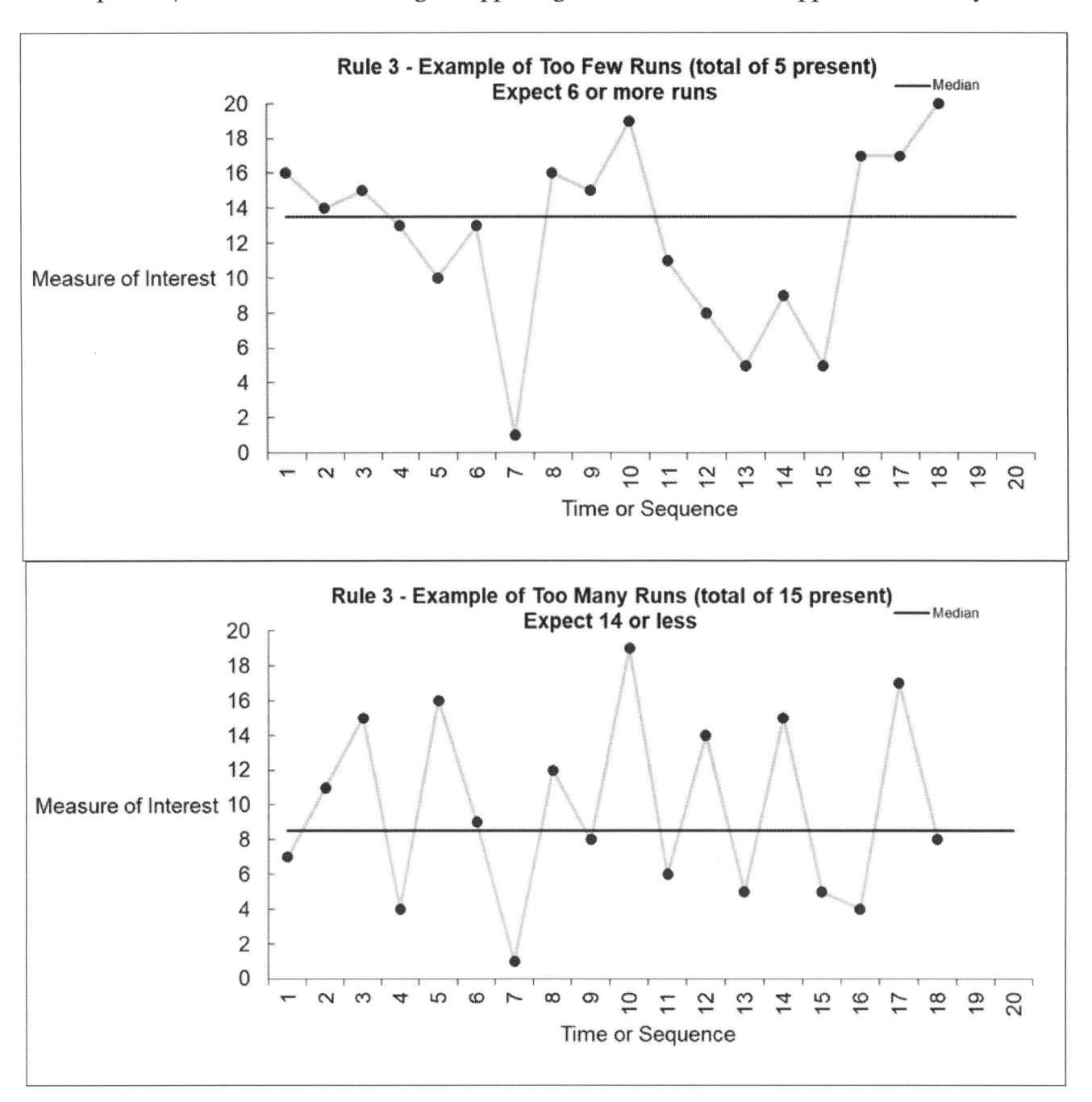

Rule 3 - Example of Too Few Runs (total of 5 present) Expect 6 or more runs

Rule 3 - Example of Too Many Runs (total of 15 present) Expect 14 or less

These two charts are good examples of Rule 3 in practice. Improvement teams looking at them and using the table provided are easily able to see that in each case, non-random variation is detected. The next step for a team would be to investigate what the cause of the non-random variation might be.

Rule 4: Astronomical value

The presence of an Astronomical value in the data is the fourth circumstance in which there is the detection of non-random variation. This is referred to as the Astronomical Value rule and is not based on a calculation of probability (see examples below). It is the subjective application of subject matter expertise to the data presented. Improvement teams will find this rule helpful when a single data value is blatantly, or obviously different, from the performance of the rest of the data points plotted. When such a data point exists, improvement teams should seek out an explanation for what happened to generate this one different level of performance. Because of the subjective nature of this rule there may be times when team members, or stakeholders disagree as to whether a single value is truly astronomical. In those circumstances, it is advisable to move the data from a run chart to a Shewhart control chart where an upper or lower limit may assist the improvement team in deciding if spending resources to learn why a data value is very high or very low is worth the investment.

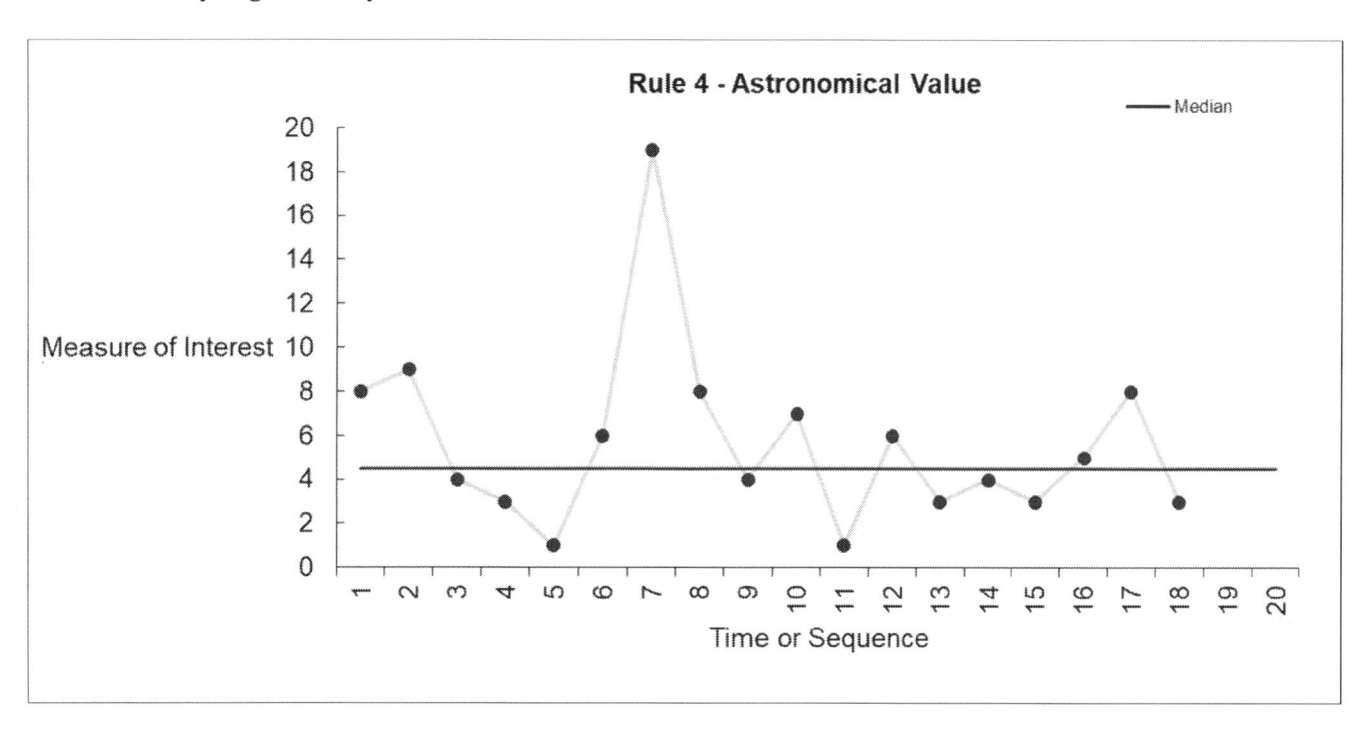

Predicting future performance and detecting change as it occurs

Improvement teams are interested to know when the changes they have made have resulted in improvement to the process or system under study. When using a Run chart to accomplish this learning, best practice is to collect enough baseline data (ideally 10 or more data points) and to calculate and display a baseline median, before any changes are made to the system. Once calculated, the baseline median is "frozen" (i.e., new data, collected in the future is not used to update the calculation of the median) and the median is extended into the future. In this way the baseline median becomes a prediction of future performance.

The prediction states, if there is no change in the performance of the system then future data points collected and plotted will be distributed randomly around the existing median (i.e., an improvement team will not observe any of the four rules in the data when there is no change to the system). The baseline median, as a prediction, now becomes a point of comparison; if one or more of the four rules for detecting non-random variation manifests as new data points are collected and plotted then the improvement team has evidence of change in the system. This is using the median prospectively as a point of prediction.

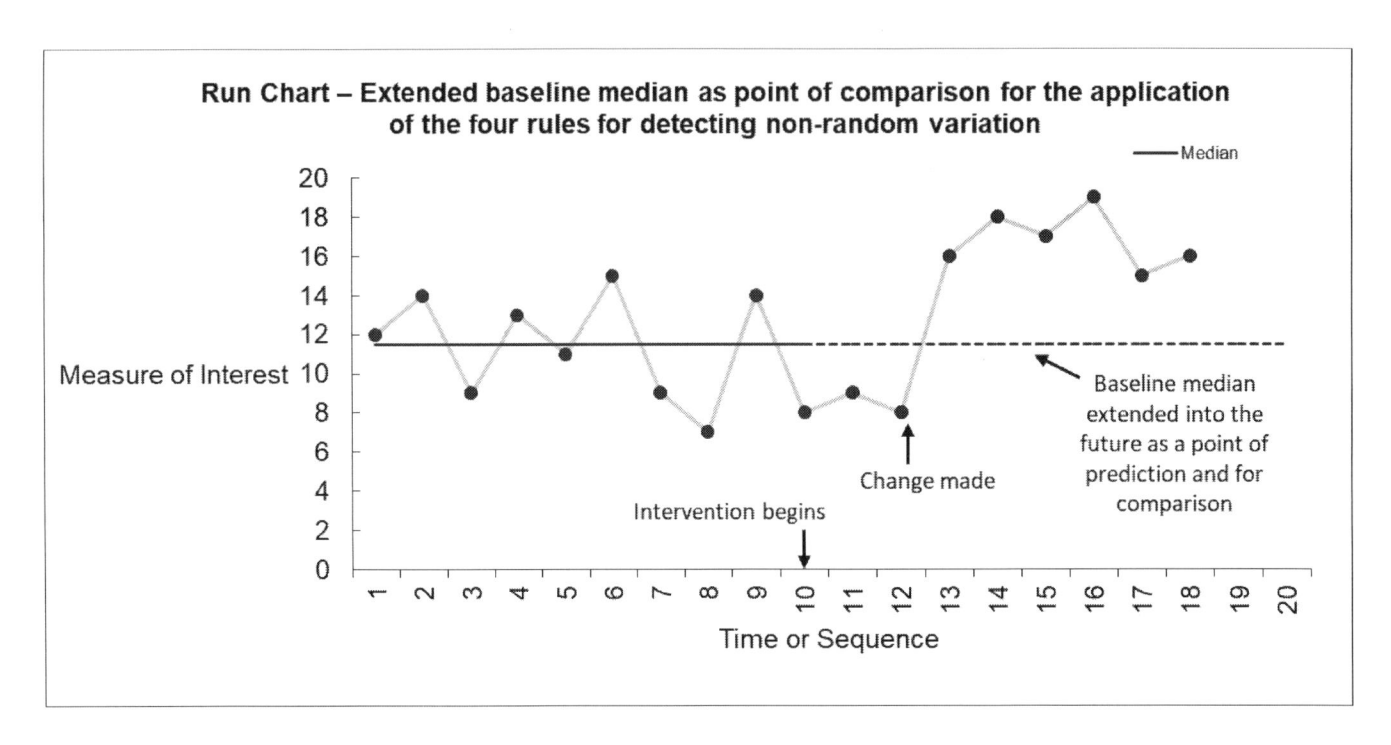

Run Chart – Extended baseline median as point of comparison for the application of the four rules for detecting non-random variation

[Run chart showing Measure of Interest (0–20) vs Time or Sequence (1–20). Data points: 12, 14, 9, 13, 11, 15, 9, 7, 14, 8, 9, 8, 16, 18, 17, 19, 15, 16. Median line at approximately 11.5. Annotations: "Intervention begins" at point 10, "Change made" at point 12, and "Baseline median extended into the future as a point of prediction and for comparison" shown as a dashed line extending the median.]

In an ideal setting, the change observed is the result of actions taken by the improvement team to improve the system and is linked in time to the performance change. Sometimes though, change is detected that is not in the direction of interest, or for which causes are unknown. In these circumstances, improvement teams are advised to investigate, speak with people who work day-to-day in the system to learn what changes might be occurring in practice (apply subject matter expertise).

Phasing Run charts - Updating our understanding of predicted performance

As improvement teams begin to observe change in performance using the four rules, their baseline data and median no longer serve as accurate predictions of what performance will likely look like in the future. A question emerges, "when should we recalculate the median?" or "when should we calculate a new median?" and "using what data?" On run charts, the calculation and placement of a new median is referred to as phasing the data, which each phase representing a period of time or a sequence in the data that displays random variation. Improvement teams choose to phase their data for many different reasons (not all of which are good practice), but the main reason to phase the data on a run chart is to achieve an accurate prediction of future performance so the improvement team can continue to apply the four rules for the detection of change.

If there were only one recommendation to give about when to re-phase the data on a run chart it would be: to only re-phase the data when the data indicates a sustained change in performance. Teams should not begin new phases simply because:

- The start of a new year, or new fiscal year: Many improvement teams, and managers are tempted to add a new median when starting a new fiscal or annual cycle, but from the perspective of the system, no real change in how things are done has been accomplished.
- The team has started an intervention: It may be a good time to freeze the baseline but remember not every change is an improvement and simply changing how the system works does not mean there will be a change in performance.

Only a sustained change in performance should lead to the creation of a new phase and new median on a run chart.

Coaching notes

Coaches working with improvement teams can be on the lookout for some predictable missteps teams make when applying and using run charts.

1) Some teams when creating run charts may be prone to applying a median too early (i.e., prior to collecting and plotting data points). In such circumstances it is useful for the coach to facilitate a data conversation, investigating why a team is wanting to calculate the median early in the data collection process. Helping teams to understand how much data is needed to create a useful run chart, and some of the pitfalls associated with applying the probability-based rules when little data has been collected can assist teams to make good choices when using a run chart.

2) Coaches may find it helpful to be on the lookout for teams who do not freeze a median representing baseline performance. Most software packages that create run charts will update the median presented whenever new data is added to the database (run chart). The addition of new data will cause a recalculation of the median, and in some circumstances may cause the median to move. Improvement teams may wonder why they are not detecting perceived changes in performances in such instances. Coaches can be on the lookout and help ensure that baseline medians are frozen and extended into the future as a point of comparison. This will help improvement teams to avoid experiencing a bouncing around effect that can sometimes occur when the median is continuously updated.

3) Improvement Teams tend to want to re-phase their data whenever they make a change in system. It is important for coaches to help improvement teams to understand that not all changes in practice result in changes in performance. As a result, coaches need to be prepared to counsel improvement teams away from re-phasing their run charts, until the run chart objectively (empirically), demonstrates a sustained changed in performance. See the section above on sustaining shifts in performance for more information on this topic. Generally speaking, good counsel is, "we don't tell the data when it has changed, rather we wait to allow it to speak for itself and tell us when its performance has changed, then and only then do we rephrase our data. All other changes, that may not result in performance change, can be annotated on the chart without rephrasing the data."

History

Plotting sequential data, particularly data that unfolds over time was first made popular by William Playfair, the Scottish political economist, during the 1700s. When comparing a static bar chart depicting data on trade (imports and exports to and from different countries with Scotland) to data plotted over time Playfair said:

"This Chart *(static bar chart)* is different from the others in principle *(time series charts)*, as it does not comprehend any portion of time, and it is much inferior in utility to those that do; for though it gives the extent of the different branches of trade, it does not compare the same branch of commerce with itself at different periods; nor does it imprint upon the mind that distinct idea, in doing which, the chief advantage of Charts consists: for as it wants the dimension that is formed by duration, there is no shape given to the quantities." *The Commercial and Political Atlas*, 1786 *(parentheses added)*

Since Playfair, people (economists, statisticians, etc.) seeking to tell a compelling story using data have often employed line charts to do so. In 1920s, Walter Shewhart, took the visualization of data plotted sequentially to a new level, combining both a statistical (probability based) and value-based analysis to these charts (known today as Shewhart control charts) and using them to assist in the management of complex manufacturing systems.

The Run chart in its current form finds its roots in the work of an American statistician named Ellis Ott. In his book, *Process Quality Control: Troubleshooting and Interpretation of Sata,* Ott explicates the use of the Run chart, defining the probability-based rules for interpreting Run charts using a statistical lens of understanding the risk of misidentifying when data indicates a change in performance. His rules for the detection of non-random variation still serve in many industries applying run charts today.

In the social sector (healthcare, education, the extension of various social services) the use and promotion of Run charts has been greatly aided by modern publication and further explication of Ott's original work. *The Health Care Data Guide*, published in 2011, by Lloyd Provost and Sandy Murray (previously available in draft form for many years prior) made available to a wide audience how to use the tool in practice and is still the excellent resource on understanding and using the tool in practice today.

Special considerations

When developing and using a Run chart there are several important considerations to be aware of and to apply in practice. Each of these is described and, in some circumstances, further study is recommended.

1) Minimum number of subgroups to develop a median: While a run chart can be started with as little as a single data point, it is recommended a median not be used for the detection on non-random variation until a minimum of 10 data points (sub-groups) has been collected and plotted. In many circumstances, this may mean waiting to start interventions until an understanding of current performance can be achieved. Improvement teams are encouraged to use historical data whenever possible, or to collect data on the performance of the system as a first step on an improvement journey. Achieving a good baseline understanding of data can assist teams in building a better theory of improvement.

2) Maximum number of subgroups to maintain a useful run chart (30 data points): Readers may note that the probability-based rules used to detect non-random variation are contingent upon the total number of subgroups collected. As Ott noted in 1975, the probabilities can change as more and more data is collected, meaning the chance of something like a shift or a trend may increase as the total number of subgroups grows. It is recommended that improvement teams who collected 30 subgroups or more of data, should consider moving their data onto a Shewhart control chart. While a run chart is still likely to be useful with more data, the probability of detecting a false positive (non-random variation that is in reality random variation) does start to increase. Though the increase in probability is marginal, in some circumstances, where the cost of investigation and learning maybe high, use of a Shewhart control chart could help to minimize the use of scare resources in understanding if and when the performance of the system is changing.

3) Run charts depend on an assumption of independence: The use of probability-based rules in the interpretation of run charts depends upon each data value being independent of all other data values. If autocorrelation is present in the data (i.e., previous data points influence or predict future data points, as in estimated weighted moving averages or "rolling averages") then rules one through three cannot be used with the run chart, rendering the tool much less effective in detecting important non-random variation that may be occurring.

4) Use of run charts with non-continuous, or attribute data: Run chart rules are based on symmetry of data around the median. They were designed to be used with continuous data however, in many

circumstances improvement teams will want to apply to them to attribute data (data which is discrete in some way: percentage, rate, Likert scaled, rounded, etc.). So long as symmetry can be maintained, use of a run chart is okay. There are instances when this symmetry breaks down though. Provost and Murray explicate these instances and what to do:

- More than half the data points fall on the median: In these circumstances the median no longer acts as a good prediction of performance or of comparison using the probability-based rules. In such circumstances it is recommended the data be plotted on the appropriate Shewhart control chart to ease interpretation of performance.
- Too many data fall on the extreme value (0%, 100%, etc.): If more than 50% of the data values fall on the extreme value of a chart then the probability-based rules associated with the use of a median do not apply for the detection of non-random variation. It is recommended in these circumstances that an improvement team consider the use of a rare events chart, counting the time or case between events rather than the rate or percent of events. Special Shewhart control charts are recommended in these circumstances.

5) Fluctuations in the size of denominators from subgroup to subgroup when plotting attribute data – If an improvement team is plotting attribute data on a run chart (i.e., percentage data, rate data, etc.) they need to be careful to maintain a consistent denominator size, with the recommendation being that the denominator for each subgroup be approximately the same (+/- 25% of the average denominator size). Percent and rate data are particularly sensitive to denominator sizes (i.e., 1/10 = 10%, 1/20 = 5%, 1/100 = 1%, etc.). If this is not adhered to, then a single data value with a small denominator size could appear extreme on the run chart (astronomical value) but its position is actually due to a fluctuation in the sample size for the single subgroup. If denominator sizes are expected to fluctuate considerably from subgroup to subgroup, then the use of Shewhart control chart is recommended.

6) Data not plotted in time or sequential order: When teams choose to display data collected in an order other than time or sequence (i.e., category) then the data should not be connected with a data line. Also, rules one through three in using probability to detect non-random variation should not be used. Only rule four (astronomical value) can be used to detect non-random variation in such cases.

7) Use of multiple measures on a single chart: Some improvement teams will be tempted to place data for multiple measures or locations on a single run chart. It is useful to reflect on recommendations for the display of quantitative information in such circumstances. For line charts, it is not recommended to exceed four data lines on a single chart. Because run charts have both a data line and a median line, best practice suggests there should never be more than two measures displayed on the same chart using a median to assist in interpretation. Beyond two data lines and two median lines, the graphic becomes visually confusing to most readers. If more data has been collected, improvement teams should consider the use of a small multiples view to display many run charts simultaneously, easing the visual burden and making interpretation simpler for readers.

References and Further Reading

- Provost L, Murray S. *The Health Care Data Guide: Learning Data for Improvement.* San Francisco: Jossey-Bass, Publication, 2011
- Ott, E., *Process Quality Control*, New York: McGraw-Hill, 1975, 39-44.

- Perla, R., Provost, L., & Murray, S. (2011). "The run chart: A simple analytical tool for learning from variation in healthcare processes." *BMJ Quality & Safety*, 20(1), 46-51.
- Swed, F. S., and Eisenhart, C., "Tables for Testing Randomness of Grouping in a Sequence of Alternatives," *Annals of Mathematical Statistics*, 1943, Vol. XIV, 66, 87, Tables II and III.
- Tufte, Edward R. *The Visual Display of Quantitative Information. (2nd Edition)* Connecticut: Graphic Press, 2001.

Histograms

Other Names: Frequency Plots, Grouped Frequency Distribution

Conceptual Links:

System of Profound Knowledge: Understanding Variation
6 Principles: Focus on variation in the process

Purpose

Histograms exist to visualize distributions of continuous data. They create a picture that:

1) Plots the location of the data collected on the scale used to measure the data.
2) Displays the spread of the data along the scale, helping users to see quickly the range of data collected.
3) Visualize the shape of the distribution created by the data collected by plotting the frequency of data occurring within various ranges of the scale presented.[64]

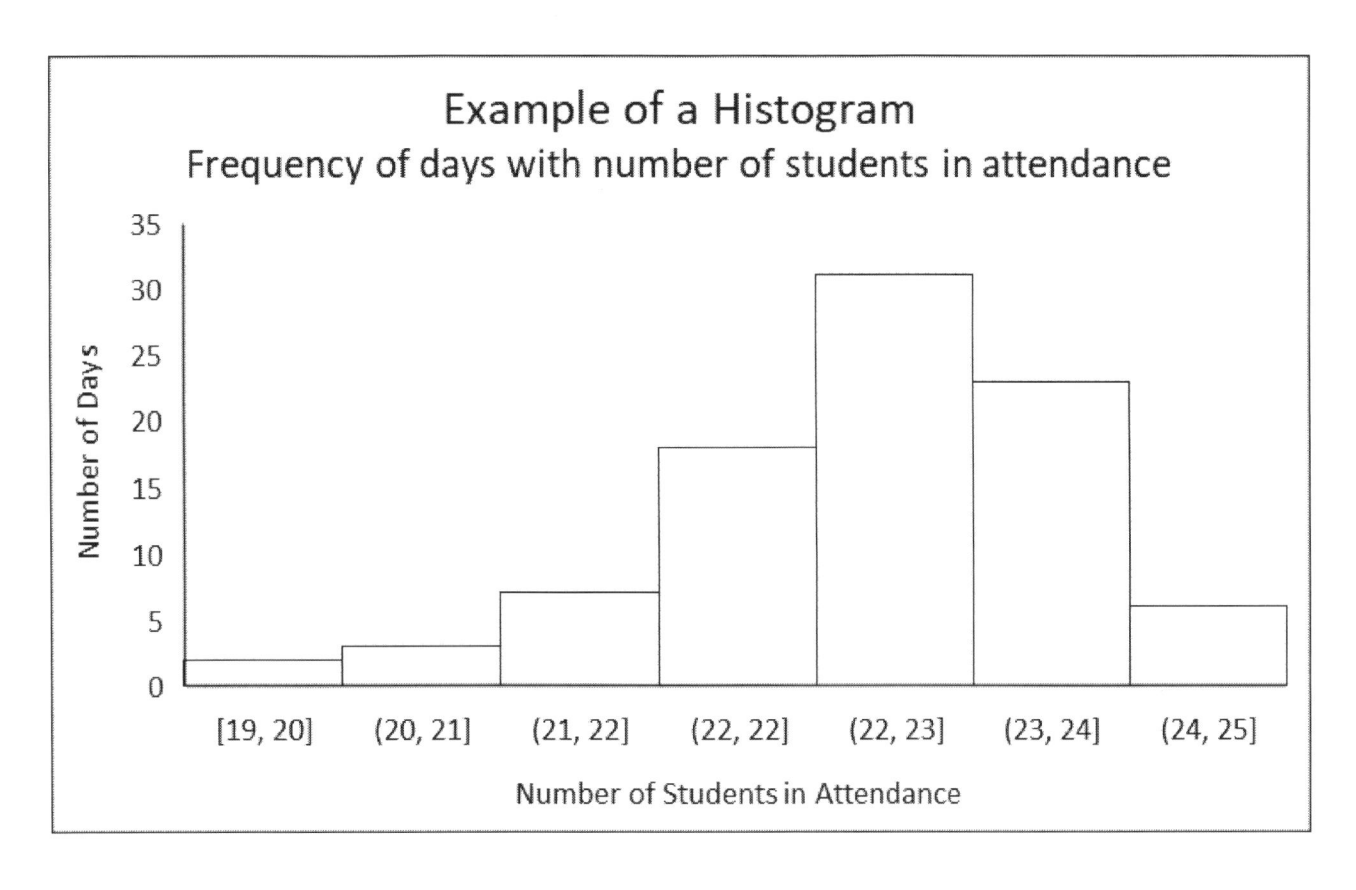

Example of a Histogram
Frequency of days with number of students in attendance

Number of Students in Attendance	Number of Days
[19, 20]	2
(20, 21]	3
(21, 22]	7
(22, 22]	18
(22, 23]	31
(23, 24]	23
(24, 25]	6

---

[64] Distributions are infinite in their shapes and sizes. Most readers will be familiar with the normal or Gaussian Distribution resembling a bell-shaped curve; however, distributions can be skewed in one direction or another, can be symmetric without being normal, can be bi-modal or multi-modal in shape, and can literally take on many other shapes. The histogram visualizes the shape of the data for the user, assisting them in seeing what type of shape is present.

When to use histograms

Improvement teams will find histograms useful in answering several questions associated with **continuous data** they have collected. Associates in Process Improvement recommend the tool for answering these:
- How wide is the spread in the data set?
- Is the data set symmetrical?
- Is there more than one peak?
- Are there isolated values in the data set?
- What is the spread of the data set relative to target and specifications?
- What percent of values are outside target or specifications?
- Is there a tendency for certain values to be present or missing?

There are two key moments in the life of an improvement initiative when the use of histograms to answer these questions can be helpful. During the early stage of discovery and diagnosis, the histogram can be useful for visualizing the distribution of historical data a team might have access to. In some instances, teams might even want to plot small multiple[65] histograms of historical data (by month or year) to understand if or how the shape of the distribution of their data has changed over time. This can be an important way to view data when the data available for analysis is collected infrequently (i.e., when data is gathered once or twice a year and may only be available for two to three years historically).

The other moment in the life of an improvement journey when histograms can be useful is in the analysis of data that is part of a project's family of measures. Typically, when a family of measures is selected for a project, teams collect data on each measure and plot the data as it unfolds over time (i.e., on a run or Shewhart control chart). If the data collected and plotted over time displays stability (as assessed by a Shewhart control chart), then histograms can be used to generate a prediction of what the shape of the distribution of data is likely to be in the near future if the stability of the measure is maintained.[66]

It should be noted histograms are intended for use with continuous data — data varying along a continuous measure. Examples include time, money, height, weight, through put, volume, and distance. Histograms are not appropriate for use with discrete or categorical data (also known as attribute data, such as: school, ward, ethnicity, etc.). If an improvement team needs to analyze such data, then a simple Bar Chart or a Pareto diagram are recommended.[67]

Elements of a histogram

There are three key elements of a histogram: the measure of interest (horizontal axis), the frequency of occurrence of a single value or range of values along the measures scale (vertical axis) and the vertical bars displaying the chart.

---

[65] See Section Six: Data Visualization Using Small Multiples for more on this way of viewing data.

[66] If a measure being collected is unstable then a histogram can only be descriptive of historical performance (the shape of the distribution in the past) but has no predictive value for what the shape of the distribution might be in the future.

[67] See Section Six: Ordered Bar Chart and Pareto Analysis for more information on these tools.

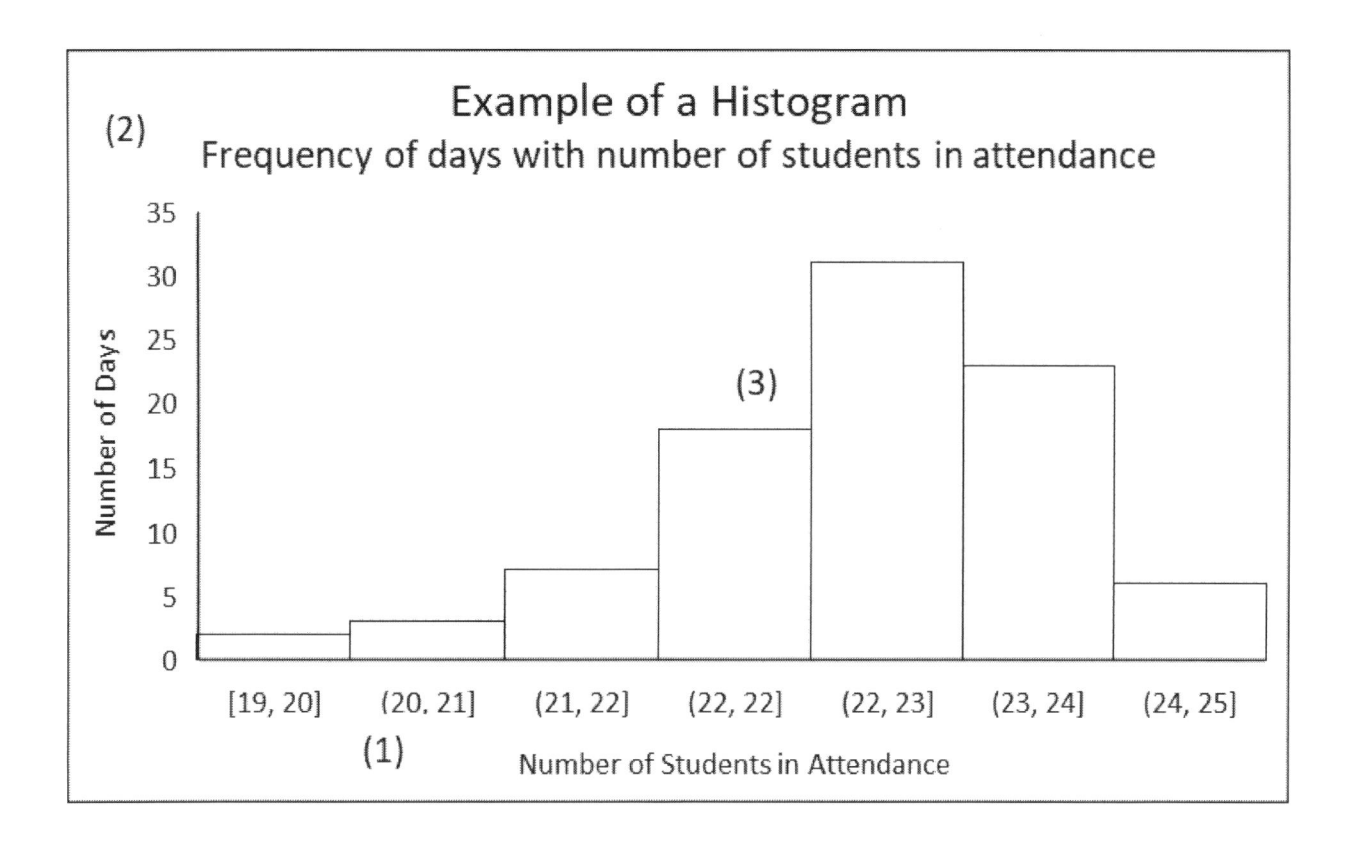

Example of a Histogram
Frequency of days with number of students in attendance

(2) Number of Days (vertical axis, 0 to 35)

(3) bar over [22, 23]

(1) Number of Students in Attendance — bins: [19, 20], (20, 21], (21, 22], (22, 22], (22, 23], (23, 24], (24, 25]

Horizontal Axis (1)

The horizontal axis on a histogram displays the scale of the measure of interest. Remember, histograms are used when displaying continuous data. Continuous data sets vary along a continuous scale. The horizontal axis of a histogram displays that part of the scale representing the values of the data set collected. The horizontal axis on a histogram is divided into "bins" or "cells." These are subdivisions of the range of data collected. The size of bins is usually chosen by considering the amount of data, as well as what would be a meaningful division of the data when interpreted by a subject matter expert.
In the example above the measure of interest is the number of students in attendance in a single classroom. The horizontal scale varies from 19 students to 25 students. This indicates that the number of students attending the class varies between 19 students and 25 students on the days for which data was collected (in this example, the 90 days of a single semester). The bin range for this example is 1, where a new bin is created for an increase in the size of attendance of the class by a single student. This may be because the size of the classroom is rather small. One could imagine a much larger classroom size (n=500) where bin ranges vary by 25 students (i.e., 1-25, 26-50, 51-75, etc.). Finally, each bin begins with (and ends with]. The] denotes a hard stop on the continuous scale for where counting for that bin ends.

Vertical Axis (2)

The vertical axis on a histogram displays the frequency (or relative frequency) of occurrence for a given range of data as identified by the horizontal axis.
In the example above the vertical axis varies from 0 to 35. When viewing the graph this tells the reader there are few occurrences when a certain number of students are present (i.e., 19 or 25) and there are many more occurrences when the number of students present is 21 or 22 or 23.

Vertical Bars displaying frequency of occurrence (3)

Histograms are a form of bar chart for continuous data. The bars plotted represent the frequency of occurrence for the bins (or ranges) depicted on the horizontal axis. The height of each rectangle present corresponds to the frequency with which data values from the data set appear in the bin or range described.

In the example above the height of the bin for 23 students (22,23] is 33, indicating there were 33 days in the semester when 23 students were present for class.[68]

Readers may notice in the example above that there are no spaces between the bars displayed on the histogram. This is a common practice when building histograms to visually communicate to readers that the scale along the horizontal (x-axis) is a continuous scale, rather than a discrete scale (like categories) which one would see in a Pareto analysis or other type of bar chart.

How to create a histogram

Drawing a histogram by hand

1) Identify the learning question to be answered through the construction of the histogram.
2) Identify what data is needed, including the source of the data (i.e., collection, accessing an existing data set or database, etc.).
3) Collect the data.
4) Find the minimum and maximum values of the data and calculate the range.
5) Divide the range into a suitable number of bins (see guidance below on selecting the number of bins).
6) Plot the horizontal axis (x-axis) including subdivisions based on the number of bins selected.
7) Plot the vertical axis (y-axis), scaling the axis to vary between the frequency of occurrences by bin.
8) Plot the data using vertical rectangles (bars) scaled to the height of the frequency of occurrence for each bin.
9) Label the graphic with a title, labels for the horizontal and vertical axes, and any important annotations that can help clarify the story presented by the data.

Drawing a histogram using point and click in Microsoft Excel

1) Identify the purpose for which you are using this chart (display the location, spread, and shape of a distribution or compare more than one distribution to each other)
2) Format your data (one column or row of continuous data)
3) Select the data you would like to include in the analysis (i.e., highlight the row or column of data for inclusion)
4) Using the Insert tab at the top of the screen, select the "Insert Statistic Chart" button and then select the Histogram button
5) Format the chart created using the normally available Format Chart Area option in Microsoft Excel

---

[68] Note, this does not include days when there were 24 or 25 students present. A variation in the use of histograms dealing with cumulative summation will be discussed later in the chapter for situations where teams may want to see a picture of cumulative occurrences.

Guidance for selecting a suitable number of bins

There is no rule for how many bins (i.e., cells or vertical bars) a histogram should have. Though users of the tool will note that when the number is too small it is difficult to see the shape of the distribution of data presented. Similarly, when there are too many bins, spaces can appear in the data presented making it difficult to see the shape of the distribution. Ideally, the user will have just enough bins to provide insight for the intended audience. All statistical software packages have a default setting for selecting the number of bins. Users may notice though, that the number of bins selected, or their size may not be intuitive for readers to understand and use the chart and so some adjustments may be helpful:

1) Adjust the number of bins and bin width to reflect intuitive breaks in the data (i.e., pay attention to subject matter relevant breaks on the scale that will make sense to readers).
2) Use guidance on bin number and width based on the amount of data being used to create the chart

   a. Ishikawa:

Number of Data Values	Recommended Number of Bins
<50	5-7
50 – 100	6-10
100 – 250	7-12
>250	10-20

   b. Ott:

   "The number of cells should preferably be between 13 and 20. However, when the number of observations is less than say 200, then as few as 10 cells may be of use. The number of cells k is a direct consequence of the cell with:"

   $$k = \Delta/m$$

   k = number of bins
   Δ = difference (delta) between the high value and the low values recorded
   m = cell width chosen

   c. Square Root rule:

   $$k = sqrt(n)$$
   The result is then rounded to the next whole number
   k = number of bins
   n = number of data values used to chart the histogram

How to use a histogram in practice

There are many instances when an improvement team may want to use a histogram to display continuous data they have collected: at the start of their projects when first investigating historical performance of their process or system, and/or after establishing stability in a measure of interest, to understand what variability and frequency they might expect in data collected in the future. Improvement teams will often use histograms to compare data from different sources or from different time periods. This use type can help communicate process change (performance change) across time or between subgroups. See example below:

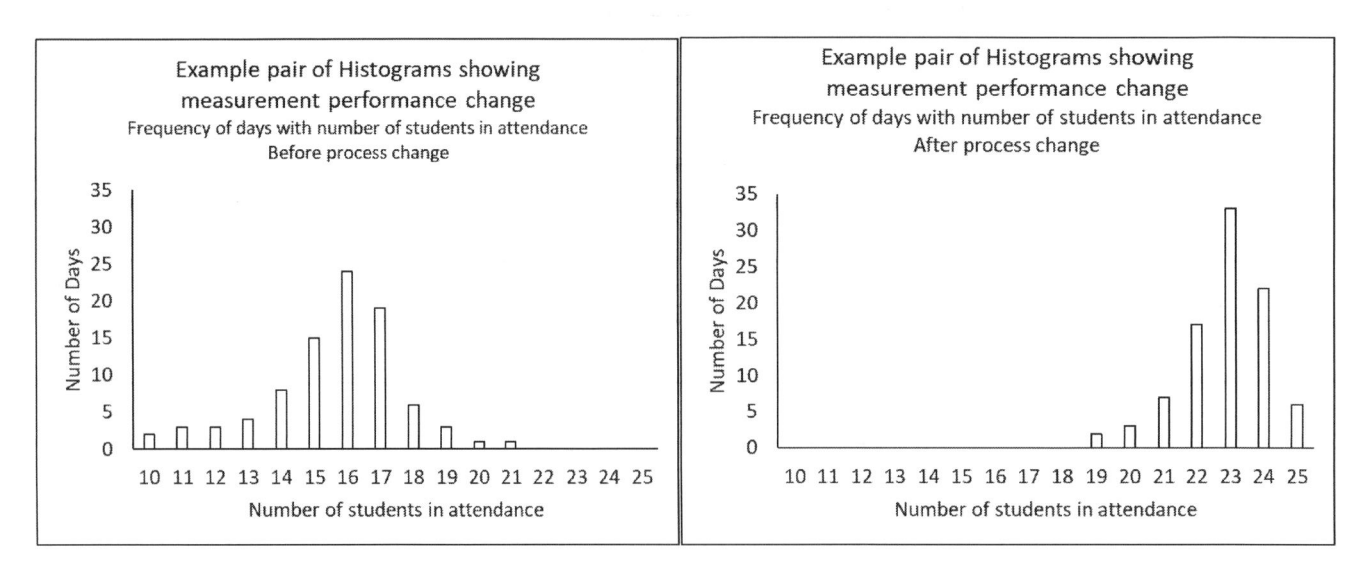

Example pair of Histograms showing measurement performance change
Frequency of days with number of students in attendance
Before process change

Example pair of Histograms showing measurement performance change
Frequency of days with number of students in attendance
After process change

When describing histograms, it can be helpful to understand and use some common terms:
Symmetric — describes when the data is evenly distributed about the mean and median, both sharing the same value for symmetric distributions. In symmetric distributions the right and left sides of the distribution (divided by the mean and median) are mirror images of each other.

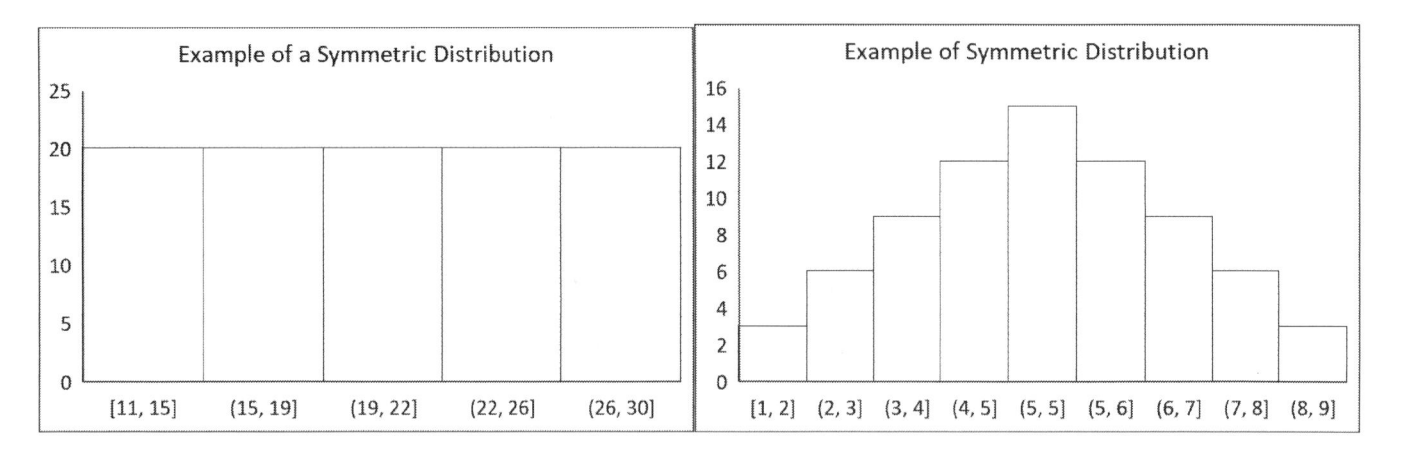

Symmetric Unimodal

This term describes a symmetric distribution with a single modal value. A normal or gaussian distribution is an example of a symmetric unimodal distribution.

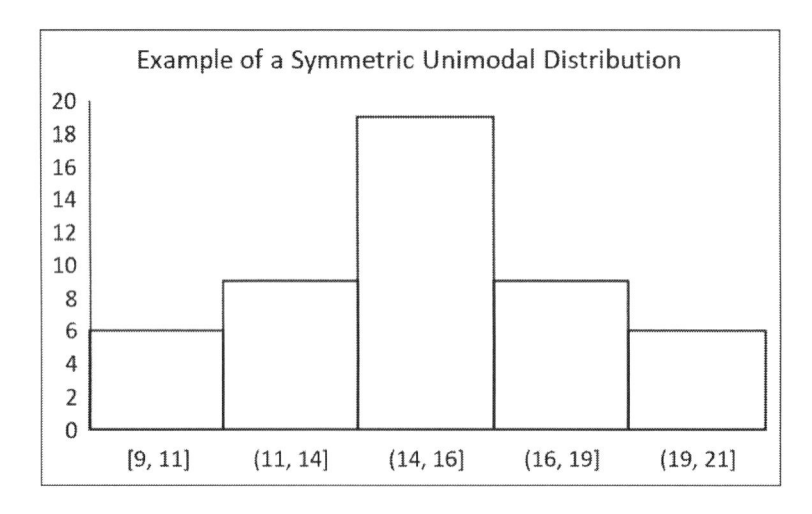

Skew

Refers to a distribution that appears to be pushed either to the left or to the right. Skewed distributions are not symmetrical, they have more of their data display to one side or the other of the mode (the most commonly occurring value).

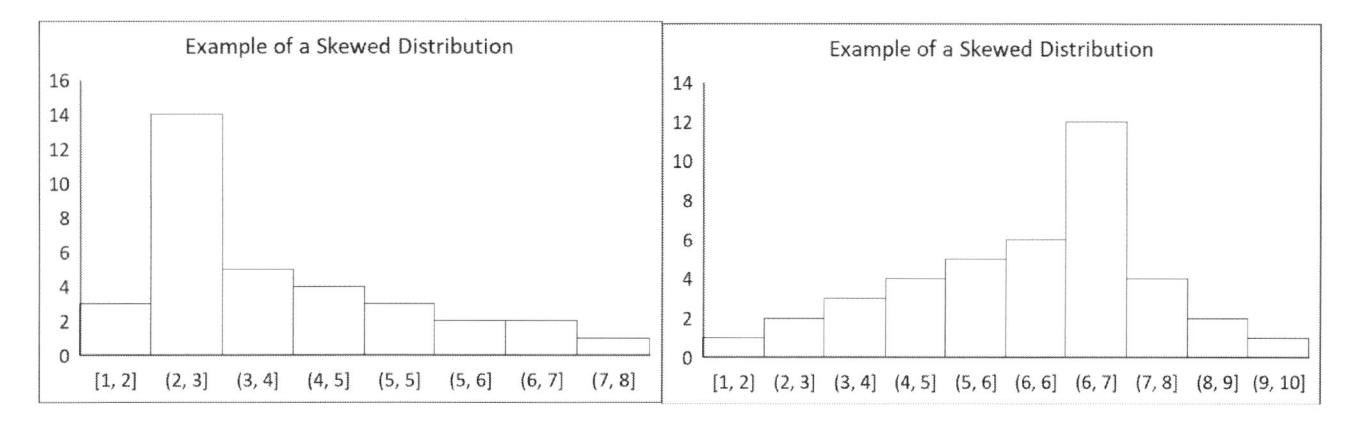

Bimodal

A bimodal distribution occurs when there appear to be two values along the scale that occur more frequently than just a single value (unimodal, see above).

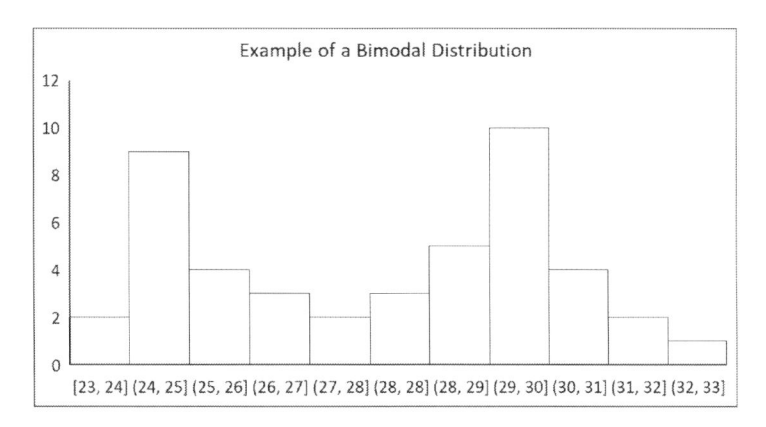

Multimodal

Like a bimodal distribution, a multimodal distribution occurs when there are more than two values along the scale that occur with some frequency making the histogram appear to have many humps or spikes in the performance of the data.

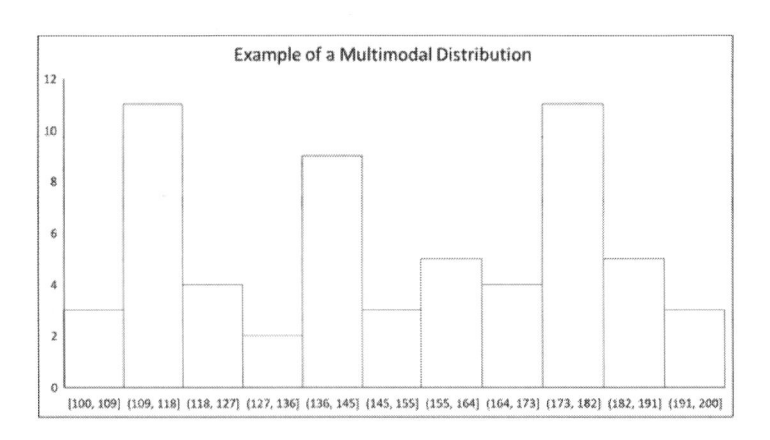

History

Described by Kaoru Ishikawa as one of the original seven basic tools for quality, the histogram has long been a useful tool for practitioners working in the field of quality improvement. The histogram was created by Karl Pearson in 1891 as a graphic tool for the quick visualization of the shape of a distribution of continuous data. Pearson introduced the tool in a series of lectures (Gresham Lectures 1891-1894) and published the tool formally in 1895 in a book chapter entitled: Contributions to the Mathematical Theory of Evolution. II. Skew Variation in Homogenous Material.

Variations

Cumulative Histogram

Unlike most histograms which show the shape of a distribution of data, the Cumulative Histogram displays the cumulative frequency of the data by bin. As the bins increase, so does the cumulative frequency of the size of the bin displayed with the largest frequency displaying the total number of data points in the data set.

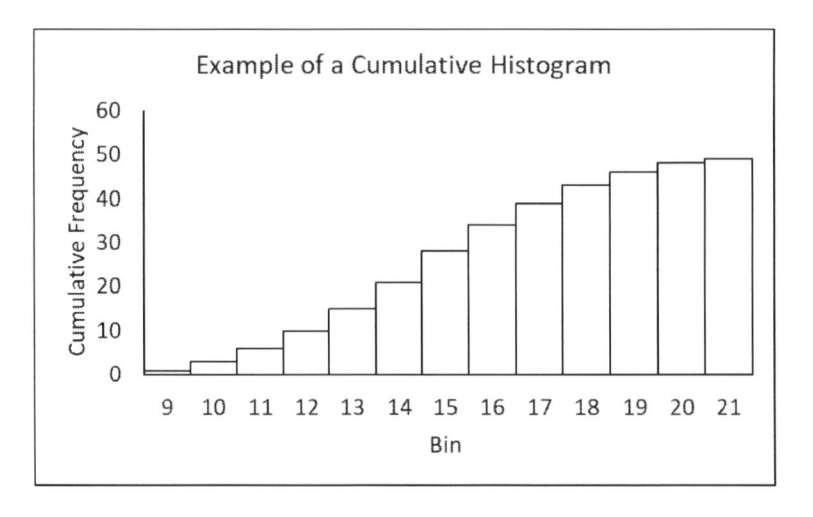

Stem and Leaf Diagram

In John Tukey's 1977 book, *Exploratory Data Analysis*, he describes an alternative to the classic histogram for visualizing and summarizing a data set. His Stem and Leaf Diagram accomplishes the same purpose of a traditional histogram, plotting the location, spread and shape of the data set while also displaying all the data in a consumable way for readers. His stem and leaf diagram allows users to reconstruct the full data set displayed. One drawback is the tool does not allow the user to reconstruct the data set in the order in which it was collected, since the display is an aggregate summary.

The stem and leaf diagram is composed of two parts: the stem and the leaf. The stem (or column of numbers to the left or right of the leaves and separated by a vertical line) generally displays the start of data at an order of magnitude larger than the leaves. Stems replace bins from our traditional histogram. The leaves represent the detail of each data point collected for each stem (or in each bin). An example below illustrates the use of stem and leaf diagram using the collected weights of individuals.

```
Example Stem and Leaf Diagram
Weight in lbs of a group of individuals

10 | 5 7 9
11 | 2 2 5 6 7
12 | 1 2 5 8 8 9
13 | 2 3 4 5 5 5 7 8 9
14 | 3 4 4 6 6 8
15 | 5 6 7 7 8 9
16 | 2 3 4 5 6
17 | 4 5 6 6 7
18 | 2 3 4 4 4 6
19 | 1 1 2 3 4 5 6 8 8
20 | 2 2 3 4 5 7 8
21 | 3 5 6 7 7 8 9
22 | 1 2 2 5 5 5
23 | 3 3 6 6 8         Legend
24 | 2 4 7             16|2 = 162 lbs
25 | 2
```

In this example, reading (or deconstructing) the stem and leaf diagram allows the user to discover the individual weights of each person measured. For example, there are three people whose weights fall between 100 lbs. and 109 lbs. Their weights are 105, 107 and 109 lbs. Because of the detail present, the tool is very powerful in both summarizing and making accessible a data set.

Special Considerations

Stability

Stability is very important concept in the field of measurement associated with quality. Data stability data refers to the performance of a measure over time and occurs when the data being examined does not display any special or assignable cause variation (variation that out of the ordinary, does not apply to every instance or time period, and does not affect all samples of the measure equally).

Within the context of quality improvement, stability is assessed using Shewhart control charts which provide insight into when the performances of measures are either stable or unstable. When measures are stable (i.e., do not display special or assignable causes) then they are said to be predictable. In these circumstances the use of a histogram (displaying stable historical data) can be helpful in communicating the location, spread, and shape of data that is expected to occur in the future barring the introduction of special or assignable causes.

When using histograms, it is very important to first understand whether the data being displayed is stable or unstable using a Shewhart control chart. If the data are stable, inferences or predictions of what to expect next can be made with some degree of belief. If the historical data is unstable then the histogram displayed can only serve as a summary of historical performance and cannot serve the purpose of inferring what is likely to occur in the future performance of the measure.

Use of Relative Frequency

In this chapter examples have been given that display the frequency of values occurring within a bin along a continuous scale. In some instances, histograms will be made displaying the relative frequency of occurrence of values within a bin rather than the absolute frequency of values. In this case the vertical axis (y axis) no longer represents a frequency count. It instead is depicted as a percent. Each bin is translated from an absolute frequency into a representation of what percent that bin contains of all the data collected.

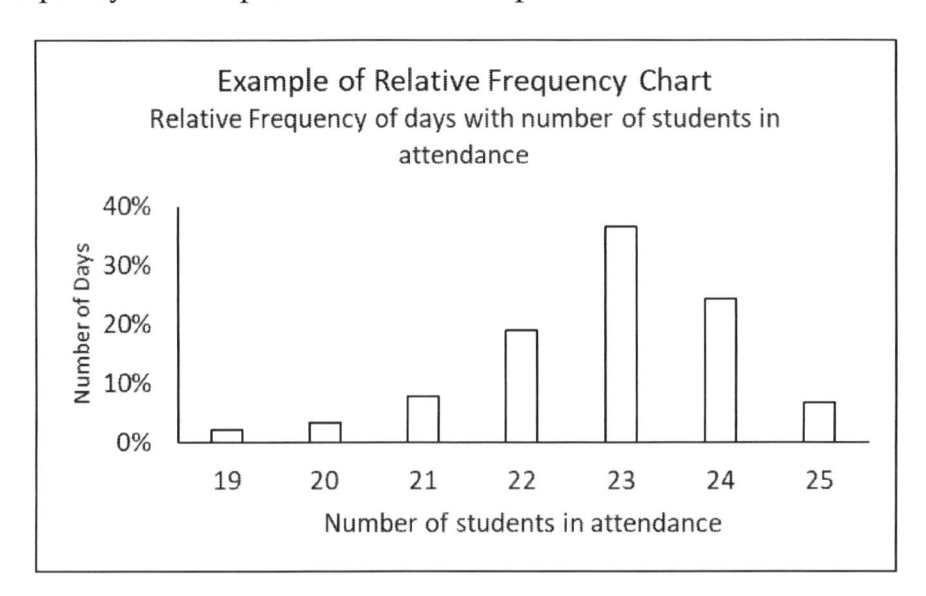

Example of Relative Frequency Chart
Relative Frequency of days with number of students in attendance

References

Associates in Process Improvement. The Improvement Handbook. Austin: Associates in Process Improvement. 2007

Ishikawa, Kaoru. Guide to Quality Control: Asian Productivity Organization. Chapter 2. 1976

Ott, E., Process Quality Control, New York: McGraw-Hill, 1975, 39-44.

Pearson, Karl. Contributions to the Mathematical Theory of Evolution. II. Skew Variation in Homogenous Material. Philosophical Transactions. pp. 343-414

Provost L, Murray S. The Health Care Data Guide: Learning Data for Improvement. San Francisco: Jossey-Bass, Publication, 2011

Rufilanchas, Daniel R. On the Origin of Karl Pearson's term "histogram". Estadística Española. Volumen 59, número 192/2017. pp.29-35

Tufte, Edward R. The Visual Display of Quantitative Information. (2nd Edition) Connecticut: Graphic Press. 2001

Tukey, John W. Exploratory Data Analysis. Addison-Wesley series in behavioral science: quantitative methods. Reading, Massachusetts. Addison-Wesley Publishing Company. 1977

Box-and-Whisker Plots

Other Names: Box Plot, Box-and-Whisker Diagram, Tukey Box Plot, Range Bar

Conceptual Links

System of Profound Knowledge: Understanding Variation
6 Principles: Focus on variation in the process

Purpose

Box-and-whisker plots are used to visually summarize the distribution of a data set. Specifically, they provide a visual representation of what is known as the five-number summary of a set of data: the maximum and minimum values, the median, and the upper and lower quartile values. In one variation on the use of the tool they also calculate a value for the identification of "outliers," and display those outliers in addition to the five-number summary described above.

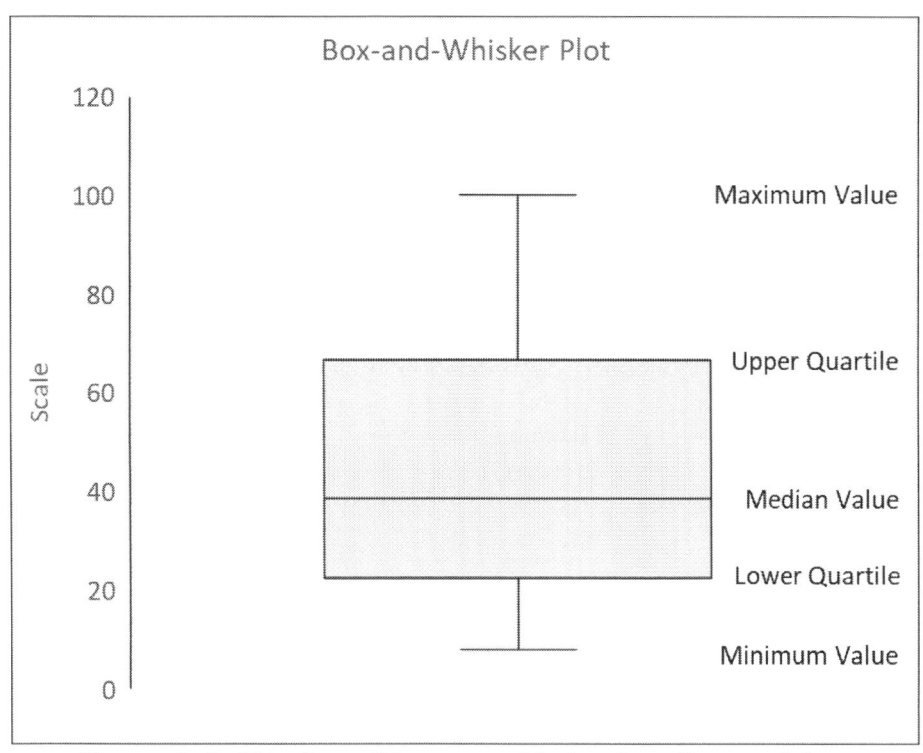

Example 1: Display of the general behavior of a set of data

When to use box-and-whisker plots

Box-and-whisker plots can be used in two ways:

- Display of the general behavior of a set of data (summarize the shape of a distribution of data)
- Display the detailed behavior of more than one set of data for the purpose of comparison (summarize, side by side, the shape of more than one distribution of data)

Improvement Teams might choose to use a box-and-whisker plot when needing to communicate the shape of a distribution of data which is collected infrequently and that is representative of a key measure or characteristic of their system they are focused on for the purpose of improvement. Box-and-whisker plots can be considered an alternative data visualization for data one might also analyze and display using frequency plots (histograms). Box-and-whisker plots are often a good choice for the communication of the data because they are familiar to many people. They also focus on summarization of data and so can be a bit easier to explain. This is much harder to accomplish using histograms (small multiples would be recommended or an alternative of a Run or Shewhart control chart).

Elements of a box-and-whisker plot

Box-and-whisker plots are most often displayed vertically and include five key elements, corresponding with the five-number summary of a data set.[69] These are:

- The maximum value
- The minimum value
- The median value
- The upper quartile[70]
- The lower quartile

Box-and-whisker plots include at least one axis describing the scale of the data being observed. Best practice in visualizing the data is to limit the number of numbers on the scale so as not to distract the reader from the important story displayed by the box-and-whisker plot. The exception to this practice occurs when dealing with small variations on the scale that may have important impacts on the interpretation of the graphic. This can occur for example with a scale displaying dates, where a particular year or month may have an important consequence to the narrative the data is intended to display. In such circumstances adding more tick marks to the scale may help the reader to correctly interpret the data displayed.

In instances when the box-and-whisker plot is being used to compare more than one data set a second axis is added to describe the different sub-groups of data being displayed (see example 2 below).

---

[69] The default setting for the creation of Box-and-Whisker Plots in most software settings (including Microsoft Excel) is in a vertical position. Exceptions to this formatting rule comes from Edward Tufte in the form of his quartile plot, which is oriented horizontally, as was Mary Elanor Spear's range plot. Examples of this will be shown in the section on variations of the tool later in the chapter.

[70] For readers unfamiliar with quartiles, a quartile can be defined in a similar way to the median. The median describes the point in the data set below which falls half of the collected data and above which falls half of the collected data. The lower quartile then is the point in the data set below which falls one quarter of the data set and above which falls three-quarters of the collected data. The upper quartile is the point above which falls one quarter of the data set and below which falls three-quarters of the collected data.

Box-and-Whisker Plots used for comparison

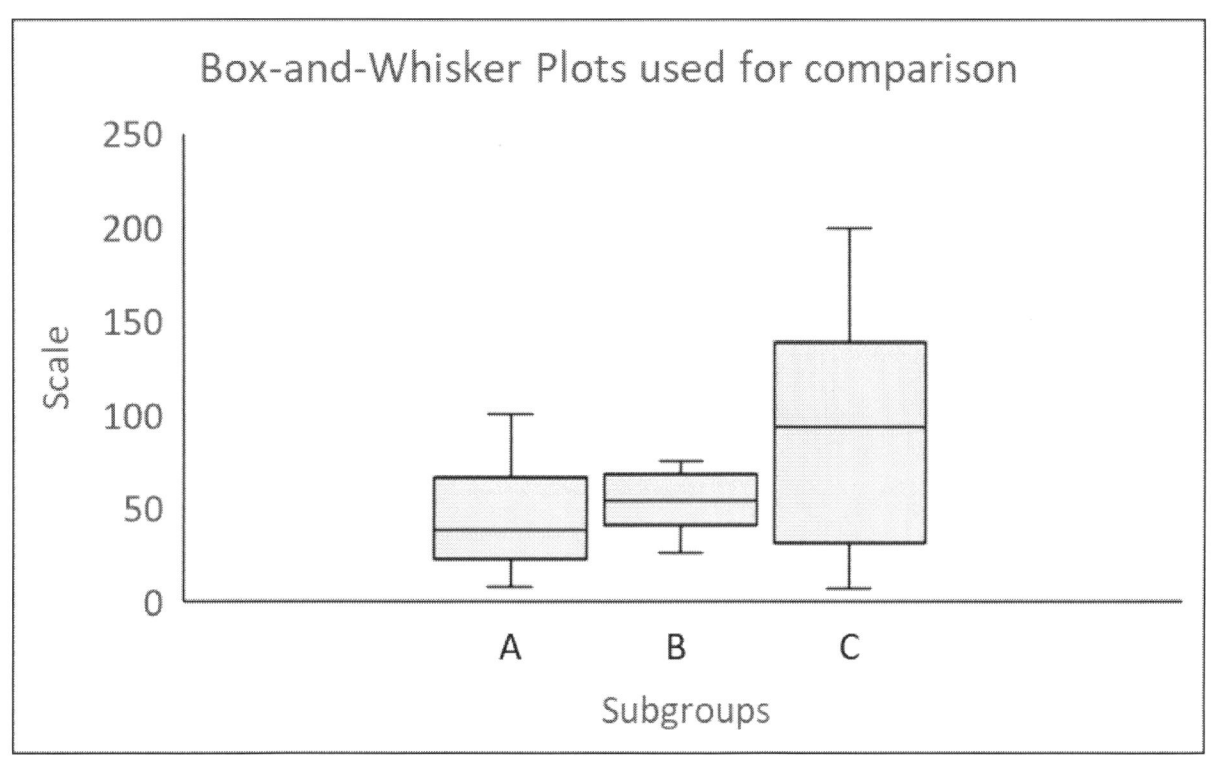

Example 2: Display the detailed behavior of more than one set of data for the purpose of comparison

How to create a box-and-whisker plot

Drawing a box-and-whisker plot by hand

1) Identify the purpose for which you are using this chart (display the general shape of a distribution or compare more than one distribution to each other)
2) Order the raw data set from largest to smallest
3) Identify the maximum value
4) Identify the minimum value
5) Calculate the median value[71]
6) Decide whether you plot the graphic horizontally (as in a range bar) or vertically (as is more common when using the box-and-whisker plot to compare data)
7) Draw your scale
8) Using your scale, draw the interquartile range (your box from the lower quartile to the upper quartile)
9) Divide your interquartile range box with a single line at the value of the median (sometimes the median is depicted using some other symbol. Using a diamond to depict the median is shown in Example 3 below)
10) Draw the whiskers of the plot ending them with a hash at the value the indicates the maximum and minimum values of the data set

---

[71] If the data set for a subgroup has an odd number of data values, then the median is found easily by counting to the middle value of the ordered data. If the data set for a subgroup has an even number of data values, then the median is found by counting to the middle and taking the average of the two most middle values in the ordered data set. Medians can also easily be found by using the =median function in software programs like Microsoft Excel or Google Sheets.

Drawing a box-and-whisker plot using point and click in Microsoft Excel[72]

1) Identify the purpose for which you are using this chart (display the general shape of a distribution or compare more than one distribution to each other)
2) Format your data (one column or row of data per subgroup)
3) Select the data you would like to include in the analysis (i.e., highlight the data for inclusion)
4) Using the Insert tab at the top of the screen, select the "Insert Statistic Chart" button  and then select the Box and Whisker button 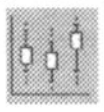
5) Format the chart created using the normally available Format Chart Area option in Microsoft Excel

How to use a box-and-whisker plot in practice

As is depicted in Example 3 below, box-and-whisker plots can summarize a lot of data (five-number summaries) and show notable change over time (or across data sets) in a single graphic (in Example 3, five-by-five number summaries for a total of 25 data points in a single graphic). An example might be when needing to communicate a summary of findings, such as responses to a survey or survey question. The box-and-whisker plot allows teams to communicate quickly and easily the shape of the distribution created by respondents to the survey. Example 3 below shows a comparison of the distributions formed when teachers in a school district were asked to rate themselves on a 1-6 scale (strongly disagree to strongly agree) on the survey item "Overall my job feels overwhelming."

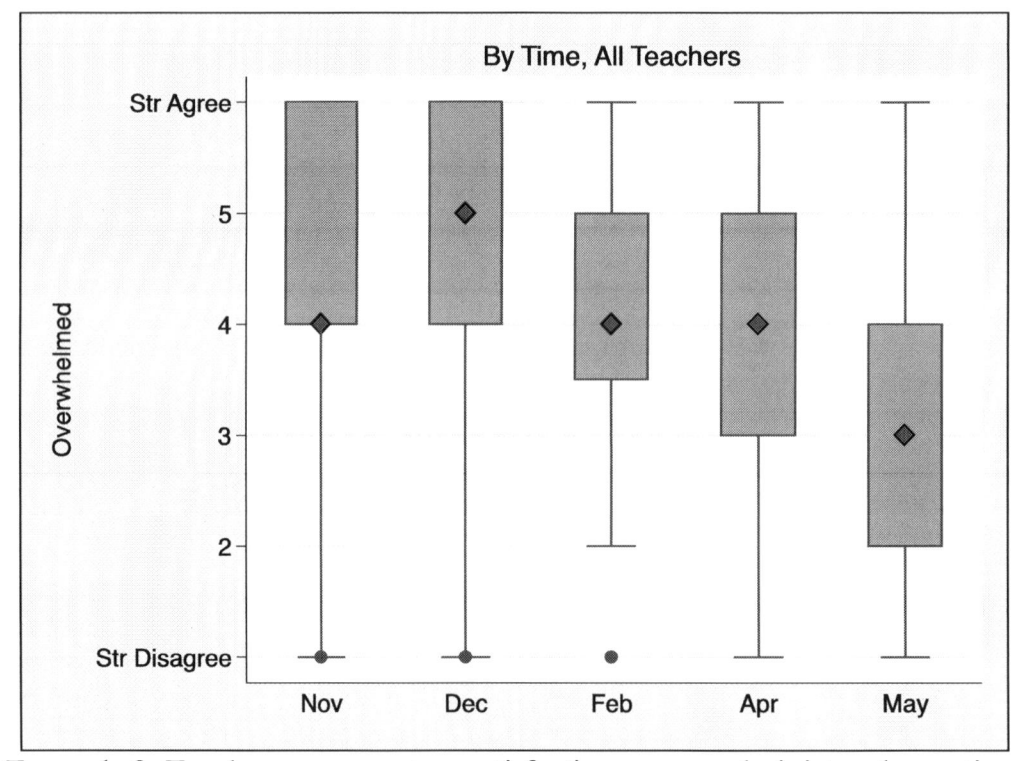

Example 3: Teacher responses to a satisfaction survey administered over time
"Overall my job feels overwhelming"

History

---

[72] This guidance will only allow for the creation of vertically oriented Box-and-Whisker Plots. Readers interested in learning how to create horizontally oriented charts using Microsoft Excel are encouraged to explore various online tutorials.

Published in 1952, Mary Spear's *Charting Statistics* is the earliest reference of what today we think of as a Box Plot. Her diagram was oriented horizontally, and she referred to as a "Range Bar." As with the box-and-whisker plot, it included a visual depiction of the range (high to low) of the data, as well as the median and an interquartile range. The tool as is commonly used today was described by John Tukey in his 1977, *Exploratory Data Analysis*. It has remained largely unchanged since then, both in terms of what data it describes and how it displays data.

Variations

Vertical or Horizontal Orientation

Readers are likely to see in the literature they come across box-and-whisker plots oriented vertically and horizontally. There is no right or wrong when it comes to orientation of the data. The choice is one of preference and convenience on the part of the person conducting the analysis and creating the visual display of the data. An example of the same data set oriented horizontally and vertically is provided below.

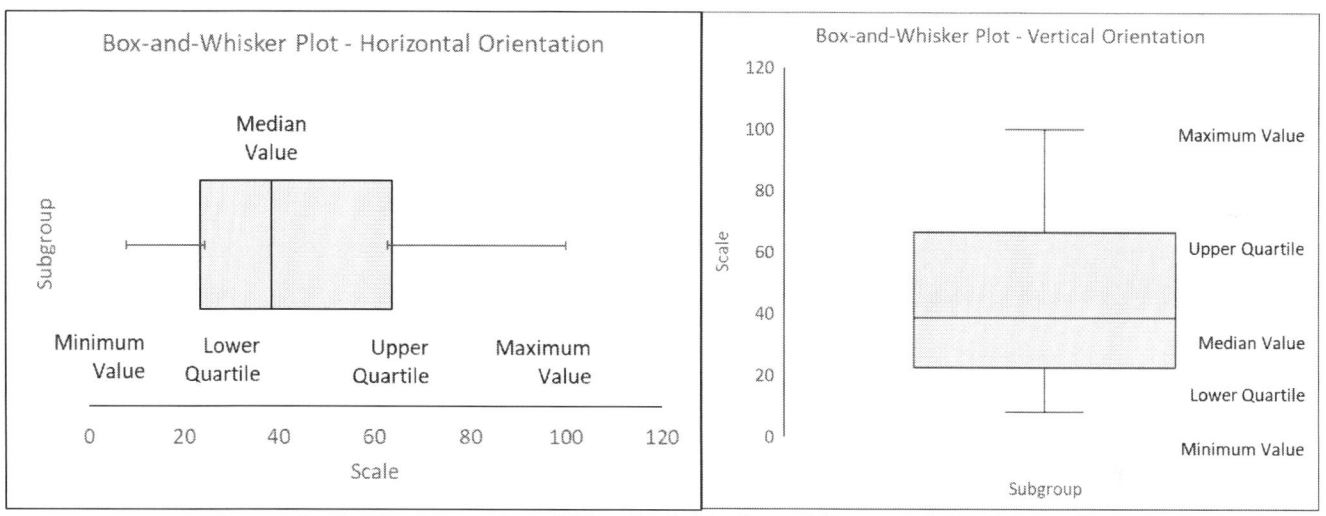

Example 4: Horizontal and Vertical display of Box-and-Whisker Plots

Outliers

Another variation in the use of box plots occurs when there is the suspicion of outliers in the data. Tukey described these data values as "straying out far beyond the others" or, in some circumstances, "straying is not so obvious, but our suspicions are alerted." Tukey suggested it is "convenient to have a rule of thumb that picks out certain values as "outside."" Because the primary use of the tool (5-number summary in visual form) relies on the minimum and maximum values to define the whiskers, a transformation/calculation is needed to adjust the whiskers to include most of the data, thus helping to identify data that is suspected to be "straying…outside."[73] The calculation for the adjustment of the whiskers is:

---

[73] It is important to recognize the creation of the rule for the detection of outliers is largely arbitrary, created by Tukey because he dealt with data sets, which at times he felt contained values that were outside the norm of what was expected. Readers will often see these adjusted box plots that identify outliers but should not assume that these outliers are akin to special cause variation as described by Shewhart control charts (the data tool most powerfully associated with quality improvement efforts). The theory for the identification of such outliers and their interpretation are fundamentally different than the "convenient rule of thumb," Tukey first described (and which has become standard practice with the use of box-and-whisker plots) in 1977.

Lower whisker = Q1 − (1.5 x IQR)

Upper whisker = Q3 + (1.5 x IQR)

Q1 = Quartile 1

Q3 = Quartile 3

IQR = Interquartile Range = Q3 − Q1

Any data point that falls "outside" these adjusted whiskers is suspected of being an outlier and may be an indication that further learning about why or what caused the value is needed.

Example 5 below demonstrates the application of the adjusted box-and-whisker plot to detect outlier values in a data set measuring patient waiting times at a health care clinic. Values outside the whiskers represent patients who waited very long times to be seen and further investigation into why their waits were so long would be recommended as a next step in trying to understand the system.

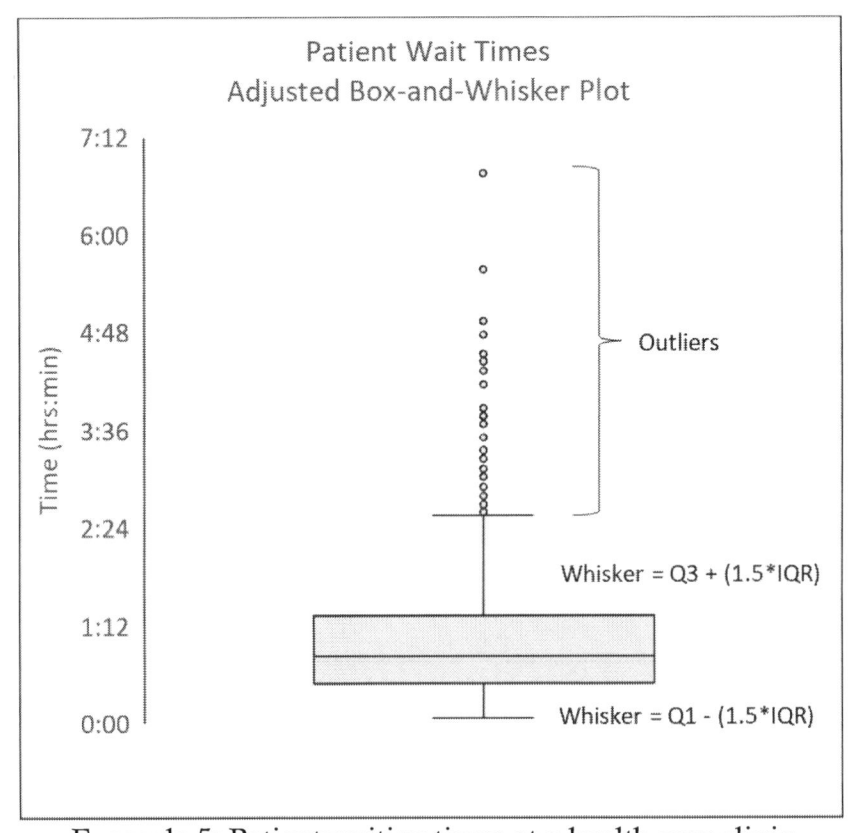

Example 5: Patient waiting times at a health care clinic

The key decision users of the box-and-whisker plot will need to consider is whether to use the simple plot or the adjusted plot (which screens the data for outliers). In most quality improvement contexts, the presence of outliers represents an opportunity for investigation and learning. This contrasts with other forms of statistical data analysis where outliers are ignored or excluded from considerations of performance. If screening using a box-and-whisker plot is done, it is recommended that further investigation is undertaken to understand why found outliers exist in the system. That information could be very valuable in informing the design or redesign of the process or system under study.

For more sophisticated practitioners, it is recommended that a Shewhart control chart is used to detect special causes of variation (outliers) in the data, as that tool is specifically designed for the purpose of detection and investigation.

There are a few other rarely used variations on the tool and include:

- **Variable width box plots** — boxes vary in size depending on the size of sample of data included in the analysis (larger boxes = larger sample sizes)
- **Notched box plots** — boxes are notched at the median creating an hourglass effect allowing for easy comparison of medians when the chart contains multiple plots.
- **Tufte's quartile plot** — focused on minimizing ink on the page while maintaining the information a box plot intends to convey (the five-number summary)

For more information on these more rarely used box-and-whisker plots, readers are recommended to read Tufte's *The Visual Display of Quantitative Information* and seek out other specific resources online regarding the production of variable width and notched box plots.

References

Tufte, Edward R. The Visual Display of Quantitative Information. (2nd Edition) Connecticut: Graphic Press. 2001

Tukey, John W. Exploratory Data Analysis. Addison-Wesley series in behavioral science: quantitative methods. Reading, Massachusetts. Addison-Wesley Publishing Company. 1977

Moore, David S. The Basic Practice of Statistics. (4th Edition) New York. W. H. Freeman and Company. 2007

Spear, Mary E. Charting Statistics. New York. 1952

Appendix A: Improvement Tools—Reference Sheets, Templates, and Checklists

In this appendix, you will find reference sheets and templates for:

- Empathy Activities
- Process Failure Analysis
    - Process Failure Analysis Template
- Process Maps
- Force Field Analysis
- Cause and Effect Diagrams
    - Cause and Effect Template
- Aim Statements
- Theory of Practice Improvement
    - Driver Diagram Template
- Plan-Do-Study-Act
    - PDSA Sample Templates (1-3)
    - Reviewing PDSAs
- Planning PDSA Ramps Template
- Assessing Scale for Testing
- Visualizing Quantitative Information
- Pareto Analysis
- Run Charts

Reference Sheets are available online at www.improvementcollective.com.

Empathy Activities

When to use empathy activities

- To elicit stories and uncover hidden needs through deep listening and asking smart follow-up questions.
- To watch what people, do and how they interact with their environment.
- To gather clues about what users think and feel and help you learn about what they need.
- To observe how a user crosses institutional boundaries.

Empathy Interviews

Empathy interviews are designed to elicit stories and uncover hidden needs through deep listening and asking smart follow-up questions.

How to Conduct:

- Before the Interview
  - Be clear about purpose
  - Write interview questions
  - Deal with data logistics
  - Decide on the number of interviews
  - Train your team
  - Find a partner
  - Attend to your own bias
- During Interviews
  - Make the person you're talking to feel comfortable
  - Encourage stories
  - Go deeper
  - Be neutral
  - Look for inconsistencies
  - Don't suggest answers to your questions
  - Capture what you hear
- After Interviews
- Prepare data for analysis
- Bring a team together to analyze results
- Debrief the process

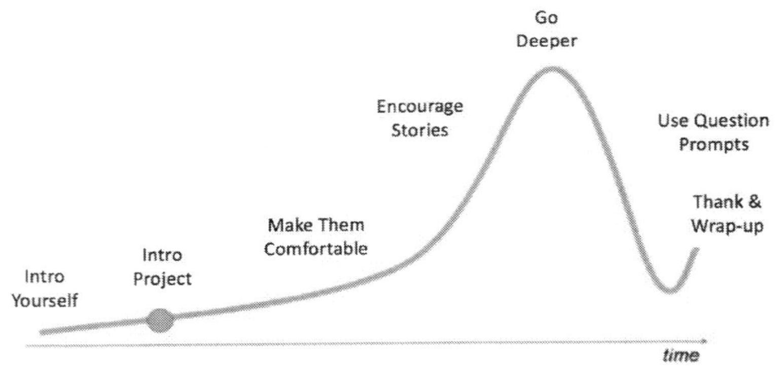

Intro Yourself → Intro Project → Make Them Comfortable → Encourage Stories → Go Deeper → Use Question Prompts → Thank & Wrap-up

time

How to Analyze:

- **Make headlines**: A descriptive summary of the data you've collected
- **Create an empathy map**: A synthesis of the interview that captures what users say, do, think, and feel
- **Conduct a point of view analysis**: Go straight from human-perspective to brainstorming change ideas

234

Empathy Observations

Empathy observations allow you to watch what people do and how they interact with their environment. Observations give you clues about what they think and feel and help you learn about what they need.

How to Conduct:
- Decide who you are observing and why
- Be a learner
- Think like a traveler
- Capture your learnings

Variations:
- Fly-on-the-Wall
- Context Inquiry
- Shadowing
- Do-it-yourself Immersion

Journey Map

A journey map is a visualization of a user's specific experience, creating a process map from the user's perspective.

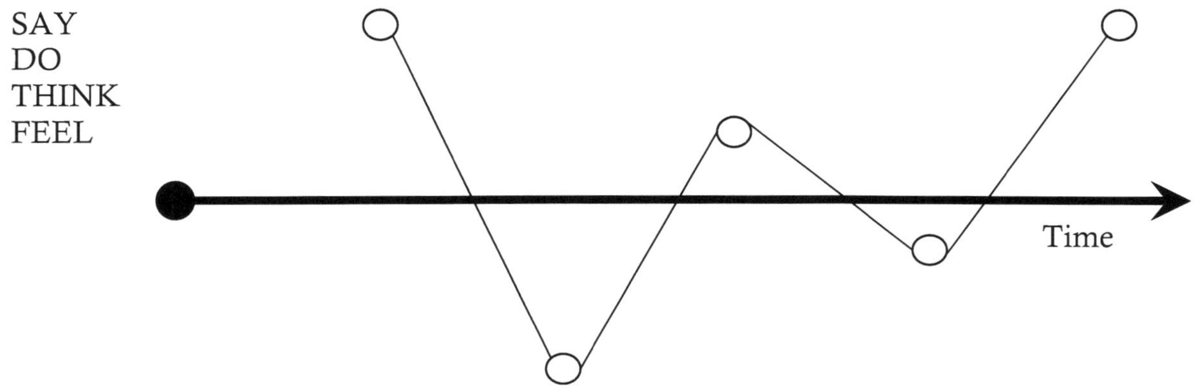

SAY
DO
THINK
FEEL

Time

How to Construct
- Choose the user you want to learn more about and identify your learning goal
- Choose the "journey" or experience you want to map; determine where the journey begins and ends
- Conduct an empathy interview and observation
- Identify the key phases of your user's journey
- Map them onto a timeline
- Add details to each phase

Process Failure Analysis Reference Sheet

When to use a process failure analysis:

Elements of a process failure analysis:

CHANGE IDEAS

FAILURE MODES

CURRENT PROCESS

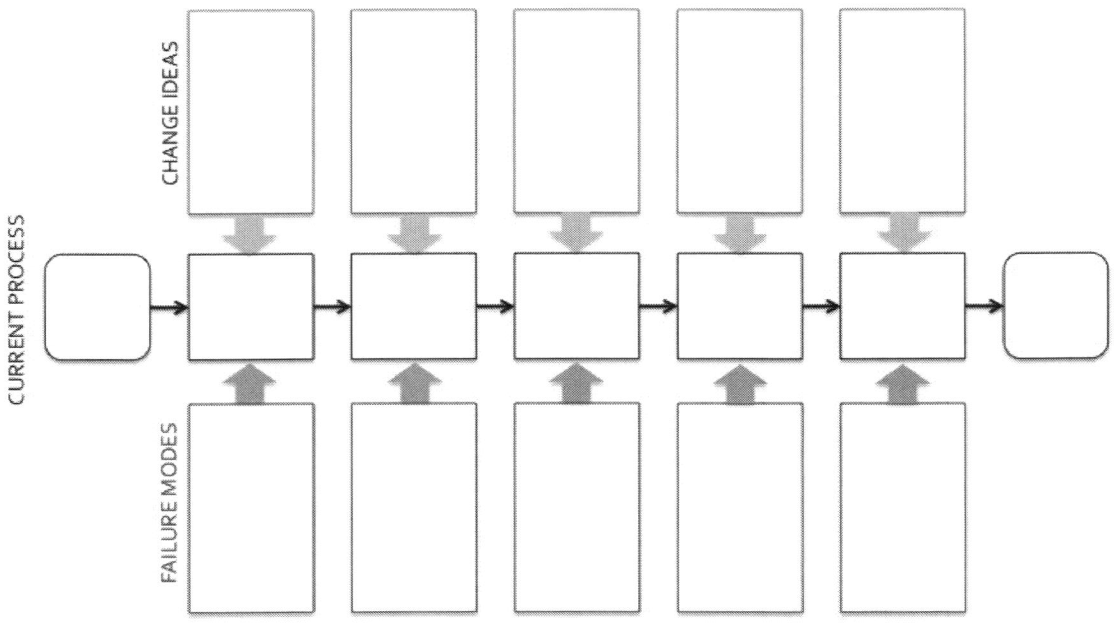

How to do a process failure analysis:

① Create a high-level process map

② Identify possible causes of failures for each high-level process

   a. Ideally you would collect data to identify the frequency of each cause

   b. Ideally you would rate how critical each possible failure is regarding the effect on the desired outcome of the process.

③ Generate change ideas for the high priority break-downs

Process Failure Analysis Template

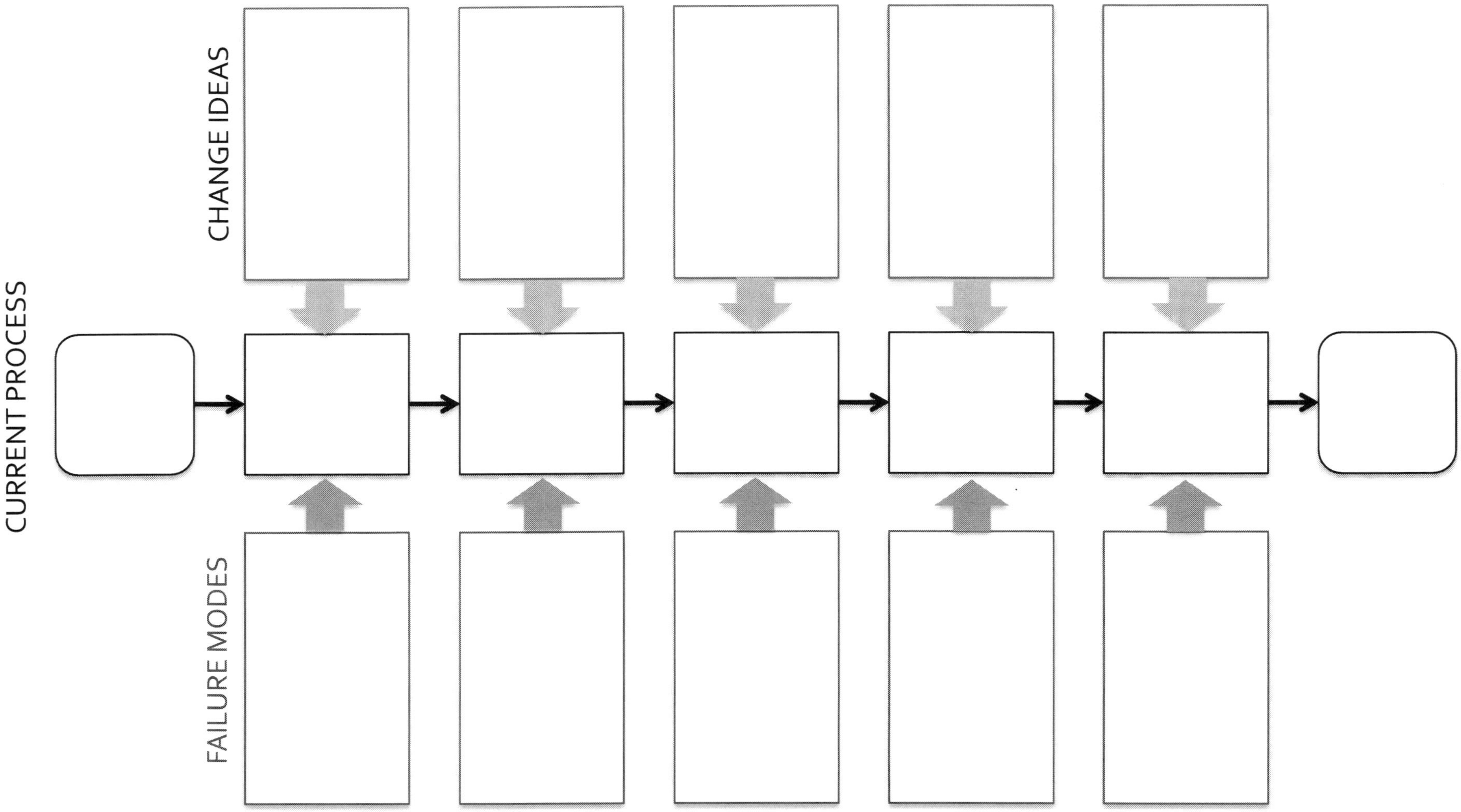

CURRENT PROCESS

CHANGE IDEAS

FAILURE MODES

Process Map Reference Sheet

When to use:

- To visualize and build a shared understanding of each step and decision point in the daily workflow for an individual, team or organization
- To capture an intended idealized design for what daily work might look like in a future state of the system

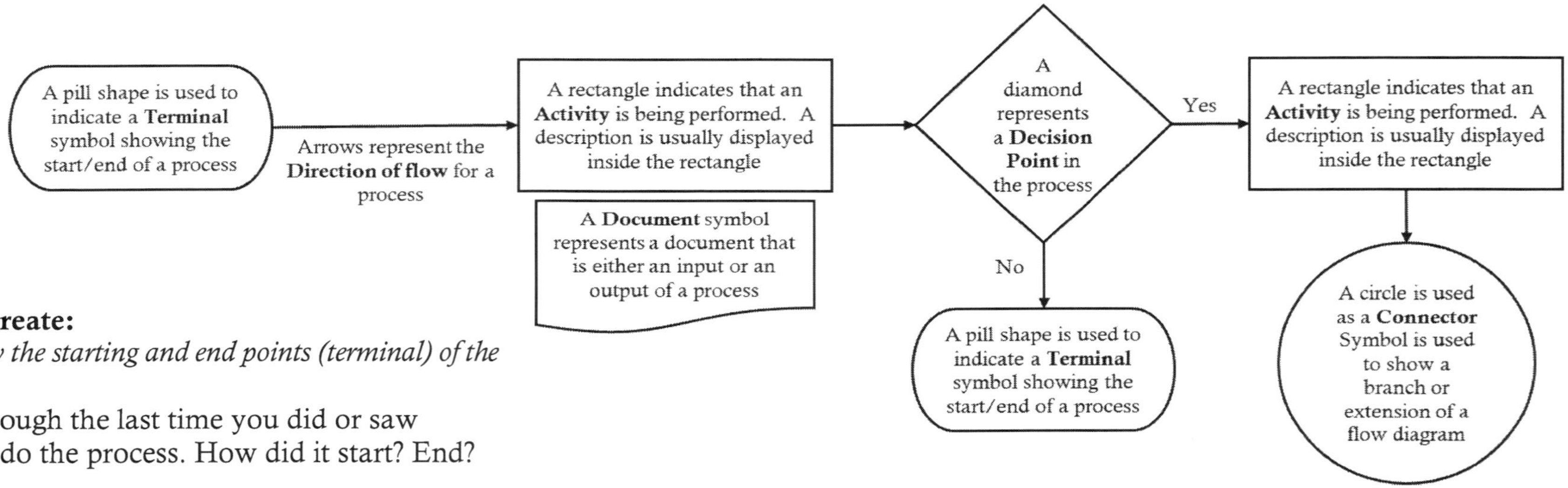

A pill shape is used to indicate a **Terminal** symbol showing the start/end of a process

Arrows represent the **Direction of flow** for a process

A rectangle indicates that an **Activity** is being performed. A description is usually displayed inside the rectangle

A **Document** symbol represents a document that is either an input or an output of a process

A diamond represents a **Decision Point** in the process

Yes → A rectangle indicates that an **Activity** is being performed. A description is usually displayed inside the rectangle

A circle is used as a **Connector** Symbol used to show a branch or extension of a flow diagram

No → A pill shape is used to indicate a **Terminal** symbol showing the start/end of a process

How to create:

1. Identify the starting and end points (terminal) of the process.
Think through the last time you did or saw someone do the process. How did it start? End?

2. Map out the sequence of steps
Ask yourself: "Then what did we do? What happened next?" Add a step for each new activity.

3. Add detail
Add detail to each step. Who did each step? When? How long did it take?

4. Reflect on the process
Write down what worked well about the process (+) and what could be improved (▲).
Use ideas to the right to help with your reflection.

Reflection ideas:

- **Time:** How long does the whole process take? Individual steps?
- **Ordering and number of steps:** Are the steps in the ideal order? Can any of the steps be combined to make the process more efficient?
- **Breakdowns:** Where are the delays and bottlenecks?
- **Outcome:** Did the process achieve what it was intended for?

Example process map

Force Field Analysis

When to use force field analysis:

- Teams may choose to produce this visualization when there is a need to create a common understanding of the system in which they work.
- When there is a desire for improvement and a team needs to examine the current forces, which might drive or restrain the system toward the desired performance.
- When a team has identified a problem of practice (poor performance) within their system and there is a need to examine the current forces reinforcing (driving) the problem and the current forces preventing (restraining) the problem from growing.

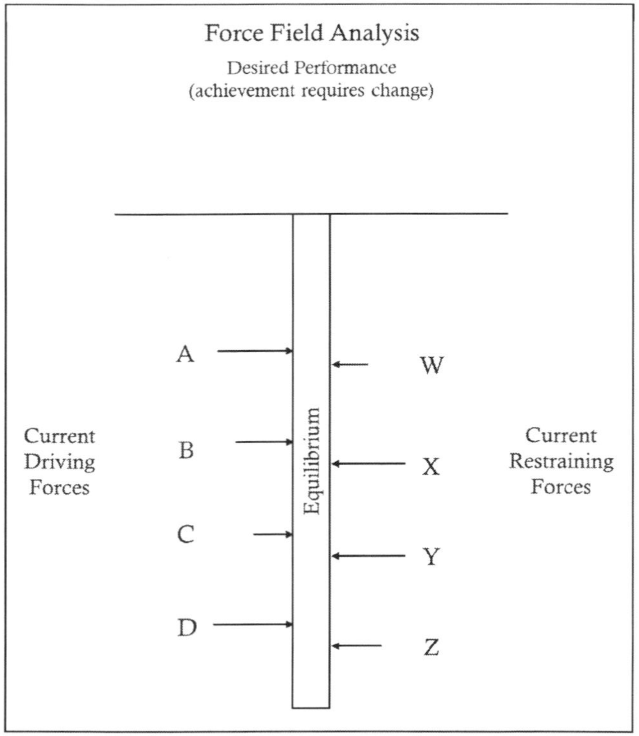

Five elements of a force field analysis:

1. A description of the desired performance.
2. The center line or line of equilibrium. This line, drawn vertically down the page represents the quasi-stationary equilibrium of the system as it current exists.
3. Driving forces — existing forces acting on the current system which are pushing performance towards the desired performance described.
4. Restraining forces — existing forces acting on the current system which are working against the desired performance described.
5. Arrow lines are drawn between each force and the center line. The length of arrow lines is an indicator of the perceived strength of the force described.

How to perform a force field analysis:

Format the diagram.
1. Identify the desired outcome for the system or process. Write this on the top of the page.
2. Draw a line from the desired outcome vertically down the page. This represents the current state of equilibrium.
3. Label the quadrants (Left = Current Driving Forces, Right = Current Restraining Forces).

Developing a shared understanding of the current forces
4. Brainstorm a list of driving forces. List these in the quadrant labeled Current Driving Forces.
5. Brainstorm a list of restraining forces. List these in the quadrant labeled Current Restraining Forces.
6. Draw an arrow from each force to the center line. Vary the length of arrow based on the strength of the force.

Force Field Analysis
Desired Performance
(achievement requires change)

Current Driving Forces: A, B, C, D
Current Restraining Forces: W, X, Y, Z
Equilibrium

Cause and Effect Diagram Reference Sheet

Cause and effect diagrams are useful for visualizing the complexity of the causes generating the observed effect or problem. They are used to:

- Identify categories of causal factors for which deeper investigation and data collection would be useful
- Summarize a team's current understanding of the main factors influencing an outcome

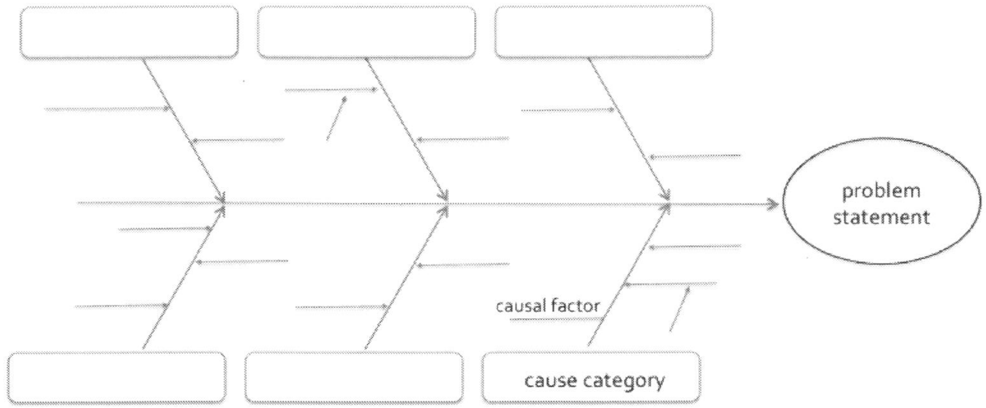

Elements of cause and effect diagram

Problem (or effect): Description of the problem of practice or gap in performance

Cause categories: Groups of related causes. These groupings can be organized by:

- General groupings: perceived similarity
- Dispersion analysis groupings: materials, methods, equipment, measurement, environment and people
- Process steps

Specific causal factors: plotted as a nested structure as offshoots of the main categories

How to construct an initial cause and effect diagram

1. Choose the effect (or problem) to be studied.
2. Create an operational definition of the problem.
3. Gather the team members and/or other key stakeholders with diverse perspectives on the problem.
4. Have each team member individually record their hypotheses about the main contributing causes based on their perspective and/or the evidence they gathered.
5. Share out proposed causes. Group causes into categories
6. Determine a method and process for deepening the understanding of the problem using evidence (quantitative or qualitative).

How to use a cause and effect diagram to investigate

1. Use the identified causes to create a check sheet
2. Collect data on the frequency with which causes are observed in practice
3. Visualize the frequency of causes using a pareto chart
4. If revealed, focus efforts on the vital few causes which emerge most frequently, or which subject matter expertise suggests may be very important for improving the system.

241

Cause and Effect Template

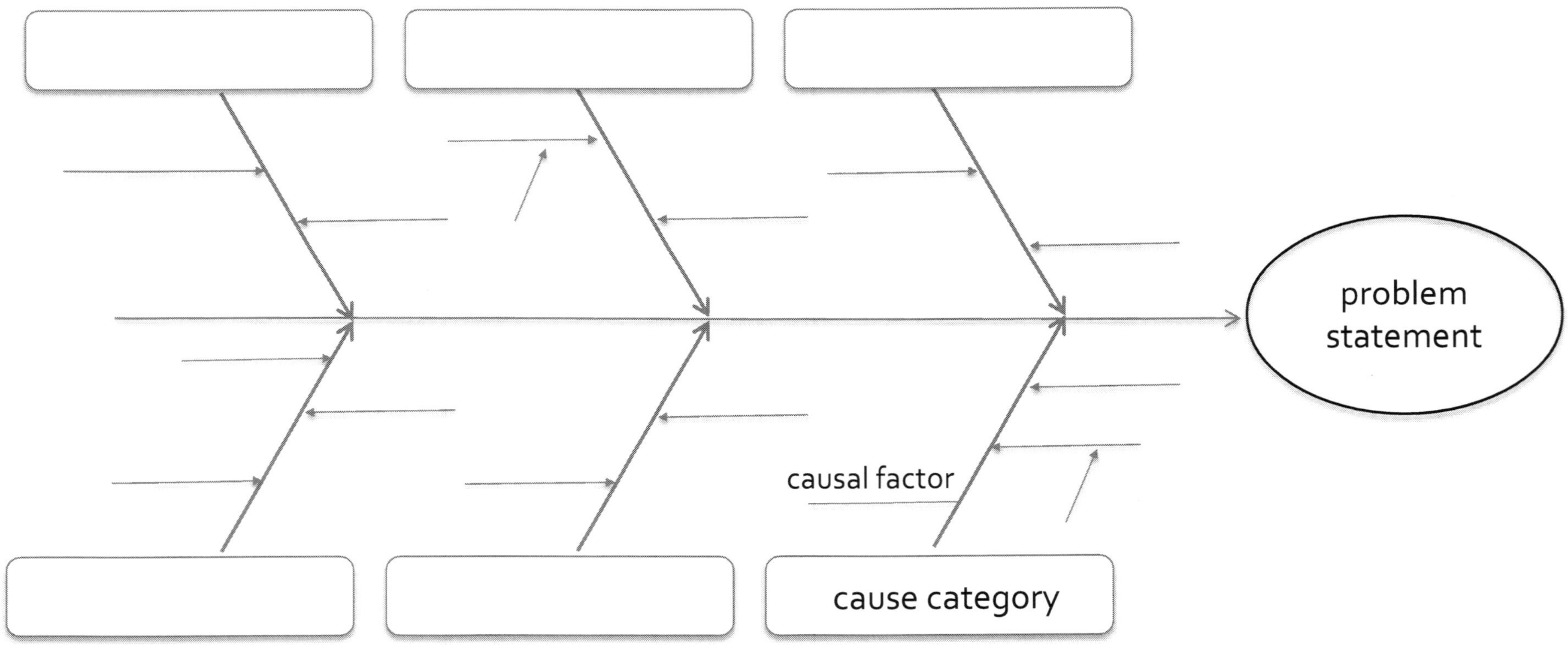

- problem statement
- causal factor
- cause category

Aim Statements Reference Sheet

When to use an aim statement:

- When the team is ready to come to agreement on the focus and direction of an improvement effort
- Return to the aim regularly to assess progress

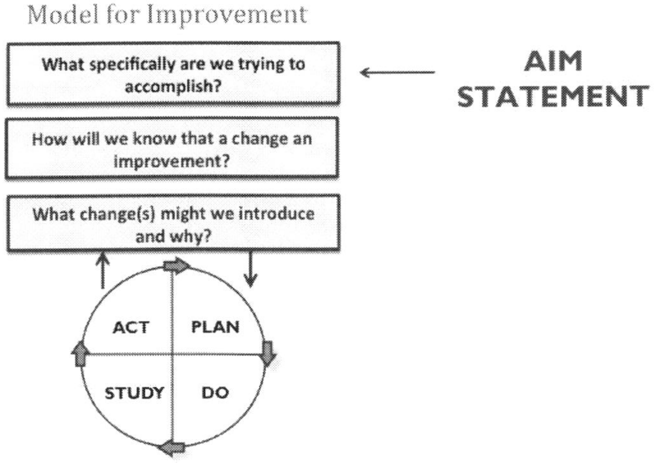

Model for Improvement

```
What specifically are we trying to
accomplish?

How will we know that a change an
improvement?

What change(s) might we introduce
and why?
```

→ AIM STATEMENT

PLAN / DO / STUDY / ACT

Elements of an aim statement:

Aim statements **clearly define success** for the improvement effort by specifying:

✓ *What will be improved?* (clear, operational definitions of all key terms)
✓ *How much?* (measurable, specific numerical goals)
✓ *By when?* (timeframe)
✓ *Where? For whom?* (target population)

How to craft an aim statement

1. Create a sentence (or two) that captures the team's current answer to: What are we trying to accomplish? Write it so everyone can see it.
    - Appropriate scope?
2. Add specificity:
    - Define key terms
    - Identify measures
    - Set targets based on baseline data
3. Settle on and record a final (for now) articulation of the aim
4. Link your aim statement to a compelling narrative motivates the specific focus selected by your team.

Theory of Practice Improvement: Driver Diagram Reference Guide

When to use a driver diagram:

- **Chartering** — During the early stage of an improvement journey the creation of an initial theory of improvement is a critical step.
- **Prioritization, direction, and measurement** — Improvement teams use the tool to decide where to introduce changes to the system and inspire what measures are needed to understand when improvement occurs.
- **Consolidation** — At regular intervals teams reconsider and update their driver diagram to reflect ongoing learning.
- **Publication** — Final driver diagrams are very useful in communicating the learning a team achieved during the life of a project.

Elements of a driver diagram

1. *Aim Statement / Outcome of Interest*: The aim statement articulates the outcome(s) of the system, the intended magnitude of the improvement, and a timeframe for completion.
2. *Primary Drivers*: Primary drivers are high level elements within the system that are believed to need to change to accomplish the aim. They can be thought of as "what" needs to change in the system. Primary drivers can be comprised of structures, processes, or operating norms found in the system.
3. *Secondary Drivers*: Secondary drivers are more actionable approaches, places, or opportunities within the system where a change can occur. They can be thought of as "where" in the system a change can be applied.
4. *Change Ideas*: Change ideas are tangible and specific in nature. They can be thought of as "how" the system will be changed. They represent very specific actions to be taken on the system.

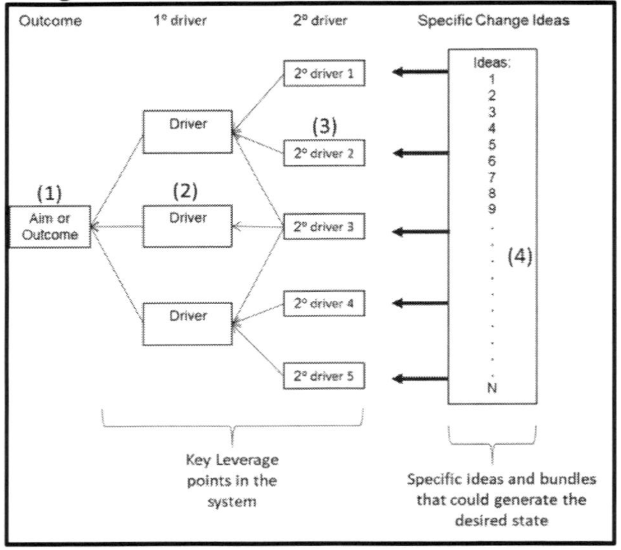

How to create a driver diagram (social process 1)

1) Develop and articulate an aim statement
2) Identify the primary drivers and place them on the visualization
3) Identify the secondary drivers that have strong influence over the primary drivers, place them on the visualization and connect the important links between secondary and primary drivers
4) List change ideas
5) Place these on the visualization, along with links to the secondary drivers they are intended to influence

How to create a driver diagram (social process 2)

1) Develop and articulate an aim statement
2) List change ideas
3) Conduct an affinity protocol on the generated change ideas to look for commonalities in what they are addressing
4) Based on the affinity protocol generate secondary drivers and place them on the driver diagram visualization
5) Determine which primary drivers represent, are influenced by, or are connected to the secondary drivers identified
6) Place primary drivers on the driver diagram visualization
7) Connect change ideas to secondary drivers to primary drivers to the aim statement

Driver Diagram Template

NAME
date

Aim statement

MEASURES:

Primary drivers

Secondary drivers

Change ideas

"Probably wrong and definitely incomplete"

Plan-Do-Study-Act (PDSA) Cycle Reference Sheet

When to use a PDSA cycle:

- Test a change idea in practice in order to learn:
  - Feasibility and user response to a change idea
  - Whether a change is an improvement
  - How to adapt the change to a new context
  - How to minimize resistance to implementation
  - How to embed a change and make it permanent

Elements of a PDSA cycle:

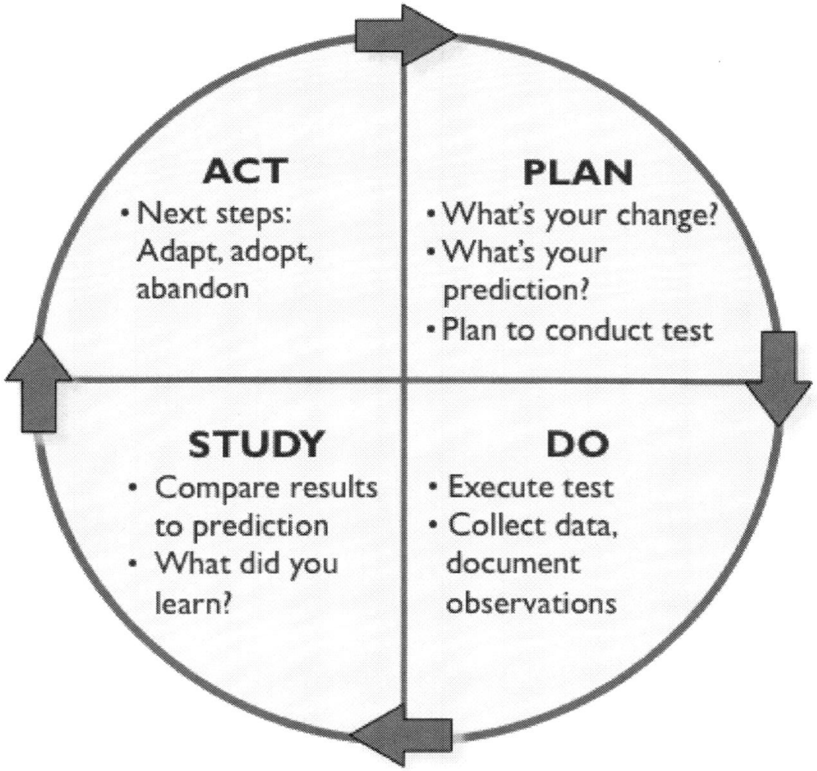

PLAN
- What's your change?
- What's your prediction?
- Plan to conduct test

DO
- Execute test
- Collect data, document observations

STUDY
- Compare results to prediction
- What did you learn?

ACT
- Next steps: Adapt, adopt, abandon

How to run a PDSA cycle:

① Identify the **change idea** you want to test

② PLAN the experiment
  - Identify a learning goal
  - Determine the scale and opportunity to test
  - Create learning questions and make predictions
  - Create a data collection sheet
  - Prepare to test the change idea

③ DO the experiment
  - Carry out the plan
  - Collect data & record surprises

④ STUDY the results
  - Compare results to predictions
  - Reflect on the initial hypothesis

⑤ Determine next steps (ACT)

⑥ PLAN the next PDSA

PDSA Example
A small scale test of a change

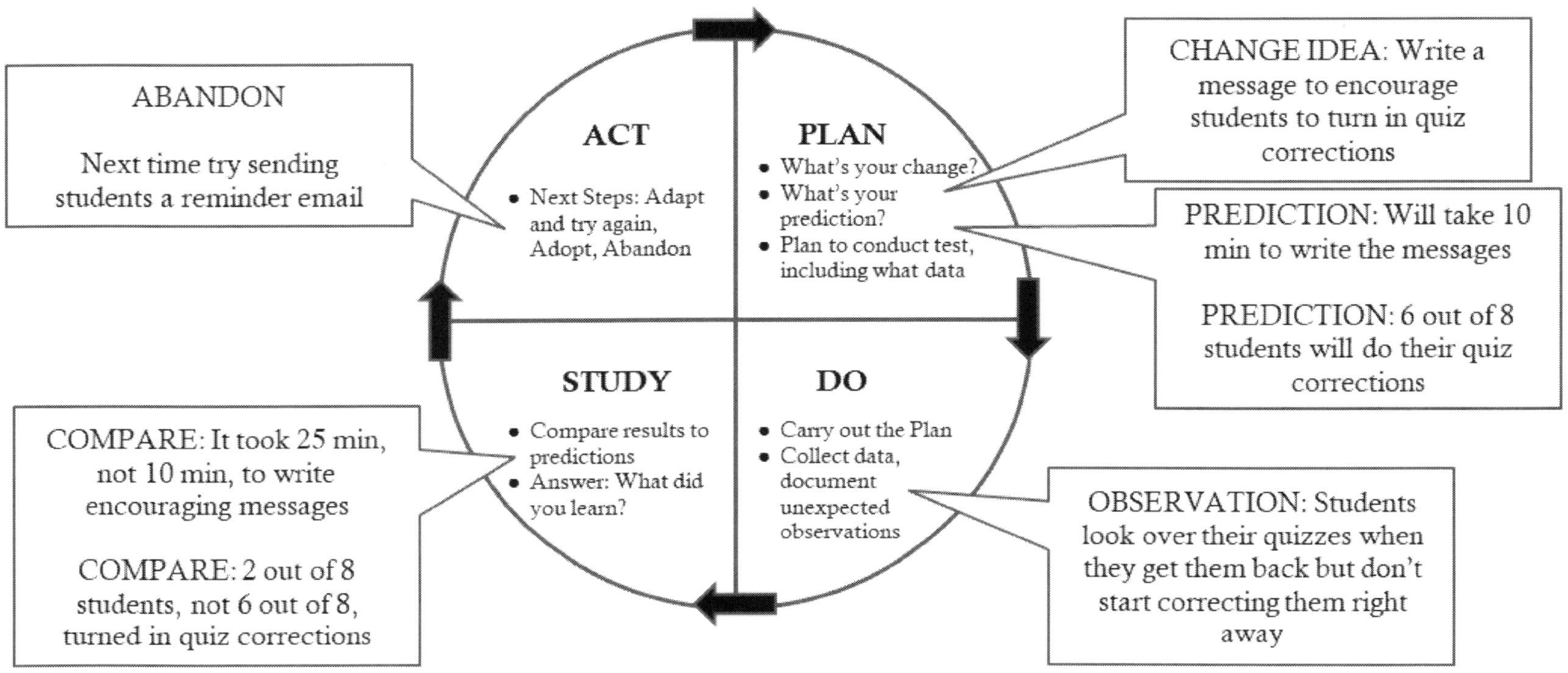

PLAN
- What's your change?
- What's your prediction?
- Plan to conduct test, including what data

CHANGE IDEA: Write a message to encourage students to turn in quiz corrections

PREDICTION: Will take 10 min to write the messages

PREDICTION: 6 out of 8 students will do their quiz corrections

DO
- Carry out the Plan
- Collect data, document unexpected observations

OBSERVATION: Students look over their quizzes when they get them back but don't start correcting them right away

STUDY
- Compare results to predictions
- Answer: What did you learn?

COMPARE: It took 25 min, not 10 min, to write encouraging messages

COMPARE: 2 out of 8 students, not 6 out of 8, turned in quiz corrections

ACT
- Next Steps: Adapt and try again, Adopt, Abandon

ABANDON
Next time try sending students a reminder email

PDSA Template 1

Test Title:		Date:
Tester:	Cycle#:	Driver:
What change idea is being tested?		
What is the overall GOAL of the test? *		

*Identify your overall goal: To make something work better? Learn how an innovation works? Learn how to text in a new context? Learn how to spread or implement?

1) PLAN

Questions: Questions you have about what will happen. What do you want to learn?	Predictions: Make a prediction for each question. Not optional.	Data: Data you will collect to test predictions

Details: Describe the who/what/when/where of the test. Include your data collection plan.

3) STUDY

What were the results? Comment on your predictions in the rows below. Were they correct? Record any data summaries as well.

☐

☐

☐

☐

What did you learn?

2) DO
(Briefly describe what happened during the test, surprises, difficulty getting data, obstacles, successes, etc.)

4) ACT
(Describe modifications and/or decisions for the next cycle; what will you do next?)

PDSA Template 2

Problem:

Aim of this cycle:

The Change Idea:

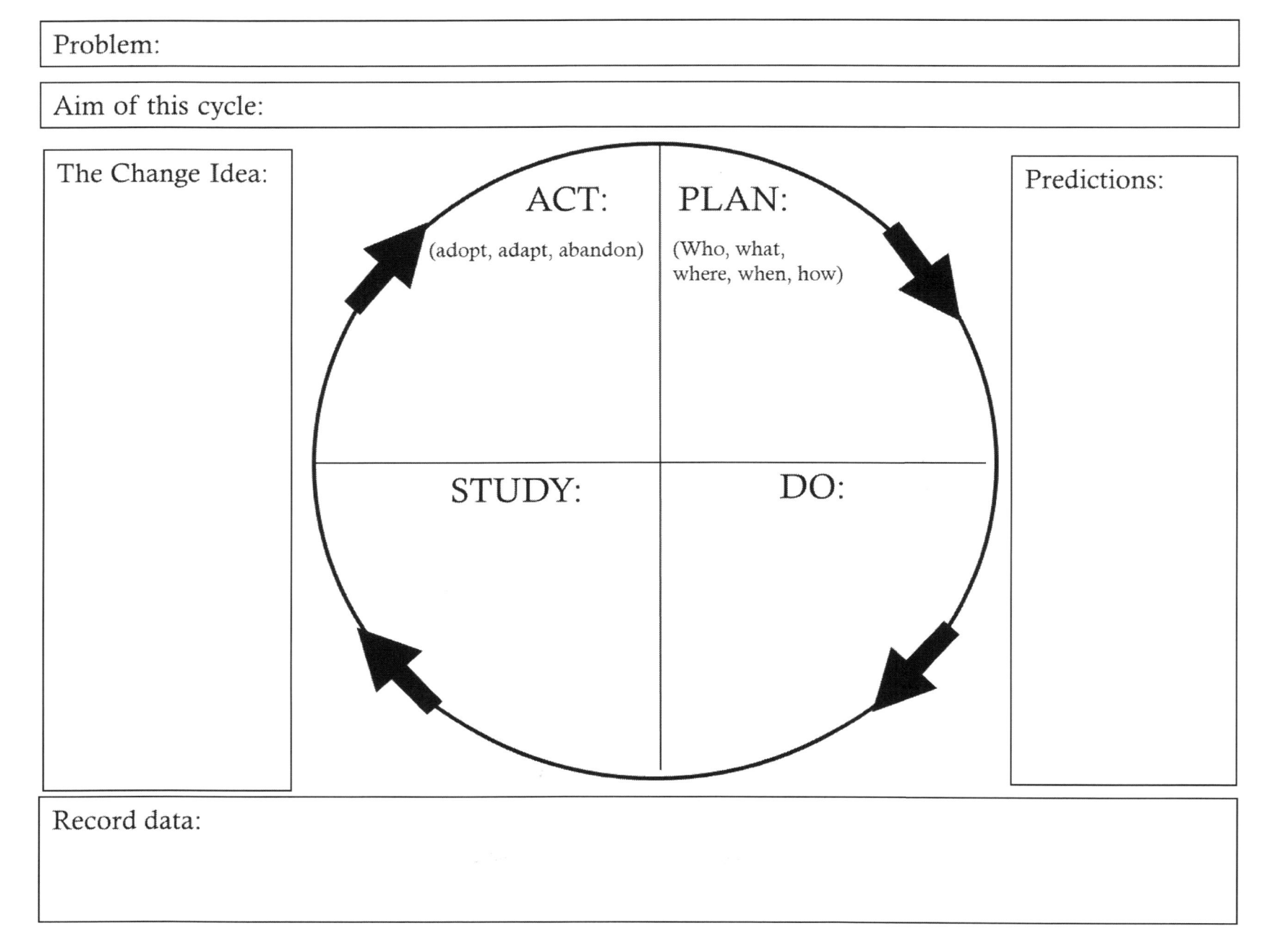

Predictions:

PLAN:
(Who, what, where, when, how)

DO:

STUDY:

ACT:
(adopt, adapt, abandon)

Record data:

PDSA Template 3

PDSA CYCLE #_____ Date:

Change Idea	Intended Result →	When and where can I try it? What do I hope to learn?

PLAN

DO

Learning Question	Prediction	Actual Result

Other observations

D
O

Use this space to do one or all of the following:
  1) Prototype your change idea
  2) Create a data collection form
  3) Capture other logistics to run the test

STUDY

ACT

1) Compare results to predictions 2) What do you conclude about your original hypothesis?	Next Steps *adopt, adapt, expand, abandon*

250

PDSA Template 4 (2 pages)

PDSA Worksheet Team Name:	Cycle Number: Cycle start date: Cycle end date:

Problem:

PLAN: Describe the change you are testing and state the question(s) you want this test to answer (If I do x will y happen?) and your predictions.

The Change:

Aim of the Change:

Question	Prediction
1.	
2.	
3.	
4.	

How will you carry out the test and collect data to evaluate your predictions?

DO: Report what happened when you carried out the test. Describe observations, findings, problems encountered, and special circumstances.

STUDY: Compare your results to your predictions.

What happened? (Match with each Question/Prediction)
1.
2.
3.
4.

What did you learn? Any surprises?

ACT: Modifications or refinements for the next cycle; what will you do next?

PDSA Checklist and Coaching Plan

QUALITY CRITERIA (look-fors)	CRITERIA PRESENT YES or NO?
PLAN: Articulation of a clear hypothesis and learning goal	
A. The learning goal of the cycle is clear?	
B. Strong change idea *(based on best practice or prior learning)*	
C. Change idea is specified and developed?	
D. Clear predictions? *(avoid yes/no predictions when possible)*	
PLAN: Design of the experiment	
E. Data collection plan? *(must be related to predictions)*	
F. Scale of the test appropriate?	
Equity Checks • Does the change idea have the potential to interrupt inequitable practices? • Are assumptions explicit so they can be tested? • Have we integrated user voice to understand the user experience of the change?	
DO: Documentation of learning	
G. Carry out the plan? *(including collecting intended data)*	
H. Record any notes and surprises that happened during the test?	
STUDY/ACT: Evaluate the original hypothesis & determine next steps	
I. Compare what actually happened with predictions?	
J. New learning or theory refinement? *(explicit reference to the original hypothesis)*	
K. Suggested next steps? *(logical next steps based on the learning from this cycle)*	
Equity Checks • Reexamine the findings: were our original hypotheses influenced by biases or deficit thinking? • Were all team members and end users given fair opportunity to voice and challenge interpretations? • Do the next steps have the potential to interrupt inequitable practices and systems?	

WHERE TO FOCUS

What can you build on? What's most important?

Key learnings to highlight/reinforce

One specific area in which you would focus? (learning goal for the coaching conference)

COACHING MOVES AND STANCE

Agenda for your upcoming 30 min team meeting

What stance would you use for each part (inquiry? facilitative? Directive?)

Note: Equity checks inspired by work at the Rennie Center and Teach Plus

Planning PDSA Ramps

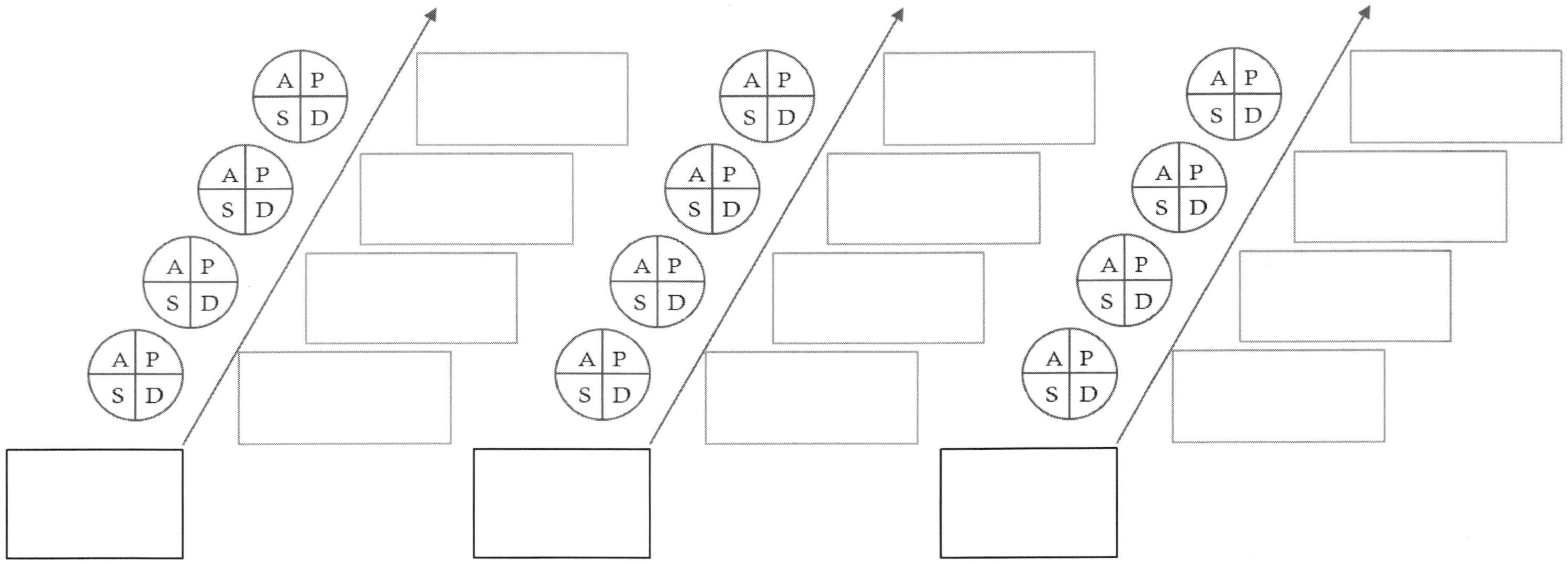

For each cycle summary it is useful to capture: any adaptations tried, who and where the cycle was completed and any lingering questions generated as a result of the cycle.

254

Assessing Scale for Testing

Staff Readiness to Make Change

Current Situation		Resistant	Indifferent	Ready
Low Confidence that change idea will lead to Improvement	Cost of failure large	Very Small Scale Test	Very Small Scale Test	Very Small Scale Test
	Cost of failure small	Very Small Scale Test	Very Small Scale Test	Small Scale Test
High Confidence that change idea will lead to Improvement	Cost of failure large	Very Small Scale Test	Small Scale Test	Large Scale Test
	Cost of failure small	Small Scale Test	Large Scale Test	Implement

Langley et al

Staff Readiness to Make Change

Current Situation		Resistant	Indifferent	Ready
Low Confidence that change idea will lead to Improvement	Limited capacity	Very Small Scale Test	Very Small Scale Test	Very Small Scale Test
	Extant capacity	Very Small Scale Test	Very Small Scale Test	Small Scale Test
High Confidence that change idea will lead to Improvement	Limited capacity	Very Small Scale Test	Small Scale Test	Large Scale Test
	Extant capacity	Small Scale Test	Large Scale Test	Implement

Visualizing Quantitative Information Reference Sheet

There are six types of graphics associated with the visual display of quantitative information.

LINE GRAPH. Used to display data unfolding over time.

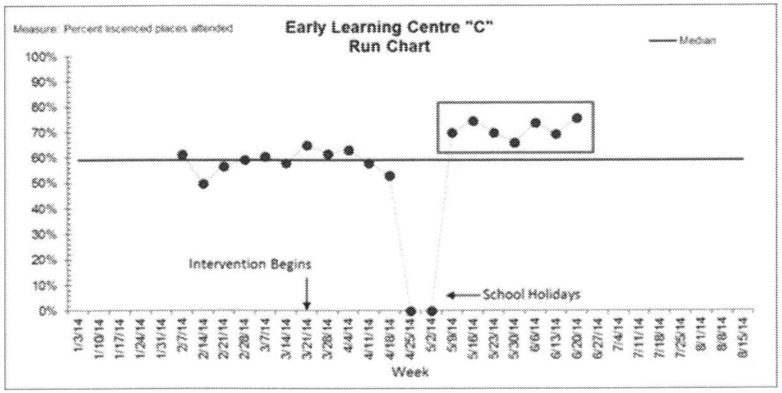

ORDERED BAR CHART. Used to display categorical data in rank order.

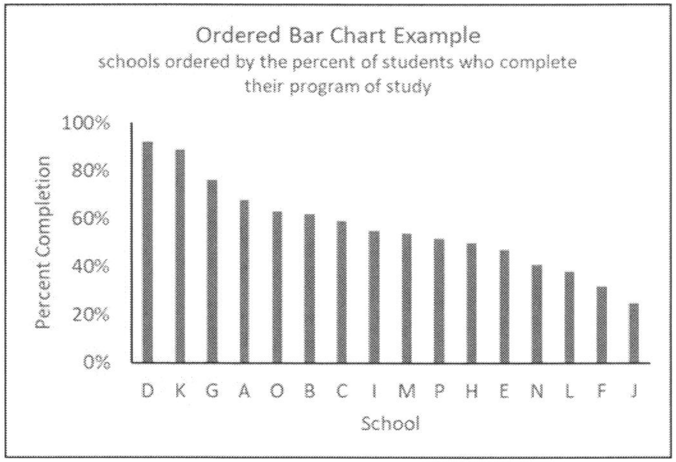

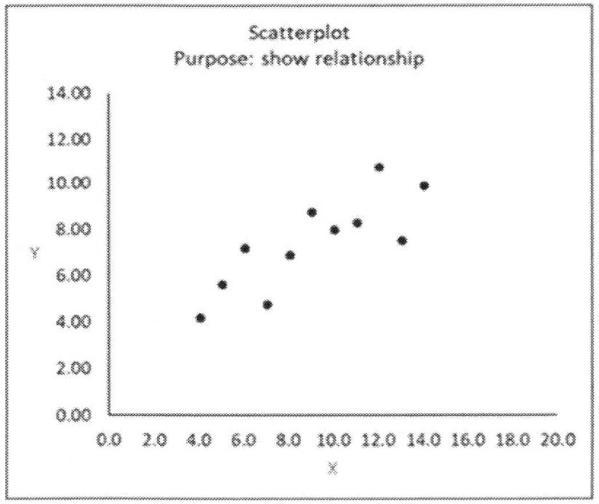

PARETO CHART. Used to understand the frequency and contribution of categorical data. Special use of the ordered bar chart

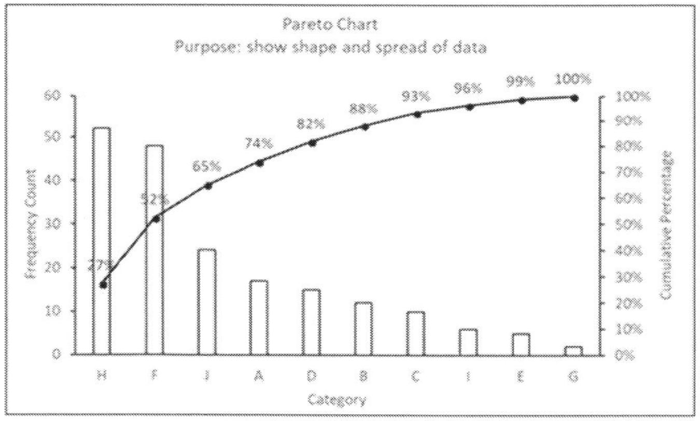

SCATTER PLOT. Used to display the relationship between two sets of continuous data.

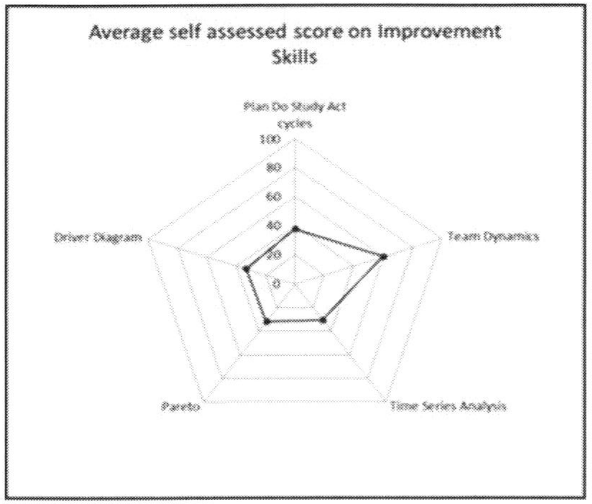

Data Visualization Checklist

- ☐ Clear title
- ☐ Axes are clearly labeled
- ☐ Scale is appropriate (and not deceptive)
- ☐ Appropriate display for the data presented
- ☐ Annotations are present (where they should be) and helpful
- ☐ Display allows for easy visual comparisons

BOX-AND-WHISKER PLOT. Used to visually summarize the distribution of a data set.

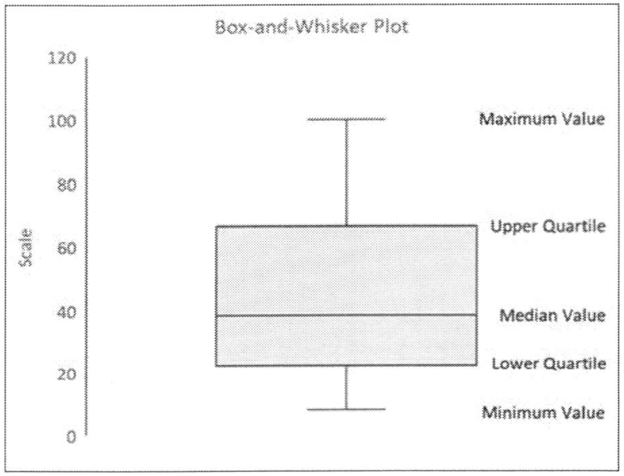

RADAR CHART (SPIDER DIAGRAM). Used to display multiple measures on a single chart.

Pareto Analysis Reference Guide

When to use Pareto analysis

Improvement teams find the use of Pareto analysis helpful for:

- Diagnosis during the initial stages of investigation of the system: understanding the gap, or problem.
- Understanding the frequency of with which various interventions, or services are being used by the system under study.
- In the communication of important learning accomplished by completing a Pareto analysis of data.

Steps for Conducting a Pareto analysis

1) Identify a learning question(s)
2) Identify what information is needed to answer the learning question
3) List possible variables that could be useful in stratifying the data collected
4) Develop any important operational definitions to clarify the investigation
5) Identify the duration and location for the collection of data
6) Devise a simple check sheet for collecting the data
7) Collect the data (minimum of 30 occurrences)
8) Draw the vertical and horizontal axes
9) Order the categories by most frequently occurring on the left to least frequently occurring on the right
10) Plot the bars using the vertical axis to scale
11) Label the graph (title, axis, data labels, categories, relevant annotations)

Optional steps if using a secondary (vertical) y-axis

12) Calculate the percent contribution of each category to the whole
13) Calculate the cumulative percent of categories moving from left to right on the graph
14) Plot the secondary axis and line graph using the cumulative percent numbers at each category

Example of a Pareto Chart

Consider pairing this tool with:

- Cause and effect diagram to analyze causes objectively using collected data
- Run charts to understand if the vital few categories identified display consistent random variation in performance over time

Run chart Reference Sheet

When to use a run chart

Consider displaying data on a run chart when:

- Collecting time series or sequentially ordered data
- There is a need to make performance visible to various stakeholders.
- There is a need to assess whether a change made to the system has resulted in a change in performance.
- There is a desire to determine whether a performance change has been sustained by the process or system.

Elements of a run chart

- X-axis (horizontal axis) — plots the order in which the data was collected, most often by time.
- Y-axis (vertical axis) — plots the measure of interest.
- Data points — plot the specific values of the data collected.
- Median — acts as a point of comparison to assist in the detection of changes in performance. Is generally included when there are ≥10 data points.
- Labels — run charts include labels for the x-axis, the y-axis, a chart title.
- Annotations — adding words to run charts helps greatly in telling a data story, including what happened when and why.

Seven steps for making a run chart

1. Formation of a learning question that is best answered using a run chart. Examples of learning questions include:
   - How many families are we serving per day (or week, or month)?
   - How many times do I reinforce positive behaviors in my classroom per class?
   - How many PDSA cycles are we as a network completing each week?
2. Develop the scale for the x-axis (horizontal axis). Largely dependent on the frequency of data collection, or the frequency with which it is valuable to have data summarized.
3. Develop the scale for the y-axis (vertical axis). The scale of the y-axis will depend on the data collected and good visual display of information practices should be adhered to.
4. Plot the data values (points) for each subgroup for which data was collected.
5. Calculate and place a median on the run chart. In most cases this should be done only when 10 or more data points have been collected and plotted on the run chart.
6. Label the run chart effectively, including labels for the title, x-axis, and y-axis, median, etc.
7. Annotate the run chart with any additional information that might help to tell the story of performance, change and/or improvement.

Four Rules for Interpreting Run charts

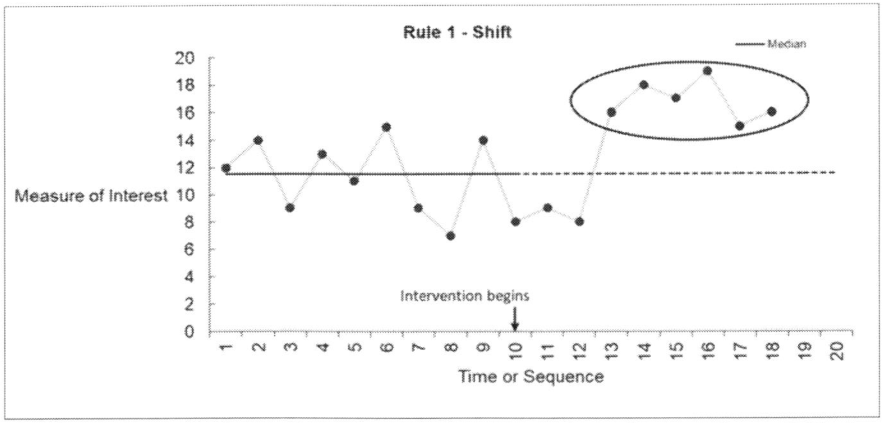

Rule 1 - Shift

Shift: Occurs when six or more consecutive data values fall above the median or below the median. Data points falling directly on the median do not count towards or against the presence of a shift.

Rule 2 - Trend

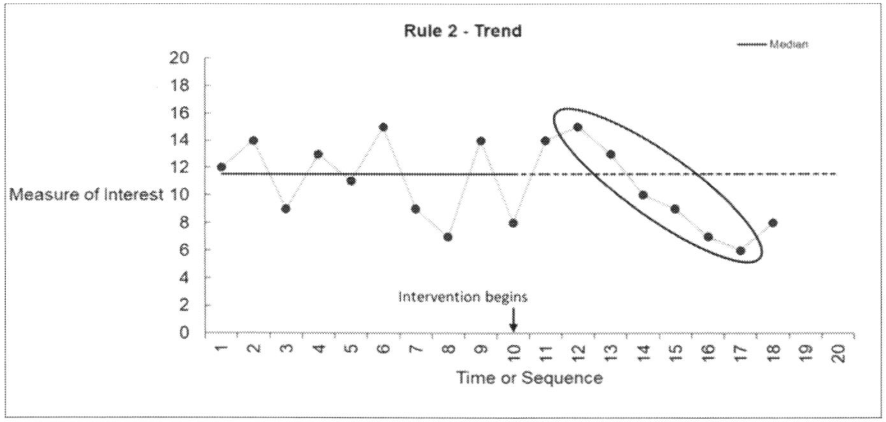

Trend: Occurs when five or more consecutive data values are all increasing or all decreasing. It is possible for two or more consecutive values to have exactly the same value. In these cases, the data points, having the same value, falling consecutively, neither make nor break the trend.

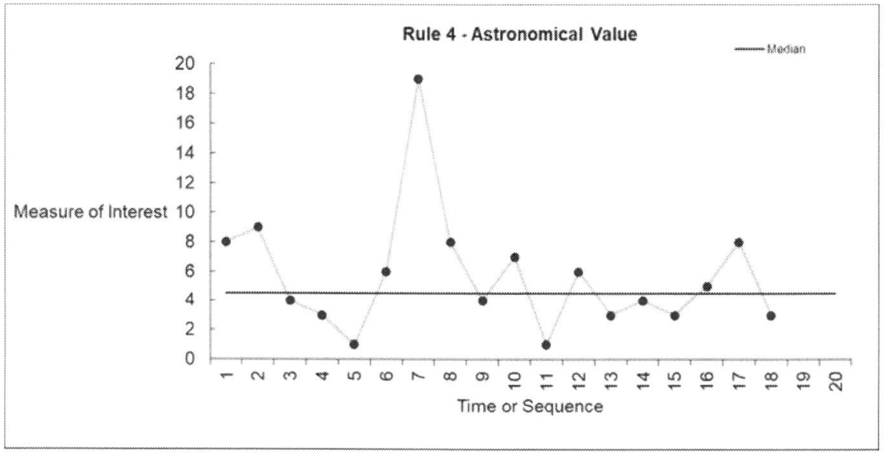

Rule 4 - Astronomical Value

Astronomical Value: Occurs when a single data value is blatantly, or obviously different, from the performance of the rest of the data points plotted. This rule is the only rule not based on a calculation of probability and is dependent on the subjective application of subject matter expertise to the data presented.

Too Many or Too Few Runs: A run is defined as consecutive data points on one single side of the median. Each time the data line crosses the median, a new run is begun. If a data point falls exactly on the median, that point does not break the run. It is ignored. To understand if there are more than or less than the expected number of runs use the table above.

Total count of number of data points displayed on the run chart (excluding any data points falling exactly on the median)	Minimum number of runs needed for random variation (if there are fewer than this number, non-random variation is detected)	Maximum number of runs allowed for random variation (if there are more than this number, non-random variation is detected)
10	3	9
11	3	10
12	3	11
13	4	11
14	4	12
15	5	12
16	5	13
17	5	13
18	6	14
19	6	15
20	6	16
21	7	16
22	7	17
23	7	17
24	8	18
25	8	18
26	9	19
27	10	19
28	10	20
29	10	20
30	11	21

Values described by Swed and Eisenhart, 1943, summarized by both Ott, 1975 and Provost and Murray 2011

Appendix B: Protocols and Agendas

In this appendix, you will find:

- Initiating Conversation: Sample Agenda (with questions and listen-fors)
- Sample Agenda of Initial Launch Meetings
- Huddle Protocol and Note Taking Form
- Team Meeting Protocol
- Data Conversation Protocol
- Learning Consolidation Protocol

Reference Sheets are available online at www.improvementcollective.com.

Initiating Conversation: Sample Agenda (with questions and listen-fors)

Objectives

- Build a relationship between the improvement coach and those initiating the improvement work
- Identify focus area and potential team members for improvement work
- Assess the group's readiness for commissioning an improvement team
- Create an action plan for commissioning an improvement team

Who should attend?

- The sponsor of the improvement work (if identified)
- Organizational leaders whose departments are impacted by the improvement work (sometimes the organization's leadership team)
- It can also be helpful to have a representative from the different levels of the organization that would participate on the team

To prepare ahead of time

- Send a note with the agenda and asking the team to bring relevant data and any other relevant docs
- Prepare questions and anticipate possible follow-up activities
- Prepare talking points on improvement science
- Prepare an outline of how you might phase the improvement work (see project proposal)

Time	Topic	Key Questions	Listen-for / Probe
2 min	Introductions and meeting objectives		

5 min	Establish a coaching relationship	- Introductions and background (if necessary)
		- Potential questions
		  o Have you had outside help with improvement before?
		  o What works for you in being coached? What should I avoid?	

15 min	Motivation and focus of improvement work	- Facilitated conversation about focus of improvement work
		- Potential questions
		  o What are you hoping to improve? What would be a win?
		  o Tell me about why this is important to you personally? To the organization?
		  o What do you know about how well you are currently doing? What are you curious about?
		- Review data (if available)
			- **Compelling motivation for the work.** Learn what matters to people both personally and organizationally. Understand their felt need.
			- **Potential focus area for improvement work and assumptions about scope.** Get a sense of how clear the improvement focus is and how much work will need to be done to scope it down to a reasonable size. Assess whether current performance is well enough understood to select sites and a focus.
			-

264

		- **Capacity and comfort with data.** Assess their ability to report on clear data (i.e., concrete numbers, appropriate visualizations) and effectively analyze data to understand what is going on. - **Level of curiosity.** Do they try to explain away potential gaps in performance or are they willing to hear and explore potential theories?

8 min	Overview of improvement	- **Provide brief overview of improvement science approach** highlighting:
		  o How an improvement science approach is different
		  o Role of an improvement coach
		  o Role of leaders in an improvement approach
		  o High-level overview of the improvement process
		- **Potential questions**
		  o What resonates with you about an improvement science approach? What are you worried about?
		- **Level of understanding of improvement science.** Assess how familiar they are with improvement science and/or experience with other types of inquiry.

10 min	Identifying people and roles	- Brainstorm possible sites and members and identify other potential stakeholders that need to be engaged
		- **Potential questions**
		  o Who would be involved in the improvement work? Do they have a felt need? Do they have the capacity (room) to focus on this right now?
		  o Who else needs to be on board for this improvement work? Are they on the same page?
		- Assign people to follow up and gauge interest and bandwidth (if necessary)
		- **Right decision-makers and expertise.** Assess if the appropriate people are in the room to decide who should be on the team and if they have access to the appropriate expertise given the focus area.
		- **Appropriate allocation of time and resources.** Assess if leaders have accurate understanding of time and resources it takes for team to engage in improvement work and is making the appropriate allocations.

5 min	Next steps	- Identify additional activities - Schedule next meeting

<u>Alternatives:</u>
- You can provide some of the questions around the motivation for the improvement work in advance and have them come prepared to share their initial thoughts on the focus and structure of improvement work.

Sample Agenda of Initial Launch Meetings

Meeting 1	Meeting 2	Meeting 3
(7 min) Go-round: "I'm 95% sure that I'm the only one on this team who…" (8 min) Introduction to improvement focus + improvement process + roles (15 min) Improvement = learning • Individual write: What do you need? What are you worried about? How can I help you as coach? • Go round: Share one of each. (10 min) Intro to understanding the problem: Getting curious. Group conversation: What is currently happening? • What do we know? • What do we want to know? (15 min) Empathy interviews • Introduction to why and how • Individual time to plan who and what curious about • Share out (5 min) +/Delta	(15 min) Go-round: Tell a story from student you connected with and why (15 min) Team norms • Bring back a list from last conversation. • Add procedural norms (meetings, communication etc.) (5 min) Reorient purpose (use language from first conversation) (20 min) Introduce next improvement activity (based on questions the team has) • Introduction • Individual time to plan • Share out (3 min) Introduce teamwork space/documentation routines (2 min) +/Delta	(15 min) Introduce conversational capacity • Self-reflection, what struggle with? What do you need? • Share and add to norms list • Prioritize norms (5 min) Reorient purpose (20 min) Introduce next improvement activity (based on questions the team has) • Introduction • Individual time to plan • Share out (5 min) +/Delta
Do and Bring Back: -Empathy interview with another student	Do and bring back: -Empathy interview with another students	

Huddle Protocol and Note Taking Form

Time	Protocol	Notes
2 min	**Go-round check-in** - One word to describe how you are feeling right now - Go in alphabetical (or other order) and use for rest of the call	
1 min	**Goals of the Huddle** - Share learning from learning cycles - Collectively problem-solve any issues - Maintain momentum of this work **Norms** - Safe to share, no judgment zone - Share information most relevant to the team - Be concise and efficient with the group's time	
15 min	**Sharing** - What change idea did you test this week? What did you learn? *NOTE: Our sharing will be as specific and relevant as possible. Have any PDSAs and data in front of you.* Suggested format: - This week I've run x PDSAs... - I've been testing x change idea... - I've learned... - Therefore, next I want to...	
6 min	**Open discussion** - Where are you struggling? - What support do you need from the team?	
3 min	**Next steps by person** - What will you do next?	

267

Team Meeting Protocol

Time	Protocol	Notes
2 min	Go-round check-in • One word to describe how you are feeling right now • Go in alphabetical (or other order)	
1 min	Goals of Team Meeting • Consolidate learning from learning cycles and data Norms • Safe to share, no judgment zone • Use evidence to support claims and ideas • Be concise and efficient with the group's time	
20 min	Data Review • Review and discuss data **Protocol** • Walk through the data—explain display (e.g. what is this a graph of, what is represented on the different axes, etc.). Does everyone understand it? • What do you see and notice? (stay descriptive) • What hypotheses or explanations do you have about what you see? What alternative theories might exist? • What questions does the data raise for you?	
20 min	Consolidation of learning • What change ideas have been tested over the past month? How many PDSAs were run around each? • What was learned? What does the information tell us about efficacy of the change ideas tested? • Did you learn anything unexpected or surprising? Did we uncover or learn about other parts of our system that might need improvement? • Which, if any, change ideas should be abandoned? Adapted and tested further? Adopted? Based on what evidence?	
15 min	Plan next PDSAs 1) Given what we have learned, what change idea(s) do we want to test next? 2) Complete PLAN section for next PDSA: What will be done, who will do it, where will it happen, when will it happen, and what data will be collected.	
3 min	Closing: • Summary of any action items for the team • Plus/delta on the meeting	

Data Conversation Protocol

Making Sense of Data Collectively

Protocol

- Walk through the data — explain display (e.g. what is this a graph of, what is represented on the different axes, etc.). Does everyone understand it?
- What do you see and notice? (stay descriptive)
- What hypotheses or explanations do you have about what you see? What alternative theories might exist?
- What questions does the data raise for you?

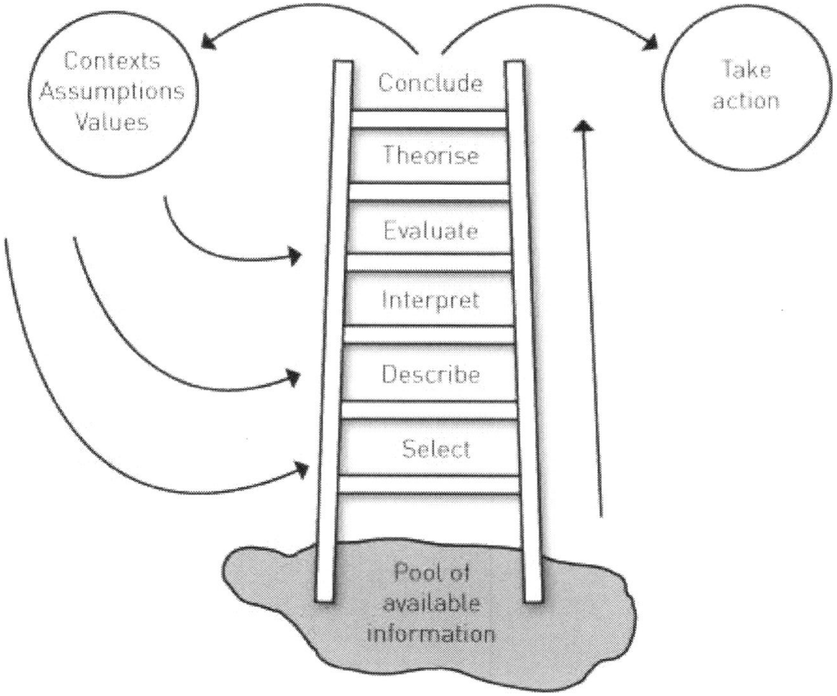

Learning Consolidation Protocol

For use in the Learning in Practice phase

To prepare:
- Create relevant data displays
- Design a facilitation plan for updating the theory based on your learning goal for the consolidation

Time	Protocol
10 min **Welcome and opening**	Go-Round Check In: • What has been your biggest "improvement win" from the last action period? Big Picture Orientation • Review aim and/or team charter • Review learning goal for the current action period • Goal of this meeting: Consolidate learning from the last action period Norms: • Safe to share, no judgment zone • Use evidence to support claims and ideas • Hard on ideas, soft on people • Lean into uncertainty

20 min
 	
What progress have we made?
	Take stock of current performance using key data displays
	• Orientation to the data display(s)
	• Individual review
	   ◦ Go round: Notice & wonder
	• Discuss:
	   ◦ Where is there evidence of improvement?
	      ■ Hypotheses and explanations?
	      ■ Key learning to investigate, capture or spread?
	   ◦ What's not moving in the right direction?
	      ■ Hypotheses and explanations?
	      ■ Next steps

30 min **What's our theory now?**	Summarize learning from testing changes (individually summarize and share out) • What change ideas have been tested over the past action period? What was learned? What does the information tell us about the efficacy of the change ideas tested? What did we uncover about other parts of the system that might need improving? Update the team's collective theory based on learning
20 min **Where do we focus next?**	• Determine focus and key learning goal for the next action period • Given what we have learned, what change idea(s) do we want to test next? • Who will do what?
15 min **Summarize & Close**	• Update the charter • Summary of any action items for the team • Plus/delta on the meeting

Appendix C: Improvement Journey — Forms, Templates, and One-Pagers

In this appendix, you will find:

- Improvement Journey Plan Template
- Learning Plan Template
- Investigation Summary Template
- Investigation Summary Look-Fors
- Charter Board Template
- Charter Form
- Charter Slide Deck Template
- Charter Assessment
- Improvement Routine Planning Template
- K-W-L Template
- Talking Points One-Pager

Reference Sheets are available online at www.improvementcollective.com.

Improvement Journey Plan Template

(1) Determine and label the LAUNCH and END POINT for your project (you may have to extend the timeline)
(2) Draw in the meetings you have with your team
(3) Determine natural phases of the project. Label with a vertical dotted line
(4) Use the Improvement Journey Map to plan a learning focus for each phase. Label the phases.
(5) Project what artifact you will produce at each phase of your journey

Timepoint 1   Timepoint 2   Timepoint 3   Timepoint 4   Timepoint 5

Learning Plan Template

Title/Team:

Iteration 1: {dates}
Driving Question(s):

Perspectives Needed:

Activities:

Iteration 2: {dates}
Driving Question(s):

Perspectives Needed:

Activities:

Iteration 3: {dates}
Driving Question(s):

Perspectives Needed:

Activities:

Investigation Summary Template

Title/Team: _____ Date/Version: _____

Team:

Important background on my local context:

DESCRIBE: Current performance (charts, graphs, quotes, observations, visualizations that describe what is currently happening)

ANALYZE: Why does this problem or need exist? (charts, graphs, visualizations that explain the gap)

GAP

GOAL or TARGET: What would success look like?

Investigation Summary Look-Fors

Title/Team: Date/Version:

Team:

Important background on my local context:

ANALYZE: Why does this problem or need exist? (charts, graphs, visualizations that explain the gap)

- Insight into the cause of the gap
- Use of an appropriate methodology to understand the gap and test assumptions
- Conclusions are supported by data (qualitative or qualitative)

GAP

DESCRIBE: Current performance (charts, graphs, quotes, observations, visualizations that describe what is currently happening)

1. A detailed understanding of current practice
2. Stays descriptive and doesn't go into higher on ladder of inference
3. Uses an appropriate methodology to get at different stakeholders' points of view
4. Uses a visual representation that can be repeatedly referred to
5. Data (when available)

GOAL or TARGET: What would success look like?

- Clear definition of what "quality" would be in this particular area
- Fits within the network goals

Charter Board Template

Team:
Members, norms, routines

What specifically are we trying to accomplish?

How will we know that a change is an improvement? *Performance measures, graphs*

What changes can we make that will result in improvement? *Driver Diagram, process map, process list, initial change ideas*

Charter Form

What are we trying to accomplish?
Problem to be addressed (Broadly defines the WHAT? Provides any necessary background information and introduces the problem that the team is formed around. Two to three sentences)

Reason for the improvement work (Defines the WHY? Makes a powerful case to all stakeholders about why improvement is needed. Four to five sentences)

Aim statement and expected outcomes (How good? For whom? By when? One to three sentences)

How do we know a change is an improvement?
(Identify appropriate measures, outcome and process measures are specified at a minimum; very brief description of how often data will be collected, not necessarily how. Four to five sentences)

What changes can we make that will lead to improvement?
(Initial changes, ideas for PDSA cycles, constraints/barriers identified and brief ideas on how to address them. Four to five sentences)

Team Information
Who is on the team and what knowledge/skills do they bring?

Charter Slide Deck Template

Slide	Content
1	Improvement Team
2	Problem and Motivation
3	Aim Statement
4	Family of Measures
5	Initial Driver Diagram or Process Map

Charter Assessment

TEAM/PROJECT: _____   REVIEWER: _____

WHAT ARE WE TRYING TO ACCOMPLISH?

Compelling Case for Improvement • Benefit for the user is clear • Rationale for the focus is motivating	Strong Partial Weak	*Suggestins and comments:*
Clear, Compelling, Reasonable Aim • Expected outcomes are clear • Specific, numerical goals • Scope is appropriate given timeframe and resources	Strong Partial Weak	

HOW WILL WE KNOW IF A CHANGE IS AN IMPROVEMENT?

Relevant Measures are Identified • At least 1 outcome and 1 process measure are identified w/ operational definitions • Process measure(s) can be tracked frequently enough to assess progress	Strong Partial Weak	
Baseline Data is Displayed • Graphs have been created to track project measures • Clear description of current performance (qualitative and/or quantitative data)	Strong Partial Weak	

WHAT CHANGES MIGHT WE INTRODUCE AND WHY?

Initial Change Ideas are Identified • Well-defined initial change ideas	Strong Partial Weak	

WHO'S AT THE TABLE?

Appropriate Team Membership • The appropriate subject matter expertise is represented on the team • An organizational sponsor is identified	Strong Partial Weak	
User Voice • "End Users" are on the team and/or have been involved in crafting the aim, measures and change ideas.	Strong Partial Weak	

Other Comments:

Improvement Routines

1) **TEAM MTGS/HUDDLES:** Identify how frequently you would like to meet as a team. If you can identify dates/times now, even better. Team meetings are usually for longer conversations (data conversations, consolidating learning from learning cycles. Huddles are no more than 30 min and usually used to maintain testing momentum (share learning from learning cycles, articulate next steps, trouble-shoot issues that arise during testing, etc.).
2) **LEARNING CYCLES:** Identify how frequently you will run learning cycles—how many PDSAs can your team run each week given what you're testing? Write down the number for each week. Ideally, you will run a <u>minimum</u> of one PDSA per week.
3) **DATA COLLECTION:** Identify how frequently you will collect data--daily? weekly? monthly?
4) **CONSOLIDATE LEARNING:** Identify when you would like to pause and consolidate what you have learned so far. Again, this will likely happen during a team meeting. Plan on consolidating once before LS5 and and once before the Improvement Reviews.
5) **DATA CONVERSATION:** Identify when you would like to review data with your team. Some teams like to review their data and consolidate learning at the same time; others like to review their data more frequently and allocate some time during huddles to do this.

	Week 1	Week 2	Week 3	Week 4 (PROGRESS UPDATE)	Week 5	Week 6	Week 7	Week 8 (PROGRESS UPDATE)
TEAM MTGS/HUDDLES								
LEARNING CYCLES								
DATA COLLECTION								
CONSOLIDATE LEARNING								
DATA CONVERSATION								

280

K-W-L Template

OUR IMPROVEMENT PROBLEM

What we **KNOW** about current performance	What we **WONDER** about current performance	What we **LEARNED**

✪ Priority questions

Talking Points for leaders @ Improvement Science

What is Improvement Science?
A disciplined way of structuring collective efforts to make evidence-based changes that lead to better outcomes, system performance and organizational **learning.**
It's a well-established approach that has been used in multiple sectors to drive organizational improvement.

How is it different?
- Engages front-line teams to **LEARN** their way into improvement
- Adds discipline to improvement efforts
- Often starts small and scales-up

Where should we focus?
- Important to the organization
- Scoped realistically
- Will, ideas and execution

IMPROVEMENT GOAL

Who?

Sponsor
Create time and space for the work
Remove barriers

Improvement Team
Weekly team meetings
On-going cycles of inquiry
Collecting and reflecting on data

Team Lead
Manage the team

Improvement Coach
Guide the learning journey

What improvement teams need:
- Protected time
- Access to improvement and content expertise
- A safe learning environment to admit and learn from failures

What can leaders do to create a vibrant learning environment for improvement?
- Communicate in word and action the importance of improvement work
- Be a lead learner; demonstrate curiosity and vulnerability
- Provide space for teams to engage in sustained improvement work.

Printed in Great Britain
by Amazon